A HANDBOOK FOR
LANGUAGE PROGRAM
ADMINISTRATORS

MARY ANN CHRISTISON
University of Utah/Snow College

&

FREDRICKA L. STOLLER
Northern Arizona University

Editors

ALTA BOOK CENTER PUBLISHERS

Proofing Editor: Louella Holter

Acquisition and Production: Aarón Berman

Production Coordination: Jamie Cross

Book Design: Cleve Gallat

Cover Art: Bruce Marion

Alta Book Center Publishers

14 Adrian Court

Burlingame, California 94010 USA

Phone: 800 ALTA/ESL • 415.692.1285 (Int'l)

Fax 800 ALTA/FAX • 415.692.4654

E-mail: ALTAESL@AOL.COM • Website: WWW.ALTAESL.COM

Printed in the United States of America

ISBN 1-882483-62-6

TABLE OF CONTENTS

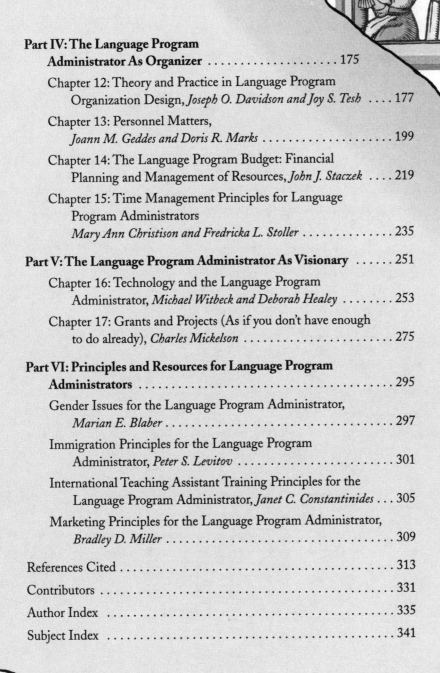

PREFACE

his handbook is designed for practicing language program administrators and administrators in training. It is the book that we wish someone would have given us when we first took on administrative responsibilities in our language programs. As we all know, the job of a language program administrator is multifaceted, requiring a wide range of skills, knowledge, and expertise. We learned to be language program administrators much like apprentices in a twelfth-century craft guild: We looked for *master* language program administrators who had learned the craft on the job and by trial and error.

This apprenticeship process is reflected in the cover artwork, which emphasizes two dimensions of language program administration: our many roles and how we learn them. In our search for artwork that captured the essence of language program administration, we realized that one graphic image would not represent what it is that language program administrators do. The cover art that we have chosen, adapted from eighteenth-century Catalan woodcuts, depicts a variety of craft guilds that symbolize how language program administrators have traditionally learned their craft and the different responsibilities that they have. Each woodblock depicts a different facet of our jobs and mirrors a section of the volume. Part I, On the Nature of Intensive English Programs, is represented by the two characters stirring ingredients in a large pot, depicting the background knowledge that we must have to be successful in our jobs. Part II, The Language Program Administrator As Leader, is depicted on the back cover by the woodblock with the people working together around the conference table. Part III, The Language Program Administrator As Promoter, is represented by the two people blowing horns, characterizing the responsibilities that we have to promote our programs and to advocate for our students and faculty. The Language Program Administrator As Organizer, Part IV, is shown on the back cover by the character seated at the desk with the contemporary in-out box. Part V, The Language Program Administrator As Visionary, is depicted by the woodcut with the modern-day computer, representing the responsibilities we have to look ahead to the future and plan for tomorrow. The final section of the book, which includes principles and resources for language program administrators, is represented by the character with the hammer and chisel; we interpret this woodblock image as a metaphor for the language program administrator who drafts guidelines and shapes principles of sound and effective administration.

Of course, craft guilds were dependent on many people working together cooperatively to produce a high-quality and marketable product. In the same way, this handook is the product of many authors who contributed their expertise in a cooperative spirit. The contributors to this volume are or have all been language program administrators; thus they have been able to not only outline critical issues in their chapters but also offer practical and useful advice based on their own experiences. Although the majority of contributors work in university-based language programs, it is our feeling that the insights they offer will be equally valuable, with some adaptation, to language program administrators in public schools and in private language institutes, both in the United States and abroad.

Robert B. Kaplan and David E. Eskey, two master administrators, start off the volume in Part I. Kaplan's chapter provides historical background on intensive English programs (IEPs) and highlights the broad diversity in program sites and structures. Eskey's chapter focuses on IEPs as nontraditional entities, arguing against the notion that IEPs should demand traditional status.

In Part II, The Language Program Administrator As Leader, Fredricka L. Stoller promotes the administrator as a catalyst for change and innovation, demonstrating how innovation can empower program personnel, invigorate a program, and lead to improved teaching and learning. Susan Carkin considers language program leadership as intercultural management; in this chapter, Carkin provides language program administrators with valuable insights about working successfully across academic discourse boundaries. Sarah J. Klinghammer explores the role of the administrator in the strategic planning process and outlines steps that administrators should follow when bringing language program personnel into the planning process. Alexandra Rowe Henry highlights the challenges that administrators face in their roles as decision makers and negotiators. Lee Ann Rawley completes this section, reporting on a study of policy formation in institutions of higher learning that focuses on two major concerns for language program administrators: the nature of policy making and how ESL professionals shape those policies.

The chapters in Part III concern the language program administrator as promoter. Frederick L. Jenks begins the section by discussing the process of building academic legitimacy and outlining the ways in which program status may be improved. Elizabeth F. Soppelsa highlights the responsibilities that language program administrators have for empowering faculty through participatory decision making and ongoing professional development. Mary Ann Christison explores four ways in which the language program administrator can serve as a second language student advocate. Finally, Rebecca Smith Murdock offers practical suggestions for outreach linkages, both on and off campus, as means for promoting the language program.

Part IV, The Language Program Administrator As Organizer, contains four chapters. Joseph O. Davidson and Joy S. Tesh discuss the theory and practice of organizational design and offer concrete suggestions for keeping records, running meetings, establishing committees, conducting self-studies, and improving communication among program personnel. Joann M. Geddes and Doris R. Marks provide an overview of personnel matters, including useful guidelines for staffing, supervision and evaluation, problem solving, and professional enrichment. John J. Staczek examines the role of the administrator in financial planning and the management of resources. The section concludes with Mary Ann Christison and Fredricka L. Stoller, who set forth time management principles for busy language program administrators.

Part V, The Language Program Administrator As Visionary, highlights two additional areas of importance for administrators: technology and grant writing. Michael Witbeck and Deborah Healey explore the promises and challenges of technology in relation to instructional practices and program administration. Throughout their chapter, Witbeck and Healey highlight the responsibilities that administrators have in guiding the general direction of change that accompanies new and evolving technologies. Charles Mickelson concludes the section with a chapter on grants and projects, focusing on the cyclical effect of grant and project activity, funding sources, proposal writing, and budgeting.

The final section of the volume highlights principles and lists resources for language program administrators in four areas of concern. Marian E. Blaber outlines principles related to gender issues, Peter S. Levitov proposes principles related to immigration issues, Janet C. Constantinides sets forth principles related to international teaching assistant training, and Bradley D. Miller presents marketing principles.

Together, the chapters in this volume provide state-of-the-art advice on many important aspects of language program administration. We hope that the volume will serve the needs of practicing administrators and also help prepare future administrators. When we first became program administrators, there were few available resources. We relied on Ralph Pat Barrett's 1982 edited volume (*The Administration of Intensive English Language Programs*), common sense, trial and error, and the conversations that we had with colleagues who found themselves in a similar situation, learning by doing. This volume symbolically represents the professional history of language program administration and literally marks the emergence of a new field: We now see more books and articles being written about language program administration and more courses and workshops being offered on the subject than when we began as administrators.

As editors of this volume, we would like to thank the contributors who took time from their busy administrative schedules to write chapters for the volume. We appreciate their continued support and commitment to the shared belief that the profession needs a practical handbook on language program administration. We would also like to thank Bill Grabe, Northern Arizona University, and Adrian S. Palmer, University of Utah, for their professional and personal support. We would like to thank Louella Holter, our editor at Northern Arizona University, who was tireless in attending to the many details of this manuscript and enormously helpful in providing feedback and commentary as someone from outside the profession. We would like to acknowledge the support of Northern Arizona University's Associate Provost of Research and Dean of the Graduate College, Henry Hooper, who made it possible for us to work with Louella at the Bilby Research Center on the Northern Arizona University campus. We are grateful to Aarón Berman and Simón Almendares of Alta Book Center Publishers, who have believed in this project and supported us in our vision from the very start. Finally, we thank you, the readers—program administrators past, present, and future. We hope that you find the volume useful and helpful and a valuable addition to your professional library.

Mary Ann Christison   Fredricka L. Stoller
University of Utah/Snow College   *Northern Arizona University*

April 1997

Glossary of Acronyms

The acronyms listed below are used throughout the volume; they are included here for the convenience of the reader.

AAAL   American Association for Applied Linguistics

AAIEP   American Association of Intensive English Programs

ACE   American Council on Education

ACT   American College Test

ACTFL   American Council of Teachers of Foreign Language

AILA   Association Internationale de Linguistique Appliquée (International Association of Applied Linguistics)

ATESL   Administrators and Teachers of English as a Second Language (section of NAFSA)

CALL   Computer Assisted Language Learning

EAP   English for Academic Purposes

EFL   English as a Foreign Language

ELT   English Language Teaching

ESL   English as a Second Language

ESP   English for Special/Specific Purposes

ETS   Educational Testing Service

F1 status   An F1 visa and F1 student status are granted to individuals who are qualified to pursue a full course of study at an academic or language institution that is authorized to admit international students

FTE   Full-time equivalent

GMAT   Graduate Management Admissions Test

GRE   Graduate Record Exam

I-20 form	Formally designated the Form I-20 A-B/I-20 ID, this is a U.S. governmental form that is used as a certificate of eligibility for nonimmigrant F1 student status for academic and language students
IEP	Intensive English Program
IIE	Institute for International Education
INS	Immigration and Naturalization Service
ITA	International Teaching Assistant
L2	Second language
MLA	Modern Language Association
NAFSA	National Association of Foreign Student Affairs: Association of International Educators
SAT	Scholastic Achievement Test
TA	Teaching assistant
TEFL	Teaching English as a Foreign Language
TESL	Teaching English as a Second Language
TESOL	Teachers of English to Speakers of Other Languages
TOEFL	Test of English as a Foreign Language
TSE	Test of Spoken English
TWE	Test of Written English
UCIEP	Consortium of University and College Intensive English Programs
USAID	United States Agency for International Development
USIA	United States Information Agency
WASC	Western Association of Schools and Colleges

Part I

ON THE NATURE OF
INTENSIVE ENGLISH PROGRAMS

Chapter 1

AN IEP IS A MANY-SPLENDORED THING

Robert B. Kaplan
Emeritus Professor, University of Southern California

he title of this chapter is intended to evoke a once very popular motion picture titled *Love Is a Many-Splendored Thing* that appeared in 1955 and won the academy award for best picture that year. In my opinion, the title of the film is the most vacuous I have ever encountered. Not so, however, when that title is adapted to intensive English programs (IEPs). IEPs are many-splendored, many-faceted organisms; they do not merely teach English syntax and lexicon to nonnative speakers of whatever designation (i.e., foreign students, immigrants, refugees, on-the-job trainees, and so forth), but they also engage in some or all of the following activities: IEPs teach grammar and lexicon to all students; teach academic skills, culture, pragmatics, paralinguistics, and kinesics, implicitly or explicitly; offer both academic and personal counseling; provide teacher training (both pre-service and in-service); purchase or prepare teaching materials; construct computer-assisted language learning (CALL) networks; design, administer, and interpret assessment instruments; train international teaching assistants; engage in the pursuit of grants; recruit students and teachers; interact with other academic and administrative entities on and off the campus; interact with educational agencies of foreign governments and with U.S. federal agencies; and engage in a multiplicity of other activities.

The many-faceted nature of IEPs makes them unusual academic units. To explore why this is so, first some historical background is provided by exploring the varying conditions under which IEPs have developed: How did IEPs come into existence? What factors influenced their current configurations? Next is a look at some of the central problems facing IEPs and IEP administrators. Finally is a discussion of some of the issues relating to the future of IEPs in their current configurations, and some of the ways in which they have responded to change.

Historical Factors

Three important factors contributed to the many-faceted nature of IEPs in their early history: the conditions under which IEPs were established, the development of the field of foreign language teaching, and the emergence of the field of applied linguistics.

The Establishment of IEPs

The first factor that influenced the current structure of IEPs was how decisions were made to establish IEPs in the first place. As Goodwin and Nacht (1983) point out, the initial decision to establish foreign student programs, including English as a second language (ESL) programs, at most U.S. colleges and universities during the 1950s and 1960s was made without any forward planning, without any clear idea why such programs should exist. As international students began to undertake study in U.S. institutions after the end of World War II, specific and unique needs surfaced and immediate responses to those needs were implemented. By 1953, some 150 U.S. institutions had some sort of ESL program for international students.

One of the needs that surfaced early on was defined as the inability of many international students to undertake the studies they had come to pursue because their language skills were insufficient to compete with native English speakers in an environment in which instruction was delivered almost exclusively in English by a random mixture of native English-speaking (including speakers of a wide variety of English dialects) and nonnative English-speaking faculty. Attempts to meet this need created interesting academic debate. The problem was initially perceived as subject to simple remediation and many of the earliest ESL classes were wrongly conceived as exactly equivalent to remedial courses for semi-literate native speakers—indeed, sometimes as sections of such courses. Local analyses, often steeped in nearly total ignorance or at least in great naiveté, presumed that language deficiencies were primarily identified as related either to writing (therefore, requiring remedial English composition) or to speaking (therefore, requiring remedial speech). In some instances, the speaking problems were further reified as "dysfluencies" and were treated clinically. Frequently, instruction was relegated largely or exclusively to teaching assistants (TAs) or community volunteers, commonly without any supervision or preparation for the task. Both the fact that there was no forward planning involved in the creation of most IEPs and that there was no agreement on how the needs should be met have been factors that have led to the many-faceted nature of IEPs.

Language Learning Controversy

Not only was there an absence of decision in creating IEPs and programs for international students, there were also powerful underlying assumptions in the field of foreign language learning that affected the development of IEPs. Foreign language teaching, when it was initially introduced in the medieval university, involved only the classical languages—Latin, Greek, Sanskrit, and Hebrew. The purpose of instruction was to achieve an understanding of the thought and art of dead civilizations. The lexicon and syntax of such languages were fixed, since they were dead languages; the literature was limited, since no new literature was being produced, and there was no point in teaching speaking skills since there were no living native speakers of those languages with whom to communicate. The activity was purely intellectual, and so enrollment was restricted to the most able students. The purpose of instruction, after all, was to achieve a proficiency that would permit students to read the canonical literature. When the teaching of modern languages was introduced into the academy in the latter nineteenth century, the assumptions that had governed language instruction for hundreds of years were simply transferred to the new activity. The grammar translation methodology was eminently suited to the purpose and was widely adopted; the same methodology is alive and well today in many institutions around the world.

Another factor that has influenced the development of IEPs has to do with the emergence, in the mid-1940s, of a new language teaching methodology and a different underlying linguistic model from the one stated above. During the years of World War II, Charles C. Fries and his colleagues at the University of Michigan had devised a methodology and a linguistic model for teaching critical foreign languages to military personnel. This work constituted the basis of instruction in United States military language institutes. In these institutes, motivation was very high because failure often meant assignment to combat duties. The military institutes were quite successful. Fries and his colleagues essentially invented both audiolingual methodology and its underlying applied linguistics (predicated on structural linguistics and Skinnerian psychology). Unlike the traditional grammar translation method, audiolingual methodology focused on developing speaking and listening skills. The activity of learning a foreign language was not considered purely intellectual since it had been developed in response to the need for speakers to actually communicate in real-life circumstances in the foreign language.

As a result of this work, the first major ESL program was born at the English Language Institute at the University of Michigan in 1941. As other IEPs like the ELI began to develop, their English language teaching methodology became greatly influenced by the grammar translation method, the audiolingual methodology, and the underlying assumptions surrounding these methods. Yet, there has been no general agreement among IEP professionals as to which methodology to employ. In addition, the field of English language teaching continues to evolve as new methodologies emerge. (See Christison, 1997, for more information on language teaching methodologies.)

The Role of Applied Linguistics

The field of applied linguistics has also greatly influenced the development of IEPs. The invention of the term *applied linguistics* is sometimes attributed to an unknown group of language teachers in the United States during the 1940s; they wanted to be identified as scientists rather than as humanists, to separate themselves from literature teachers, and to ally themselves with scientific linguists (Mackey, 1966; Palmer, 1980). But the term did not acquire substance until the late 1950s and the early 1960s. (A chronology of key events in the development of applied linguistics may be useful at this point and is presented in the Appendix.) Language teaching within IEPs has been inextricably tied to the field of applied linguistics for the principle reason that a great many English language teachers within IEPs have been trained by professional applied linguists; indeed, the principles underlying materials preparation and assessment also derived from work in applied linguistics. In a paper delivered before the American Association for Applied Linguistics, Angelis (1987) reported on a number of empirical indices of the contemporary scope of applied linguistics. He examined articles published in the journal *Applied Linguistics* over the first eight years of its existence as well as articles in the *TESOL Quarterly* over the first ten years of its existence and the indexical descriptors employed in the ERIC System under the broad category Applied Linguistics. Grabe and Kaplan (1992) augmented exploration by examining the articles included in the *Annual Review of Applied Ling* between 1980 and 1990, the applied linguistics articles included in the Oxford University Press *International Encyclopedia of Linguistics* (Bright et al., 1992), and the names and activities of the scientific commissions of the International Association for Applied Linguistics. Something on the order of half of the items in these several indices were, as late as 1992, in some way related to language teaching and learning. These items included areas of pedagogical importance within IEPs, such as second language acquisition and educational language testing. Thus, language pedagogy, in particular language pedagogy within IEPs, remains to this day a significant focus of the work in applied linguistics.

Challenges for IEP Administrators

Historical factors contributed to the multifaceted nature of IEPs. More contemporary issues such as the location of IEPs on their campuses, students' changing proficiency profiles, institutional reporting hierarchies, and the evolving role of IEP directors represent some of the challenges facing language program administrators today.

Location of IEPs

The many-faceted nature of IEPs has created some interesting challenges for IEP administrators, one of which has to do with the location of IEPs on their home campuses. Because there was no forward plan in establishing IEPs, they were not clearly defined in relationship to other academic units within the university. Consequently, no definitive placement for IEPs exists within the university framework. Fry (1986), in her careful study of NAFSA Field Service consultations over the first 20 years of the existence of the consulting program, shows the wide variety of sites in which ESL programs were founded. Some of the earliest ESL programs were uncomfortably housed in Departments of English and Departments of Speech. These sitings were uncomfortable because (a) the ESL programs were alien to the missions of those departments, (b) the ESL programs were tangential to the curricula which had been in place for decades, and (c) the ESL faculty did not do the sorts of things that the regular faculty of those departments did, such as conduct research and publish papers. In some other cases, ESL programs were attached to departments of foreign languages on the dubious rationale that foreign language departments were expert in language teaching. A smaller number of ESL programs were organized on the student personnel services side of the house on the assumption that ESL teaching was not, in a strict sense, academic; thus, programs were attached to foreign student advisors' offices. Other ESL programs were attached more broadly to the responsibilities of the dean of students' office.

Many ESL programs were sited in divisions of continuing education or in other tangential academic structures. It was believed that the greater administrative and budgetary flexibility offered in those tangential sites would permit ESL programs to earn even larger incomes and return more "surplus" to the institution. Because numbers of international students coming to study in U.S. institutions were growing by leaps and bounds (the average growth rate between the late 1950s and the early 1980s was about 10% per year), it dawned on some academic administrators that the ESL program was a potential cash cow. It became an unstated assumption in academic circles that ESL programs not only could stand on their own budgetary bottoms but could also be expected to produce cash surpluses that might be used for other institutional purposes. Programs also employed graduate teaching assistants, part-time teachers, or even volunteers, none of whom were eligible for fringe benefits. Such hiring practices required little investment by the institution and added to the notion of the IEP as a cash cow. IEP students not only paid basic tuition, but often paid additional special fees for the privilege of taking these courses. The courses were often structured so that the units provided were not tied to actual instructional time, since academic credit was rarely involved.

In the meantime, particularly during the 1960s, departments of linguistics (but not necessarily of applied linguistics) proliferated in U.S. academic institutions. (According to the Institute for International Education, by 1969 there were 23 institutions offering graduate work in teaching English as a second language [TESL] and applied linguistics and at least 40 more offering ESL methods courses.) In some cases, ESL programs were attached to such departments on the grounds that linguists presumably knew about language teaching. This siting was as uncomfortable as the siting in English and speech departments, since most autonomous linguists were no more interested in language teaching than were professors specializing in Cervantes, Goethe, Milton, or Shakespeare, or for that matter, physics or chemistry.

In the same time period, schools of education began to develop curricula for teachers of English as a second language to serve the growing immigrant and refugee populations arriving in the United States and enrolling in the public school systems, particularly in large coastal cities. More recently, schools of education have turned their attention to the preparation of teachers for bilingual programs and for multilingual/multicultural environments. As these events occurred, some ESL programs were attached to schools of education. Frequently, in these situations, the programs also became sites for teacher training, so the graduate teaching assistants who delivered instruction in ESL programs were actually also receiving in-service training and practice teaching. This latter development constituted an important improvement, since the instructors in ESL programs began to receive not only preparation for the task at hand but some supervision as well. This change did not require greater investment by the institutions in running the ESL programs, since the teaching assistants—augmented by variously sized pools of part-time instructors—were still ineligible for faculty status, fringe benefits, or competitive salaries.

Student Proficiency at Entrance

Another challenge facing IEP administrators is in the policies and practices concerning English language proficiency at entrance. Obviously, a problem recognized early on in the history of program development was the efficient academic placement of students on arrival. Again, because IEPs did not evolve from a coherent and unified plan, a great diversity of student profiles soon evolved, requiring the general placement of students at various levels of proficiency, as well as the need to determine strengths in various skill areas, and to determine, in some cases, admissibility. A great number of assessment instruments have evolved in response to these needs, including the various well-known tests developed at the English Language Institute at the University of Michigan (collectively known as the Michigan Tests), as well as an instrument developed at the American Language Institute, Georgetown University, although many institutions employ locally developed tests (e.g., the International Student English Placement Examination at the

University of Southern California), or employ various combinations of instruments. In the mid-1960s, Educational Testing Service of Princeton, NJ, developed the Test of English as a Foreign Language (TOEFL), which is administered internationally; this test, to a large extent, became the standard measure of English language proficiency for U.S. colleges and universities. The existence of the TOEFL created a new need in the international student population. Since TOEFL scores became a standard for admission to many U.S. tertiary institutions (indeed, even a standard for acquisition of the Immigration and Naturalization Service's form I-20 which allows students to acquire a visa to enter the United States), students needed instruction to achieve appropriate scores on the TOEFL.

Reporting Hierarchies

The multiplicity of sitings for ESL programs, as well as the multiplicity of program configurations, produced a wide variety of reporting structures, each of which is marked by its own special problems. ESL units housed in humanities departments, such as English or foreign languages, normally report to the dean of the humanities division, either directly or indirectly through the chairs of the departments from which the ESL program is suspended. (ESL units are rarely housed in social science or hard science units, though there are cases in which a school of engineering, for example, may have its own ESL program.) ESL units housed in continuing education commonly report to the dean of continuing education, often directly since continuing education units tend not to be departmentalized. ESL programs housed in student personnel services offices commonly report directly to the head of the service to which they are attached; for example, a unit attached to the foreign student advisor's office normally reports to the director of that office, whatever that person's title may be.

The dean of humanities has a quite different agenda than does the dean of continuing education. ESL programs housed in humanities units compete for resources with other humanities departments and programs. A dean of humanities is much more concerned about recruiting distinguished literature specialists than about recruiting language teachers. Under these conditions, ESL programs are at a distinct disadvantage, since they frequently lack regular faculty (i.e., tenure-eligible individuals with the normal guarantees of academic freedom and due process as well as competitive salaries and fringe benefits). The structure of ESL programs tends to be rather different from the structure of humanities departments both in terms of credit-bearing courses and in terms of content, with the ESL content perceived as being less academic. The ESL program director is not perceived as a peer among departmental chairs but rather enjoys a kind of second-class citizenship.

ESL units housed in continuing education, or for that matter those attached to student personnel services offices, are also disadvantaged, in part because they may be the only units in the configuration delivering courses in the administrative sense, as opposed to courses earning continuing education units or structured as some sort of noncredit activity. Continuing education units (and student personnel services units) are not departmentalized so there is less competition for resources, or at least there are fewer powerful voices speaking for limited resources. Thus, in this environment, the ESL program director may carry more prestige than directors of other activity centers. In continuing education units, ESL programs may have access to a greater range of resources and may be able to negotiate an arrangement in which some portion of earned surplus may be returned to the ESL program to enhance instruction in various ways (though not generally to enhance salaries).

The variety of reporting hierarchies has implications for the position of ESL faculty. In most cases, however, that faculty is perceived as somehow less than regular faculty, as engaged in less academic activities, as delivering work that does not deserve academic credit, and as not deserving of normal faculty status.

The Role of the Director

The many-faceted nature of IEPs creates variables that impact on the role of the director. Historically, ESL programs consisted of individual courses, listed in university catalogues under the departments in which the courses were sited. Gradually, either because the number of courses and students reached a critical mass, or because the home departments wanted to be freed of the burden of administering such courses, the courses were actually organized into programmatic (sub) units, and some individual was designated to oversee the lot, often with the title of coordinator, sometimes director. It is to the functions of such an administrator that attention will now be directed.

Many of the early coordinators/directors not only lacked administrative experience, but were isolated from their administrative peers by virtue of the peculiar nature of the programs they oversaw, by virtue of the siting of ESL programs, and by virtue of the fact that there was no collective experience on which they might draw. (See Carkin, this volume, for additional information on marginalization of IEPs.) Many of these new administrators did not possess a doctorate, as the doctorate was generally not available in TESL and because the task—in the view of academic administrators—did not require a doctorate.

The tasks for which they were responsible grew increasingly complex as program size and diversity increased; in many cases, the scope of work was more comparable to that of a divisional dean than a departmental chair, although both of those titles are rare in the history of ESL programs. As ESL programs evolved into intensive English programs, the duties of directors became still more onerous. The scope of responsibility of the director of a large IEP is diverse indeed. Clearly, it is impossible to anticipate all of the variation that will occur across institutions, but an attempt is made in Table 1 to sort out some of the duties and to provide a brief taxonomy of them. As suggested in the table, directors are responsible for the academic content of the courses offered (and for the measurement of achievement), the administration of a large unit (often employing dozens of instructors and staff), cross-institutional linkages with academic and administrative units from the rest of the institution, political linkages in the external world (both in terms of recruiting and in terms of relations with educational agencies of the U.S. and foreign governments), the fiscal operation of the unit (including the pursuit of grant proposals), and the intellectual management of the unit (including forward planning for both personnel and physical facilities and including all of the intricacies of personnel management in the contemporary world of intersecting local and federal regulations and faculty rights).

Clearly, it is impossible to construct a complete list of tasks; different institutional structures will add or subtract items in each of the categories. Load distribution will vary according to the personality of the director; some directors will be better at or will prefer certain categories while delegating others. However, every director should be competent at least in academic, administrative, and managerial functions. In the ordinary course of events, most directors are consumed by administrative, management, and fiscal issues and are forced either to delegate other functions or to leave them undone. A key issue involves the ability of directors to delegate wisely and to limit the span of their authority. It is not possible for all employees of an ESL program to report directly to the program supervisor; rather, it is necessary to construct some sort of reporting hierarchy that limits the number of individuals with whom the director interacts on a regular basis. If fiscal constraints will permit, the director ought to be assisted by at least an academic director and a fiscal manager; larger programs will, obviously, call for a more detailed subdivision of effort, possibly including a CALL administrator, a materials specialist, or a testing officer.

Table 1. **Six of the Primary Duties of a Language Program Director**

Academic Responsibilities	*Administrative Responsibilities*	*Institutional Responsibilities*
Curriculum design	Operations	Liaison with higher level
Testing	Policy development	administrators
Syllabus development	Policy implementation	Committees (e.g., admissions,
Student placement	Infrastructure planning	governance, language
Teacher evaluation	Long- and short-term budget	education, faculty)
Articulation among levels	Organizational planning	Student/faculty advocacy
Test development and	Staff development (in-service/	
curriculum trialing	pre-service)	
Teacher training	Record keeping	

Political Responsibilities	*Fiscal Responsibilities*	*Managerial Responsibilities*
Liaison with clients	Budget development	Staffing
Institutional policy	Day-to-day control of expenses	Running meetings
development	Purchasing	Structuring committees
External professional	Equipment maintenance	Hiring
organization involvement	Planned acquisition of office and	Firing
Liaison with accrediting	instructional equipment	Dealing with grievances
agency, funding agencies,	Grants and contracts	Counseling
sponsors, international		Legal action
agencies		Personnel records
		Personnel harmony
		Personnel searches

Variables Affecting Language Program Change

English language teaching programs in institutions of higher education will continue to evolve, creating more diversity in overall program design and curricula. There are three impeti for change that are important for IEP administrators to recognize: changes in the student population, changes in the requirements of other sectors of the institution, and paradigmatic changes in the structure of the field itself (i.e., in linguistic theories of second language acquisition and in pertinent educational theories). How an IEP responds to change will be very important to its future.

Changes in Student Population

When the international student population in the United States shifted toward more graduate students, the population in ESL programs changed and the language needs of that population also changed. Graduate students in science programs, for example, are often engaged in lock-step programs of disciplinary studies and have little time to devote to language study. Their language needs are different; their entry-level proficiency is likely to be higher, and English for Specific Purposes (ESP) instruction is likely to be more appropriate than more generalized English for Academic Purposes (EAP) instruction. This shift in the instructional paradigm requires a parallel shift in methodology and materials, achievement assessment, and certain other levels of the director's job. Reporting lines for graduate students engaged in science study will be more departmentally focused, and institutional linkages with graduate departments will be more diversified than such linkages typically are for undergraduate students (i.e., departmental graduate advisors in many units rather than one undergraduate advisement office). The disciplinary faculty will wish to play a larger role in determining the kind of proficiency they wish their students to have than would be typical of undergraduate advisors. The variables that affect program change are indicated in Table 2. These variables reconfigure themselves in response to change and thereby redefine the program and the roles of the various players.

International Teaching Assistant Training

IEPs have responded to other changes in the academy by creating special programs to train international teaching assistants (ITAs). In the sciences, in particular, ITAs are used to teach lower division undergraduate science courses, to supervise laboratories, and to assist the teaching faculty in other ways. Without the involvement of teaching assistants, science departments would be hard pressed to cover all instruction. Furthermore, international graduate students are often in dire need of some sort of financial assistance to be able to undertake graduate study at all. The use of international graduate students represents a solution to both problems; that is, ITA awards constitute both a teaching resource for their academic departments and a mechanism for funding international graduate students. But there are problems. Native English-speaking undergraduates frequently complain that they cannot understand their ITAs and that as a consequence they are being deprived of a reasonable opportunity to do well.

Problems with ITAs have escalated in the past decade, and a number of state legislatures have become concerned, as have the boards of trustees of both public and private institutions. In some cases, state legislatures have mandated some sort of assessment of

ITA language ability as a condition of appointment; in other cases, institutional adminis-trations have mandated ITA training. Since the issue is perceived to be one of language, the task of providing such instruction has fallen to ESL programs, particularly to large IEPs. But the problem implicates language only to a certain extent (Kaplan, 1989).

It is undoubtedly true that, in some cases, the English pronunciation of ITAs is suffi-ciently deviant from standard English to pose a real problem for some native speakers. It is undoubtedly also the case that the deviant pronunciation of some ITAs could provide a handy excuse for the failure of an undergraduate to grasp the subject, particularly if the subject matter is difficult or if the student lacks the background to comprehend it. But there are a number of other issues involved.

ITAs may have quite standard English pronunciation and syntactic fluency but may lack the pragmatic knowledge to perform in front of a classroom. They may not rec-ognize the thrust of a student's question, may not understand the semantic limitations of various lexical and syntactic forms (see Biber, Conrad, & Reppen, 1996), may not know the politeness rules that are required between teachers and students, may lack presenta-

Table 2. **Variables That Affect Program Change**

Student Characteristics		
Student Background	*Student Objectives*	*Desired Emphasis*
Academic experience	Academic: general (EAP) and specific (ESP)	Computer literacy
Competencies	Business: general and specific	Conversation
Language abilities	Social	Grammar
Personal goals	Survival	Listening
	Vocational	Pronunciation
	Adjunct	Reading
	Sheltered	Study skills
		Writing

Program Options				
Program of Study	*Pedagogy*	*Schedule*	*Classroom Management*	*Classroom Formats*
Full time	Audiolingual	Hours per day	Team teaching	Listening lab
Part time	Functional	Hours per week	Self-instruction	Computer lab
Intensive	Notional	Weeks per term	Cooperative learning	Reading lab
Open entry	Situational		Single-teacher	Writing center
Set entry	Task based		managed classroom	Teacher-managed
Voluntary	Content based			classroom
Compulsory	Communicative			Self-access learning
	Eclectic			center
	ESP			
	VESL			
	TPR			
	Natural Approach			
	Immersion			
	Silent Way			

tional skills (e.g., may talk to the blackboard), may be shocked by the informality of U.S. undergraduates, and so on. All of these issues need to be addressed in ITA training classes provided through ESL programs. ITAs may be perfectly conversant with the lexicons of their special fields, so ESP materials and methodologies may not be appropriate for this population. Furthermore, it is important to recognize the extreme pressure on ITAs. They may have a limited time in which to complete graduate study—that limitation implicit in the duration of the visa provided at entry, in the constraints placed on the student by a home-country employer or educational agency, and certainly in available funding. While the support provided by the award of an ITA-ship may be very attractive, the possession of an ITA-ship is already a powerful constraint on the international graduate student's available time; it may significantly slow progress toward a degree.

It is unfortunately the case that some science departments exploit ITAs. ITAs now find themselves in the United States enrolled in a graduate degree program, but their ability to continue may depend entirely on the resources provided through the ITA-ship. Their lives are suddenly and sometimes unexpectedly complicated by the interposition of an English-language proficiency assessment instrument and by the possibility that failure on the assessment instrument may mean loss of the ITA-ship, a further extension of the time toward the degree, or, in the worst case, the requirement to return home without a degree—a genuinely face-threatening alternative. No wonder there is a powerful tension between the science department and the ESL program, and between the international graduate student and the ITA instructor.

Until recently, commercial materials available for ITA instruction have been quite limited, although new materials are appearing with reasonable frequency now. The same is true of assessment instruments. Here the problem is particularly thorny, as one wants to use an instrument that is both valid and reliable, that has been normed for the greater population of ITAs, and that is readily available, reasonably inexpensive, and easy to score (since speed of placement is a critical issue). At the same time, the assessment instrument has to be applicable within the particular constraints of the individual campus. Educational Testing Service (ETS) offers a standardized examination for this purpose (the Speaking Proficiency English Assessment Kit or the SPEAK Test), though there have been some problems reported with its use. Probably the best assessment instrument involves having the subjects teach a real class, but such a procedure is time consuming and expensive, and may lead to reliability and validity problems.

The challenges associated with ITA training are but one example of how IEPs must respond to change. Again, because there is no forward plan for ESL programs (including ITA training) at most institutions, ESL programs respond to the immediate needs of the institution and once again add to the many-faceted nature of IEPs. (See Constantinides, this volume, for additional information on ITAs.)

Proficiency of ESL Students

Another example of how IEPs have responded to change concerns how ESL programs have responded to the effects of the ETS-generated TOEFL. Because a TOEFL score is now required for entrance into most universities, the emphasis among students has been for more assistance in achieving higher scores on this exam. Some ESL programs have TOEFL preparation courses, although these courses normally involve much more than studying English. They often address test-taking skills, time management, and the mechanics of managing a machine-scored multiple-choice answer sheet. Courses of this type are often administered as adjunct to courses in English, so students enrolled in an ESL program often take TOEFL preparation courses as a supplement to the basic curriculum; a successful TOEFL score often constitutes the exit criterion for ESL programs.

In the 1980s, the TOEFL was augmented by ETS's Test of Spoken English and the Test of Written English. These tests, in turn, have created a new curricular need. In the same time period, the University of Cambridge Local Examinations Syndicate developed a series of tests that largely became the standard for British colleges and universities. In the British sphere of influence, courses sprang up to aid students with these instruments.

These various language assessment instruments have, over time, indicated a gradual upward shift in the level of proficiency at entrance, at least for U.S. institutions, and IEPs have responded to this change. In the earliest period of ESL program evolution (before sending countries were able to provide predeparture English language instruction), the great majority of enrolled students required intensive elementary level or low-intermediate level instruction; a large percentage of these students were admitted for undergraduate study. Gradually, as sending countries became more sophisticated about their work force needs, as those countries were able to develop their own tertiary institutions, and as the geographic focus of arriving students changed with international political and economic events, the distribution of international students shifted in the direction of graduate education, and the language needs of arriving students shifted toward high-intermediate and advanced levels of instruction. Because a greater proportion of students were in fact going to study at the graduate level, the focus of instruction also shifted, from a generalized EAP focus to a variety of ESP courses.

Responding to Change Through Needs Assessment

Program directors must be prepared to conduct periodic needs analyses, not only among the student population enrolled, but also among the academic units served. ESL programs are, perhaps more so than most traditional academic units, at the mercy of market forces; after all, they do not control institutional student recruitment but must be prepared to serve populations admitted by other departments. It is this constant reconfiguration of program populations and their needs that accounts for the great diversity among ESL programs.

While there are detectable national trends, institutions respond to those trends variably and develop their own trends based on their individual histories, their instructional pool, and their individual objectives (e.g., the population at a state college will be different from that at a private full-service university, which in turn will be different from that at a community college). These differences are in part the result of differing institutional mission statements. Some institutions, as a consequence of historical patterns, focus on particular sending countries or regions (though it may be a long-term hazard to enroll too large a population from any given polity), whereas others seek greater diversity in their international populations. In addition, of course, there are some proprietary programs, operating in the absence of parent institutions, that are frequently driven by a more explicit profit motive. Such proprietary programs are at the same time more flexible and more constrained: They are able to make curricular changes and to respond to market forces more quickly on the one hand, but they are more constrained by the need to produce profit on the other. Indeed, teacher salaries in such institutions directly reflect the fiscal bottom line, often dictated by distant owners or stockholders.

Conclusion

The preceding discussion has attempted to show that IEPs are indeed many-splendored organisms. The great diversity in program sites and program structures is the result of the rapid growth of the population served as well as the result of the varying conditions under which programs were begun. Figures 1 and 2 attempt to summarize different aspects of their diversity. Central problems lie in the great variety of functions for which the IEP is responsible, in the conditions under which directors are appointed, and in the practical administrative constraints under which such directors operate as compared with the multiplicity of tasks they are expected to accomplish.

As this discussion has attempted to demonstrate, the units currently known as IEPs (or, more generally, ESL programs) came into existence largely over a relatively brief historical period—essentially between 1940 and 1980. They were organized to serve immediate needs as perceived by host institutions. Regrettably, in most cases, the units were unplanned; they grew like Topsy, without much forward planning, without much understanding of what functions would be served, and without much sophistication about the activities that would be undertaken. They have been augmented as new needs became apparent. Their faculties have tended to consist of individuals who are not typical of tertiary academic faculty, who perform a restricted number of functions—functions perceived as nonacademic—and who, as a consequence, tend to be perceived as second-class citizens (though many of them publish with greater or lesser frequency, but not in journals recognized by their more academic peers). As a class, these individuals are underpaid and undervalued.

There are many questions about the future of IEPs that remain unanswered and that are worthy of future research. For example, is it the case that international students who test out of ESL programs are generally more able than those who move through them? Is it the ESL program—or only the fact of immersion in an English-speaking environment—that serves to improve the language proficiency of ESL program clients? Are ESL programs teaching the appropriate aspects of language? How important is grammatical knowledge in intercultural communication? Are the methodologies typically employed in ESL programs appropriate to enhancement of communicative skills? Are the materials typically employed appropriate to student needs? Does the availability of computer-assisted language learning contribute significantly to improved language proficiency? How good are ESL teachers?

These are questions that need to be addressed, and the future of the field depends to a significant degree on the ability to respond to change and to find answers to these questions. In the interim, IEPs and other ESL programs are likely to move forward with modest success as the many-splendored organisms that they are, as long as the flow of international students supports the need for such services.

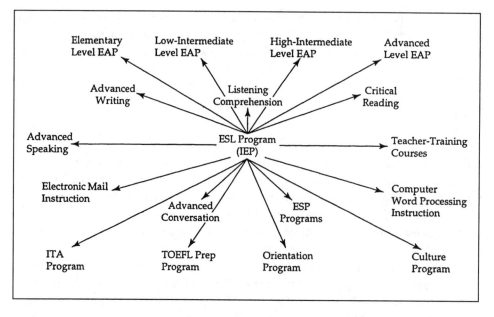

Figure 1. **Some instructional features of an IEP.**

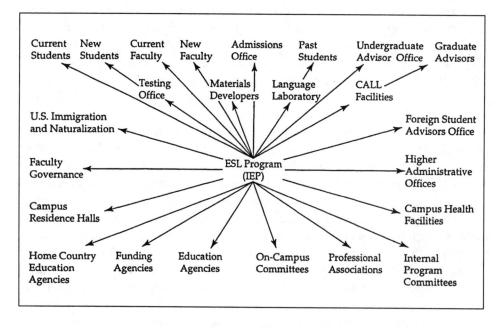

Figure 2. **Some possible contacts for an IEP.**

Discussion Questions and Activities

1. Why do you think IEPs came into existence with so little preplanning? In general, what has been the result of such limited planning in many institutions?

2. What is the role of applied linguistics in the operation of an ESL program?

3. To what extent is it really possible for a director to be expert in administration, management, fiscal planning, and curricular planning (including materials development, assessment, and CALL)? If a director is not an expert in some of these areas, how should s/he go about meeting the needs of the program in these areas?

4. To what extent is it reasonable to expect a director to be proficient in maintaining effective relationships with a variety of entities on the campus as well as a variety of very different entities away from the campus?

5. Should ESL programs offer academic credit? If so, what sort of credit? Why?

6. Assume that you have just been asked to develop a plan for an ESL program (which you are likely to direct) on a campus that has no previous history of admitting international students and no prior history of ESL instruction. Develop a plan for an ideal program and an argument to present to the dean that articulates the rationale for the program as you have devised it.

Suggested Readings:
A Supplementary Bibliography for Language Program Administrators

Alderson, J. C., Krahnke, K. J., & Stansfield, C. W. (Eds.). (1987). *Reviews of English language proficiency tests*. Washington, DC: TESOL.

Ballard, B., & Clanchy, J. (1984). *Study abroad: A manual for Asian students*. Kuala Lumpur: Longman Malaysia.

Ballard, B., & Clanchy, J. (1991). *Teaching students from overseas*. Melbourne: Longman Cheshire.

Barber, E. G., Altbach, P. G., & Myers, R. G. (Eds.). (1985). *Bridges to knowledge: Foreign students in comparative perspective*. Chicago: University of Chicago Press.

Brown, J. D. (1995). *The elements of language program curriculum: A systematic approach to program development*. Boston, MA: Newbury House.

Brumfit, C. J. (Ed.). (1988). *Annual Review of Applied Linguistics, 8*. New York: Cambridge University Press.

Byrd, P. (Ed.). (1986). *Teaching across cultures in university ESL programs*. Washington, DC: NAFSA.

Byrd, P., & Fox, L. (1988). Survey of college ESL credit: A report from a subcommittee of the Committee on Professional Standards. *TESOL Newsletter, 22*(2),11–12.

Fry, M. E. (1986). *Selected perceptions of English-as-a-second-language programs in postsecondary institutions in the United States*. Unpublished doctoral dissertation (2 vols.), University of Southern California, Los Angeles.

Goodwin, C. D., & Nacht, M. (1983). *Absence of decision: Foreign students in American colleges and universities.* New York: Institute for International Education.

Grabe, W., & Kaplan, R. B. (Eds.). (1992). *Introduction to applied linguistics.* Reading, MA: Addison-Wesley.

Henning, G. (1987). *A guide to language testing.* Cambridge, MA: Newbury House.

Jenkins, H. M. (Ed.). (1983). *Educating students from other nations.* San Francisco: Jossey-Bass.

Kaplan, R. B. (1987). On ESL program administration. *Communique: An Occasional Publication of Interest to University and College Intensive English Programs, 3,* 2–4.

Lee, M. Y., Abd-Ella, M., & Burks, L. A. (1981). *Needs of foreign students from developing nations at U.S. colleges and universities.* Washington, DC: NAFSA: Association of International Educators.

Matthies, B. F. (1983). *A study of characteristics, qualifications, and perceived roles of the directors of ESL programs.* Unpublished doctoral dissertation, University of Illinois, Urbana.

NAFSA. (1983). *NAFSA self-study guide: A guide for the self-assessment of programs and services with international educational exchange at postsecondary institutions.* Washington, DC: Author.

Pennington, M. C. (1985). Effective administration of an ESL program. In P. Larsen, E. Judd, & D. Messerschmitt (Eds.), *On TESOL '84: A brave new world for TESOL* (pp. 301–316). Washington, DC: TESOL.

Pennington, M. C. (1989). Faculty development for language programs. In R. K. Johnson (Ed.), *The second language curriculum* (pp. 91–110). New York: Cambridge University Press.

Stoller, F. L. (1992a). *Analysis of innovations in selected higher education intensive English programs: A focus on administrators' perceptions.* Unpublished doctoral dissertation, Northern Arizona University, Flagstaff.

Stoller, F. L. (1995b). *Managing intensive English program innovations.* (NAFSA Working Paper No. 56). Washington, DC: NAFSA: Association of International Educators.

TESOL. (n.d.). *Standards and self-study questions for postsecondary programs.* Washington, DC: Author.

TESOL. (1984). *Statement of core standards for language and professional preparation programs.* Washington, DC: Author.

Valdes, J. M. (1986). *Culture bound: Bridging the culture gap in language teaching.* New York: Cambridge University Press.

Yalden, J. (1983). *The communicative syllabus: Evolution, design and implementation.* Oxford: Pergamon.

Young, R. (Ed.). (1989). [Special issue] *English for Specific Purposes, 8*(2).

Appendix

Chronology of Major Events in the Early Development of Applied Linguistics

1941   Foundation of the English Language Institute (ELI), University of Michigan (C. C. Fries, Director)

1950   *Language Learning: A Journal of Applied Linguistics* began publication from the ELI at the University of Michigan

1956   Inauguration of the School of Applied Linguistics, University of Edinburgh (Ian Catford, Director)

1958   Opening of the Center for Applied Linguistics (CAL), Washington, DC (Charles Ferguson, Director)

1964   Formation of the International Association of Applied Linguistics/Association Internationale de Linguistique Appliquée (AILA)

      Peter Strevens appointed first Professor of Applied Linguistics in the United Kingdom, at the University of Essex

1966   Teachers of English to Speakers of Other Languages (TESOL) organized by a consortium including the Center for Applied Linguistics (CAL), the Modern Language Association (MLA), the National Association for Foreign Student Affairs (NAFSA), the National Council of Teachers of English (NCTE), and the Speech Association of America (SAA) (see Alatis, 1993, for details)

1967   International Association of Teachers of English as a Foreign Language (IATEFL) organized

      TESOL Quarterly began publication from TESOL

      British Association for Applied Linguistics (BAAL) organized

1973   S. Pit Corder's *Introducing Applied Linguistics* published by Penguin

      J. P. B. Allen and S. Pit Corder's *Readings for Applied Linguistics: The Edinburgh Course in Applied Linguistics* (vol. 1) published by Oxford University Press

      R. B. Kaplan appointed first Professor of Applied Linguistics in the United States, at the University of Southern California

1975   Allen and Corder's *Papers in Applied Linguistics: The Edinburgh Course in Applied Linguistics* (vol. 2) published by Oxford University Press

1976   Applied Linguistics Association of Australia (ALAA) founded

1977   American Association for Applied Linguistics (AAAL) organized

1980   *Applied Linguistics* began publication from Oxford University Press

      Annual Review of Applied Linguistics (ARAL) began publication from Newbury House, subsequently published by Cambridge University Press

      R. B. Kaplan's *On the Scope of Applied Linguistics* published by Newbury House

Chapter 2

THE IEP AS A NONTRADITIONAL ENTITY

David E. Eskey
University of Southern California

he first intensive English program (IEP) in the United States, the University of Michigan's English Language Institute, was established a little more than 50 years ago (1945); one of its founders, Dr. Robert Lado, died as recently as 1995. Since the total history of such programs is thus still somewhat shorter than one average person's life expectancy, it is hardly surprising that IEPs cannot be described as "traditional" academic programs; IEPs are clearly new kids on the academic block. But there are other, more fundamental reasons why they may *never* qualify as traditional programs:

1. They serve nontraditional student populations.

2. They employ nontraditional faculty.

3. They feature nontraditional curricula directed toward nontraditional academic objectives.

4. They are usually locked into nontraditional administrative and budgetary structures.

Each of these facts and their consequences is explored here, including a discussion of future prospects for IEPs as nontraditional entities, arguing in opposition to the currently cherished notion that IEPs should demand, or at least lobby for, traditional status in U.S. universities.

Why Are IEPs Nontraditional Entities?

IEPs represent nontraditional entities when compared to traditional academic units. An examination of IEP students, faculty, curricula, and administrative and budgetary structures illustrates the nonconventional nature of these programs.

IEP Students

Students enrolled in an IEP are, by definition, international students who are short-term visitors (at least officially) on F-1 visa status; they are planning to earn U.S. university degrees, but they have almost nothing else in common with other university students. They come from many different countries and different ethnic groups within those countries, and they vary dramatically with respect to prior educational experience, proficiency in English, expectations, motivation, and, most of all, academic and career goals. Some are graduate students and some are undergraduates, and they plan to major in virtually every field. There are, of course, trends; in any given year, larger numbers come from certain parts of the world (the Middle East in the 1970s, the Far East in the 1990s), mainly as a consequence of economic and political factors. Most students eventually major in such fields as science, engineering, and business; the group is disproportionately male. But trends change with the times, and there are many exceptions. IEP students are, in short, a heterogeneous bunch with no obvious place in the academic pecking order and few natural advocates among university administrators, especially high-level administrators, or among faculty in more traditional fields. Faculty tend to advocate for students in their academic specialties without regard to foreign or domestic status. Since the great majority of IEP students have not yet been admitted to degree programs, they do not attract much faculty support. In fact, among the faculty as a whole, IEP students, like other international students, have more enemies than advocates. Staczek and Carkin (1985) provided a summary of faculty attitudes toward such students based on Goodwin and Nacht's (1983) extensive interview sampling. They observed that the faculty interviewed fell into three groups, only one of which, the smallest, was unequivocally committed to international students.

The first group, committed to international educational exchange, included faculty who were involved in technical-assistance programs with overseas extension and those who were former Peace Corps volunteers. The second group of faculty perceived that their own areas of expertise were dependent on international student enrollments in programs such as agriculture and hotel management, which had grown beyond the U.S. demand for them. These faculty welcomed international students. In other areas, such as engineering, physics, and computer science, international students were appreciated as educational consumers and as laboratory or research assistants, but they were often regarded as fillers in a temporarily depressed program that was expected to recover and eventually become "re-Americanized." Within this group, Goodwin and Nacht (1983) reported that "some of the faculty seemed to feel shame at their dependence on foreign students and that having to recruit abroad dented morale" (p. 9).

The third group had no real self-interest in international students, even though some of the faculty taught in programs of international studies. Goodwin and Nacht noted, to their surprise, that "there was a prevailing apathy, and in some cases, hostility to the foreign presence. It was frequently observed [by faculty] that foreign students retard the educational process and are an annoyance to be minimized" (1983, p. 9). When questioned about their reasons for negative feelings toward international students in their classrooms, faculty usually referred to the amount and types of additional help needed by the students and the inscrutability of such students, citing examples of passive classroom behavior, negotiating behaviors with grades, and obsequious attitudes toward authority. Goodwin and Nacht concluded that there were strong feelings behind some of the complaints and unflattering comments about international students in U.S. classrooms that emphasize the need for accurate information about and reasoned attention to the subject from all concerned.

This is not the total picture, of course. In addition to the faculty and staff of the IEP itself, there are people on most U.S. campuses who serve as advocates for international students. Most obvious are the people who provide admission, immigration, and advisement services to such students, but there are also miscellaneous faculty and staff who are committed to international educational exchange as valuable, even essential, to these students and to their host institutions. Unfortunately, such people are rarely major policy makers, which raises the larger issue of the role and status of international students on U.S. university campuses. Much can be inferred from the title of the best single study on that subject—Goodwin & Nacht's *Absence of Decision* (1983)—which demonstrates quite convincingly that most U.S. universities (there are some happy exceptions) simply have no coherent policy regarding international students besides welcoming the increased tuition income that these students represent. (See Rawley, this volume, for additional information on policy.)

IEP Faculty

It seems crucial to begin any discussion of IEPs by clearly distinguishing between two kinds of English as a second language (ESL) faculty: those who hold professional rank in tenure-track appointments (assistant, associate, or full professors) and those who are full- or part-time ESL instructors. People in the field like to fudge this distinction in the interest of improving the lot of faculty in the latter category, who are frequently exploited in universities and many other kinds of programs.

For tenure-track faculty (who normally hold a doctorate in some appropriate field), ESL represents a focus for research, just as physics does for physicists; typically they teach a few graduate courses (6 to 9 hours a week) to future scholars and practitioners in departments of English or Linguistics, Schools of Education, or international centers of some kind. There is, of course, no reason why they should not also teach in IEPs, and some do, but the great majority do not. Like other university faculty, they make their reputations, and qualify for promotion and tenure, more on their research and publication than on the quality of their teaching.

For ESL instructors (who normally hold a master's degree in an appropriate field), whether full or part time, the situation is quite different. They teach much heavier loads (typically 15–20 hours per week). For part-timers who would prefer full-time status, this often means teaching on several different campuses. They do little or no research or research-related publication because their job requirements rarely include this. Their job security often depends on evaluations of their teaching by program administrators and students. At a few institutions full-time instructors can earn tenure, but this is quite rare.

In discussing IEP faculty, then, we are discussing instructors, not professors. Instructors differ from traditional faculty with respect to academic qualifications, focus and scope of work, and access to tenure. That being the case, they are often excluded from traditional faculty functions such as service on committees that determine, or at least have a major say in, issues such as program structure, budget, admissions policies, faculty governance, and working conditions. They have much less influence on university policies concerning these issues than faculty in traditional disciplines. Predictably, then, they rarely achieve the kind of control over program structure and working conditions that their colleagues in other fields take for granted.

Another problem for these instructors is the pervasive belief that anyone who can speak a language can teach it. Despite their graduate degrees and sometimes extensive experience in the United States and abroad, ESL instructors are often not regarded as having any special expertise because what they teach is their own language, which any native speaker knows in some sense. In this regard, academic colleagues may be part of the problem. They may see ESL as a convenient dumping ground for unemployed colleagues in their own specialties or even for spouses looking for a little part-time work.

IEP Curricula

One hallmark of traditional academic disciplines is that students major in them. IEP students may eventually major in any of the traditional disciplines, but none will major in ESL, which means that IEP course work—like IEP students and IEP faculty—is, in many ways, nontraditional.

As the word intensive suggests, most IEP curricula include many more instructional hours—often 25 to 30—than the typical academic course load requires, hence the heavy teaching loads for instructors. Moreover, the final objective of this work is not the acquisition of a body of knowledge, as in most traditional fields of study, but the mastery of a particular set of language skills—the English skills required for success in U.S. university degree programs (i.e., a particular version of English for Academic Purposes). Work of this kind also occurs, of course, in professional fields like engineering, medicine, and education, but in these fields such work is regarded as supplementary to a core program based on a body of content. To put the case more abstractly, ESL is regarded, accurately enough, as a means, not an end—a *pre*requisite to academic study—and therefore something very different from such traditional fields as literature or chemistry, the mastery of which at degree levels is recognized as an end in itself. One unfortunate result of this is that ESL students, especially those enrolled in pre-admission IEPs, are often confused with native-speaking students who have failed to acquire the language skills required for successful university-level performance—that is, students in need of remedial course work. Thus, ESL courses are often considered remedial courses (i.e., courses for weak students or for students who have not been properly prepared) and are therefore conducted at a lower intellectual level than traditional academic classes. Finally, IEP courses—and ESL courses in general—are nearly always *non*credit courses, which further marginalizes ESL instruction in a university context where accumulating credits toward a specific degree is the usual academic practice. Even *non*remedial, noncredit courses are generally regarded as a kind of self-improvement (like modern dance or karate), not to be confused with serious academic study.

IEP Administrative and Budgetary Structures

A final category in which IEPs nearly always differ from traditional academic programs is the administrative structure to which their universities assign them. They may be attached to academic departments, such as English or Linguistics, but they are almost never regarded as academic departments themselves. They may be assigned to international centers of some kind, along with various service units for international students (like international student admissions and advisement), which is an unfortunate arrangement that drives the IEP even further from the academic mainstream. They may also function as free-standing units, most often in Extension or Continuing Education, where they commonly report to relatively minor administrators and often have no meaningful relationship to academic programs in applied linguistics or language teacher education despite their overlapping concerns. None of these models provides IEPs with anything like traditional academic status; the differences among such models amount to being the smallest fish in a big puddle (like a School of Arts and Sciences) or being, at best, the biggest fish in a very small puddle (like Continuing Education).

In addition to low status, IEPs are often burdened with oppressive budgetary arrangements. Most are required to be self-supporting and many are frankly regarded as cash cows that are expected to generate large surpluses for the support of more prestigious programs. (The attachment-to-an-academic-department model is particularly vulnerable to this. Many such departments use money generated by IEPs for projects dear to the hearts of tenured faculty, which rarely include the IEP itself.) This means maximizing income and minimizing costs, which in practice means radical understaffing, low salaries for both staff and faculty, large numbers of part-time faculty with few or no benefits, and major corner-cutting with respect to equipment, facilities, and faculty perks such as support for curriculum development, in-service training, and attending professional conferences. Obviously, universities differ in their treatment of IEPs—not all are exploited to the maximum and some are reasonably well treated—but I know of no university that accords its IEP full academic departmental status. Both academically and administratively, IEPs are nontraditional entities and seem likely to remain so for at least the foreseeable future.

Where Do We Go From Here?

Not much has changed since Staczek and Carkin's mid-1980s analysis of the relationship between U.S. IEPs and their universities (Staczek & Carkin, 1985). In terms of their subtitle, Practices and Promise, the practices are pretty much the same, and the promises remain largely unfulfilled. The truth is that nothing much has changed in the lifetime of such programs. A great many new IEPs were established in the 1970s in response to a rapidly expanding international student population and a widespread perception, probably accurate at the time, that such programs were sure-fire money makers. Newly established IEPs created new jobs for faculty and staff; then, during the 1980s as enrollments leveled off, the increased number of IEPs around the country created increased competition for IEP students. But, to the best of my knowledge, the new programs do not differ much from the old. Those that are successful continue to provide a useful service for international students who can afford to study English in the United States, and much-needed revenues for their universities, which, in most cases these days, find themselves in financial difficulties. But IEPs show no signs whatsoever of achieving parity with more traditional programs and departments. In fact, quite the opposite is true in a time of tight budgets when both student enrollments and support for research are shrinking at most U.S. universities.

For those of us who administer these programs, this is bad news. We and our faculties and staffs remain the Rodney Dangerfields of academia: we are still in demand, we do (in most cases) a good job of teaching English to our students—a job that certainly needs to be done—and we maintain much higher professional standards than our situation warrants. But we "don't get no respect" because we remain nontraditional entities in a culture in which traditional status means power and prestige.

Institutional Commitment

There are a few interesting developments that could lead to changes for the better. An increasing number of U.S. universities have committed themselves to some form of greater internationalization. Science and business, in particular, have become such international enterprises that universities must follow suit if they are to attract good students. Schools of Engineering, for example, have discovered that their need for international students to fill classes, especially at the graduate level, and to serve as teaching and research assistants, has not diminished—as many had thought it would. The need for international students may, in fact, be a permanent condition of their continued existence. Meanwhile, business students must learn to compete in a worldwide market economy, and many are choosing to study Asian languages and cultures and are actively seeking overseas experience. Engineering and Business are large and influential schools on many U.S. campuses, and some are pushing their institutions to commit significant amounts of money and resources to the development of many kinds of international programs and partnerships, some on campus, some in overseas locations. Often these programs have ESL components, and some IEPs are doing a land-office business, sometimes in conjunction with other departments, in special contracts for wealthy overseas clients. This increased international activity certainly does not assure better treatment for IEPs in the future; it could, however, provide a wedge for prying open the door to negotiations leading to a higher status for such programs commensurate with their new roles in these important new ventures.

Accreditation

There has been movement within the profession toward providing IEPs with stronger indicators of quality. For a number of years, both NAFSA and TESOL have been providing opportunities for structured self-study. This is useful for enhancing a program's own sense of its strengths and weaknesses and its reputation within the profession, but is less effective for improving its image with either universities or the general public (see Byrd & Constantinides, 1991). Now, however, TESOL has agreed to serve as an official accrediting agency for IEPs (Harshbarger, 1994; Paiva, 1996; Price, 1995), thus providing the kind of official stamp of approval awarded by a prestigious peer agency that other academic disciplines enjoy, especially disciplines linked to respected professions such as Law and Medicine. The obvious intent is to demonstrate to people outside the field that IEPs have come of age and have achieved true professional status, but support for this idea is far from universal. Smaller, folksier programs are concerned about meeting accreditation criteria—which are likely to include minimum standards of academic preparation for faculty (thus eliminating talented amateurs)—and are *very* concerned about the costs involved. Larger programs which have made what they consider acceptable arrangements with their universities (this includes IEPs at some very prestigious schools) see no need for this kind of accreditation. Many of these programs would prefer to be evaluated as an integral part of their departments or schools by the established accrediting agencies (e.g., WASC) for universities in particular regions. These IEPs see themselves as academic and not professional programs, and therefore not in need of separate, professional accreditation which might in fact serve to reduce their status in the eyes of their academic colleagues. In this debate, IEPs are facing a very old trade-off in human social endeavors between more freedom and more power. Compared to other academic fields, we are currently free of arbitrary constraints and much of the petty snobbery that follows from evaluations by leaders in the field whose qualifications to serve as such may be open to question. On the other hand, we clearly do not have the clout of more traditional academic disciplines or prestigious professions such as Law and Medicine, which routinely require accreditation of programs, partly because no one will take a profession seriously that cannot state what its minimum standards are and what constitutes exemplary practice.

Options for IEPs

The movement toward greater internationalization on many U.S. campuses and TESOL's system for formally accrediting programs may both have positive effects on the future role and status of IEPs. Yet neither, by itself or in combination with the other, seems likely to produce any major changes unless IEP directors take a more proactive role in specifying and actively pursuing the kinds of changes that we believe should be made. Before we can act to effect such changes, however, we will need to agree on what we actually want for our programs. There are two major options. We must lobby, perhaps even fight, either for traditional academic status or for completely new arrangements more in keeping with the real strengths and needs of IEPs. Staczek and Carkin (1985) argued for the former. They took the position that IEPs are not different in any significant way from more traditional academic programs and that IEPs are therefore entitled to the same kind of treatment as other academic units. In their view, an IEP

> is an administrative and academic enterprise with a comprehensive mission to provide ESL training, using qualified professionals in a logical and developing sequence of courses to guide the student to a level of mastery of the English language that will lead to eventual success in a degree or certificate program in an academic institution. This applies equally to ESL as it does to any other discipline: foreign language, English, history, accounting, chemistry. (p. 294)

Such a program should be

> an autonomous unit, that is, independent of another academic department but certainly responsible to an academic officer of the university, be it a dean or a vice president for academic affairs. This kind of organizational relationship contributes to an image that an IEP is a legitimate organization within a university and is bound by the same policies and standards as are other programs or departments. As such an autonomous unit, its budget may then be expected to be internal to the university, generated by a formula, or external to the university, generated by a comprehensive fee for services that covers all academic, administrative, support, and overhead costs. Any surpluses would be used by the program for its development of curriculum, faculty, and resources. (pp. 295–296)

IEP instructors are, as they see it, no different from other academic faculty.

> [They] have contributed to the development of the field as a profession as they have done research, developed materials, made conference presentations, published articles in scholarly journals and published textbooks. These professionals

are not unlike other academic professionals. The argument that the master's level terminal degree is not equivalent to the standard terminal degree for an academic position is untenable. Certainly the performing and creative arts do not require the doctorate and their practitioners are recognized as legitimate members of a university faculty with all the same rights and privileges. (p. 296)

Finally, as a faculty of professionals engaged in an academic enterprise,

the IEP faculty need to be able to determine their course of development, their program governance and their mission, so long as the priorities and goals of their mission are consonant with those of the university. Academic freedom, advancement, tenure, merit evaluation and opportunity for faculty development ought to be among the rights and privileges of the faculty. Moreover, the IEP faculty should have the right to nominate, select and evaluate its leadership within the existing governance structure of the university within which it operates. (p. 296)

This is an attractive line of argument, but it is also, I believe, mainly wishful thinking. For all of the reasons discussed above, IEPs are not—and probably never will be—traditional academic programs as that phrase is understood in the culture of U.S. universities. More specifically, traditional programs do not regard training that will lead to eventual success as their primary mission; they teach the content of their disciplines and consider the acquisition of that content to be the end of education in those disciplines, not, like language training, merely a preliminary means to that end. In their world, the teaching of skills does not equate to teaching specific academic content. With respect to program autonomy, no academic unit that I know of has automatic access to any surpluses in the money it generates. Such money is always distributed in accordance with the university's, not the unit's, priorities. As for IEP instructors, few have job descriptions that include a research and publication component (as those of traditional faculty do), and most are too busy teaching heavy hourly loads to do much research or to publish in scholarly journals. At most U.S. universities (and certainly at the more prestigious schools) arguing that a master's degree is equivalent to a doctorate would be a waste of time; the doctorate is the scholar's degree, and most faculty members in traditional programs would maintain that it is Staczek and Carkin's argument that is untenable in this regard. Like faculty in Law and Medicine, faculty in the arts substitute their professional work, not simply their teaching, for more traditional scholarship, and universities have long since decided that conference presentations and textbooks, though useful contributions, are no substitute for research and publication. The only ESL faculty that I know of who are treated like tenure-track faculty are those who in fact have tenure-track appointments in some traditional discipline like English, Linguistics, or Education. No one confuses these people with master's-level IEP instructors.

Instead of pursuing traditional academic status by means of arguments that can easily be refuted in the current version of U.S. university culture, I believe we would do much better to insist that our host universities recognize IEPs for what they are: a new kind of nontraditional unit that is nevertheless important to the future of U.S. universities in a rapidly internationalizing world where English has become the world's second language. From that vantage point, we could argue for the kinds of support, and the kinds of rights and privileges for IEP instructors, that our programs and faculties actually merit.

It is certainly well beyond the scope of this paper to lay out in detail exactly what we should ask for, but I believe that most of what Staczek and Carkin listed in the final paragraph cited above could—with the major exception of tenure—be obtained from U.S. universities. There are in fact IEPs today that have come close to achieving most of what is on their list for faculty and staff—some control of program mission and development, academic freedom, opportunity for advancement, merit evaluations, and a major voice in choosing and evaluating program leadership. There are also IEPs that enjoy good working relationships with more traditional scholars in the field who provide education, and sometimes training, for current and future IEP faculty. In the best situation, cross-fertilization routinely occurs between IEPs and tenure-track faculty in the field, although no one confuses professors with instructors even when the professors do some teaching in the program.

Such programs are, of course, the exception today in a field where IEPs are more often mistreated or, at best, neglected at many U.S. universities, but they do provide models for what the profession might reasonably aspire to in seeking better treatment for these important programs. The first step would be for IEP leadership to develop an agenda that most of us could support, then to sell that agenda to the rest of the profession, and finally to aggressively promote that agenda in every U.S. university that hosts, or plans to host, an IEP. This would entail supporting all those programs—and there might be quite a few—whose host institutions simply refuse to meet the minimum conditions specified; the ensuing confrontations would certainly be something new for TESOL. In its brief history, our profession has never mounted such a challenge, and we have never taken a stand for something new and fought for it. Unless we choose to do so in this case, however, the next century will be much like this one for IEPs as nontraditional entities.

Discussion Questions and Activities

1. What are the major problems that faculty and staff in your IEP face compared with the faculty and staff of more traditional academic units within your institution?

2. Eskey describes the nontraditional status of university-based intensive English programs. In what ways are other types of language programs that you are familiar with (e.g., high schools, community colleges, private language schools) similar to or different from university-based programs?

3. List three reasons for supporting the accreditation of IEPs. What are some reasons against it? Would large IEPs in university Continuing Education programs be likely to support IEP accreditation? Why? Why not? How about small IEPs in community college settings?

4. In what ways are the faculty and staff of an IEP like—and unlike—those of more traditional academic units within a university? Write a memo to a senior administrator arguing for better treatment for your staff and faculty on the grounds that IEP faculty and staff are much like those in other academic units.

5. Do you agree with Eskey's basic premise concerning the future of IEPs as nontraditional entities? Why? Why not?

6. If you were asked to serve on a university committee that was to propose recognizing IEPs as a new kind of nontraditional unit within the university, what would your arguments be?

7. How could those of us in the profession pursue better treatment for our language programs? Specify what the needs of your language program are, and then develop a plan for obtaining what is needed.

Suggested Readings

Goodwin, C., & Nacht, M. (1983). *Absence of decision: Foreign students in American colleges and universities.* New York: Institute of International Education.

In this book-length study of U.S. universities' policies and practices related to international students, the authors demonstrate very clearly (a) that there is no accepted model for addressing the needs of international students in institutions of higher education and (b) that universities vary wildly with respect to what they expect of, and provide for, their international students. The ambivalent feelings about international students that U.S. universities display go a long way toward explaining their equally ambivalent feelings about nontraditional programs—like IEPs—that serve this population.

Harshbarger, B. (1994). TESOL task force urges accreditation of intensive English programs. *NAFSA Newsletter, 45*(6), 1, 28–31.

In this article, Harshbarger succinctly outlines the history of and current issues concerning the accreditation of IEPs. He focuses on three major issues underlying current discussions of accreditation: (a) problems with how IEPs are currently evaluated, (b) the perceived division between university-operated IEPs and independent language programs, and (c) the potential for governmental intervention in IEP accreditation.

Staczek, J., & Carkin, S. (1985). Intensive English programs fit in traditional academic settings: Practices and promise. In P. Larson, E. Judd, & D. S. Messerschmitt (Eds.), *On TESOL '84: A brave new world for TESOL* (pp. 289–300). Washington, DC: TESOL.

The authors, well-respected and experienced IEP administrators themselves, argue that IEPs should be treated like other, more traditional, academic programs. Their discussion of IEPs in traditional academic settings, the only published treatment of the subject, is both well informed and informative.

Part II

THE LANGUAGE PROGRAM
ADMINISTRATOR AS LEADER

Chapter 3

THE CATALYST FOR CHANGE AND INNOVATION

Fredricka L. Stoller
Northern Arizona University

lthough rarely listed in our job descriptions, one of our most important responsibilities as language program administrators is to serve as catalysts for change and innovation. Through strong leadership and involvement in programmatic change and innovation, we can enhance many aspects of our programs, creating greater job satisfaction among faculty and staff, better learning conditions for students, improved reputations for our programs, and more effective management of program resources. Despite the fact that innovation is a fundamental component of thriving and progressive programs (see Baldridge & Deal, 1983), our role as advocates for change and innovation is no simple task. Innovations, by their very definition, require adjustments in attitudes and behaviors and they challenge the status quo, necessitating modifications in standard, routine practices. Thus, they often provoke discomfort, angst, insecurity, indignation, differences in opinion, and turf battles; and they mobilize opposition groups that we never knew existed (see McWhinney, 1992). In addition, innovations almost always require increased workloads, some form of retraining, and costs in terms of time, energy, and resources.

Whereas innovations inevitably bring with them levels of uncertainty, they also energize those involved in their development and implementation. They empower language program personnel who forge new paths, pilot novel ideas, see improvements, and reap the benefits of their labors. The exhilaration that comes from such exploration can invigorate a program and lead to improved teaching and learning.

The successful management of innovation—whether introduced by administrators, faculty, students, or outside consultants—requires leadership from the language program administrator. An understanding of innovation diffusion can help administrators to guide the multidimensional processes associated with diffusion, mobilize those looking to innovate, and deal with the inevitable resisters. A discussion of the following topics will help facilitate that understanding:[1]

1. Differences between change and innovation.
2. Impetuses for innovation.
3. Characteristics of language programs that stimulate innovation.
4. Characteristics of language programs that hinder innovation.
5. Paths to successful innovation diffusion.

The discussion concludes with a set of principles that can guide language program administrators in their efforts to promote successful innovation while they simultaneously juggle the multifaceted demands of their administrative positions.

Differences Between Change and Innovation

Although much of the literature on *change* and *innovation* uses the terms interchangeably, I find it useful to make a distinction between the two. Change is often identified as one of the most stable features of organizational life (Baldridge & Deal, 1983). In all settings, including language programs, change is predictable and inevitable, always resulting in an alteration in the status quo but not necessarily in improvements. Language programs experience change when, for example, members of the faculty and staff leave the area or assume other jobs in the institution; student enrollments increase or decrease; student demographics fluctuates because of, for instance, international politics, global economics, and the value of the dollar; mandates are imposed by governmental or institutional legislation; educational costs increase; and policy makers question the value of internationalization or the services provided to our students. Language program administrators usually spend a great deal of time responding to changes such as these despite the fact that we have little, if any, control over them.

Innovation, on the other hand, results from a deliberate and conscious effort that is perceived as new, is intended to bring about improvement, and has the potential for diffusion, that is, the process by which an innovation spreads over time through an organization or program (Hamilton, 1996; Nicholls, 1983). While change is inevitable in language programs, innovation is the key to raising standards in that it facilitates self-renewal, promotes a sense of well-being, enhances teachers' careers, prevents burnout, improves instruction, and allows programs to be responsive to changes that are likely to impact them (see Hamilton, 1996).

It should be noted that the notion of *newness* runs throughout most discussions of innovation even though the element of newness is relative; what may be new in one program may be considered old hat in the next (see Levine, 1980). That so-called standard practices in one program may be viewed as innovations in another should not diminish the significance of the innovations themselves; rather, it reveals the local, context-specific nature of innovation diffusion.

Despite the positive connotations associated with the term *innovation*, managing and implementing an innovation represents an administrative challenge. The very same innovation (e.g., the conversion from a discrete-skills syllabus to an integrated-skills, content-based syllabus, or an e-mail pen-pal program) can be enthusiastically endorsed and implemented with little or no resistance in some settings, and harshly criticized and strongly rejected in others. To complicate matters, the simple generation of an innovative idea is seldom sufficient on its own; many administrators often rely on the supposed merit(s) of the innovation itself simply because they are unaware of the diverse factors that actually influence successful reform efforts (Bottomley, Dalton, & Corbel, 1994; Henrichsen, 1989). Even when innovations are grounded in strong academic theory and sound practical considerations, they rarely take hold simply on account of their own merits. This might explain why the same innovation can be strongly accepted in some language programs and vigorously criticized in others.

Impetuses for Innovation

It is said that "some innovations spring from a flash of genius but most stem from a conscious, purposeful search for innovation opportunities" (Drucker, 1991, p. 9). What actually inspires innovation, however, is highly variable and is dependent on the environment in which it occurs. The impetus for innovations can emerge from a variety of circumstances, including unexpected occurrences or critical incidents, incongruities, a desire for greater efficiency, demographic shifts or market changes, new knowledge (from action research, research, conference attendance, and so forth), dissatisfaction with the status quo, strong leadership, shared interests, a power imbalance, or outside recommendations (see De Lano, Riley, & Crookes, 1994).

In a study of innovation in intensive English programs (Stoller, 1992a, 1995a, 1995b), survey respondents, who were directors of language programs, identified numerous incentives for programmatic innovation; five of those incentives, discussed below, are particularly noteworthy because of their applicability to a wide range of language program contexts.

Dissatisfaction With the Status Quo

The most frequent impetus for innovation is dissatisfaction with the status quo; innovations most often occur when current practices are viewed as needing to be improved, upgraded, renewed, or replaced (Jones & Lewis, 1991). Innovations that emerge from dissatisfaction impact any number of areas within the language program, such as curriculum, personnel, placement, evaluation, recruitment, orientation, and management. So, for example, when faculty are unhappy with the results of placement procedures semester after semester, their dissatisfaction may mobilize them to generate a new and possibly innovative set of placement procedures. When students complain loudly and often that they have too few opportunities to speak with native speakers, a student counselor might set up an innovative conversation partner program, linking language students with native speakers. When faculty are discontent with working conditions, language program administrators may introduce an innovative plan for rewarding accomplishments, adjusting teaching schedules, or empowering faculty through self-governance structures.

Need for More Professionalism

The desire to enhance working conditions, improve hiring practices, and provide faculty with more professional growth opportunities often provides the incentive for language program innovations. Examples of successfully implemented innovations[2] that represent language program responses to a need for more professionalism include the following:

1. Developing a career ladder policy in which teachers are rewarded for professional development in teaching, administration, curriculum development, or assessment.

2. Peer observation of faculty using nonjudgmental approaches.

3. Redefining full-time faculty responsibilities.

4. Forming a council, with administrators and faculty, that deals with program-wide procedures and policies.

5. Funding professional development seminars and conference attendance.

Explicit and Implicit Support, Mandates, and Requests

The momentum needed to introduce and implement an innovative proposal often stems from support or encouragement from individuals in the higher administration; mandates or new expectations from professional organizations, the home institution, or governmental legislation; requests or complaints from students enrolled in the program; and suggestions or concerns voiced by non-language-program faculty. For example, a mandate—from a university president or board of regents—to internationalize the university could lead to the following innovations:

1. A new credit-bearing language program course (cross-listed with Anthropology) that facilitates cross-cultural exchanges among nonnative and native speakers enrolled in the course.

2. A promotional video or four-color brochure.

3. Language program participation in an international fair and food festival (with institutional support).

Student Needs and Desires

Recognizing new student needs or desires is another common motive for innovation. For example, the realization that computer literacy is required of language students in the workplace or in mainstream classes has provided many language programs with the impetus to develop computer facilities and accompanying instruction. As students enter programs with increasing proficiency in word processing skills, for example, we have been propelled to bypass keyboard instruction, which was considered essential just a few years ago.

Faculty Interest and Suggestions

The interests of faculty commonly provide the needed incentive for programmatic innovation. Faculty often return from conferences, seminars, and workshops with new ideas from which they can develop innovations appropriate to their own language programs. In addition, individual faculty interests—professional and personal—often lead to innovative instructional practices. For example, a faculty member who is particularly interested in vocabulary acquisition may experiment with new approaches to vocabulary instruction and may develop an innovative approach that is adopted by others; faculty interested in desk-top publishing may propose an innovative course combining writing instruction and newsletter publishing; faculty with theater arts backgrounds may propose innovative elective courses that integrate acting, pronunciation instruction, and project work.

In sum, understanding all of these impetuses for innovation can help administrators stimulate programmatic improvements. When introducing innovations to faculty, stu-

dents, funding agencies, or higher-level administrators, or when trying to inspire innovation in others, administrators should try to link proposals to specific impetuses: dissatisfaction, a need for more professionalism, explicit or implicit mandates, student needs, faculty interests, or any other signs that might indicate an environment conducive to innovation. When contemplating innovative proposals submitted by others, administrators
should determine the underlying motivation for the proposal by requesting that the inno-
vator provide a principled justification for it that identifies the intended beneficiaries and
probable costs. The resulting dialogue can help clarify the appropriateness of the proposal
and lay the foundation for later stages in the innovation diffusion process.

Characteristics of Language Programs That Stimulate Innovation

Successful language programs avoid stagnation by evolving and innovating "rather
than remaining routinized and standardized" (White, 1988, p. 138). Administrators can
stimulate innovation by recognizing programmatic characteristics that enhance the potential for innovation. With this awareness, language program administrators can understand
why some programs can manage and sustain innovative efforts while in others innovations
seem to fizzle out. This heightened understanding enables administrators to provide the
leadership needed to harness the forces that bring about innovation (Hamilton, 1996).

In the Stoller study mentioned earlier, survey respondents were asked to identify
those aspects of their programs that most positively influenced programmatic innovation.
The four most commonly cited characteristics are described below.

A Stable Core Faculty

Having a stable core faculty has a positive influence on programmatic innovation. As
administrators, we need to nurture stability, professional working conditions, and a sense
of belonging or permanence, whenever possible. Faculty who demonstrate creativity, flexibility, initiative, commitment, professionalism, and a willingness to communicate with
peers are likely to contribute to the innovative potential of a language program, if given
the opportunity to do so. Thus, when hiring and later evaluating faculty performance,
administrators should make sure that faculty are aware that such behaviors and attitudes
will be valued and rewarded (see Barsi & Kaebnick, 1989).

Administrative Leadership and Dynamism

Innovation most often takes place in contexts of leadership, though it is important to
keep in mind that "monolithic central controls stifle innovation" (Hamilton, 1996, p. 3).
Even if initially proposed by and later carried out by faculty, successfully implemented
innovations can usually be attributed partially to responsive, flexible, and supportive language program administrators who demonstrate a commitment to high standards and
who exhibit trust and respect for faculty.

As language program administrators, we need to reflect on our attitudes towards change
and the status quo to determine the degree to which we are contributing to the potential for
innovation in our programs. Administrative involvement, though not necessarily direct
involvement, is important. Most essential, however, are a willingness to explore innovative
alternatives with faculty and an inclination to make provisions for faculty "freedom."

We must also recognize that the potential for innovation in language programs is nourished when there are individuals who have links to other academic units, institutions, and sources of ideas. Thus, we need to encourage faculty to attend conferences, become active in professional organizations, and serve on professional committees; the professional networks and exposure to new perspectives that result from such activities can contribute positively to language program innovations.

Similarly, we should support course development projects and faculty research, including action research, because they often lead to innovations. If we become too attached to the status quo, and we are unwilling to experiment with new ideas, stagnation is likely to set in, and faculty burnout and disenchantment will become widespread. Provisions for pilot courses and release time—to explore new perspectives or develop new materials—are crucial for promoting innovation.

A Flexible Organizational Framework

It is difficult to disassociate the attitudes of administrators from the organizational and philosophical frameworks of their language programs. Language programs that are open to change, are flexible, and grant freedom to faculty have greater potential for innovation. Such an atmosphere necessitates trust, an openness toward experimentation, a desire for self-renewal, and the acceptance of possible failure as one step toward innovation. A language program that supports its faculty by means of reasonable teaching loads, rewards, and opportunities for professional development positively influences its innovative character. Provisions for participatory mangagement influence faculty commitment to and involvement with innovation as well.

As language program administrators, we play an instrumental role in shaping the organizational and philosophical framework of our programs. We should analyze the underpinnings of our programs to determine whether or not faculty have been granted enough freedom to innovate and whether or not there is sufficient fluidity in the curriculum to allow for faculty experimentation. We must structure our programs so that the possibility for innovation is built into them, and we must share the responsibility for innovation with our faculty so that innovation has the potential to spread.

Responsiveness to Mandates for Change

Responsiveness to explicit and implicit mandates for change is another variable impacting the innovative character of a language program. When language programs respond directly to mandates stemming from changes in student needs, parent institution expectations, market demands, student enrollment, trends in the field, or dissatisfaction with the status quo, the results can sometimes be innovative.

The explicitness of certain mandates—for example, a change in United States immigration regulations, a direct request from the president or principal of one's institution, or student hostility—often obliges immediate action. The recognition of implicit mandates for change, however, requires a concerted effort on the part of program administrators and faculty. To recognize less visible mandates for change necessitates an ongoing assessment of student needs and institutional climate, and an understanding of the professional needs of faculty. Equally important, we need to be sensitive to and informed about parent institution policies that could impact student enrollment and hiring practices. In programs serving the language learning needs of international students, it is important to be aware of international market demands and enrollment trends that are influenced by global politics and economics. A familiarity with and tracking of issues such as these can help us identify implicit mandates for change and then act upon them in a deliberate fashion.

Characteristics of Language Programs That Hinder Innovation

While there are many programmatic variables that contribute positively to the potential for innovation, there are other variables that hinder it. Two obstacles that we should all be aware of are the very nature of innovation itself and the marginality of language programs. Although there are no easy ways to sidestep these hindrances, recognizing them and learning to overcome them are keys to successful innovation diffusion.

Innovations As Hindrances

Innovations, by their very definition, require changes in attitudes and behaviors because they challenge the status quo and necessitate modifications in routine practices. As a result, they often provoke disagreements and insecurity, they often involve retraining and increased workloads, and they always require time, energy, and resources. In addition, innovations are most often viewed differently by the person advocating the innovation and the person who is being asked to implement it; when innovators fail to take into account the adopter's viewpoint, difficulties are likely to arise (see White, Martin, Stimson, & Hodge, 1991).

Furthermore, the normal stages of innovation diffusion usually require more time than originally anticipated (Markee, 1997). In the first stage, a small number of individuals will be involved in the introduction of the innovation. In the second stage, only "early adopters" can be expected to implement the innovation willingly. In the middle stages, the majority, influenced by the early adopters, accept the innovation. And finally, the late adopters "give in" while a minority steadfastly refuse to adopt. (See Rogers, 1983, and White, 1988, for further discussion of the stages of innovation diffusion.)

Although there is little we can do to counter the inherent nature of innovation, there are five general guidelines to follow while promoting innovation in our language programs:

1. We can only provide the leadership needed to sustain the lengthy innovation process if we ourselves are willing to usher in new policies and practices.

2. We need to recognize willingly the time and patience required to move from the first stage to the final stage of the process.

3. We must accept the fact that there may always be a few stalwart resisters to programmatic innovation.

4. We must take into account and deal with the difficulties adopters are likely to experience. If we do not, those who initially endorse an innovation will become disillusioned and join forces with the resisters, resorting to past practices and old ways.

5. We must recognize the need to provide adequate administrative support in the form of release time, resources, or retraining opportunities.

Marginality of Language Programs

That language programs are viewed as marginal—physically and educationally—by our home institutions represents a second major hindrance to programmatic innovation. Many of our programs are housed in temporary bungalows, in basements, or on the periphery of our campuses. Our students are viewed as "different" because of their diverse linguistic, educational, and cultural backgrounds. Our instruction is often perceived to be remedial, developmental, or compensatory. It is frequently assumed that any speaker of English can do what we do in the classroom, resulting, at times, in unqualified teachers' being assigned to our classrooms. And our faculty often have a nonstandard status on campus because they are part time or they do not have the terminal degree expected of others on campus. The so-called oddity of our language programs often contributes to their perceived second-class status, which in turn deprives us of the prestige and funding opportunities needed to innovate.

The questionable status of language programs represents a serious obstacle to programmatic innovation. As long as ignorance, lack of appreciation, or misperceptions about our programs exist, our innovative efforts may be thwarted. In order to get out of the academic basement, we can combat these misperceptions in the following ways:

1. We need to educate (and sometimes re-educate) those with whom we deal in our institutions and communities so that they appreciate the value of our instruction, students, and faculty (see Stoller & Christison, 1994).

2. We should avoid using terms that carry negative connotations (e.g., remedial, compensatory instruction, or student deficiencies) when referring to our programs and students, as they generate stereotypes for those unfamiliar with the mission of our instruction. This misconception detracts from the professional work being carried out in our programs. Conversely, we should adopt positive terms.

3. We should publicize more assertively the professional activities and accomplishments of our faculty and students in addition to curricular innovations that may have applications in other units in our institutions.

4. We should make known our association with professional organizations, such as TESOL and NAFSA: Association of International Educators.

5. We should familiarize others with the professional journals and publications of our discipline, as they are usually unknown to those outside the field. Furthermore, we need to publish in these forums and make our efforts known to others in our home institutions.

Paths to Successful Innovation Diffusion

Innovation diffusion is a complex process not only because motivating individuals to embrace new ideas and abandon the comfort and security of the status quo is challenging, but also because of the multiple variables that interact to either facilitate or inhibit the acceptance and implementation of innovations. (See Henrichsen, 1989, for a discussion of the multidimensionality of the innovation process.) We must consider the following variables in language program contexts:

1. The language program itself, including its faculty, students, administrators, mission, status, and facilities.

2. The characteristics of the home institution, along with its priorities, policies, and resources.

3. Variables beyond our institutions, including social, political, and fiscal events in the global arena.

4. Innovations themselves and their perceived qualities.

The ways in which potential adopters/supporters perceive innovations—often reflecting the way in which innovations are introduced to them—can influence their receptiveness to new policies or practices. Language program administrators must understand the role of perceptions in the innovation diffusion process so that they can use that knowledge wisely when soliciting the approval of potential adopters.

Innovations reportedly have many characteristics that interact in various ways with one another, generating much complexity in the innovation diffusion process. The most often cited set of properties attributed to innovations was proposed by Rogers and Shoemaker (1971) and later refined by Rogers (1983). The five properties, based on the conclusions of more than 1,500 empirical and nonempirical studies, are listed and defined in Table 1. Rogers claims that these five attributes influence the adoption of an innovation in different ways. Three of the five attributes—relative advantage, observability, and trialability—positively influence the adoption of an innovation. In the case of *relative advantage*, innovations that are perceived to be better than the ideas they supersede are more likely to be adopted than innovations that are perceived to be no different than current practices or only slight improvements over past practices. The greater the perceived advantage, the greater the likelihood of adoption.

Table 1. **Attributes of Innovations**

Attribute	Definition of attribute
Compatibility	The degree to which an innovation is consistent with already existing philosophies, policies, practices, and beliefs.
Complexity	The degree to which an innovation is perceived as difficult to use or understand.
Observability	The degree to which the results of an innovation are visible to others.
Relative advantage	The degree to which an innovation is perceived as better than the idea it supercedes.
Trialability	The degree to which an innovation can be experimented with on a limited basis.

(Rogers & Shoemaker, 1971; Rogers, 1983)

Similarly, innovations that are clearly visible and *observable*, such as new software or improved hiring policies that are easily identifiable, are more likely to be adopted than less-visible innovations, such as a new philosophical approach to teacher supervision. In a similar way, innovations that can be piloted (i.e., those that are *trialable*) are more likely to gain the support of potential adopters than innovations that cannot be piloted. For example, teachers may be more likely to accept a change in curricular focus—from a discrete skills approach to an integrated skills approach—if the new curriculum can first be piloted and then evaluated by the faculty.

Complexity, on the other hand, is said to be negatively related to adoption; the more complicated an innovation is perceived to be, the more resistance is exhibited by potential adopters. At times the innovation itself is not actually very complex, but if it is perceived to be difficult, regardless of reality, the innovation is likely to encounter resistance and possible rejection.

Compatibility, unlike the other four attributes, is variable in that it can either accelerate or retard the rate of adoption of an innovation. If an innovation is perceived to be too compatible with current practices, potential adopters may not think that the innovation is worth the time, trouble, or expense to adopt. At the same time, if an innovation is not at all compatible with current practices, it may be seen as too radical, and thus be rejected.

Table 2. **Attributes of Innovations**

Attribute	Definition of attribute
Acceptability	Match between institutional philosophy and the innovation.
Feasibility	Match between institutional resources and the innovation.
Relevance	Match between perceived student needs and the innovation.

(Kelly, 1980)

Table 3. **Factors Contributing to the Acceptance or Rejection of Innovations**

Factor	Role of factor in acceptance/rejection
Balanced divergence	Favorable attitudes develop towards an innovation when potential adopters view the innovation as sufficiently divergent but not too divergent from current practices.
Dissatisfaction	The presence of some degree of dissatisfaction with the status quo will facilitate the implementation of an innovation.
Viability	The more viable an innovation is perceived to be, the more likely its adoption.

(Stoller, 1992a, 1994b, 1995a, 1995b)

A smaller set of attributes, outlined in Table 2, is proposed by Kelly (1980), who concludes that three perceived attributes of innovations correlate *positively* with rate and success of innovation diffusion. Based on Kelly's findings, adoption of an innovation will most likely occur when the innovation is perceived to be highly acceptable, feasible, and relevant by adopters/supporters. Kelly's conclusions introduce two attributes that are not fully accounted for by Rogers and Shoemaker's set, specifically feasibility and relevance; Kelly's notion of acceptability corresponds closely to Rogers's compatibility.

In my study (Stoller, 1994b, 1995b), three factors were identified that play a role in the acceptance or rejection of innovations. They are listed and defined in Table 3. The *balanced divergence* factor actually combines six attributes from the innovation literature (i.e., compatibility with past practices, complexity, explicitness, flexibility, originality, and visibility). At first glance, the factor appears to combine a disparate set of attributes, which seem to play diverse roles in the innovation literature. For example, previous research claims that visibility facilitates the acceptance of innovative proposals whereas complexity does not. Contrary to the literature, which suggests that such attributes are generally positively or negatively related to adoption rate, the balanced divergence factor suggests that adoption rates depend on a perceived "middle range." That is, when certain attributes are "sufficiently" present and fall within a perceived *zone of innovation*, adoption rates are likely to increase. Conversely, their perceived absence or excess can be detrimental to adoption because they lead to unfavorable attitudes towards the innovation and subsequently undermine potential support for the innovation.

What seems to be at issue with the balanced divergence factor is something akin to a Goldilock's syndrome whereby attitudes towards an innovation can be too cold, too hot, or just right. When attributes making up this factor are perceived to fall outside the zone of innovation, the innovation is perceived to be too cold or too hot, undermining potential support for the innovation. When the attributes are perceived to be sufficiently present (or just right), favorable attitudes towards the innovation develop that result in support for the innovation. Figure 1 illustrates, in visual form, this zone of innovation phenomenon.

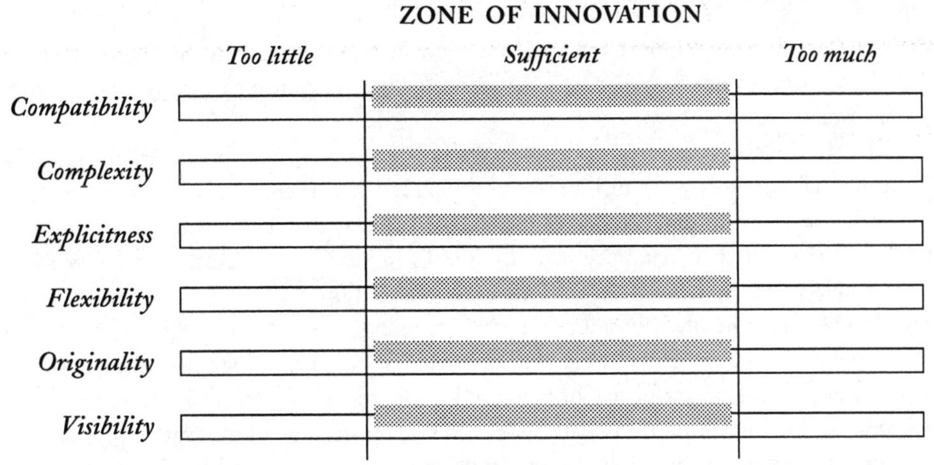

Figure 1. **The zone of innovation that motivates individuals to support innovations.**

A few examples should suffice to illustrate this phenomenon. When an innovation is perceived to be sufficiently visible, favorable attitudes towards the innovation are more likely to develop and thus motivate potential supporters. Conversely, if an innovation is not perceived as sufficiently visible, the support of potential backers will be difficult to obtain. At the same time, there are indications that excessive visibility can threaten the acceptance of an innovation because highly visible system-divergent practices threaten individuals who are satisfied with the status quo, leading to a mobilization of the opposition (see Berg & Ostergren, 1979).

A similar phenomenon exists with perceptions of complexity. If an innovation is perceived as overly simplistic, the innovation may not be viewed as significantly different from what is currently in practice; as a result, the innovation would not be considered worth the time, effort, and resources needed for development and implementation. If the innovation is perceived as excessively complex, few would consider it worthy of adoption.

Similarly, if an innovation is too compatible with current practices (i.e., similar to current practices), it will not be viewed as an innovation; in such cases, the innovation will be perceived as a minor adjustment in or a simple tinkering with current practices. At the same time, if the innovation is perceived as totally incompatible with current practices, the innovation is perceived as unacceptably divergent from current expectations. These findings support Rogers's (1983) observation that acceptance of an innovation can be undermined if an innovation is perceived to be either too compatible or not compatible enough with current practices.

The concept underlying the zone of innovation phenomenon has implications for the promotion of language program innovations. When soliciting support for an innovative idea, we must be sensitive to the role of the balanced divergence factor. Innovations should be presented so that the salient characteristics of the innovation are perceived to fall within the zone of innovation.

The second factor, *dissatisfaction*, depicts the degree to which individuals perceive a need for change because of varying levels of satisfaction or dissatisfaction with the status quo. The study suggests that dissatisfaction with the status quo and the perceived need for improvement represent converse perspectives on the same general notion of satisfaction. The close relationship between the two perspectives suggests that a useful method for soliciting support for an innovation involves promoting the innovation as both (a) an improvement over past practices and (b) a response to dissatisfaction with current practices.

The third factor, *viability*, is positively related to adoption rate. There are indications that potential adopters view an innovation as viable when there is a match between the innovation and institutional resources and a match between the innovation and student needs (cf. feasibility and relevance in Kelly, 1980). In addition, innovations are perceived to be viable when they are practical and useful. The more viable an innovation is perceived to be, the more likely its adoption.

So what do the results of these studies mean for language program administrators? Acknowledging the powerful role of perceived attributes is one step towards better management of the innovation diffusion process. When promoting an innovative proposal in our language programs, we should orchestrate our efforts with the knowledge that certain attributes are more likely to lead to acceptance and others are likely to lead to rejection. An honest and persuasive presentation—one that guides events and presents innovative ideas so that they are likely to be accepted and implemented—requires that we do the following:

1. Present innovative proposals so that the advantages (relative advantage, observability, trialability, relevance, feasibility, viability, or acceptability) outweigh the disadvantages (invisibility). If we truly believe in the innovation that we are advocating, the benefits should outweigh the difficulties without manipulation.

2. Point out how the proposal is a response to dissatisfaction of students, faculty, staff, administrators, the upper administration, or sponsoring agencies. Identifying the beneficiaries of the innovation and the ways in which they will benefit can demonstrate how the innovation is an improvement over past practices.

3. Highlight issues related to the usefulness, feasibility, and practicality of the proposed innovation; by pointing out these features, we should be able to show how viable the innovation actually is.

4. Introduce innovations so that they are viewed as neither excessively divergent nor too similar to current practices. Keep in mind the zone of innovation phenomenon when planning your introduction.

Guiding Principles for the Successful Management of Innovation

Language program administrators must view the management of innovation (rather than change) as one of their most important, and challenging, leadership roles. The following nine general principles can guide us in this complex task.

1. *We need to accept change as an inevitable part of our jobs.* Change is the most predictable aspect of the work place. We should not, however, be complacent with change. We should strive for innovation and work towards deliberate, rather than unplanned, efforts to promote innovation. If we see change as inevitable, but innovation as desirable, we can work towards creating an environment within our language programs that will lead to innovations. With an openness towards new alternatives, experimentation, and creativity, and a willingness to entertain differences of opinion, innovative energies can more easily be brought to life in our programs.

2. *Language program faculty play a significant role in bringing about programmatic innovation.* Thus, we need to create stability in the work place and help faculty develop a sense of belonging. We should encourage and reward creativity, initiative, commitment, and professionalism. In addition, we should support professional development activities among our faculty; they often lead to new perspectives that stimulate innovative practices.

3. *Managing innovation is a complex process.* There is more to the adoption of an innovative proposal than simple acceptance or rejection. Adoption often involves an extended (and sometimes complicated) decision-making process. By recognizing the complexity of the process and the interacting variables that come into play, we are likely to be more successful in our attempts at innovation.

4. *We need to be willing to experience failure.* According to Rogers (1983), 75% of all innovations fail. We need to be willing to fail on some attempts in order to succeed on others. Viewing "mistakes" developmentally can be helpful.

5. *The responsibility for innovation must be shared and should not be left to chance.* Innovations cannot sustain themselves without a team of steadfast supporters. Thus, we need to identify faculty leaders, support risk-takers who are willing to explore new and potentially improved paths, and develop mechanisms for teamwork and collaborative decision making.

6. *Innovations are not equal.* Although all innovations can be seen as improvements in the status quo, they share few other similarities. Their visible differences are obvious to us all; for example, an innovation in computer-aided instruction is clearly distinct from the introduction of a database management program into the front office. What we do not often consider, however, are the "invisible" characteristics that can so easily sway potential adopters' opinions. The extent to which innovations are accepted by potential adopters/supporters is strongly influenced by perceived attributes of innovations. Some attributes (visibility, trialability, or feasibility) often lead to positive responses to innovative proposals. Others (complexity) can create immediate barriers. Our thoughtful consideration of these attributes can lead to more successful innovation efforts.

7. *Subjective perceptions are more powerful than objective viewpoints.* The subjective perceptions of potential adopters of an innovation influence their attitudes towards that innovation. When an innovation is perceived to be complex (whether it is actually complex or not), it is difficult to solicit support for it. Because of the power of subjective perceptions, it is important to find out how potential adopters view proposed innovations. Our discoveries can help us plan the ways in which to frame our introductions and solicitations for support.

8. *Every work place environment has its resisters to change and innovation.* Change and innovation challenge the status quo and often upset levels of comfort and stability in the work place. Many educational units have personnel who are content to maintain the status quo, rather than entertain new alternatives, simply to preserve the balance and predictability of the work environment. We must strive to alleviate the fears of resisters and stimulate their willingness to at least entertain innovative proposals.

9. *Innovation diffusion requires leadership.* All innovations need a strong and steadfast supporter, someone who is willing to champion the innovation from the early introductory and developmental stages through implementation and diffusion. Language program administrators can provide the necessary leadership. Faculty are normally willing to spend extra time to bring about an innovation when there is administrative support.

Endnotes

1. Other aspects of innovation in English language teaching settings are covered in Bowers (1983), Brindley & Hood (1990), Cumming (1993), Holliday (1992), Kennedy (1987, 1988), Markee (1993, 1994, 1997), Stoynoff (1989, 1991), Tomlinson (1990), White (1993), Young (1992), and Young & Lee (1985).

2. See Stoller (1992b, 1995b) for a more complete listing of intensive English program innovations.

Discussion Questions and Activities

1. List the variables and conditions identified that encourage innovations to flourish in language programs. Based on your own experiences with change and innovation, can you add any variables/conditions to the list to make it more complete? Which variables or conditions do you think are most crucial? Least crucial? Why?

2. What do you think are the greatest challenges facing administrators who want to encourage innovation in their language programs? What can administrators do to overcome those challenges?

3. It is said that innovations are more likely to be successfully implemented in language programs that grant some degree of freedom and flexibility to faculty. How would you translate this notion into practice? (Consider the teacher's role in programmatic areas such as classroom teaching, curriculum development, textbook/software/materials selection, program governance.)

4. Imagine that you are a director of a language program. For the past few years, you have been following the development of a curricular innovation (through professional publications and conference presentations/workshops) that you think would enhance the language teaching and learning that take place in your program. Set up a general plan that identifies the steps you would take to introduce, pilot, implement, and then evaluate the innovation. Consider how you would identify faculty leaders who might help you implement the innovation and how you would deal with stalwart resisters.

Suggested Readings

De Lano, L., Riley, L., & Crookes, G. (1994). The meaning of innovation for ESL teachers. *System, 22*(4), 487–496.

The authors review the literature on educational innovation in an attempt to generate an extended definition of innovation that is appropriate for second language teaching settings. They explore three major causes of innovation (i.e., critical incidents, research findings, and change agents). They conclude by examining the role teachers can play in bringing about innovation in second language programs.

Kennedy, C. (1988). Evaluation of the management of change in ELT projects. *Applied Linguistics, 9*(4), 329–342.

Kennedy analyzes innovation as a process operating within a complex hierarchy of interrelated social subsystems. He convincingly argues that if innovations are going to have some chance of long-term impact, teacher-implementers must feel some sense of ownership; they must also feel that the gains associated with the innovation outweigh losses. He concludes with a set of questions innovators must consider when planning for and managing ELT innovations.

Markee, N. (1997). *Managing curricular innovation in second and foreign language education.* New York: Cambridge University Press.

Based on the premise that language professionals should know about the management of change and innovation, Markee presents lessons to be learned from authentic examples of curricular innovation. After outlining a general framework for understanding the theoretical issues that should inform any attempt to manage change, he illustrates how a curricular innovation was managed at a U.S. university. He concludes with principles that can guide language professionals in the management of educational change.

Stoller, F. L. (1995b). *Managing intensive English program innovations* (NAFSA Working Paper No. 56). Washington, DC: NAFSA: Association of International Educators.

In this monograph, Stoller reports on the results of a study examining innovation in intensive English programs. Practical implications of findings are discussed throughout, with the language program administrator in mind. An annotated bibliography of select references related to innovation in English language teaching settings concludes the monograph.

White, R. V. (1993). Innovation in curriculum planning and program development. In W. Grabe et al. (Eds.), *Annual Review of Applied Linguistics, 13: Issues in Second Language Teaching and Learning* (pp. 244–259). New York: Cambridge University Press.

White provides a review of literature related to innovation in curriculum planning and program development. He examines the innovation process from a variety of educational and ELT perspectives and explores the role of teacher development and evaluation in that process.

White, R., Martin, M., Stimson, M., & Hodge, R. (1991). *Management in English language teaching.* New York: Cambridge University Press.

This book, a practical guide for newcomers to the field of ELT management, has one section that focuses on managing curriculum development and innovation. The basic premise of the section is that change is not only a question of introducing new practices; it also involves changing people's behavior and attitudes. The authors outline steps for managing the implementation of innovations as well as examining factors that both facilitate and hinder the process.

Chapter 4

LANGUAGE PROGRAM LEADERSHIP AS INTERCULTURAL MANAGEMENT

Susan Carkin
Utah State University

The school as a model and reflection of the dominant culture will be unlikely to change in order to incorporate the cultural diversity represented among immigrant students. The school is preferred as a melting pot institution; it is not meant to diversify but rather to maintain the status quo. (Grey, 1991, p. 94)

his quotation describes the mindset faced by immigrants in English as a Second Language (ESL) programs in the United States, but the same scenario is experienced by international students in U.S. higher education. Although there have been various diversity and internationalization initiatives in our schools, including the use of salad, stew, and mosaic metaphors in place of the melting pot, the attitude of U.S. educational institutions toward their culturally diverse clientele is still best described as assimilationist—a one-way process of acculturation, with the burden of change toward institutional norms borne almost exclusively by the international or immigrant student.

Out of this melting pot arena have arisen relatively unique academic enterprises known as intensive English programs (IEPs). These programs are often associated with colleges or universities and carry a mission to provide accelerated English instruction in intensive time frames, ranging from 20 to 30 hours per week. IEPs in the United States often have a curious relationship with the mission, administration, governance structure, budget, and professorate of their host institutions. Most IEPs in higher education are characterized by their distance from the mainstream of institutional operations. ESL programs in K–12 public schools are similarly positioned as sheltered and pull-out classes, and their students are distinguished as nonmainstream. This distance from the center of instructional norms often puts ESL and some bilingual education efforts at the margins of public education.

The interface of ESL program with institution is characterized by the presence of boundaries. Boundaries are encoded in administrative hierarchies that represent lines of communication and power. Disciplinary fields, too, establish their own criteria for admission and valorized ways of knowing and talking through direct teaching and socialization. The obverse of boundaries, frequently stressed by universities, is communities. There is the academic community, administrative community, various discourse communities, the student body, the professorate, and so on. Whether one acknowledges the function of these groups as communities or as boundaries is largely a matter of perspective. The participant's perspective is one of communities, whereas the marginal sees boundaries.

Participating in various communities and institutional hierarchies is one key to establishing the identity and agenda of a language program. Effective language program administrators are able to negotiate across boundaries, which can be viewed as an act of intercultural communication. To work successfully across academic boundaries requires knowledge of the institution, its governance structure, and its discourses. In short, to be a successful negotiator of boundaries on behalf of marginalized programs and peoples, one must be a skillful intercultural manager who has knowledge of institutional discourses, who knows how to communicate across cultures and hierarchies, and who is able to negotiate from multiple perspectives.

Marginality

The concept of marginality can be applied to IEPs on a number of fronts: English language programs are often departmentally segregated from other educational units, ESL students are rarely mainstreamed with their native-speaking peers, and ESL professionals usually have different academic roles than their colleagues in more traditional disciplines. The use of marginality as a lens with which to view L2 students, ESL educators, and English language programs can extend our understanding of their interactions with educational institutions. (See Bennett, 1993; Billson, 1988; Goldberg, 1941; and Grey, 1991, for relevant perspectives on marginality and marginalization.)

Intensive English programs are seen as serving a group of unique students, and on this basis they are often isolated, by both geography and status, from other instructional programs that the institution offers. Teaching the English language in an English-medium institution is not often perceived as a credit-worthy curricular goal. (See Carkin, 1988, for the history of how one IEP became credit bearing.) The university presumption is that English should have been learned earlier and elsewhere. (See Eskey, this volume, for further discussion of this issue.) Some institutions go so far as to designate the IEP as a remedial endeavor. The status of an IEP on a university campus (i.e., how distantly it is located from the centrality of the institutional mission) is a fair indicator of how thoughtfully the institution has balanced its educational concerns for culturally and linguistically different students with its need to support graduate students who may teach in the IEP as teaching assistants and its concern for profit from the IEP's operation.

The university experience for international and immigrant ESL students cannot be presumed to be like the experience of other students, even though it may take place on the same campus and under the same general policies. International students studying in the United States are marginals by definition: "they are shaped and molded by one culture" and brought by education into "contact with a culture of a different content" (Goldberg, 1941, p. 52). The marginality of international students requires a number of support services to assist their transitions from the margins.

IEP faculty experience marginality as well. Their marginality is based in part on differences in their most commonly held terminal degree, usually a master's degree in Teaching English as a Second Language; most higher educational institutions recognize doctorates as terminal degrees. These professionals teach heavy loads in intensive instructional formats that vary in emphasis from English for Academic Purposes, English for Science and Technology, and English for Professional Communication (Scollon & Scollon, 1995) to short language and culture study tours.

The marginality of IEP faculty is also related to the travel, foreign work experience, and professional development that they bring with them to the workplace. Their professional identity is enhanced by their world travel and intercultural interests. Scollon and Scollon (1995) discuss in some detail the "professional discourse" that unites ESL teachers in their attempt to provide support, contacts, and resources to members of the ESL community while pursuing their own individual career development. In addition to being members of an ESL professional discourse community, ESL professionals in higher education are simultaneously members of the university discourse community. The potential for marginality (and conflict) stems from the competing demands of the two different systems.

If one is to successfully span the boundaries resulting from the marginalization of intensive English students, faculty, and programs, it is necessary to understand university priorities. Such perspectives are not taught, but are gained through socialization within the institution. Few formal resources are available to language program administrators in higher education to help them fully understand academic organization and culture. To gain that understanding, one can read the institution's governance documents, mission statement, and related materials, but language program directors should also employ anthropology's time-honored way of learning about a new culture: Use a cultural informant, a trusted person inside the culture who can interpret the actions of the university and offer interpretation. Few IEP administrators will have the opportunity to be part of the mainstream discourse of the institution; they rarely participate in the faculty senate or other venues of institutional governance, and they seldom serve on tenure and promotion committees or formulate student and curriculum policy. Becoming knowledgeable about the institutional context in which the IEP operates is a critical determinant in the overall effectiveness of a language program administrator.

The Nature of Higher Education

Universities express their nature and purpose through the academic culture, which consists of "beliefs, ritual practices and art forms" (Kane, 1991, p. 241, borrowing from Swidler, 1986). Universities encode their beliefs in mission statements that are interpreted through curriculum and policy. They abound in ritual practices, from graduation to final exams. Their artifacts, to name but a few, include educated graduates, scholarly papers, grant income, journals, learning technology, and art. Membership in the university is gained through socialization into the academic community, through valorized academic talk, beliefs, values, and attitudes. Within the discourse communities associated with particular academic fields, there are also valued ways of knowing, talking, evaluating, and writing. Knowledge of these discourse-specific conventions is an important tool for effective interaction between IEP administrators and the institutional culture. However, administrative talk and discipline-specific talk are not the same. A successful departmental administrator knows that to gain positions, equity, or equipment from a university, it is essential to frame one's departmental request with the institutional mission and the current administration's priorities in mind.

Universities represent cultures that are influenced by the knowledge they create and the traditions from which they were created; they reflect larger sociocultural norms and, at the same time, create and provide information that challenges those norms. These socially and historically situated forces are inescapable in higher education; for a language-based discipline such as ESL whose students are culturally different, they pose some dilemmas that are not easily resolved.

The educational uniqueness of IEPs challenges traditional university norms. Because IEPs teach English as a second language, and do so in an English-speaking environment, they risk the perception of "teaching the known." Members of the larger society in which IEPs operate often fail to understand what teaching (and learning) one's first language encompasses (Buttjes, 1991). A common presumption is that being a native speaker is necessary and sufficient for teaching the native language. Another aspect of teaching the known is its interdisciplinary nature. ESL draws from a variety of disciplines, including cognitive psychology, reading research, composition studies, text analysis, education, and applied and formal linguistics. ESL can be naively viewed as not only teaching the known, but also as borrowing from more mainstream disciplines that are firmly established in traditional academic departments.

ESL is taught in an academically unique context. American universities have some familiarity with accelerated learning, all-day and week-long workshops, and other intensive training formats, but a sustained 1- or 2-year intensive learning program with multiple admission periods has no peer in higher education. The absence of such a model from higher education is a disadvantage for IEPs. Administrators not directly involved with IEPs, their students, or their faculty will have little basis for comparison. They are therefore likely to base decisions of general support (i.e., resource and space allocation, staffing, student-teacher ratio, professional development opportunities, leave, and long-term planning) on their perception of the program's status and their perception of the nature of English language teaching and learning. Those same administrators are unlikely to have an understanding of the stress resulting from a long-term, intensive-format educational enterprise that deals with students who need special support services. (See Smith Murdock, this volume, for a discussion of these special needs.) Nor are they likely to understand fully the needs of IEP faculty that result from high teaching loads in year-round programs with multiple admission, orientation, and assessment periods.

IEPs often have a somewhat different financial responsibility than mainstream departments. Many pay some kind of overhead to their administering department or institution, and many IEPs need to make a profit to support other endeavors and priorities within the institutional community. This profitability makes IEPs unique institutional units and is one of the reasons for the steady increase in number of both proprietary and university-affiliated language programs around the country.[1] One consequence of IEP profitability is the potential for an unfriendly takeover, that is, a change in administrative venue that typically satisfies a more powerful department or university office. Such takeovers usually occur when there is an unequal power relationship between IEPs and other university bodies, and when there are no advocates for ESL students and the ESL profession at the negotiating table when decisions and policies are being made. ESL professionals must work within institutional hierarchies and across diverse discourses to be invited into the institution's policy-formulating processes.

Intercultural Management

Universities operate through boundaries that are defined by status and power. In a hierarchical system, "participants recognize and respect the social differences that place one in a superordinate position and the other in a subordinate position" (Scollon & Scollon, 1995, p. 45). IEPs are most always in subordinate positions in this academic hierarchy, lacking the power of departmental status and professorial rank to participate in academic self-governance. Accompanying this difference in status and power is a difference in discourse communities and professional cultures. One way to bridge these differences is through skilled intercultural communication and management.

Samovar and Porter (1991), Scollon and Scollon (1995), and Gee (1990) offer suggestions and insights about intercultural communication that can help language program administrators develop the intercultural skills necessary for successful language program management. Samovar and Porter (1991) offer seven precepts based on their intercultural work that are applicable to all cultures, including university and IEP cultures. These maxims are meant to facilitate intercultural communication in the traditional sense of speaking across different culture and language groups:

1. Know the attitudes, opinions, and biases that influence the way the world looks at you.

2. Understand how you are perceived by others.

3. Know your own communication style.

4. Encourage feedback because it allows you the opportunity to change and to adapt future behaviors.

5. Ask questions that encourage participation.

6. Cultivate nonverbal behaviors for displaying open attitudes.

7. Make an honest effort to learn the language/discourse of those with whom you communicate.

Scollon and Scollon use the term *interdiscourse communication* to refer to the use of a single language in professional communication settings where participants are simultaneously members of multiple discourse systems. In their 1995 work, Scollon and Scollon note general strategies that can be used to talk across different discourse communities. They suggest that an increase in shared knowledge is critical and that miscommunications are to be expected in professional dialogue where speakers are members of different discourse systems. Most important is the realization that one cannot assume to be an expert in the discourse system of an outgroup:

> A person who understands the outlines of the pattern of differences and commonalities, but fully recognizes his or her own lack of membership and state of non-expertise, is likely to be the most successful and effective communicator. (Scollon & Scollon, 1995, p. 252)

Gee (1990) makes the point that when one is "socialized" into a discourse communi-ty, there is much beyond language that must be understood, including values, attitudes, and beliefs. Sharing the code, therefore, is important for marginalized programs and peo-ples. IEP professionals who do not interact directly with the values and assumptions of the university, except to experience the effects of decisions made without their input, miss opportunities for socialization because of their marginal status.

Marginality is not without its benefits, although the benefits generally take the form of knowledge and are difficult to translate into power. While discussing how international students can deal with marginality, Bennett (1993, 1995) finds ways for marginalization to be empowering. She notes that marginalized individuals can respond to conflicts and stress by becoming either encapsulated or constructive. The encapsulated marginal is trapped by marginalization.

> In contrast, by maintaining control of choice and the construction of boundaries, a person may become a "constructive marginal" who is able to construct context intentionally and consciously for the purpose of creating his or her own identity. (Bennett, 1993, p. 113)

In Bennett's conceptualization, constructive marginality is an asset, a desirable and healthy response to living "at the edges where two or more cultures meet" (Bennett, 1993, p. 113).

Barak and Breier (1990) introduce the notion of "boundary spanners," individuals who can work between administrative offices and academic communities during a formal program evaluation. Boundary spanners are needed not only for program evaluation, but even more importantly for program articulation. Language program administrators should equip themselves to be boundary spanners; they need broad knowledge of institu-tional values and priorities to work across boundaries and discourses on behalf of their students, faculty, and programs.

If participation in the university is valuable to IEP professionals, then how do they go about learning and participating in the discourse systems of the academic hierarchy? Without opportunities to participate in institutional governance, policy formation, and decision making, and with few possibilities for providing feedback to the academy on ways that they and their students are affected by its policies and agendas, ESL profession-als are simply cut off from learning the discourse that allows them to be effective commu-nicators and that might allow them to understand institutional decisions and policies bet-ter. The dilemma is somewhat circular: Marginal program status keeps ESL professionals out of the mainstream of academic discourse, and their nonparticipation in academic dis-course hinders their ability to influence their marginal status. Moving from the margins means breaking the circularity. IEP administrators must develop proactive initiatives and target people and programs that will benefit from information dispersal. Such initiatives and information must be moved forward with a clear and consistent agenda that empha-sizes that the success of international students benefits the institution's mission.

Integrating the IEP into the University

Intercultural expertise is requisite for a program administrator to become a success-ful boundary spanner and to integrate the IEP into the university hierarchy. The language program administrator communicates across traditional and diverse academic discipline areas and institutional power structures to explain the nature of ESL and the goals of the program to people who may have outdated beliefs about how English is learned. In such circumstances, it is critical for the administrator to encourage feedback rather than summary judgments, to demonstrate code sensitivity (Samovar & Porter, 1991) for the language of the disciplines as well as the language of the power structure, and to engage in information sharing (Scollon & Scollon, 1995) about the particular needs of ESL students.

There are strong reasons—cognitive, affective, political, sociocultural, and administrative—to integrate educational programs for language-diverse students into the educational mainstream. In addition to the obvious "membership" benefits that could accrue to students and programs, there is also the opportunity for the mainstream to learn from the program and the students.

Given that IEPs are much more flexible than institutions, and in some collective sense they possess meta-knowledge about the different discourse realms in which they operate, it makes sense for IEPs to take the initiative to improve their marginal status. The list below represents 10 ways through which an IEP can begin to integrate itself into the academy. This list is not intended to be exhaustive. It suggests a variety of approaches to be taken by a language program administrator when the program recognizes advantages for its students, faculty, and programmatic status in moving toward the university mainstream. The suggestions below are generally relevant and adaptable to a wide range of language programs, including ESL and bilingual programs in public schools.

1. Agree upon a mission statement. An English language program should have a mission statement that connects its work to the wider goals of the home institution's mission statement. If the language program is housed in a department or division, it should also write a mission or role statement describing how it fits into that unit. The statement should be sent through the appropriate channels for feedback and approval, helping higher level administrators see how the language program complements institutional and departmental missions.

2. Draft individual role statements. Language program faculty and administrators should have role statements that parallel the role statements of regular faculty in as many ways as possible. Where differences exist, especially in definitions of scholarship and teaching loads, those differences in expectations should be stated clearly and with a rationale. A role statement is a powerful tool for faculty development and program management. It allows faculty to set annual and long-term goals and to maintain a coherent professional perspective. It allows management to observe, evaluate, and reward the goals that are accomplished.

3. Pursue academic credit for ESL courses. If English language teaching faculty are qualified (with master's degrees or records of relevant scholarship) and the ESL curriculum is detailed and specified in ways similar to the mainstream curriculum, it might be useful to write a proposal to request some kind of academic credit for English language study. There are many kinds of credit that can be sought: pass/fail, lower division, lower and upper division (on par with foreign language credit), elective, and even continuing education units. Such a move requires an understanding of the advantages that credit would bestow to the program as well as to the home institution.

4. Work across disciplines. English language programs can demonstrate their interest and commitment to language students by following them into mainstream academic classes. For example, university-based language programs can conduct studies or surveys of the classes that international students take by examining course syllabi and textbooks, analyzing class assignments, observing lectures and class sessions, and interviewing professors (Bame, 1995; Horowitz, 1986; Rogers, 1995); the results of such studies can be used for a basic needs analysis and can provide the basis for meaningful curricular change. Such cross-disciplinary activities demonstrate the role of language in every facet of student learning and the responsibility that language programs have undertaken to understand the evolving needs of students.

5. Involve U.S. students. By including U.S. students in ESL classrooms and extracurricular activities, English language programs can involve all students in institutional internationalization efforts. It is fairly easy to find ways to use U.S. students as cultural informants in culture classes, as aides in conversation classes, as tutors in writing courses, and as conversation partners with social roles outside of class. (See Jenks and Smith Murdock, this volume, for more information on integrating U.S. students into language program curricula and Mitchell, 1995, for information on integrating international students into mainstream courses.) The role of ESL programs and their students and faculty, as both cultural mediators and purveyors of new knowledge to U.S. students, should be carefully spelled out in program mission statements.

6. Conduct a self-study. One way for a program to demonstrate its quality and its commitment to long-term goals and professional development is to study itself. By undertaking a self-study, a language program declares itself interested in the assessment of its quality and the outcome of its teaching mission, and committed to long-term change and professional growth. Wintergerst's (1995) edited volume on self-study is a useful place to begin to investigate the process and its potential benefits to an ESL program. A program may want to consider the effects of bringing in outside evaluators as part of the self-study process (Carkin, 1995). The self-study undertaking should be familiar and valued by most educators and administrators.

7. Join professional organizations. Language programs and personnel should consider membership in several professional organizations. Some organizations have more stringent membership criteria than others, but all serve to promote language program quality, advocate for ESL students and second language education, and connect professionals and programs in a field that is relatively dispersed. The following organizations should be considered:

- NAFSA: Association of International Educators encourages institutional membership, and its ATESL section (Administrators and Teachers of English as a Second Language) provides important professional forums that are familiar to most U.S.-based higher education ESL professionals.

- TESOL is an international organization with individual and institutional memberships; it is a powerful source of information for ESL and EFL professionals.

- UCIEP, a consortium of intensive English programs in U.S. higher education, focuses on the advancement of professional standards and quality instruction.

- · AAIEP is a broad-based organization for proprietary and public IEPs in the United States. It is involved in setting student recruitment and program standards.

8. Recognize student and faculty accomplishments. Language programs should develop systems to recognize and reward excellence. Without such systems, outstanding students and faculty are missing tremendous opportunities for professional development, motivation, publicity, and enhanced credibility. In settings where language program status restricts institutional forms of recognition, language program leadership should develop a plan internal to the program to recognize teaching excellence and student scholarship. Language programs could bestow other awards as well, such as for excellence in advising, curriculum development, or course design, or for outstanding alumni; determination of such awards should complement the program's agreed-upon values, goals, and mission.

9. Encourage research and scholarship. Language program administrators should encourage active engagement in research and scholarly activity. Systematic analysis of data on student progress, teacher performance, student satisfaction, placement procedures, assessment measures, administrator performance, textbook effectiveness, match of curriculum to student needs, and so forth, is imperative to maintain program quality, accountability, and face validity. ESL professionals, like members of any other discipline, must be free to define their own kind of scholarly work.

A great deal of creativity and leadership is needed to promote a sustainable research agenda for individual teachers because year-round teaching and intensive teaching formats usually result in limited time for formal study and outside research. Providing incentives for collaborative and individual scholarship—in the form of release time, raises, recognition, merit of some sort, and reasonable teaching loads that allow time for scholarship—can benefit a language program, and its personnel, in many ways.

Another opportunity for scholarship should appeal to language program administrators as well as instructors interested in discourse analysis. The hierarchical structure of educational institutions provides a setting in which discourses of power and prestige abound. An analysis of ways that language is used in the institution by persons in different positions within the administrative hierarchy, across various discourse communities, and for various purposes, would be a valuable contribution to several professions and would be useful information for other marginalized programs and peoples.

10. Engage in boundary spanning. Language program administrators should find a mentor (another administrator or experienced faculty member) who is willing to serve as a "cultural informant." This informant can guide the language program administrator through the maze of institutional policies and procedures as well as the tacit assumptions and values that characterize mainstream academic operations.

Conclusion

Universities carry within their mission and values hundreds of years of traditions. These traditions reflect mainstream social norms in an educational organization that is highly stratified by traditional academic values and rewards, and by disciplinary communities. The conflict between elite academic traditions and new disciplinary and social cultures appears almost inevitable. The most adaptable of the marginal programs and peoples will learn to assimilate themselves into the institutional culture, whereas the others will remain on the margins. This probably requires that IEPs, their faculty, and their students learn to function within the various discourses of the institution. (See Gee, 1990, for a discussion of "mushfake discourse.") To succeed in such an endeavor, language program administrators will need all of their professional experience and expertise regarding language, culture, discourses, and power as they negotiate institutional boundaries and enter diverse discourses on behalf of international and immigrant students and the professionals and programs that serve them.

Endnotes

1. The Institute of International Education reports that in 1978–79 there were 23,607 international students enrolled in a total of 163 IEPs; 15 years later, a total of 43,522 international students were enrolled in 494 IEPs (Palmer, 1995).

Discussion Questions and Activities

1. Review a situation in which you perceived yourself or others to be marginalized. In what ways were you or others marginalized? In retrospect, how might the individuals involved have brought themselves to the "inner circle"?

2. Assume that you have just been appointed as a language program director or ESL/bilingual coordinator. How do you propose to go about educating the institution, the college, or the department that you are a part of? What public resources can you use? What other resources are available to you?

3. The author recommends 10 ways in which language programs can integrate themselves into their home institutions, thereby minimizing their marginalized status. Considering a language program with which you are familiar, identify three of the steps that you think represent good starting points. Provide a rationale for your selections.

4. The author promotes the idea of language program administrators as intercultural managers and as boundary spanners. What do you perceive to be the main responsibilities of intercultural managers? Of boundary spanners? Considering all of the responsibilities that language program administrators have, how important do you think the roles of intercultural manager and boundary spanner are?

5. Design a brief questionnaire (about five questions) to examine beliefs about how people think language (English) is learned. The content should center on issues such as the difference between learning through socialization (a child's first language experience) and through education, that is, consciously deploying cognitive resources (the adult L2 school experience). Questionnaire items might be phrased as statements that respondents agree or disagree with: "Any adult who lives in a new country long enough will automatically learn the language" or "Formal language instruction is the best way an adult can learn a language well enough to attend a college using that language" or "Adults learn language in the same ways that children do."

    Administer the questionnaire to three groups (e.g., university administrators, ESL faculty, and nonuniversity people) and compare their answers. You might use a scale of agreement or a simple true-false format. Based on the results, how would you go about educating those individuals or groups who need to understand the language education of nontraditional students?

Suggested Readings

Bennett, J. M. (1993). Cultural marginality: Identity issues in intercultural training. In M. Paige (Ed.), *Education for the intercultural experience* (pp. 109–135). Yarmouth, ME: Intercultural Press.

This chapter deals with the psychological stages and processes surrounding the marginality experienced by individuals who operate within two or more cultures. Of particular interest is Bennett's discussion of the encapsulated marginal and the constructive marginal. Intercultural educators can benefit from understanding the factors involved in shifting frames of reference and intercultural identity. The relevance of Bennett's work for ESL professionals is in gaining self-awareness as one works between the discourses of the profession and those of the institution.

Gee, J. P. (1990). *Social linguistics and literacies: Ideology in discourses*. Bristol, PA: Falmer Press.

The emphasis of this volume is on the relationship between discourses and their speakers. Gee asserts that discourses carry with them the values, signals, norms, and ways of being in different societies, cultures, and institutions. In short, discourses are intimately wedded to identities. The author argues that discourses are not well adapted to being apprehended through formal education, but that individuals who want to learn a discourse other than their home-based one learn best through apprenticeship and acceptance.

Grey, M. A. (1991). The context for marginal secondary ESL programs: Contributing factors and the need for further research. *Journal of Educational Issues of Language Minority Students, 9*, 75–89.

Grey provides a valuable discussion of marginality in secondary ESL programs, taking readers through the historical development of the concept, which originally applied to individuals who spanned two or more cultures. The author demonstrates how six sets of factors contribute to the marginalization of ESL programs. The article is one of few to address the concept of marginality in an ESL educational context.

Samovar, L., & Porter, R. (1991). *Communication between cultures*. Belmont, CA: Wadsworth.

This is a basic and important text about communicating across cultures. It includes key concepts and clear explanations of how intercultural communication works in a number of critical settings, including international business, education, and health. The volume concludes with solid, if somewhat basic, advice on how to facilitate such communication in a broad sweep of settings.

Scollon, R., & Scollon, S. (1995). *Intercultural communication.* Cambridge, MA: Basil Blackwell.

This book on intercultural communication is remarkably satisfying. The focus is on professional communication in organizations through analyses of diverse discourses. The authors coin the term *interdiscourse communication* to describe what happens when people talk across boundaries that are formed by age, gender, occupation, status, and other types of group membership. The chapter on the professional discourse of ESL/EFL teachers ought to be required reading for all ESL/EFL professionals.

Chapter 5

THE STRATEGIC PLANNER

Sarah J. Klinghammer
University of Oregon

Lou is the new director of an established university-based language program. Having worked up through the ranks and accrued the requisite credentials (i.e., a doctorate, 17 years in the profession as an ESL instructor, professional activity outside the program, and a good working relationship with members of the unit), Lou is a logical choice for the position, being accepted as such by both university academic units and language program staff. Lou has had no management training or administrative experience, but this lack of expertise is not seen as a problem since few other academic unit heads and deans begin with administrative training either.

Within the first year, Lou is faced with a series of management problems: Finances are uncertain, several key classified staff and core faculty positions have become vacant, the technical coordinator needs to update the computer inventory as programmatic demands require new technology, the college has asked the program to design a new curriculum for matriculated students, university space problems are affecting scheduling, several faculty want to involve the unit as a whole in extensive research projects, the opening of new language programs around the country has created more competition, and other language programs are becoming more proactive in their search for students by attending recruitment fairs and by advertising.

Operating with insufficient information and no long-term vision, Lou begins to feel harassed, uncertain, and hesitant to make decisions. Decisions made are based on other people's opinions and on what seems right at the moment. The director's office becomes a roadblock to action. Lou needs help with planning; more specifically, the program needs to engage in strategic planning.

 trategic planning has proven helpful for administrators like Lou, although language programs need not be in trouble to benefit from strategic planning. The strategic planning process highlighted here has been developing since the early 1970s, replacing long-range planning as the dominant theory. Long-range planning, based on a belief in unlimited market growth, forecasts the future by projecting existing trends; the approach has proven inadequate for dealing with marketplaces that are now dominated by rapidly changing technology, volatility, and resource constraints. Strategic planning has a different orientation; it is defined here as the process of determining the long-term vision and goals of an enterprise and the means for fulfilling them (Bean, 1993). Strategic planning originally grew out of the need for multinational companies to create a central mechanism for the direction and coordination of their diverse, and often geographically distant, operations (Taylor, 1987). Current processes associated with strategic planning vary with different organizations. The flexible nature of the strategic planning process makes it possible for various types of organizations, including language programs, to benefit from its emphasis on (a) the external environment of an organization, (b) the demands for change arising from that environment, and (c) market competition, rather than the unlimited market growth associated with long-range planning (Makridakis & Héau, 1987).

The Pros and Cons of Strategic Planning

Language programs can benefit from strategic planning in many ways, although there are four advantages worth highlighting (J. Blakely, personal communication, January 13, 1995):

1. The strategic planning process rallies language program personnel around common goals. The ideal planning process builds individual empowerment, program-wide synergy, shared vision, and community consensus, thereby revitalizing the language program by focusing effort and encouraging innovation. Program-wide consensus allows programs to expend human and financial resources on issues important to the unit as a whole.

2. The strategic planning process creates a framework for wise decision making, enabling administrators to be proactive, think holistically, plan ahead, respond to internal and external changes, and create new opportunities inside and outside the program.

3. The strategic planning process educates and trains current and future language program leaders. The process results in the development of strategic thinking that can set the tone of a program, shape organizational values, energize personnel, and build consensus (Burton & McBride, 1991).

4. The strategic planning process helps identify features of a program that differentiate it from other language programs. The process assists in identifying areas that, if sufficiently developed, could create a strong niche in the market for the language program.

Language program administrators often get bogged down in the minutiae of daily operations, such as meetings, correspondence, e-mail, personnel and student issues, and faculty and staff supervision. The focus on immediate internal issues can blind administrators to external factors that affect the program and can result in a reactive, emergency-room culture characterized by crisis management. Language program administrators who engage themselves and their programs in the strategic planning process arm themselves with direction, a framework for decision making, and supportive personnel, making it easier for them to respond to the internal and external challenges faced by the program.

The benefits that can accrue from an effective strategic planning process are many and varied. But good strategic planning is challenging and requires a commitment of time and resources; the process is demanding both cognitively and in terms of human interaction. In addition, it may create program-wide anxiety by illuminating the need for internal changes, the uncertainty of future events, and the influence of a shifting external environment (Munro, 1987). Securing a commitment to the process from language program faculty and staff is often difficult for two additional reasons: (a) Language program personnel may have invested time, emotion, and energy into past planning processes, only to witness their recommendations ignored; and (b) language program personnel may perceive a loss of freedom if the results of the planning process commit them to activities that complement a newly defined mission rather than personal interests (see Munro, 1987). To counter these fears, administrators must be committed to staff involvement, implementation, and a synergy that increases the likelihood of success.

The Strategic Planning Process

There are many factors that contribute to a successful strategic planning endeavor. Advocates of strategic planning describe the process with varying terminology and procedural detail (see Bean, 1993; Burkhart & Reuss, 1993; Burton & McBride, 1991; Cook, 1994; Holloway, 1986; Merson & Qualls, 1979). Yet, basic to all of the discussions is a simple three-part procedure involving the development, implementation, and evaluation (and revision, if necessary) of the strategic plan. Each part of the process is discussed in more detail below, followed by a case study illustrating how strategic planning was utilized in a real language program, and concluding with a discussion of related issues that should be of interest to language program administrators who want to take on the role of strategic planner.

Development of the Strategic Plan

The strategic planning process begins with the formation of a planning team, usually a group of administrators and faculty, most often from within the language program, who will be most responsible for developing and later implementing the strategic plan. The plan results from work done at a series of meetings and from tasks assigned to various committee members in preparation for those meetings. A team facilitator, the individual who is in charge, can make sure that meetings are run efficiently and effectively (Burton & McBride, 1991). Although the facilitator could be the program director or another program leader, optimally it should be an outside consultant who is knowledgeable in strategic planning. An outsider is the better choice for two other reasons:

1. The head of the language program should be part of the planning process and therefore cannot be spared to serve as an impartial facilitator.

2. An outside consultant has the advantage of having no preconceived ideas about or history with the language program, and therefore has no personal agenda.

Hiring an outsider as facilitator can be costly; nonetheless, it is an option worth serious consideration for the person's neutral stance, expertise in strategic planning, and increased objectivity.

Team members must consider two complex sets of issues that provide the foundation for developing a strategic plan. The first set relates to establishing a planning framework, and the second set requires conducting analyses to collect pertinent information for the plan.

Establishing a planning framework. A good strategic plan includes the following six elements: vision, values, purpose, mission, goals, and strategies. These are common to most planning frameworks, but are defined in various ways in the literature. Sometimes they are combined into rather fuzzy, catch-all terms that lack the focus necessary to make them useful (J. Blakely, personal communication, January 13, 1996). They are defined here separately for the purposes of this discussion.

A *vision* is a statement of direction and destination. A vision statement specifies where a language program is going in the long term and what its members hope to accomplish (Collins & Lazier, 1992).

Values are the principles that guide the conduct of a language program. When a program states that its first responsibility is to its students, this core belief should dictate what the program and its leadership do and how they conduct themselves.

Purpose refers to the basic reason(s) for an organization's existence, giving meaning to the work of the language program. Formally articulated purpose statements, in general, are global and enduring, describing how the program impacts the world and fulfills human need—for example, "Our purpose is to enhance individual growth and global understanding in the international community through English language and intercultural learning, teaching, and research opportunities."

Mission refers to a clear and compelling statement that "serves as a focal point of effort" (Collins & Lazier, 1992, p. 73). It is the time-bound (2–5 years), action-based part of the vision, which needs to be both achievable and measurable. A mission statement such as, "By the year 2005, this unit will be recognized internationally as a leader in the field of ESL," is both unachievable and unmeasurable, and is therefore much more likely to create cynicism than energy in the program. A more workable mission statement might be something like this: "Reaching the new century as a language teaching and learning community, this unit will be (a) diversified, (b) on the cutting edge of the ESL profession in terms of research and professional development, and (c) recognized on campus and externally as an excellent program."

Goals are time-bound steps that define the parameters of each arm of the mission. A goal can be quantitative (e.g., increasing enrollment by 50 new students by Fall '98) or qualitative (e.g., providing an environment that fosters research and development).

Strategies are the methods and activities used to achieve goals. Effective strategies maximize the match between internal structure, resources, and expertise, and external opportunities and threats.

Conducting analyses. In addition to establishing a planning framework, the team gathers information pertinent to developing the strategic plan. A Stakeholder Analysis, Situation Analysis, and Critical Success Factor Analysis are particularly useful in this regard.

A *Stakeholder Analysis* identifies individuals, groups, and organizations with an interest, or stake, in the successful operation of the language program. Some stakeholders will actually be part of the strategic planning process. When designating planning teams, each language program must decide for itself who to include in the process (e.g., program management, faculty, classified staff, a representative of the larger academic department, someone from the dean's office, or a student). A Stakeholder Analysis helps determine who all of the stakeholders are, including those directly participating in the planning process, how each stakeholder or group of stakeholders impacts the language program, and what their objectives are.

A *Situation Analysis*, which provides information about the internal and external factors that impact a language program, actually has two components:

1. The SWOT Analysis objectively examines a language program's internal *strengths* and *weaknesses* in addition to external *opportunities* and *threats* to the existence or successful operation of the language program.

2. The Competitive Analysis examines the strengths and weaknesses of competitors (e.g., other departments, other language programs in the area, or programs competing for the same grant funding; see Collins & Lazier, 1992).

A *Critical Success Factor Analysis* evaluates "characteristics, conditions, or variables that, when properly sustained, maintained, or managed, impact on the success" of a program (Leidecker & Bruno, 1987, p. 333). Success factors can originate from within the program (e.g., high-quality teaching) or from outside the program (e.g., competitively low tuition rates or favorable Immigration and Naturalization Service regulations). Negative factors can include poor-quality teaching, high tuition, and unfavorable changes in INS regulations.

In sum, the development stage of the strategic planning process requires that the team agrees upon a planning framework by reaching a consensus on program vision, values, purpose, mission, goals, and strategies, while gathering pertinent information about stakeholders, the competition, and the strengths and weaknesses of the program itself. The team will then draft a strategic plan that includes a unit-wide commitment to specific strategies for implementation. The plan will be most effective if viewed as a pliant agreement subject to revision as goals are met or revised and new goals are established (J. Blakely, personal communication, January 13, 1996).

Implementation of the Strategic Plan

Implementation, the second stage of the process, is key to the success of the strategic planning endeavor. A strategic plan is ready to be implemented only when the following conditions exist:

1. Each goal must be *clearly stated* so that everyone involved in its implementation agrees on what it means, how it can be achieved, and which resources are required to achieve it.

2. The plan must include a detailed *timeline* that specifies when each goal is to be accomplished; in this way, the plan can proceed in a timely fashion.

3. Lines of *communication* must be clearly established with all participating members of the language program community firmly within the network.

4. The strategies for reaching goals should include short-term, *visible performance achievements*, so that those involved can clearly see that their efforts are succeeding (Kotter, 1995).

5. The outcome(s) of each goal must be *measurable* so that everyone can see and agree that the step has been successfully completed.

6. Someone with the authority to, for example, make decisions, allocate resources, delegate responsibility, and problem solve should be responsible for the successful completion of each goal. Assigning individuals from the planning team to different goals enables the team to apportion responsibility, use individual expertise effectively, and establish *accountability*.

If implementation is the key to a successful strategic planning process, people are the key to successful implementation. Despite the importance of strategies for successful implementation, their execution is not likely to be achieved without skilled and committed individuals (see Tichy & Charan, 1995). Program leadership must create an environment in which implementation teams have the authority to make decisions and proceed. Team members must feel free to speak up and be confident that they will be heard. Rewards for responsible team members are appropriate when goals are reached. Rewards do not have to be large or even pecuniary; public recognition, access to professional development opportunities, and merit points represent some forms of reward.

Each implementation team should contain individuals with the required expertise, in addition to one or two people who are interested in learning about the targeted area. An illustrative example involves technology. An implementation team formed to reach a technological goal should include the language program faculty member or administrator who has the most expertise in this area; it should also include several people who are interested in improving their technology skills, thus broadening the pool of technology-literate staff. Such an arrangement not only spreads out the work and the responsibility, but also trains people and ensures a broad ownership of the process.

Evaluation and Revision of the Strategic Plan

The third part of the process represents a natural and important extension of the implementation stage: evaluation and revision, if necessary, of the strategic plan. Bean (1993) recommends an evaluation early in the implementation process to make sure that the language program is on track and to make necessary adjustments based on early implementation experiences. An ongoing review enables the language program to revise goals and strategies as they are tried, thus minimizing unproductive endeavors and ensuring that the plan is being implemented.

A Case Study:
Strategic Planning in an Intensive English Program

The strategic planning process, outlined above in general terms, can be better understood by examining the process as it actually took place in Spring 1996 at the University of Oregon's American English Institute (AEI). The AEI is an academic unit operating as part of the Linguistics Department in the College of Arts and Sciences at the University of Oregon, reporting to both the department chair and the dean's office. The strategic planning team consisted of the AEI director, the budget/office manager, three program coordinators representing different curricular areas, the technology coordinator/instructor, and an outside facilitator—a strategic planning consultant who donated his time for the development stage of the planning process. We began with the general development-implementation-evaluation framework in mind, although what is reported here relates only to the first two stages because, at the time of this writing, we were just beginning the implementation stage.

Development Stage

After naming members to the strategic planning team, the first steps were to agree on a schedule of meetings within a specific time-frame, to outline the type of preparation needed at each stage of the process, and to determine the point at and the extent to which various stakeholders (e.g., the dean, the department head, faculty, and classified staff) would be involved in the strategic planning process. The team held all-day sessions off campus to allow for a more relaxed, neutral atmosphere. Different elements of the plan were discussed, debated, and agreed upon during each meeting. Some of our key discussions are highlighted here.

Setting the scene. Our team facilitator began the strategic planning process by posing the question, "Where do we want to be by the year 2001?" Before the first meeting, each team member wrote a response to the question. The facilitator compiled all the responses into one overall scenario, which became the focus of discussion at our first meeting. While commenting on the scenario at that first meeting, the strategic planning group brainstormed lists of core values, identified stakeholders, and began to draft a purpose statement. Before the next meeting, members were expected to engage in several tasks that represented follow-ups to the first meeting topics; for example, they categorized values, mapped stakeholder interests, and reviewed and edited the purpose statement. The facilitator compiled data resulting from task assignments and used them as springboards for discussion and decision making at the second meeting. This cyclical procedure—including group brainstorming, individual tasks, data compilation, and group discussion—became the standard operating pattern for our group.

The team discussed issues related to program vision, values, purpose, mission, goals, and strategies early in the process to lay the foundation for further discussion. The group had particular difficulty drafting a mission statement, rewriting it several times until, still unsatisfied, members of the team decided to table it and return to it after working further through the process.

Determining program values. To reach group consensus on program values, the team followed Burton and McBride's (1991) holistic approach for determining core values (cf. Bean, 1993, for another approach to determining core values). Initially team members worked on their own to create a list of what they felt the language program's values were or should be. After categorizing items individually, two members of the team grouped the items and created a worksheet (see Table 1), which was used later, by the group as a whole, to draft a one-page statement of program values.

Conducting the Stakeholder Analysis. When conducting our Stakeholder Analysis, the strategic planning group identified broad categories of stakeholders, and then further divided each category into more specific subcategories. We then brainstormed the characteristics of each group (see Table 2). This information was used to map the interrelationships of various stakeholders with our language program (see Table 3). The Stakeholder

Analysis was conducted while we were drafting our vision statement to ensure that all interests were being represented in the planning process.

Table 1. **Program Values Worksheet**

Values	*We strive to ...*
Excellence: We are dedicated to top quality in everything we do.	• Have top-quality faculty and staff. • Be at the forefront in teaching, curriculum design, and research. • Promote excellence actively in all areas of our organization and in all daily activities. • Improve upon our work by means of continual reflection and evaluation. • Foster professional cooperation and collaboration.
Balance: We recognize the desirability of balance in life.	• Balance service and scholarship. • Balance individuality and teamwork. • Balance cultural diversity and global community. • Balance work and play.
Involvement: We want to promote positive change in our communities.	• Be responsible citizens of many communities, including our language program, the university, the surrounding community, and the world. • Make a positive contribution to these communities to enhance global understanding. • Promote an open exchange of ideas and participation in decision making. • Advocate intercultural involvement.
Integrity: We insist on the importance of basing our actions on integrity.	• Promote integrity within our organization and with people with whom we work. • Be perceived by others and each other as honest, accountable, and reliable. • Defend our values in the face of external pressures.
Service: We take pride in enabling people to communicate across cultures.	• Provide skills, information, and knowledge that enable others to communicate in English.
Employees: We honor our employees' contributions to the organization.	• Support employees in their professional endeavors. • Provide professionally competitive wages and benefits. • Respect individual needs.
Financial Responsibility: We recognize the need to be financially secure and to control our own finances.	• Manage program resources in ways consistent with our values.

Table 2. **Intensive English Program Stakeholders**

Stakeholder categories	Stakeholder subcategories	Characteristics
Students	University-bound	55% want TOEFL
	English-only	45% want practical conversation and computer instruction
	Special short-term	Need individualized programs
Faculty	2-year contracts	10% of faculty; benefits and salaries
	1-year contracts	40% of faculty; benefits and salaries
	Term-by-term contracts	50% of faculty; benefits and salaries
Management	Director/assistant director	3-year rotation
	Program coordinators	3-year rotation; 50/50 teaching/administration
	Specific-function coordinators	75/25 teaching/administration
Classified staff	Office manager/assistant	Classified position
	Secretary/receptionist	Classified position
Student employees	Graduate teaching fellows	4–6 total; salary for set teaching load
	Tutors	40–50 per term; hourly rate, training needed
	Clerical workers	3–4 per term; training needed, scheduling needed
Host institution	Dean/academic department chair	Lines of authority/vested interests
	Office of International Education and Exchange	I-20 policies
	Registrar/Admissions	Set procedures; deadlines
	Computing center	Timelines; policies
	Bookstore	Timelines; services
Sponsors	Host families	Orientation; follow-ups
	Community sponsors	Liaison
	Embassies/companies/agencies	Liaison; updated information
Government agencies	Immigration and Naturalization Service	Regulations; potential changes
Suppliers	Publishers	Need for desk copies; copyright permissions
	Office-supply stores	University purchasing policies
Competitors	Regional language programs	Networking; basis of competition

Note: Information in this table represents a sampling of the information that can result from a Stakeholder Analysis.

Table 3. Worksheet Identifying the Wants, Needs, and Expectations of Key Stakeholders

Area of Concern	Key Stakeholders					
	Students	Sponsors	Faculty	Staff	Linguistics Department	College of Arts and Sciences
Marketing and finance	Affordable tuition	Good value for money	Longer term contracts	Recognition	Graduate teaching assistant support	Public relations revenue
Program quality and delivery	Knowledgeable faculty	Program flexibility	Resource availability	Reasonable workloads	Academic expertise	Quality teacher supervision/training
Teaching and learning environments	Access to labs and technology	Small classes & individualized instruction	Respect from peers & administration	Cross-cultural training	Training for teaching assistants	Academic preparation
Support systems	Academic advising	Security and safety	Good working conditions	Adequate work space	Classroom visitation opportunities	Involvement in budgetary planning
Communication	Feedback on abilities & progress	Timely responses	Involvement in decision making	Clear job description	Input into training	Program advertised as part of college offerings
Personal and professional growth	Improved TOEFL scores	Satisfied students	Sense of accomplishment	Respect	Research possibilities	Academic expertise
Sense of community	New friends	Extracurricular student activities	Cooperative colleagues	Pleasant working environment	Collaboration with training	Program viewed as part of college

Note: Information in this table represents a sampling of the information that can result from a Stakeholder Analysis.

Conducting the Situation Analysis. As part of our Situation Analysis, we conducted SWOT and Competitive Analyses, focusing on the issues listed in Table 4. We believed that the success of the planning process depended upon the entire language program staff's feeling a sense of ownership and involvement in the process and its results; therefore, everyone was encouraged to participate in the Situation Analysis. After naming 4–7 members for each Situation Analysis group, the strategic planning team held its first all-staff meeting where the facilitator explained the value of conducting Situation Analyses, proposed a focus for each group, and distributed instructions to group members.

Table 4. Focus of SWOT and Competitive Analyses

Internal assessment	*External assessment*
Strengths and weaknesses	Opportunities and threats
Resources	Professional/market trends
Innovations	Technology trends
	Competition (other programs)
	Social/regulatory environment
	Student demographics

(Adapted from Collins & Lazier, 1992)

We began with the SWOT Analysis. Each group met briefly to clarify assignments after which group members gathered information on the program's current strengths, weaknesses, opportunities, and threats. The information was compiled and categorized by the strategic planning team member who was assigned to and participated in the group. After prioritizing the group's deliberations, the list was forwarded to the team facilitator, the strategic planning team, and other groups. These results were reviewed by the strategic planning team and were used to refine the mission statement.

The groups met again to conduct a Competitive Analysis. Group members were asked to identify key competitors along with their strengths and weaknesses and their competitive advantage (i.e., the single most important characteristic that made them strong competitors). Groups were then asked to identify our own program's strengths and weaknesses in relation to each competitor and specify, if possible, our competitive advantage. Group deliberations were distributed to the strategic planning team facilitator, team members, and other group members for consideration.

Finally, the strategic planning group, using all the collected information, decided on three core strategies that would enable the program to achieve its 5-year mission.

Implementation Stage

The implementation process began by developing a comprehensive list of required activities for each core strategy. The strategic planning team divided up into smaller groups to brainstorm and prioritize implementation strategies. For the highest priorities, the team agreed upon a timeline for completion, the necessary resources, and the critical success factors.[1] Table 5 illustrates the results of our deliberations on one particular goal.

Table 5. **Example of a Strategic Goal Implementation Sheet**

Strategic goal	Increase the diversity of student groups.
Present status	Program is dependent on two major sources of student groups.
Strategy for accomplishment	Develop a marketing plan.
Resource requirements	Funds are needed for advertising, travel, new marketing coordinator position, and perhaps an outside consultant.
Responsible individual	Mary Rodan
Reports to	Director
Estimated completion date	June 1, 1999
Authorization	_____
Comments/critical success factor	Because the program has no space to expand and already has as many students as it can accommodate in its classrooms, if this strategy is followed, there needs to be some reconsideration of admissions policies.

The Role of Language Program Administrators in the Process

Successful strategic planning requires an atmosphere of strong leadership (see Johnstone, 1990; Stoller, 1995b). To be effective leaders, language program administrators must realize that although individual vision is important, strategic planning requires that administrators recognize patterns that are emerging inside and outside of language programs. Therefore, as language program strategists, we must be active inside and outside of our programs, keeping in personal contact with other professionals, attending meetings and conferences, and accepting positions in professional organizations. We must understand the details of our own programs to help create an atmosphere that stimulates other program personnel to think strategically (see Mintzberg, 1987). We must also be able to recognize the need for change. We need to know when it is time to think about renewal, when it is time to formulate a new strategy, and when it is time for stability and continuance (Mintzberg, 1987). We must keep in mind that our faculty, staff, and students cannot do their best when operating in an atmosphere of constant upheaval and change.

In addition, we must be open to working with management teams, a characteristic of the strategic planning process that stems from total quality management (TQM). TQM endorses the "flattening" of organizations into more horizontal management entities, with broader opportunities for capable employees through management teams. (For further discussion of TQM, see Domb, 1993; Hradesky, 1995; and Sashkin, 1993.) Because a more horizontal management style contributes to the success of the strategic planning process, language programs may have to reorganize their administrative hierarchy.

As strategic planners, we must also be aware of other issues that can contribute to the success of the strategic planning process—specifically the timing of strategic planning and resource management. Furthermore, we should be cognizant of potential roadblocks to strategic planning so that we can avoid or overcome them.

Timing

Planning is often motivated by crisis situations when, for example, enrollment is falling, internal strife between management and faculty is strangling effective practice and resulting in resignations, or the host institution has decided to take 50% of program income as overhead. Critical situations such as these tend to narrow the focus of planning efforts; they rarely lead to strategic planning.

The best time to engage in strategic planning is during a positive period, when, for example, enrollment is steady, the unit is making a profit, administration and faculty have a good working relationship, or modifications in internal and external environments are creating a need for change. At such times, faculty and staff are more likely to reach consensus in the development phase of the strategic planning process, and the unit is likely to have resources for implementation and evaluation.

Resource Management

A large amount of information is collected, compiled, and analyzed during strategic planning processes. Considerable time and energy is often expended to create detailed collection instruments (e.g., schedules, worksheets, interview forms), diverting resources from subsequent implementation and evaluation stages. To manage resources most efficiently, the number of instruments used during the development phases of the process should be kept to a minimum, and the design of the instruments should be kept simple. A review of the literature and model instruments can help stimulate thinking and can aid in the development of program-specific instruments (see Bean, 1993; Burkhart & Reuss, 1993; Burton & McBride, 1991; Cook, 1994).

Roadblocks to Effective Planning

Before beginning the strategic planning process, language program administrators should be aware of possible roadblocks to effective strategic planning. Bean (1993) identifies the "Big Three" enemies of effective planning—ego, politics, and bureaucracy—in their negative manifestations. To that list could be added complacency and poor or ill-equipped leadership.

Ego, in this context, refers to the mismanagement of self: a director who has a personal agenda, who must always be right, who needs to "be the boss," who does not want a plan implemented—either from fear, laziness, or just petulance—and who is in a position to prevent it from being implemented. A problem ego among faculty and staff can often be dealt with by a good facilitator, but a problem ego among leadership subverts the whole process.

Negative *politics* refers to the mistreatment of people and to inappropriate political maneuvering within the host institution. Mistreated personnel (because of, for example, unethical hiring practices and poor remuneration) will rarely commit themselves to the strategic planning process; likewise, it is difficult to engage in any planning if the host institution is unpredictable in its treatment of the program, especially regarding its finances.

An obstructive *bureaucracy* can subvert planning with an overload of policies and procedures. For example, rigid hiring procedures established by the host institution can make it impossible for a language program to hire an individual with the special skills needed to implement a particular strategy.

Complacent and ill-equipped leadership often leads to a blatant disregard for a changing external environment or competition, disrupting the strategic planning process. Administrators who enjoy the familiarity of the status quo create a true roadblock to any kind of effective planning. Complacency among faculty and staff is treatable with good leadership; among the leadership, however, it serves to short-circuit the planning process before it begins.

Conclusion

Strategic planning can be a highly productive process for language programs to undertake if (a) the planning is carefully tailored to fit the organization, (b) the whole unit is engaged in the process, and (c) the development-implementation-evaluation stages allow for fluidity and revision. Strategic planning is a flexible process with a combined top-down and bottom-up approach to planning. The emphasis on emergent strategies, strategic thinking, and close interaction between planning and implementation (Wall & Wall, 1995) can be altered and adjusted to fit each language program's needs and organizational framework. The process described in this discussion can provide programs with a sense of focus and direction and the ability to serve their teachers, students, and communities better.[2]

Endnotes

1. Note that we engaged in a modified form of the Critical Success Factor Analysis. Instead of engaging in the analysis as part of the development stage of the strategic planning process, we chose to focus on critical success factors as part of the implementation process, when trying to determine the feasibility of various action strategies.

2. Special thanks to Jerry Blakely, strategic planning consultant in Eugene, Oregon, and to editor extraordinaire Peggy Dame of the American English Institute, University of Oregon, for their expertise, clear-thinking, and generous contribution of time to the production of this chapter.

Discussion Questions and Activities

1. Create a graphic representation of the strategic planning process that illustrates the relationships among the fundamental components of the process.

2. Review the benefits associated with the strategic planning process. Rank-order the

benefits from most to least beneficial. Provide a rationale for your decisions.

3. Review the disadvantages of the strategic planning process. Can you think of any other disadvantages? In what ways can a language program administrator who is interested in strategic planning avoid or overcome these disadvantages?

4. Using Table 4 as a guide, conduct a SWOT Analysis of a language program that you have either worked in or are very familiar with. If you haven't been associated with a language program, use an academic degree program or business that you know well to conduct the analysis.

5. Using a language program that you know well as a point of reference, draft six statements that illustrate the meaning and distinctions among the following terms: vision, values, purpose, mission, goals, and strategies.

6. Imagine that you are a language program administrator who wants to initiate a strategic planning process. You anticipate that the majority of your faculty and staff will support your decision, but you know that a minority will feel that it is a waste of time and effort. Draft an outline of the presentation you will make at a faculty/staff meeting that will strengthen the support of the majority and alleviate the fears and doubts of the minority.

Suggested Readings

Collins, J. C., & Lazier, W. C. (1992). *Beyond entrepreneurship: Turning your business into an enduring great company.* Englewood Cliffs, NJ: Prentice Hall.

This text is divided into two parts, the first being an excellent blueprint for developing a strategic planning process, with real-world examples and illustrations. The second part contains suggestions for creating a company atmosphere that stimulates ongoing innovation. The text does not cover implementation processes.

Domb, E. (1993). Total quality management: Strategy for success through continuous improvement. In W. C. Bean (Ed.), *Strategic planning that makes things happen: Getting from where you are to where you want to be* (pp. 247–268). Amherst, MA: Human Resources Development Press.

This volume provides a useful summary of what total quality management (TQM) is and how it forms a basis for strategic planning.

Drucker, P. F. (1973). Managing the public service institution. *Public Interest, 33*(3), 43–60.

Drucker, P. F. (1994). *Innovation and entrepreneurship.* Boston: Butterworth-Heinemann.

Drucker has been writing about management, business, economics and society, and politics for more than 50 years. He does not specialize in strategic planning per se, but includes it in his discussions. These two volumes are good basic references for anyone interested in management.

Wall, S. J., & Wall, S. R. (1995, Autumn). The evolution (not the death) of strategy. *Organizational Dynamics, 24*(2), 7–19.

The authors discuss some of the problems associated with the strategic approach to planning. They explain how recent changes in the approach have created a stronger, more responsive process.

Chapter 6

THE DECISION MAKER AND NEGOTIATOR

Alexandra Rowe Henry
University of South Carolina

anguage program administrators are faced with numerous administrative challenges that require skills in negotiating and decision making. To be an effective negotiator and decision maker, administrators must have expertise in a wide variety of areas, both academic and nonacademic, including instruction, materials development, recruitment, program research, budgets and finances, employment conditions, interpersonal relations, interdepartmental politics, and global events. Language program administrators who have learned how to negotiate and how to make decisions effectively, using their knowledge of these many different areas, can help maintain the stability essential to language program quality and success.

Language programs in general, and intensive English programs (IEPs) in particular, are often both a part of and apart from the educational contexts in which they operate. This "apartness" makes the language program distinctly odd, and this oddity is both a strength and a weakness, an opportunity and a threat (Stoller, 1995b). An examination of the context in which most IEPs operate illustrates the ongoing need for language program administrators to engage in decision making and negotiating. Parallels exist for language programs of other types.

Even though an IEP exists within the culture of the university at large, the IEP culture contrasts sharply with the institution of higher education, and as a university entity it is often misunderstood. The culture of the IEP nurtures students and colleagues and submerges egos; institutions of higher education generally highlight individual egos. IEPs often regard people idealistically, even altruistically; institutions of higher education regard people realistically and pragmatically. Santos (1992) claims that the reverse is true for instruction. Instructionally, IEPs are realistic and pragmatic, while institutions of higher education are often idealistic. IEP faculty and staff behave more similarly to parents, coaches, and counselors; faculty and staff at institutions of higher education often act like team captains. IEPs are characterized by noncompetitive teamwork, whereas higher education supports individual competition. IEP faculty and staff are, for the most part, nonpolitical within the program; institutions of higher education, on the other hand, are highly political. IEP faculty share information to help the program succeed; higher education faculty often withhold information so that each may succeed individually within the system. IEP faculty and staff make decisions together, thereby sharing power; higher education faculty and administrative staff wield power and make decisions by themselves (Henry, 1994, 1995).

Considering the differences between IEPs and institutions of higher education, it is not surprising that contact between the two entities often results in misunderstandings and conflicts. Essential, then, to the success of any academic program is the ability of the administrator to negotiate effectively and make wise decisions so that conflicts are minimized and an atmosphere of collegiality is obtained.

Out of necessity, most language program administrators have learned to negotiate and make decisions by trial and error. Staczek (1991) comments that "we have received the intellectual training characteristic of our discipline, but not the training necessary to make decisions affecting programs, financial resources, and people" (p. 21). In general, language program administrators can benefit from more formal attention to and guidance in decision making and negotiating within the context of the language program. To meet these needs, six major challenges that language program administrators face in decision making and negotiating are addressed here, along with suggestions that can guide language program administrators in developing the skills required for confident decision making and effective negotiation.

The First Challenge:
The Scope and Diversity of Decisions and Negotiations

The first challenge that language program administrators face in decision making and negotiating is understanding what types of decisions must be made. Each operation within an IEP for which the language program administrator has responsibility requires that an action be decided or negotiated. These responsibilities include recruiting students, marketing the program (externally and internally), providing services to students, hiring appropriately trained faculty and staff, developing and assessing personnel, and purchasing textbooks, resource materials, equipment, and supplies to support program operations. The language program administrator's decisions and negotiations facilitate all of these operations, as well as other functions such as processing immigration documents, providing insurance for students, and securing and maintaining classroom and office space. Within any single working day, the language program administrator may sign 10 to 20 documents, have four or five meetings, teach a class or two, and write a proposal to bring in a special group of students. All of these activities require that decisions be made. Ultimately, the language program administrator can potentially be involved in deciding or negotiating everything—from recruitment trips to paper clips.

Language program administrators often feel overwhelmed with the number, complexity, and types of decisions awaiting them. Areas of particular concern that relate to decision making and negotiation can be divided into four main areas: delegation of tasks, budgetary considerations, strategic considerations, and responsiveness to decisions made by others.

Delegation of Tasks

Who makes decisions is a very important consideration in any language program. A language program administrator would not want to be responsible for making all decisions. With the pressure that would accompany such responsibility, one could maintain neither the rationality nor the sanity needed to manage the program effectively. Making all operational decisions and engaging in all negotiations represents inefficient microman-agement and sets a negative and unproductive example for program personnel.

Delegating decision making of certain types and developing a system for doing so is crucial for the efficient management of a language program (and the sanity of the director). However, even when language program administrators delegate decision making and nego-tiating responsibilities to others, they need to be aware of all decisions made and negotia-tions under way. Thus, a system of reporting that will keep the administrator abreast of these activities must be established and understood by language program personnel.

Budgetary Considerations

The administrator is essentially held accountable for all operations that impact the overall quality of the program and the bottom line for the budget. As Hyson (1991) so aptly puts it, "the ultimate responsibility for making ... decisions rests on [an administra-tor's] shoulders" (p. 69). The fact that many language programs must be financially self-supporting often guides, if not mandates, decisions and negotiations. In light of these budgetary constraints, the language program administrator must determine what to decide or negotiate individually and what others—both inside and outside the program—should decide or negotiate. Whatever happens, the result must be programmatic stability and budgetary solvency, both of which are interdependent and essential to the success of the language program. Without stability, program quality and productivity on all levels will decline, which may lower enrollment and the revenues accruing from that enroll-ment. Without solvency, the language program ceases to exist.

Although language programs vary from context to context, language program admin-istrators typically have full responsibility for maintaining the budget, even though they do not usually have singular signatory power for overseeing the budget. Budgetary decisions are most often made after thoughtful consideration of questions such as those in Table 1. (See Staczek, this volume, for more information on language program budgets.)

Strategic Considerations

Language program administrators should not make decisions in a vacuum. Strategic decisions that are based on adequate data and feedback guide the program in its ongoing operations and provide for constant improvement. Strategic decisions are best made con-sensually within a language program. The kinds of questions that lead to strategic deci-sions are listed below. (See Klinghammer, this volume, for a more detailed discussion of the strategic planning process.)

1. How can we determine the quality of the language program?

2. How can we improve the quality of the language program?

3. What do we value most in the language program?

4. What type of curriculum best meets student needs?

5. What do we need to do to support this curriculum?

6. What kind of language proficiency testing is needed for accurate student placement?

7. What qualities are we looking for in faculty?

Table 1. Questions That Impact Budgetary Decision Making

Areas of Budgetary Concern	Sample Questions
Instruction	How many teachers does the program need?
	How will the program cover instructional expenses?
Staffing	How many support staff does the program need?
	How will the program cover support staff operations?
Recruitment	How much recruitment is needed to maintain enrollment?
	What types of recruitment tools will be used?
	How many students are needed to support the budget?
Professional Development	What is the level of professional development needed to maintain or improve program quality?
	What professional development activities can the budget afford?
Resources	What resources are needed to help faculty and staff do their jobs?
	What resources need to be upgraded to maintain program quality?
	What new resources will help the program improve its services?

Responsiveness to Decisions Made by Others

Some decisions that directly impact the language program (e.g., salary scales, official titles for program personnel, whether an additional staff member can be hired, new space targeted for instruction) are made by individuals outside the language program. This situation has nothing to do with the capabilities of language program faculty, staff, or administrator(s), but rather has to do with constraints imposed by the institutional or corporate culture within which the language program operates. How a language program administrator responds to these already-made decisions may either help or hurt the language program. A language program administrator must decide which issues are worth the battle. Surviving and flourishing within a bureaucracy that does not share the language program's values often means that there are more battles to be fought than there is energy and resources to pursue them. Program administrators need to choose their battles wisely.

The Second Challenge:
The Process of Decision Making and Negotiating

Language program administrators must be involved in all levels of program operations to have access to the information needed to make wise decisions on their own or to guide others in thoughtful decision making. When making decisions,

> a leader does not base decisions on hunches or good ideas; rather he or she is involved enough in the process to understand the situation, what the options are, and what effect those options will have on the organization as a whole. Without a clear understanding of why the organization exists and where it is headed, the leader will have difficulty determining the most promising course of action. (Hyson, 1991, p. 67)

In determining how decisions will be made and who is involved, language program administrators have three basic options: They may decide or negotiate by themselves; they may involve others in the decision-making process through participatory, consensual governance; or they may delegate, as previously discussed.

Deciding and Negotiating Independently

There are times when it is appropriate for the program administrator to make decisions independently, without consulting language program staff and faculty. In these situations, the administrator may be the only person, by virtue of where he or she sits, who has a view of the program as a whole, who has had contact with the surrounding cultures that exert external pressures on the program, and who has access to critical information. In addition, decisions that involve confidential matters (e.g., disciplinary actions or salaries) are often confined to the administrator's desk. Decisions that require an immediate response prevent administrators from bringing program personnel together for participatory decision making because of time constraints. When time is not a factor, however, administrators face the challenge of determining which decisions should be solitary endeavors. When it is determined that the decision has to be made alone, administrators need not work in total isolation; in such situations, it is helpful for an administrator to consult with mentors, trusted institutional colleagues, colleagues outside the program, or other language program administrators who can be objective in helping the administrator sift through the mass of details and potential consequences that relate to the issue at hand. At times it is very stressful to make decisions on one's own. In such situations, it is important to remember that the language program administrator has been entrusted with making the hard calls. At such times, as Bray (1995) comments, "we must be willing not to be loved," a difficult concession to make for administrators who are keenly aware of the affective domain and demands of the language program culture.

Shared Decision Making

In developing a participatory process for decision making, language program administrators must rely on language program personnel. Typical language program personnel are committed to helping others. They tend to function best as a team, collaborating on tasks and projects. The language program administrator is wise to use this culture-specific behavior to support the processes of decision making and negotiating within the program.

There are advantages and disadvantages to shared decision making. Group decision making strengthens an overall program. It leads to decisions informed by multiple perspectives and sources of input, rather like the conclusions of research supported by diverse triangulated data. According to Stoller (1995b), "giving faculty [and staff] decision-making powers through committee work, shared governance, administrative responsibilities, and open forum discussions can nurture a sense of belonging and commitment" (p. 20). Thus, shared decision making leads to empowerment, thereby countering the feelings of disempowerment and marginalization often present among language program personnel. For shared decision making to be effective, the participatory process must be perceived as fair. There needs to be open and frequent communication, a climate of mutual trust among all personnel, including trust in management (which must be earned), and a program-wide commitment to success (Johnson, 1996). The language program administrator contributes to the decision making process by not only sharing his or her own perspective but also sharing information to which only he or she may have access and which is vital to the process. All of these factors are important for consensual decision making and the eventual implementation of decisions made. (See Soppelsa, this volume, for a fuller discussion of participatory decision making.)

For all of the positive features of shared decision making, it is also important to recognize its limitations. Shared decision making complicates language program administration because the more people involved in making decisions, the longer the process takes. Sometimes, even though participatory management is preferable, a language program administrator will opt to make an independent decision because there is simply not enough time to bring key personnel together to consider the full range of issues at hand.

The Third Challenge:
Distinctions Between Decisions and Negotiations

Another challenge facing language program administrators is determining when to decide and when to negotiate. To clarify the differences between the two terms here, the following definitions will be used. To *decide* means to determine or settle an issue conclusively, either individually or consensually. The process is based on multiple perspectives and reliable data, resulting in a policy that is then consistently implemented. To *negotiate* means to reach an agreement, never alone and sometimes temporarily, that results from often widely variant perspectives, sometimes adversarial or culturally abnormal in nature, that are expressed in debates, rebuttals, offers, and counter-offers. The result of the negotiating process is then reconsidered after a time, and renegotiation may ensue. Program needs and goals, as well as the locus of the actual decision, influence whether deciding or negotiating is preferable.

Within a language program, an appropriate management strategy is to decide. When decisions are made, especially those that are determined by the group, they become policy. Consider decisions that are related to determining criteria for hiring faculty. When criteria are decided upon (e.g., a master's degree in the field, 3 years of experience, and evidence of professional involvement and commitment), the criteria become the policy for current and future faculty searches. (See Geddes and Marks, this volume, for more details on hiring new program personnel.) Establishing policies may seem bureaucratic, but having consensually decided policies contributes to the group perception of equity, commitment, and stability (Johnson, 1996). And, stability is integral to language program success.

Rarely is negotiation necessary within language programs, except in a case where something outside the norm is at issue. For example, a faculty member may request to be absent from classes for a short time to engage in a professional growth activity. Two cultural norms are in conflict in this case: quality instruction and professional development. Whether the former or the latter takes precedence within any single language program varies. If both are equally valued within the program, then the administrator must negotiate with the teacher so that both may be achieved. Typically, the agreement reached between the parties is relevant only to the individual case. Therefore, the negotiation may inform policy making but does not become policy.

Outside the language program, negotiation is more common. The language program administrator often operates cross-culturally and faces different cultural norms. The cultures may be those of the institution of which the language program is a part, or they may be off-campus service providers, frequently businesses providing services or products that the language program needs or wants. Negotiating can be an effective management strategy in such cross-cultural situations. (See Carkin, this volume, for more detailed insights on cross-cultural management.)

Opportunities for Negotiating

The oddity of language programs, often depicted as a weakness in language program literature, can actually be a strength in negotiations. Language programs generate funds all year, and these funds are often not bound by the same restrictions as other institutional funds. Therefore, the language program administrator may have more budgetary flexibility than mainstream administrators. Such circumstances suggest that the language program administrator can offer funds in negotiating for what the language program needs (e.g., space).

Being absolutely dependent on student satisfaction, language programs are extremely student- and service-oriented, a strength that administrators can use in negotiating. Outside service providers share this value. When outside service providers discover this language program orientation, they seek out the language program for reciprocal services. Community agencies, schools, retirement homes, and children's homes want international programming for their students and clients; language programs want their students to have as much contact with native speakers as possible. The community agencies can provide the purpose and the place for the contact; language programs can provide the students and logistics.

The Fourth Challenge:
The Time Factor in Deciding and Negotiating

Considering the multitude of decisions that the language administrator must make or facilitate daily and the personal needs that often accompany requests for decisions, it is tempting to rely on one's own sense of equity and rationality. It is often perceived to be efficient to make a decision swiftly and go on to the next pressing administrative task. Acting decisively and making decisions quickly is frequently regarded as a highly valued American managerial characteristic. When managers do not behave decisively, they may be perceived as wishy-washy, certainly a negative image for an administrator. The opposite image, however, would be the administrator who "shoots from the hip," a manager who is not only unsupportive but also potentially detrimental to the program. Such an administrative style does not consider all consequences before making decisions.

Seldom is time the major determining factor in making a language program decision. Therefore, making decisions quickly is generally inadvisable, except when there is no choice, as may be the case during a crisis. To act swiftly may be to act precipitously because to do so ignores the chief strength of effective decision making in language programs—the power of group decision making.

During times of high stress for the program, especially at the beginning or end of a term, it is not unusual for someone within the program, a student, for example, to demand that a decision be made on the spot. Unless the decision relates to a medical emergency, the most appropriate response at such a time should be, "Let me think about it and talk with (whoever may be affected by the consequences of the decision) and get back with you as soon as possible." Such a response enables the language program administrator to gather the data needed to make an informed decision. Such times are not crises, and therefore do not require the sorts of quick decisions that are often required in true crisis management.

The Fifth Challenge:
Crisis/Conflict Management

Crises occur in language programs for several reasons. First, students lacking the linguistic and cultural skills necessary to express their needs and problems sometimes panic in a situation that would have caused minimal difficulties in their first languages. The very process of second language learning places students in high-stress situations, thus creating the potential for crises to develop.[1] Program crises may also result from external forces over which neither students nor language program personnel have control. For example, global economics, politics, conflicts, and the value of the dollar affect language program enrollment, the chief source of revenue. Language programs are also vulnerable to crises imposed externally by their home institutions, such as the sudden and wholesale elimination of program classroom and office space. A third reason for language program crises is that even though language program administrators are crucial in effectively handling crises, they are themselves vulnerable. They may not have job security if, for example, they are not tenure eligible. The status of a language program administrator can affect that administrator's abilities to manage program crises effectively.

Strategies for Crisis Avoidance

To deal with crises, whether they involve a single student or a program-wide dilemma and whether they are caused by internal or external forces, the ideal managerial strategy is crisis avoidance because it is proactive rather than reactive. Many language programs, however, operate by perpetual crisis management. Administrators simply react to situations with no plan or process in place for taking steps to avoid crises and conflict. In such programs, administrators spend their time "putting out fires" and dealing with negative situations that arise as a part of the management process. The predictable result of such a management style is program instability and personnel burnout, both of which lead to decline in program quality and productivity. To avoid such stressful situations, language program administrators must strive to be proactive rather than reactive (Hyson, 1991). They must develop strategies and techniques to avoid conflict rather than react to it. A language program administrator must be prepared to operate from a position of strength rather than from a position of weakness.

Stoller and Christison (1994) articulated two effective strategies for managerial proactivity. Both strategies are useful when crises arise due to external forces. The first of these strategies is accurate record keeping, which "facilitates the smooth operation of a [language program], aids in critical decision-making processes, and facilitates reasonably accurate projections" (p. 18). Accurate record keeping is vital to crisis management and crucial for crisis avoidance. Accurate and extensive program information contributes to an administrator's comprehensive understanding of the program culture, providing views of the "little pictures" and the "big picture" of programs as they exist within their contexts; it also enables program administrators to have rapid access to data in times of program crises, thus informing decisions that must be made in situations requiring crisis management.

Another strategy for crisis avoidance involves creating consciousness-raising documents (Stoller & Christison, 1994). Producing documents that present and analyze program information, both synchronically and diachronically, keeps program personnel and institutional administrators aware of the state of the program. Such documents also contribute to the perception of program stability. According to Stoller (1995b), administrators "need to create stability whenever possible" (p. 19), especially in the midst of a program crisis, which by its very nature creates a period of instability.

A third proactive managerial strategy for crisis avoidance is planning for the future. In planning for future program needs, language program administrators need to be aware of institutional plans and international trends. For example, a language program administrator who is aware of possible enrollment growth prepares to meet future program needs by creating a pool of available temporary faculty to pull in should enrollment meet expectations. The same planning would be necessary for enrollment decline or budget cutbacks. A language program administrator monitors these trends and makes plans to handle the effects accordingly.

Another effective strategy for crisis avoidance is to network with colleagues, on and off campus. Talking with other program administrators at regional and national conferences is vital. Seasoned institutional administrators know very well the power of information and the means to obtain it. Networking can include chats over lunch, casual visits to other offices, interchanges during committee meetings, and conversations with support staff. Sharing program brochures, institutional mission statements, strategic plans, and job description documents, so that they are available for easy reference, can provide support for language program administrators in need.

A recent strategy for networking involves the use of electronic mail and list serves, both providing administrators with information concerning social, political, and economic trends that could potentially affect language programs. By being on-line, a language program administrator shares questions and concerns with colleagues around the world. It is not unusual for program administrators to seek counsel on-line, for example, when they are planning a recruitment trip or attempting to resolve a conflict within their own institution.

When a language program administrator is in the midst of a crisis, big or small, other program administrators provide perhaps the greatest source of support and strategies for program management. Some useful networks include the ATESL (Administrators and Teachers of English as a Second Language) section of NAFSA: Association of International Educators and the Program Administration and Intensive English Programs Interest Sections within TESOL (Teachers of English to Speakers of Other Languages). Two other important networks are AAIEP (American Association of Intensive English Programs) and UCIEP (Consortium of University and College Intensive English Programs.)[2]

Suggestions for Crisis Management

Even though the ideal managerial strategy for language program administrators is crisis avoidance, crisis management is sometimes inevitable. When crisis management is necessary, the following suggestions may prove useful:

1. Clarify the nature of the crisis and gather the information necessary to understand the crisis fully. Decide who should be involved in managing the crisis. Crisis management may involve the administrator alone, staff, faculty, students, or all personnel. Gather information yourself or delegate the task to others, with specific instructions about what information is needed.

2. Consider the relationship between time and the crisis. If there is little time before the consequence(s) of the crisis becomes a reality, act swiftly. If time is not critical, take more time to gather information and evaluate the crisis.

3. Develop a plan, including procedures and a timeline, for managing the crisis. Include tasks that contribute positively to the process. The ultimate goal of the plan should be to maintain program stability.

4. If appropriate, involve other program staff who are affected by the crisis. Do not withhold vital information or try to manage the crisis yourself (V. B. Lanier, personal communication, May 25, 1992).

5. Keep the program's mission and strategic plan in mind as you manage the crisis. It is most important to maintain smooth program operations during these crises and to remember the program's vision for the future. Continuing to serve currently enrolled students well is important for program stability.

6. Consult other program administrators through e-mail, letters, and the telephone. If confidentiality is an issue, private telephone calls are the most secure.

7. Keep a log of what happens during the crisis, who does what and when. The log may become important for documentation and negotiation during and after the crisis.

8. If necessary and appropriate, involve other institutional colleagues in managing the crisis. Inform them of the crisis, solicit their counsel, and involve them in a resolution.

9. Be prepared to negotiate. Determine what you will be willing and able to negotiate. Listen before making an offer.

10. Let staff and faculty know about the crisis in progress and when it has been resolved. Be sure to acknowledge and thank all individuals who helped bring about crisis resolution.

The Sixth Challenge:
Language Program Administrators As Servant Leaders

Yet another challenge for language program administrators is discovering how to create the support structure for decisions and negotiations that will lead to program quality, stability, and success. Despite the fact that language program administrators are accountable for all program decisions and negotiations, whether or not they actually make the decisions themselves, language programs are strengthened by group solidarity accruing from consensual, rather than hierarchical, decision making and negotiating.

Developing a plan for consensual decision making is perhaps the biggest personnel challenge that administrators face. Consensual decision making must occur as often as possible to retain unity of purpose. Unlike the top-down organizational structure of so many educational institutions, language programs might consider a more bottom-up organizational structure that allows for consensual decision making. (See Davidson & Tesh, this volume, for a detailed discussion of language program organization design.) In a consensual decision-making model, the administrator becomes a "servant leader" (personal communication with G. Rice on December 15, 1995), simultaneously leading and serving colleagues collaboratively and effectively. In becoming a servant leader, a language program administrator might consider serving as a participant rather than a chair of a committee. Such actions create opportunities for all interested faculty and staff to take the lead in the decision-making process. Soliciting input from as many faculty and staff members as possible is essential for decisions and negotiations. Consider the English Programs for Internationals group on the University of South Carolina campus that used this decision-making process to complete a TESOL-guided self-study in 9 months and then moved on to informed, ongoing implementation of the recommendations resulting from the self-study. As a result, program personnel and the program itself became stronger (Henry, Hamrick, & Porter, 1995). These changes, in turn, underscored program quality and success.

Conclusion

Becoming an effective decision maker and negotiator takes time. These are not skills one learns in a few months or years. In fact, the learning never stops; it is an ongoing process that continues throughout one's career as a language program administrator. The following suggestions can be helpful in guiding administrators to develop the skills needed for confident decision making and negotiation:

1. Learn the institutional or corporate culture within which the language program operates. Learn how to communicate effectively within this culture. Chances are that the rhetoric of the home institution culture is very different from that of the language program culture (Henry, 1995).

2. Develop a "solid, diversified knowledge base" (Pistole & Cogdal, 1993, p. 7) that includes comprehensive language program data in addition to knowledge of the institutional mission, organizational structure, policies, and procedures.

3. Develop good listening skills. Language program administrators should listen more than they speak. It is through listening that one develops an understanding of critical issues and different points of view.

4. Learn to ask the right questions. This is a skill that results directly from careful listening. What is "right" is contextually relative. Answers vary from context to context, and from administration to administration.

5. Seek mentors within the institution and within the profession. One should always have a mentor. When you feel ready, consider the possibility of becoming a mentor yourself.

6. Develop skills in mathematics and technology. Both are critical for budgeting, data collection and analysis, and other administrative tasks.

7. Delegate responsibilities. Language program administrators cannot nurture faculty and staff, counsel students, or be effective in the decision-making process if they are overextended or on the verge of burnout.

8. Take sensible risks. Establish and maintain a program environment supportive of professionalism and innovation.

9. Nurture faculty and staff. Teachers are the "inviolable core" of the language program, and support staff create the engine that makes a program run (Stoller & Christison, 1994).

10. Create solidarity among your faculty and staff so that they can work together in the consensual decision-making process. Group solidarity allows a program to operate from a position of strength.

In sum, language program administrators can simultaneously lead and serve colleagues collaboratively and effectively if they are skilled in decision making and negotiating. Whenever possible, language programs are strengthened by group solidarity, accruing from consensual, rather than hierarchical, decision making and negotiating. Thoughtful and strategic decision making and negotiating, driven by hard facts and relevant data, must recur as often as possible to retain program unity of purpose and strength.

Endnotes

1. A preliminary study of the types of illnesses most common among intensive English students treated by the University of South Carolina student health center in one calendar year indicates a high percentage of stress-related problems.

2. Note that only university-based programs qualify for UCIEP membership; AAIEP is open to both university-based and proprietary programs.

Discussion Questions and Activities

1. Why is it important for a language program administrator to develop skills in decision making and negotiating?

2. What is the difference between deciding and negotiating? Give two examples of each as they relate to language program administration.

3. What are the advantages of a consensual decision-making process? What are the disadvantages?

4. What is the difference between crisis avoidance and crisis management? Why is crisis avoidance the preferred managerial style for language program administrators?

5. Although there are many benefits to a consensual decision-making model, there are times when a language program administrator must make decisions alone. Can you think of a situation that would require a language program administrator to make a solitary decision?

6. Why does the author suggest finding a mentor? In what ways can a mentor assist a language program administrator in the decision-making process?

7. Imagine that you are the director of a university-based ESL program. You are facing a budget cutback in the coming year despite growing enrollment in your program. What steps would you take to involve the faculty and staff of the program in a consensual decision-making process for dealing with the changes that must result?

8. Give an example of a decision that must be made "on the spot." Explain why this decision could not be delayed.

Suggested Readings

Hyson, R. J. (1991). Point seven: Institute leadership. In R. I. Miller (Ed.), *Applying the Deming method to higher education for more effective human resource management* (pp. 65–73). Washington, DC: College and Personnel Association.

Hyson applies Deming's method to university leadership and discusses leadership as an approach rather than a collection of techniques. According to Deming, three points are central to leadership: a concern with people, a commitment to constant improvement, and a view of management as a holistic process.

Pistole, M. C., & Cogdal, P. A. (1993). Empowering women: Taking charge of our university careers. *Initiatives, 55*, 1–8.

Pistole and Cogdal highlight various strategies for female administrators to use while negotiating effectively within university contexts. The intent of the article is to provide informed insights into how women can foster "career achievement and professional development" within their institutional settings.

Chapter 7

THE LANGUAGE PROGRAM ADMINISTRATOR AND POLICY FORMATION AT INSTITUTIONS OF HIGHER LEARNING

Lee Ann Rawley
Utah State University

 y the year 2000, minority students will constitute a third of the student population in U.S. schools (Murray, 1992). Already in the nation's largest cities, more than half of the overall student body is of minority background (McLaughlin, 1992). As educators face the challenges of growing linguistic and cultural diversity in public schools, many are hopeful that policy makers will create policies supportive of curricula and assessment procedures that accommodate culturally and linguistically diverse students. Foreign language educators, in both K–12 public schools and higher education, are making the case for teaching foreign languages as a way to build bridges among diverse groups of people (Willis, 1996).[1]

As a response to this change in demographics, one current focus in higher education is on globalizing the curriculum. Educators and policy makers seek to prepare today's students for a culturally diverse society, with political and economic ties worldwide. Educators working with linguistic and cultural minority students in colleges and universities, as well as those teaching foreign languages, are hopeful that national, local, and institutional policies aimed at diversity issues will enhance the educational experiences of their students. But as Fullan and Miles (1992) remind us, "wishful thinking and legislation have deservedly poor records as tools for social betterment" (p. 752).

It will take more than wishful thinking for U.S. schools, colleges, and universities to become places that truly promote diversity. Language teachers and administrators concerned with educating linguistic and cultural minority students, and introducing all students to global perspectives, face unique challenges that require looking beyond their own classrooms, subject matter, students, and administrative exigencies to consider the broader public milieu within which schools exist and within which policies affecting schools and students are made. Whether or not an institution has clear policies affirming the value of international and immigrant students and the study of foreign or second languages affects the way language program directors interact with the systems within which they work.

Two major issues of relevance to language program administrators are addressed here: (a) policy making that governs the educational experiences of international students in U.S. institutions of higher learning, and (b) attempts by ESL professionals to shape those policies. This chapter reports the results of a qualitative study that investigated how the directors of intensive English programs (IEPs) at colleges and universities view their roles within the policy formation contexts of their institutions. Rather than prescribe how language program administrators should approach their roles as policy makers, this study presents the perspectives of actual IEP directors who have considerable experience negotiating within the higher education environment with the hope that their approaches and solutions to the policy puzzle will illuminate possible strategies for other language program administrators.

Background

To understand issues related to policy formation and the role of language program personnel in that process, it is useful to review previous studies on international student and international education policy, national influences on policy, and the role of intensive English programs in international student education.

The history of policy directed toward international students and the educational units that serve them in U.S. institutions of higher education has been one of nonpolicy and ambiguity. Each year institutions of higher education in the United States open their doors to hundreds of thousands of students from other countries,[2] but policies designed to support their educational experiences in the United States have not kept pace. Institutional responses to these students and to policies affecting their educational experiences have varied greatly. Some schools actively recruit international students, whereas others rely on the school's reputation, faculty contacts abroad, and recommendations from former students. How international students are perceived and treated when they arrive at a U.S. institution also varies greatly from school to school. Some colleges and universities have clearly articulated policies, whereas others operate on an ad hoc basis, forming policy in reaction to needs and problems only when they become pressing (American Council on Education, 1982).

The American Council on Education (ACE) and the Institute for International Education (IIE) have both examined how institutions of higher learning respond to international students on their campuses. The ACE report, *Foreign Students and Institutional Policy: Toward an Agenda for Action* (1982), characterized policy on international student admissions, education, and social accommodation as varying from nonexistent to ad hoc and expedient. The absence of national policy concerning international students in the United States reveals the need for institutions to accept more responsibility for planning for these students and making policies that deal with them fairly.

The IIE report, *Absence of Decision: Foreign Students in American Colleges and Universities* (Goodwin & Nacht, 1983), reached many of the same conclusions as the ACE report. Goodwin and Nacht studied institutions ranging from large research universities to community colleges in Ohio, Florida, and California. They also included Columbia University in New York and Michigan State University in the study as representatives of schools with a known commitment to international education. They interviewed 183 people including state education officials, institutional administrators, faculty, and service personnel whose jobs required direct involvement with international students and international education. What Goodwin and Nacht found, as indicated by the title of their volume, was a lack of policy regarding international students. Despite the fact that institutional responses varied from "nonpolicy" to "ad hocism" and "designed ambiguity" (p. 21), most of Goodwin and Nacht's respondents recognized a need for a carefully formulated institutional policy to address the needs of international students on campus.

As the ACE report notes and the IIE report corroborates, there is no national education policy governing international students in U.S. universities and colleges. The federal policy with the greatest impact on the education of international students is immigration law, which regulates who can enter the country and how long they can stay. U.S. immigration laws affecting international students and scholars are dynamic and complex; the details of the laws change frequently, sometimes from day to day, in response to political situations throughout the world (Wernick, 1992).

In the absence of any coherent national policy, IEPs play a central role in the educational experience of students attending, or preparing to attend, U.S. colleges and universities. IEP administrators and faculty have professional expertise in international education and language teaching, and many have had international experience themselves. Because their work brings them into daily contact with international students, they are affected both directly and indirectly by the policies, or lack of policies, governing their students. Despite the fact that Staczek and Carkin (1985) identified IEP faculties as among the best-qualified personnel at U.S. colleges and universities for dealing with issues related to international students, IEP faculty are not often included in the formal policy-making structures at their institutions. Sadly, the role of ESL professionals was virtually ignored by Goodwin and Nacht in their 1983 study of policy formation.[3] One possible explanation for the failure of ESL professionals to become fully enfranchised members of their institutions may be related to the low status of international students on U.S. campuses. Because many institutions of higher education do not generally acknowledge the presence of international students on campus, these institutions are not likely to acknowledge the contributions of those who deal exclusively with these students (Staczek & Carkin, 1985). Thus, if institutions are not actively making policy that provides for international students, they are not likely to be interested in creating channels for input from IEP directors or faculty. (See Wadden, 1994, for a discussion of the low status of IEP faculty on university campuses.)

In the years since Goodwin and Nacht (1983) and Staczek and Carkin (1985) conducted their studies, throngs of students from around the world have continued to come to U.S. institutions to study, and increasing numbers of universities and community colleges have added intensive English programs to their curricula. In fact, the number of IEPs in the country tripled between academic years 1978/79 and 1993/94 (Davis, 1994). But research has not kept pace with these trends in international education. Given today's highly charged national climate surrounding language and cultural issues, it is important to examine how U.S. institutions of higher learning are responding to international students in the 1990s, and how intensive English programs are contributing or failing to contribute to policy formation at their institutions.

Description of the Study

Past studies and more recent literature on international education lack information regarding the role of IEP directors in policy formation at institutions of higher education. To fill this void, this chapter presents a descriptive, multisite case study that was designed to determine how IEP directors at institutions with substantial international student populations view the ways in which their institutions define and provide for the needs of these students on campus.

The study was conducted at two community colleges and two research universities located in a state in the western United States. The sites were selected to represent varying programmatic and institutional configurations; the four institutions examined in the study differ in terms of the number and type of international students on campus, the placement of the IEP within the structure of the school, institutional policies directed toward students studying ESL, and the status and background of each IEP director.

The first institution in the study is a large research university in an urban setting; the school admits both undergraduate and graduate-level international students. The total student population is approximately 26,000, with the international student population varying between 8% and 10% of the total. The IEP at this institution serves about 200 students per academic quarter. Of those, about half are matriculated students seeking a degree and taking English classes in addition to classes for their academic majors. The remaining half are nonmatriculated students studying English full time. All ESL classes at this institution are non credit bearing. Students must earn a 500 on the Test of English as a Foreign Language (TOEFL) to be admitted to the university as matriculated students. The IEP is housed in the division of continuing education where the director and faculty have non-tenure-track contracts. The director of the IEP, who established the program in 1989, has a master's degree and has been active in the field of ESL and in TESOL (Teachers of English to Speakers of Other Languages) for some 15 years.

The second institution, a land-grant research university in a small town, also admits undergraduate and graduate-level international students. The total student population is approximately 15,000, with international students comprising about 6–7% of the total. Of the approximately 75 students attending the IEP each academic quarter, half are undergraduate students and half are graduate students. The IEP is an autonomous program within a college; the IEP director reports to the dean. IEP students are admitted to the university, but must demonstrate proof of English proficiency—by exam or successful completion of the IEP—before beginning regular university courses. All IEP courses carry university credit; for undergraduate students, 25 of those credits can be applied toward graduation. The IEP director and instructors are lecturers without faculty status. The director, nearing completion of a Ph.D. in instructional technology, has been active in the field of ESL and in TESOL for some 20 years; he has taught ESL at this institution since 1987, and has been the IEP director for 3 years.

One of the community colleges in the study is located in a rural setting. The college serves undergraduate international students seeking associate of arts (AA) or associate of science (AS) degrees, preparing to transfer to 4-year schools, or spending a year abroad to learn English. The international student population is approximately 8% of the total. Until 2 years ago, internationals were almost 12% of the total, but a sharp increase in international tuition at the school is associated with a decline in international student numbers. Students receive credit for all ESL classes, but only the credit from the advanced classes is applied toward graduation. In addition, completion of the IEP satisfies the foreign language requirement for an AA degree. The IEP is an autonomous department at the college; IEP instructors and the director have faculty status and tenure-track positions. The IEP director has a Ph.D. in linguistics and has been an active member of the ESL profession and TESOL for close to 20 years. She established the IEP at her institution 17 years ago.

The other community college in the study is located in an urban setting. It is an open-entry college with a basic skills, vocational training mission. The total student population is approximately 12,000; of those, 4% are international students. Internationals come to the school to earn an associate's degree before transferring to a 4-year school, or to learn English so they can gain admission to a university. The college and the IEP also serve a large number of immigrant students; in fact, up to two thirds of the students in the IEP are immigrants. The IEP is situated in the division of Developmental Studies; the instructors and the director have faculty status and tenure-track positions. The director has a master's degree and has been active in ESL and TESOL for the past 15 years.

The picture of IEPs that emerges from these profiles is typical of that found throughout the country in several respects:

1. The program directors are qualified professionals, but their status varies from institution to institution.

2. Faculty status is varied as well, although in community colleges ESL instructors are more likely to have tenure-track positions.

3. IEPs are housed in diverse units within home institutions. (See Staczek & Carkin, 1985, and Kaplan, this volume, for additional information on IEP placement.)

Formal interviews were conducted with the IEP directors at each of these four institutions, using a loosely structured set of questions. Each director was asked approximately the same questions, although the conversations varied somewhat because informants were allowed to introduce topics of their own. The interviews, conducted over the telephone, lasted from 45 minutes to an hour. The interviews were audiotaped and transcribed verbatim for analysis.

Study Findings

The purpose of the study was to determine how directors of intensive English programs view the process of policy formation at their institutions. In an attempt to portray accurately the views of the administrators themselves, what follows is a narrative that weaves together their voices and my interpretations.

According to the IEP directors interviewed for this study, nonpolicy remains the norm. Neither increased international student enrollments nor the 1990s focus on curricular globalization has brought about carefully drafted policies to address the needs of international students. None of the interviewees' institutions actively recruits international students; students seem to appear on campus "by accident." One IEP director reports that his institution had not planned to have international students at all; it "just happened, and is continuing to happen without much forethought or planning involved." Another describes his institution's whimsical international student policy this way: "International policy ... just happens. The administration gets concerned if numbers are low, but they don't do anything about it. If numbers go up, they don't do anything. They just take what happens."

The directors characterized existing policies as vague and lofty, or negative and discouraging. The directors referred to institutional mission statements and administrative invocations of the term *diversity*—meant to send the message that international students have value because they bring diversity to campus—as symbolic, hollow, insincere, and unsupported by policy to facilitate the educational experiences of international students.

Several of the directors characterized existing institutional policies as negative, inflexible, and reactionary. They pointed to unbending admission policies, health insurance regulations, and registration restrictions that set up hurdles for students and send them discouraging messages about their value to the institution. The IEP directors felt that negative policies often emerge in reaction to problems that involve only a small number of students. For example, knowing that a student had entered a degree program without completing ESL courses might lead to stricter enforcement of admissions policies. On the other hand, knowing that a student was kept in ESL classes longer than necessary is unlikely to generate a change in policy to ensure that rules are flexible enough to accommodate students. From examples such as these, it would seem that many institutions will make policy decisions based on pressures from the institution but are less likely to make changes when students themselves may be harmed. This biased approach to forming policies, in the view of the IEP directors, often stands in the way of making sound decisions based on a coherent institutional plan for internationalization.

The IEP directors were of the opinion that their presidents, vice presidents, and deans were well aware of the financial benefits associated with having international students on campus and wanted to protect that income. One director interpreted his institution's interest in international students as driven solely by money rather than by an interest in diversity. "People are speaking out in favor of diversity, and people are counting money," he said. This director was not alone in his rather cynical view, linking international students with large sums of money. At three of the institutions studied, the tuition paid by IEP students is not returned to the language program itself; rather it goes into the school's general fund. One program in the study is self-supporting; even though it receives the monetary resources that the program brings in, the director thinks the IEP is viewed as a potential source of revenue for the institution.

The IEP directors interviewed for this study regularly monitor what goes on at their institutions, paying special attention to policies that might affect international students. Unfortunately, all interviewees expressed a sense of disenfranchisement, of being separate from the governing bodies that make policy. In general, channels for IEP input into institutional policy-making processes are limited. Without institutional structures to facilitate their participation in making policies that govern their programs, their status, and their students, all of those interviewed have felt isolated and apart from policy formation.

Because these IEP directors operate from a position of perceived marginality, it cannot be said that they *make* policy at their institutions. However, they have all found ways to *shape* policy. These IEP directors have identified how the policy-making process works at their institutions, and they have learned how they can best influence it. They also have an awareness of the constraints they face and have identified a role that they think is important for IEP administrators in higher education. Some of their approaches to policy formation are discussed here.

Understanding the Process of Policy Formation

Policy formation processes seem to be idiosyncratic to the institutions studied, but each director is able to describe the process as he or she believes it works. In fact, all four directors think that becoming familiar with institutional policy-making processes is essential; understanding the system gives IEP directors the means to devise ways of influencing it. That is to say, because channels that invite the participation of IEP directors typically do not exist, the directors have had to create the channels themselves. For instance, one director reports that she created a structure for policy formation herself because there was no policy regarding international students when she began working at her institution, and it was not forthcoming from the administration. Currently, when she sees that the lack of policy is causing or is likely to cause problems, she writes a policy, with input from the IEP faculty. Then she passes the document along. She describes the process this way:

> How it generally works is that there will be no policy, so we will suggest one; it will take some time for [the upper administration] to talk about it or reach a decision, I'm not sure what happens there because we are sort of out of the loop. But our vice president will eventually get back with me and ask me some questions; then they will generally approve what we have put forward as policy.

All the directors I interviewed have given their role in the policy-making process considerable thought. They have spent time learning how the system works, and they have found ways of providing input that meet their institution's expectations and that they are comfortable with. The director quoted above is one of the most proactive of the group. Her strategy is to anticipate problems that are likely to arise. She spends time discussing related issues with the IEP faculty, urging them to decide how they want to deal with the situation so problems can be avoided. Another proactive director sees her role as an initiator of programs and ideas to support international students.

> You have to initiate a lot. I must initiate creative solutions; I initiated the ITA [international teaching assistant] workshop, the teachers' workshop, even content courses. I'm constantly initiating ... because I feel that if I don't initiate ..., no one on campus is going to come to me and say, "we've got a problem."

However, taking a proactive stance is not always possible; the directors report having to react to immediate problems most of the time. For example, one director described his institution this way:

> I think the way they make policy around here is that everybody makes policy for their own little "kingdom," independent of what's going on elsewhere. And if their policies affect us adversely, then we have to react to them. We're always reacting.

In response to adverse policies, this director writes memos explaining what the IEP position is, and how he thinks the policy will impact international students. At his decentralized institution, the memos are usually sent directly to the office, or "kingdom," that has drafted the policy. The IEP director, however, is scrupulously careful about sending copies of his memos to his dean, often soliciting the dean's approval before sending off the memo. If a new policy represents a major issue, he reacts by taking his concerns directly to the dean. Attention to the chain of command and proper channels was common to all four directors. Keeping superiors informed and not stepping out of line was a theme throughout the interviews, as these statements from two of the directors attest:

> The chain of command is important. If the dean doesn't agree with something, we won't be successful. It stops right there. That's why I think it's necessary to work with [the dean]; sometimes we have to compromise to get what we want. The dean has to be convinced. Nothing goes forward if he doesn't want it to.

> I'm very careful because once you offend someone, you can't get much done. So I usually start with my immediate superior, get him to buy into it, make sure he's in the loop. Then I go to the vice president and ask him to go to the president. I've learned that this is very, very important.

Another of the directors characterizes her institution as heavily invested in maintaining the status quo regarding international students. In this institutional culture of strong, inflexible policies, the IEP director looks for creative ways to negotiate the system without actually changing policy.

> When I have forced issues, there has been tremendous resistance. They tell me, "This is the policy, and we cannot change policy." I have been forced into becoming very creative.

In effect, this director recognizes the constraints of the system in which she works; by creatively introducing conflict, she is able to initiate modifications in the status quo. For example, on her own, this director applied to the U.S. Immigration and Naturalization Service and received I-20 granting status for her program. Having the ability to issue I-20s signifies that her IEP can admit students to the program for English study only. Because the home institution has a firm policy of only admitting students who have already demonstrated English proficiency, this director can admit students that her institution would otherwise turn away. She says of this:

> So, I find these creative solutions which I know eventually will irritate people. I know that. But that's okay. When I'm called on, I have the documentation that says, well, we [in the IEP] do issue I-20s, so now what do we do?

One of the IEP directors has given much thought to the best ways of using existing structures at his institution to provide input on policies affecting international students. He sees various avenues open to him.

> One would be sitting down and talking with the international student advisor, and then having her work through her hierarchy, including the director of admissions and the director of student services, making changes in student policy that way. Another would be through the faculty senate.

In this particular setting, the institution had just hired a new international student advisor and had used this change in personnel as an opportunity to establish a formal chain of command that did not exist before. The new advisor was told, for example, that she could not make policy as her predecessor had; she was directed to take proposals up the ladder. The IEP director took advantage of this new well-defined hierarchy to establish his own channel for input.

Using Personal Relationships

When an institution does not have structures in place to encourage input from those who consider themselves to be "out of the loop," personal relationships become critical. IEP directors typically do not have status or power at their institutions, making "who they know" all the more important. The IEP directors interviewed for this study stressed the importance of establishing and maintaining personal relationships with those who have power as well as with those who might be potential supporters of international students and the IEP. One director indicated that she knows most of the 150 faculty members at her institution, and they know her and her faculty. These relationships open the doors to discussion centered on individual students as well as policy issues that concern the students. The director from a larger institution also considers personal relationships to be a key to influencing policy successfully:

> Someone in my position needs to have been on campus for a fairly long time. That's important so that people know who you are and trust you. I think it makes a difference when you've been a familiar face for a long time. And second, you cultivate relationships. In order to get something done,... you've got to be able to cultivate relationships.

Personal relationships rather than formal policy often determine what happens to students and programs. In the case of the director who can now offer input through the international student advisor, channels of communication were not so open with the previous advisor:

> There was very little I could do. If we did have meetings with the foreign student advisor and her immediate supervisor, the meetings usually came off badly. They left without having made any changes, and the ESL staff felt very frustrated.

Striking a Balance

Being constrained by who IEP directors know and how well they get along is linked to another constraint that was mentioned by the two university IEP directors in the study: Policy makers are rarely interested in problems facing international students. One of the directors was told by her dean that "nobody wants to hear about ESL." Another director believes that the institutional administration does not value the perspective of the IEP. "I don't think we are listened to—we're too far down inside the pyramid," he said. In spite of this perceived attitude from above, both of these directors continue to work at making their influence felt where and how they can. In this regard, all of the directors attempt to maintain a delicate balance. Three of them spoke directly about learning to "push policy" without going too far, learning whom to push and when. "We are constantly pushing policy ... but just so hard that we don't get into too much trouble," the first told me. Another agreed with the need for careful balance:

> If you push ... too much, there is the potential for very negative results. I think you have to be real careful. We could push for more centralization, but I think we're comfortable reporting to our dean, at least at the moment. If the dean changes, we might not be. Or if the dean changes attitudes, we might not be. But I guess my fear is if we push too hard, it might have an adverse effect on the IEP.

All four of the directors attempt to counter this "nobody wants to hear it" dilemma by making their programs and their students more visible by publicizing curricular innovations, faculty accomplishments, special events, and contributions to the institution and community. In this way, IEP directors make sure that the higher administration and community do not associate the IEP solely with problems or policy questions.

Educating Institutional Personnel

The IEP directors interviewed agree that one of their most important administrative functions is to educate the college or university community. There is a general sentiment that those who are not directly involved with international education do not understand the problems that international students face, the process of acquiring a second language, or the intricacies of cross-cultural communication. This lack of knowledge complicates the policy-making process.

> There is so much opportunity for misinformation. ... I want to tell them how it is before anybody else has a chance to jump to the wrong conclusions. So I've stopped avoiding the issues.

Accurate information that is repeated and reinforced in different forums is crucial for bringing about institutional change and policy making. When misunderstandings or problems arise with individual faculty members or departments, one director handles it by "talking with faculty members, working through their problems, and educating them." For another director, the educational process includes listening to faculty when they express concerns about the international students in their classes and bringing about a mutual understanding that can lead to new policies.

Conclusions

Many of the findings reported here may strike a familiar note with language program administrators in other contexts. First is the perception that nonpolicy and ad hoc approaches to policy are still the norm in higher education. It is rather jarring to learn that very little has changed in the almost 15 years since the ACE (1982) and Goodwin and Nacht (1983) reports first called attention to the failure of institutions of higher education to set policies purposefully regarding international students.

Second, all of the directors interviewed were conscious of how the larger social milieu might affect their programs and students. They were greatly concerned about the attitudes toward immigrants that are prevalent in the media today, fearing that these attitudes will translate into policies that discriminate against any student who is culturally or linguistically different.

A third finding is that IEP directors feel that they operate from positions of powerlessness, preventing them from being as effective as they might be. Because there are no clearly established channels for their input, IEP directors depend heavily on personal relationships with key individuals to accomplish their goals. In addition, if they want to influence policy making at their institutions, they must devise their own structures for doing so.

Although the IEP administrators in this study share a sense of powerlessness, they also exhibit valuable leadership qualities. Their ability to see the IEP as an integral part of the institution as a whole has opened the way for them to identify how their individual institutions operate, and to use this knowledge to devise ways of shaping policy for their students and programs. None has continued to operate purely within the boundaries of the IEP, even when faced with institutional nonpolicy, seemingly arbitrary policy making which excludes them, or inflexible policy geared to the preservation of the status quo.

These IEP administrators provide models for coping with the constraints that they identify as blocking their full participation in the governance structures of their institutions. These coping strategies include maintaining a delicate balance between knowing when to push policy and when to wait, creating positive visibility for the IEP and the institution's international students, and educating other administrators and faculty on issues of cross-cultural communication and language acquisition.

The situations and solutions of the IEP directors presented here do not represent those of all language program administrators. Hopefully, however, their voices can provide insights that will encourage other language program administrators to examine their own situations and ask questions about how their institutions function so that they can best influence policy formation.[4]

Endnotes

1. Despite the call for foreign language instruction, widespread policies supporting foreign language study do not exist. Willis (1996) reports that only one state, New York, requires foreign language study for high school graduation, and only a third of U.S. public middle schools offer year-long foreign language courses.

2. In 1994, the Institute for International Education (IIE) put the figure of international students in U.S. institutions at 449,749 (Davis, 1994).

3. Of the 183 people interviewed by Goodwin and Nacht, only a handful were ESL professionals. Because their study is one of the few published investigations of policy making with regard to international students in higher education, this represents a serious omission.

4. The author would like to thank the following individuals for their thoughtful comments and conversations on policy and international students: Mark A. Clarke, Jeanne E. Hind, Nancy Sanders, Sheila Shannon, Al Smith, Ravay Snow-Renner, and the IEP directors who participated in this study.

Discussion Questions and Activities

1. What questions would you pose to language program administrators to determine how they perceive their roles in helping make policy?

2. Make a list of strategies that language program administrators can use to become involved in the policy-making processes of their home institutions.

3. How might proprietary IEPs differ from IEPs that are housed in academic units at colleges and universities in terms of how they interact with institutional policy formation?

4. Consider an IEP you are familiar with. Do clear policies exist for the admission and accommodation of international students? What areas do existing policies cover? What essentials are left out? Do similar policies exist for U.S. students? How do policies governing the educational experiences of U.S. students and internationals differ?

5. Consider a public school system or institution of higher education that you are familiar with. How do policies regarding the teaching of foreign languages compare with policies governing second language instruction and bilingual programs?

6. Determining how a language program is connected to its home institution is essential if program administrators are to influence institutional policy making. One way to determine the part that a language program plays in the larger institutional system is to imagine how the institution would look if the higher administration decided to do away with it. List the people who would be affected by such a decision. Now list the institutional offices (e.g., academic departments, student services) that would be affected.

Suggested Readings

Birnbaum, R. (1988). *How colleges work: The cybernetics of academic organization and leadership*. San Francisco: Jossey-Bass.

Birnbaum provides IEP directors and others interested in thinking about how IEPs fit into academia with a basis for understanding the organization and governance of institutions of higher learning. He analyzes the elements that define colleges and universities with an emphasis on why understanding and managing them is often problematic. In addition, he examines four traditional models of how colleges work: the collegial system, the bureaucratic system, the political system, and the anarchical system. Then, he integrates the models using a new model of colleges and universities as cybernetic organizations that rely on negative feedback to be adaptive and self-regulating. His chapters on how cybernetic systems operate are especially helpful.

Bolman, L. G., & Deal, T. E. (1991). *Reframing organizations: Artistry, choice, and leadership*. San Francisco: Jossey-Bass.

Using examples from business, health care, and education, the authors explain how to reframe issues, that is, how to look at situations from more than one vantage point.

They consolidate key concepts from organization theory into four perspectives or frames: structural, human resource, political, and symbolic. The structural frame relates to establishing and maintaining formal roles and relationships in an organization. The human resource frame focuses on motivating people and benefiting from their ideas and skills. The political frame offers insight into managing the competition for scarce resources, and the symbolic frame emphasizes the culture of an organization and the importance of meaning as evidenced through ritual and ceremony. This book can help IEP administrators and faculty make sense of the multidimensional nature of work environments.

Goodwin, C. D., & Nacht, M. (1983). *Absence of decision: Foreign students in American colleges and universities*. New York: Institute of International Education.

Goodwin and Nacht's report on policy formation is a must for IEP professionals. It is the classic work on policy issues concerning international students. The authors determined that for most of the college and university officials in their study, international students have low priority, and most institutions have not thought through the economic, educational, political, and organizational issues associated with the presence of internationals on campus. The issues that this report raises are still a significant aspect of educating international students in the 1990s.

Part III

THE LANGUAGE PROGRAM ADMINISTRATOR AS PROMOTER

Chapter 8

THE QUEST FOR ACADEMIC LEGITIMACY: BUILDING FOR LANGUAGE PROGRAM ENTRY INTO INSTITUTIONAL AND COMMUNITY INFRASTRUCTURES

Frederick L. Jenks
Florida State University

 anguage programs—no matter what their origin, location, institutional affiliation, organizational position, or size—have certain inherent characteristics that distinguish them from most other educational entities, especially those at postsecondary levels (Barrett & Parsons, 1985). Some of these distinguishing features are significantly different from traits of the host institution; it is these marked differences that prompt many to question the relationship between language programs and their host institutions, and hence their legitimacy. The focus here is on the relationship between intensive English programs (IEPs) and the college or university with which they are affiliated, although the issues raised have direct relevance to other types of language programs.

How parent institutions view the issue of academic legitimacy directly affects the manner in which IEPs are enjoined with institutional governing structures (Jenks, 1991). In general, academic legitimacy tends to be determined by circumstances related to three factors: *Nascence*—by what means and for what reasons did the IEP come into existence? *Nurturing*—which university offices, officials, and faculty leaders accept responsibility for the IEP's development and well-being? *Symbiosis*—what do the university and its students gain in terms of services and direct financial support from the IEP, and what does the IEP gain in terms of support from the university? Facets of each of these legitimizing factors are reflected in the following questions:

Nascence

Was the formation of the IEP a response to a legal mandate   Yes   No
(e.g., legislative funding for ESL preparation for linguistic
minority citizens)?

Was funding made available from either an outside agency or   Yes   No
an intra-institutional program for IEP start-up and continuation?

Is the IEP's existence derived from a broad-based perception   Yes   No
of need by an academic department, academic policy committee,
minority student group, or student affairs office?

Nurturing

Do IEP administrators and faculty hold positions that are   Yes   No
recognized by the host university as equivalent to those of
other university administrators and teachers?

Are the role and nature of the IEP communicated to the entire   Yes   No
academic community through institutionally initiated regulations,
publications, and protocols?

Do university officials turn to the IEP for expertise, assistance,   Yes   No
and advice when addressing issues related to international
education and second language learning/teaching?

Symbiosis

Does the parent institution rely on the IEP to perform   Yes   No
academic functions deemed to be important to the institution's
academic, student affairs, and international missions?

Are the IEP's primary goals directed toward assisting linguistic   Yes   No
minority students who need further language education at the
parent institution or preparing international students for regular
admission to the host university?

Does the IEP offer ESL courses for academic credit?   Yes   No

Is the IEP the only unit offering ESL instruction for   Yes   No
nonmatriculated or matriculated linguistic minority students?

Does the IEP serve as a financial resource that supports other   Yes   No
academic or student service units at the host institution?

Does the university support the IEP by providing access to   Yes   No
services, facilities, and other resources?

While not a comprehensive list of questions, positive responses suggest a perceived legitimacy for the IEP; negative responses seem to place the IEP in a marginal, less salubrious position within the institutional hierarchy. The substance of these questions is addressed here in general terms, providing examples of the positive and negative effects on IEPs. In addition, numerous suggestions, some proven and some speculative, will be offered to IEP administrators as possible means for altering the perception of IEPs as marginally aligned academic programs.

Paths to Legitimacy

To gain legitimacy and build some degree of symbiosis for their programs, IEP administrators must engage in a variety of activities, including acquiring governmental and nongovernmental support, assisting the parent institution in fulfilling its mission, building cooperative linkages, communicating with different constituencies, and promoting service connections. What follows is a discussion of each of these paths to legitimacy.

Acquiring Governmental Support

Receiving tax-derived dollars to support new and existing programs is a major goal of most universities. The mere act of receiving governmental recognition as a site for tax-derived support tends to legitimize programs and raise their status. Federal monies *are* spent on the development and delivery of English as a second language (ESL) instruction.[1] ESL instruction is provided at federal expense for many "local" (non-U.S. citizen) employees in overseas U.S. embassies and consulates, nonnative speakers on U.S. military bases stateside and overseas, and students enrolled in Department of Defense Dependent Schools.

Federal funding has also promoted ESL in public education. As a result of various legislative decisions, funding has been provided for the English language components of bilingual programs, "compensatory" education, adult or retraining grants, and certain civil rights–oriented programs. In addition, governmental funding is provided for a myriad of programs that address the language learning needs of migrant children, war and political refugees, and naturalization aspirants.

State funding is provided to support adult education through public school systems as well. In many states, ESL classes are the major adult education offering. For example, in Florida, ESL students constitute more than half of the entire adult education student population. Thus, adult education funding often represents funding for ESL instruction.

Through numerous legislative mandates, intensive or semi-intensive ESL instruction is fiscally supportable under specified conditions. The impact upon university-level IEPs, however, has been negligible except via internationally oriented programs such as those sponsored by the United States Agency for International Development (USAID), the United States Information Agency, and the Organization for American States. Organizations such as these often sponsor groups or individuals to undertake intensive English instruction in preparation for advanced studies in U.S. universities.

Affiliations with established and widely recognized educational organizations such as the International Research and Exchange Commission, AMIDEAST, or the ministries of education of other countries tend to bring respect by association to IEPs. In actuality, most IEPs are partially supported by foreign governmental or institutional funds that are provided to matriculated students for IEP tuition and living expenses, yet this often goes unnoticed by, or is unknown to, the host institution. It is important for IEP administrators to publicize these organizational connections and their level of support.

Since an IEP can enhance its acceptance by the host institution and community by acquiring tax support for its programs, the IEP administrator should be engaged in preparing proposals for funding that focus on the language training of international students and scholars sponsored by established agencies such as USAID or the Department of State through programs such as the Edmund Muskie Fellowship Program. IEP administrators can also forge linkages with other departments or schools that are preparing contract/grant proposals in the international education arena.

Gaining Nongovernmental Support

The acquisition of fiscal support from reliable nongovernmental sources can also validate an academic program. Given increasingly limited resources, colleges and universities must actively seek new revenue to fund academic offerings. Businesses, alumni, friends of the institution, and even other nations are viewed as potentially supportive entities.

It is incumbent upon the IEP administrator to submit well-documented requests for funding to university capital acquisition offices on a regular basis. Because officials in fund-raising offices are constantly seeking new contributors, appeals to special populations, such as international alumni, may be approved. When recognized as a donor site by fund-raising campaign literature, the IEP is viewed not merely as a member of the institutional community, but as an active, prioritized member in need of support. Thus, the IEP administrator who maintains close contact with fund-raising offices can make major gains in developing both on-campus and off-campus recognition for the language program; such recognition is vital to becoming a valid academic entity.

Because the economic health of many communities and states is partially dependent on international business or an English-proficient labor force, many IEP administrators have found positive results by devoting time to speaking at trade fairs and business conferences, discussing workplace language issues with industrial training officials, interfacing with tourism agencies, and serving on international issues committees. Outreach activities such as these have frequently led to IEP instruction for hospital personnel, hotel and restaurant staffs, and international trade organizations. In short, the IEP gains credibility and institutional recognition when links are made to businesses and service agencies within the institution's region.

As more public school districts consider privatizing auxiliary services, opportunities may arise for IEPs to deliver language instruction in lieu of public schools. Field-based English classes for migrant workers, for example, may be offered by IEP teachers if the IEP is subcontracted by a local educational agency to provide these services. If the IEP is perceived as an educational partner with, or a suitable replacement for, a publicly funded educational agency's program, its validity as an organization and its perception as a bona fide program is strengthened.

Although most universities and colleges are urged by the local citizenry to reach out to the community, they are often uncertain as to how to do so effectively, and with what programs. Efforts by IEP administrators to join university mandates for nontraditional, off-campus, off-hour classes can go far in building the recognition and standing of the IEP. Because few academic programs are more seasoned in the development of alternative class schedules, specialized curricula, and client-relevant instruction than IEPs, IEPs are in a good position to provide community outreach.

Assisting the Parent Institution

Circumstances occasionally awaken members of university decision-making groups to the need for enhanced learning opportunities for nonnative English speakers (and native speakers as well). When this happens, there may be opportunities for the IEP to assist the institution through direct instruction, the development of new courses, or IEP-directed research. Receiving approval to provide such services is, indeed, an ideal way for the IEP to be viewed as a fully recognized member of the academic community. When the IEP becomes involved in campus-based and campus-supported research, it strengthens its role as a supportive entity in the development of policies affecting the institution (Kennedy, 1984).

As an example, in states where the higher educational authority (e.g., Board of Regents, University System Headquarters) administers system-wide achievement tests to measure each undergraduate's grasp of minimum competencies, there are many students who fail to obtain mandated scores. An IEP-initiated background investigation of failing students may reveal that a disproportionately large percentage are nonnative English speakers who lack the requisite language skills (see Niendorf, 1994). Such a discovery, replete with affixed issues of equity, cultural bias, and discrimination by origin, may lead to an administrative decision to provide the students with additional language-building instruction via the IEP. Ergo, funding. Post ergo, legitimacy … if the IEP can demonstrate that its program yields the desired results.

The professional acumen and networking abilities of the IEP administrator are perhaps best demonstrated by seeking and finding ways to buttress the home university's established programs and policies as well as foreseeing ways to join forces with legitimized programs in pursuing new goals. IEP administrators must never brood about not being among the "in" crowd; they must find or create ways to become members without giving the impression that the quest is self-serving to the IEP and its administration.

Building Cooperative Linkages

IEP administrators can enhance the reputation of their programs by building cooperative linkages. For example, as universities seek to promote multiculturalism and diversity, opportunities arise for IEPs to reiterate their roles as "multicultural Meccas." It is the IEP administrator's responsibility to publicize the important role that the program plays in recruiting, preparing, and supporting future degree-seeking international students. Data from national surveys (Davis, 1995), backed up with one's own IEP data, can prove to be enlightening.

Through informed collaboration, many universities and IEPs have chosen to provide conditional I-20s to admissible international applicants who require additional English instruction; the conditional admissions status serves to ensure both the school and the students of a smooth and assured path toward matriculation and long-term studies. It also eases initial student adjustment and facilitates acculturation of the international student into the academic culture of the university.

As more universities deliver courses with global perspectives, the IEP administrator, faculty, and students are able to offer direct assistance to professors and U.S. students. Certainly no TESL degree program should lack a "contact" component wherein TESL students are paired with IEP learners for social, academic, or English tutorial purposes. In addition, many less obvious pairings are possible. For example, a professor teaching Cross-Cultural Communications may want to pair IEP students with domestic students in 1 hour per week cross-cultural partnerships. And, who is better equipped to give a guest lecture in a credit course on comparative or international education than a staff member of the IEP who has significant experience teaching EFL and living as an educator overseas?

Such initiatives require additional work from the IEP staff, but the effort enhances the university's curriculum by supporting multicultural goals, by permitting university students to move from theory to practice, and by recognizing IEP students as campus assets. Thus, for the IEP to be viewed as an equal entity, its administrators must build cooperative links with established programs and departments, always with an eye toward supporting the university's primary mission, namely the education of its regularly enrolled students.

Communicating With Different Constituencies

All too often, few influential university committees recognize and invite IEP representatives to serve as regular members. When opportunities to serve on existing committees are limited, the IEP leader can be instrumental in forming a new, focused team, such as an IEP advisory board, composed of key university personnel who are dedicated to learning more about IEPs and creating support for and awareness of the IEP's mission. To merit nurturing from the parent university and to establish symbiosis, it sometimes becomes necessary for the IEP leadership to recruit advocates who will assist the IEP in showing itself off.

Another logical route to building linkages is through former IEP students who have subsequently commenced degree programs at the host institution. By maintaining contact through e-mail, newsletters, and semesterly "homecoming" events at the IEP, and by developing an IEP-alumni committee, the IEP administrator can build program recognition while making its role and scope more obvious to academic departments.

A short form letter from the IEP administrator to the chairperson of each department in which former IEP students are matriculated as majors should carry the messages that (a) the students named therein are continuing their education toward degrees, (b) the IEP program was the student's first academic base, (c) the IEP administrator is eager to assist the chairperson and professors if the student experiences language-based problems, and (d) the IEP administrator seeks feedback from the department. Letters of this nature emphasize the academic-preparation mission of the IEP through its concern with the future of its "graduates" and their presence in degree programs; at the same time, the letters carry a message of partnership, which is a critical factor in the search for legitimacy.

The IEP can communicate with other constituencies by preparing different versions of an annual report, rather than merely one report for the ranking administrative official.

Typically, an annual report contains a general information update (enrollments per country, majors), a status report (enrollment trends), and a fiscal year budget report. Slightly different versions of the annual report should be prepared for delivery to different officials. For example, I send abbreviated annual reports to the chairperson of the TESL department, the dean of the college that houses the TESL department, the director of international programs, and the chairpersons of all departments in which collaborative efforts have borne fruit. Each annual report is prepared to present and highlight the information of most interest to the receiving party; however, each report carries the common message that "we're in this together, and we at the IEP are here to help."

Promoting Service Linkages

By providing auxiliary services to the university community, the IEP may be able to build some recognition as a supportive entity. For example, many universities administer the Test of English as a Foreign Language (TOEFL) per the Educational Testing Service's international testing schedule; others do not offer it at all. The institutional TOEFL, administered frequently by IEPs, can serve as a valid and reliable substitute for the international TOEFL, and it can be administered on dates convenient to the IEP, the home institution's admissions office, and matriculated international students.

Language evaluations of nonnative speakers of English who serve as professors, teaching assistants, and instructional associates are legally mandated in many state university systems (Freeman, 1995). How the evaluations are conducted, and by whom, is a critical issue, one that may be addressed by the IEP if its faculty have earned proper credentials. If IEP faculty have successfully completed American Council of Teachers of Foreign Language (ACTFL) training through its Oral Proficiency Interview workshops, or Educational Testing Service rater-training workshops for Test of Spoken English or Test of Written English evaluators, the IEP administrator is in a stronger position to seek approval for the IEP as an alternative on-campus language-testing site.

Many university students aspire to work or live overseas. The IEP can provide information and materials related to teaching ESL and working and living overseas by maintaining a library of relevant textbooks, catalogs, overseas job listings, TESL program brochures, and reference materials. IEP administrators and faculty also have the ability and resources to provide assistance to public schools requesting information on, for example, standardized tests of language proficiency or workshop presentations on germane topics; to university officials in search of interpreters for visiting international dignitaries; and to faculty members requesting international guest speakers. Providing assistance to the university community and local public schools in these ways represents a viable legitimizing strategy; when the IEP and its students are considered academic resources by members of the community, legitimacy is strengthened.

Many universities have translated the national call for greater individual responsibility into the (oxymoronic) notion of "compulsory volunteerism" by undergraduate students. This has required that new projects and new linkages with the community be designed, many of which provide academic credit to the student volunteers. Is there not a place for the IEP as a provider of experiential opportunities for undergraduate students through conversation partnerships, cultural adjustment assistance, and multicultural support? If undergraduate students are accorded volunteerism credit for tutoring migrant children or assisting immigrants who are striving to build English literacy skills, the IEP leadership has grounds for building the case for acceptance as a site for student volunteer involvement, perhaps for credit.

In the ongoing search for outside financial support, many academic departments pursue contracts to provide educational services to international agencies. Commonly sought contracts provide for the financing of international scholars' degree studies in predetermined academic specializations; by acquiring these contracts, the departments receive prepaid students (plus administrative charges) in exchange for providing specific training. What is frequently overlooked or underprioritized by the departments is the language-training component so oftentimes required by or implicit within the contractual accord. Too many IEP administrators have been placed in "doomed to fail" positions due to poorly planned, but funded, international contractual accords that, for example, include English language training as an afterthought or an addended short-term component rather than as the critical entry component. Therefore, the IEP administrator is advised to seek ways to educate grant writers about the "givens" of second language learning, such as the time required, the complexities of acquiring high English proficiency, and the need for ongoing language support services to the grantees and the role the IEP can play in the delivery of quality language support. Interprogrammatic partnerships are hallmarks of intra-institutional symbiosis.

Hurdles to Legitimacy

Perhaps the most sensitive issue for IEPs is academic credibility. IEPs are not alone in being perceived as marginally academic programs. Programs that serve nontraditional students, hold classes in diverse settings and in diverse time frames, or offer instruction that "enriches" enrollees but does not yield degrees or academic credit tend to be perceived by many as secondary, if not extraneous, to the school's academic mission. To earn the support of the home institution and its regular faculty and staff, such programs must plan and promote "inreach" as well as outreach.

Faculty Status

The quest for legitimacy is eased greatly if IEP administrators and faculty are accorded rank and salaries equal to those of other program administrators and faculty members. If the IEP leader receives university faculty or administrative status, his or her involvement in academic affairs is recognized and assured. Committee memberships, for example, provide the IEP leader with opportunities to address broader issues from the IEP's perspective. The privilege of teaching regular classes within an academic department goes far in legitimizing ESL and TESL as academic areas. At the very least, the IEP administrator and highly qualified faculty should seek courtesy or adjunct faculty status in a language or related department.

When IEP employees are appointed to their positions via academic departments, they tend to be viewed more frequently as legitimate colleagues. In such cases, the quest for equality becomes a moot one; faculty and staff members are immediately perceived as being equals, receiving similar rights, responsibilities, salaries, and benefits. But, as higher education administrators strive to downsize staffs, increase institutional productivity, focus on delivering the basics of university instruction, and seek ways to maintain flexibility in fiscal decision making, the quest for professional equality becomes more difficult for IEP personnel. If the university has made no fiscal or philosophical investment in the development and continuance of the IEP, it is doubtful that administrators will take on this responsibility post facto. It is the IEP administrator's responsibility to seek ways to make the case for professional recognition, and it is a task that may present insurmountable obstacles, especially if the IEP staff lacks professor-level credentials.

To receive recognition, IEP employees must confront many bureaucratic obstacles, academic traditions, and fiscal realities. No IEP employee lacking a doctoral degree in an academically relevant field can expect to receive faculty or administrative status equal to that of tenure-track, doctorate-holding professors. Unless the IEP employee's research, scholarly activity, teaching record, and service activities transcend those of regularly appointed faculty, chances are slim that faculty status will be granted by the host institution. However, when the IEP teacher's record of professional achievement is equivalent (or superior) to that of some faculty members, chances of establishing cooperation and approval are more robust. Ultimately, faculty status will depend on the IEP's fiscal reliability and its ability to finance the yeoman's share of faculty salaries and benefits. Faculty status is more readily achievable when the IEP provides the comprehensive fiscal support; initially, that status may have to be bought and paid for by the IEP.

Academic Credit

The credit-instruction issue is related to faculty status. Many universities view intensive English instruction as being preparatory to college studies and, as such, not worthy of carrying academic credit (i.e., semester hours). The credit issue is typically addressed through a lengthy process of committees, hearings, and policy discussions. If the IEP staff is not involved through membership in various university committees, the chances of ESL courses being approved for credit are lessened. After all, why would an institution grant approval to a program—perceived to be preparatory, remedial, or nonacademic—to deliver credit classes taught by nonuniversity faculty to nonmatriculated students?

The IEP administrator must enlist advocates from among university faculty—spokespersons who realize that real benefits will accrue to their own departments if ESL courses grant academic credit. Real benefits normally enhance existing departmental goals, primarily through the generation and dissemination of additional funds, and may include teaching assistantships, research opportunities, teaching internships, expanded departmental enrollments (which translate into increased departmental funding from the university's central administration), practicum opportunities for the department's students and faculty, or logical extensions of existing faculty interests.

Students who successfully complete advanced ESL studies possess English-language skills far stronger than those of matriculated students who have majored in a foreign language, such as French or Russian; this is obvious to IEP educators. Yet, no academic credit is provided for international students whose foreign language knowledge is measured at the near-native level; at the same time, U.S. students whose foreign language abilities are much weaker receive academic credit or even academic honors. The only difference is that the international students' foreign language is English.

Overlapping Programs

It is not uncommon for a large university to house several programs with responsibility for providing ESL services to international or linguistic-minority students. International teaching assistants and matriculated students with targeted weaknesses in specific language skills may receive ESL services from regular university faculty or from language tutors employed by student-support offices; in these cases, the IEP's role is minimal or nonexistent. If the IEP is perceived as a competitor to currently approved programs, the quest for legitimacy is gravely impaired.

The Power of Public Relations

The failure of many IEPs to be accepted and recognized as integral parts of the university community may be related to the IEP's failure to make its existence and its mission well known. Recognition is not achieved passively; it is the result of concerted efforts to publicize the beneficial role of the IEP and its ties to the parent institution, community, and respected organizations. An active IEP must publicize itself and its accomplishments, thereby validating its uniqueness as an educational asset within the university and beyond. All of this must be done with positivism, enthusiasm, and professionalism ... and with an absence of sentiments of inferiority, nonrecognition, and inequity. Whether the information is released through community and campus newspapers, faculty and staff newsletters, or promotional publications designed and disseminated by the IEP itself, the intent is the same: Let others know about the IEP's role in a plethora of positive activities. Publicizing IEP activities that enhance and enrich the educational environment will inform the citizens of the community and parent institution of the dynamism, cooperation, and energy generated by the IEP.

The IEP can reach influential decision makers in the university and community through local or campus media, or through its own promotional efforts. Topics of possible interest to decision makers are listed in Table 1.

To reach an even larger audience, the IEP leadership must initiate and establish direct, personal contact with (a) campus media relations personnel, (b) local and campus newspaper editors, (c) members of the local chamber of commerce, and (d) student affairs administrators. After personal contacts have been made, weekly or monthly news releases prepared by the IEP staff must be sent to each. The high quality and usability of desktop publishing software and image scanners make possible the in-house production of an informative and visually striking IEP newsletter. A widely dispersed newsletter can solidify the IEP's identity, tie the IEP's mission to the university at large, portray its broader impact, and promote the multifaceted presence of the IEP as a vibrant, active, and ubiquitous member of the parent institution. Newsletter entries can address (a) profiles of and interviews with satisfied and successful IEP students; (b) IEP student demographics; (c) international news items; (d) new links between the IEP and the university's ongoing programs; (e) IEP involvement in new university efforts (such as distance education, community volunteer services, and web home pages); and (f) faculty and staff activities, including publications, conference papers, international travel, and recognition of outstanding teaching.

Table 1. Topics of Potential Interest to Influential Decision Makers

1. The high percentage of matriculated international students who began their studies at the IEP.

2. The overall economic impact of IEP students upon the university and community, providing number and dollar estimates.

3. The IEP's contractual accords with international ministries of education, international organizations, and U.S. sponsoring agencies (remember that each sponsored student represents a contract between the IEP and the sponsoring agency).

4. The quantity of international student recruitment and public relations that the IEP performs for the university through international mailings of IEP brochures that contain information about the university and community, advertisements in international education publications, and participation in international language school fairs (Williams, 1994). It is likely that the IEP is the university's major investor in international recruiting and its primary vehicle for marketing the university worldwide.

5. The IEP as a self-supporting entity which generates revenue that supports other university programs (see Simerly, 1993).

6. The many "no-cost" auxiliary services provided to the university and the community by the IEP, including language testing, academic and career advising, and international student speaking bureaus.

7. The human resources represented by the IEP faculty, staff, and student body, including knowledgeable international speakers, professional educators with expertise in language learning theory, language policy, and cross-cultural communication.

8. The professional associations in which the IEP faculty and administrators actively participate through service on governing boards and committees.

9. The quantity and quality of IEP faculty and administrators' research, publications, and invited professional presentations, including information as to the magnitude of their scholarly productivity within the field of second language education.

10. The partnerships that have been established with academic departments through the mutual preparation of proposals for funding international education activities and research.

11. Human interest stories about IEP students and events including IEP student visits to public schools, successful former IEP students, and special social events at the IEP, such as the annual end-of-Ramadan potluck dinner and party.

The newsletter's banner should contain the IEP's name plus an explanatory slogan or phrase, such as "Where the world comes to learn English," that informs the reader of the program's mission. Multiple type fonts, one or more color photographs, and high-quality paper should be used; the professional appearance of the publication will prove crucial in forming positive, enduring impressions among readers. Finally, distribution should be as wide as possible. By using available address lists, all students, administrators, and faculty can be reached via campus mail at low cost. Personal contacts with community-agency leaders may yield permission to include the IEP newsletter with agency mailings. Adult education personnel, volunteer literacy program managers, and community-based international organizations (e.g., sister-city groups) may aid the IEP in distributing the newsletter as well. These IEP-produced publications may indeed be the most important tools in the IEP's effort to acquire the visibility so necessary for acquiring nascence by adoption, gaining influential supporters, and validating actual and potential symbiosis.

Concluding Remarks

Administrators of IEPs often fail to accept or confront the many subliminal and negative perceptions of the IEP mission and its students: IEP students are not often U.S. citizens and are thus not equals. IEP students do not speak English fluently and are thus targets for English-only political groups. The IEP student body is composed of racial, ethnic, and religious minorities. IEP students are not considered to be fully matriculated university students even though they are enrolled in 20–30 hours of instruction per week. And there is a sentiment among provincially minded academicians that learning ESL (and learning it to a high level) is "basic" and prerequisite to academic entry. In an era when immigration laws and practices are under much scrutiny, and when traditional sources of educational funding are being reduced, what can the IEP administrator do to improve the program's perceived status? Is it the IEP's fate to be viewed by university faculty and administrators in the same way as they view the IEP's student clientele and subject matter … as being marginal, inferior, or even illegitimate?

The basic message here is that language program status may be improved by educating different constituencies through available media; the participation of staff, faculty, and students in community and university activities; and IEP-produced literature designed to present the educational benefits associated with the program's existence and the economic impact of the IEP. In addition, IEPs can gain legitimacy by acquiring governmental and nongovernmental support, buttressing home institution programs, and offering academic credit for IEP courses. None of these campaigns is short-lived; on the contrary, all are ongoing and essential in the effort to build a reputation as a stable, high-quality, institutionally supportive educational center. It is incumbent upon the IEP leadership to create an image of the language center as a benefactor of the university, and to make known the benefits derived by university students and staff from its presence.

Visibility is improved through these activities while, simultaneously, more people become aware of the IEP's existence and mission; the resultant awareness promotes both nurturing and recognition. Program recognition is enhanced by "doing good things" (sometimes differently) and making these activities known to potentially interested or nurturing parties. And, not least, let the fiscal enrichments derived from the IEP's existence be known to university administrators and the local business community.

Finally, chief administrators of IEPs must strive to be academic and business leaders both within and outside the university. To do so effectively, they must seek to (a) educate others, (b) maintain objectivity and positivism instead of defensiveness and inferiority, (c) be spokespersons for language and intercultural learning, (d) spearhead public relations efforts in a positive and ongoing manner, (e) master strategic financial management, and (f) be active participants in the life of the home institution and profession. For the IEP to be perceived as a legitimate academic partner, the director must remember not to bemoan the IEP's status publicly or to assume a defensive posture when there is the possibility of an offensive posture. The director must embody all the requisite characteristics that lead to institutional acceptance of a new member in the collective effort to provide a solid, comprehensive education for all.

Endnote

1. No distinction is made here between English as a second language (ESL) and English as a foreign language (EFL) instruction.

Discussion Questions and Activities

1. According to the author, program legitimacy is determined in part by circumstances related to three factors: nascence, nurturing, and symbiosis. In your own words, how would you define each concept? Of the three legitimizing factors, which do you think is most important? Provide a rationale for your answer.

2. Consider the status of a language program with which you are familiar. Take into consideration the status of the language program administrators, faculty, staff, students, and curriculum. What can be done in this setting to enhance the status of each?

3. Imagine that you are writing a proposal to start up a new language program or to restructure an existing one. What provisions will you make in your proposal to ensure a perceived legitimacy of your program? Consider issues related to nascence, nurturing, and symbiosis.

4. Consider these seven paths to legitimacy: acquiring governmental and nongovernmental support, assisting the parent institution in fulfilling its mission, building cooperative linkages, communicating with different constituencies, promoting service linkages, enhancing faculty status, and offering credit for language program courses. Can you think of any other paths to legitimacy? Which paths to legitimacy will you pursue to enhance the perception of a language program that you know well?

5. Imagine that you, as a language program teacher or administrator, want to form a discussion group of representatives of other programs or departments at your university that might be perceived organizationally or administratively as marginal programs. Determine which features characterize a university program as being marginal, nonmainstream, or nontraditional. Then, based on your list of traits, design

a rationale for establishing communication among representatives from such programs and developing strategies for building some common goals.

6. Imagine that you have 10 minutes to address the entire university faculty on the IEP's role, mission, and impact at its annual meeting. Assume that faculty members know little about IEPs and language teaching; also keep in mind that their notions of what is important may differ significantly from yours. What issues or topics would you include in your address?

7. Imagine that you direct an established IEP on a major university campus and, as such, provide the only noncredit ESL instruction on campus. The International Student Services Office has just announced that it will hold semi-intensive, noncredit ESL classes, taught by university student volunteers, for free. How would you address this issue so that the volunteer ESL program does not jeopardize the IEP? To whom would you address your concerns? How would you deal with this issue in a professional, yet concerned, manner?

Suggested Readings

Davis, T. M. (Ed.). (1995). *Open Doors 1994/1995: Report on international educational exchange*. New York: Institute of International Education.

This annual publication is the primary source of information regarding international students' academic status, origin, and major fields in U.S. higher education. Companion data concerning IEP enrollees is included.

Jenks, F. L. (1991). Designing and assessing the efficacy of ESL promotional materials. In M. C. Pennington (Ed.), *Building better English language programs: Perspectives on evaluation in ESL* (pp. 172–188). Washington, DC: NAFSA: Association of International Educators.

Jenks focuses on the creation of IEP promotional materials, offering strategies for mapping their effectiveness in recruiting new students.

Simerly, R. (1993). *Strategic financial management for conferences, workshops, and meetings*. San Francisco: Jossey-Bass.

Simerly is a nationally recognized authority on strategic planning in continuing and distance education. In this volume, he sets forth step-by-step procedures for "costing out" a short-term program so as to assure that no fiscal problems will impede successful delivery.

Solomon, L., & Young, B. (1987). *The foreign student factor: Impact on American higher education* (IIE Research Series No. 12). New York: Institute of International Education. (ERIC Document Reproduction Service No. ED 311 836)

Solomon and Young present information, based on periodic censuses of international student populations in the United States, that is helpful in determining the extent of internationalism at one's university. Demographic data on student nationality, language background, and academic major facilitate comparisons between one's home university and other institutions. The benefits derived from enrolling international students are discussed in the volume as well.

Williams, T. (1994). *An investigation into factors influencing student selection of intensive English programs in the southeastern United States.* Unpublished doctoral dissertation, Florida State University, Tallahassee.

Via a survey instrument completed by UCIEP-affiliated programs in the southeastern states, Williams determines which factors weigh most heavily in students' initial selection of intensive English programs.

Chapter 9

EMPOWERMENT OF FACULTY

Elizabeth F. Soppelsa
University of Kansas

hat is faculty empowerment? In the most general sense, empowerment of faculty involves the ceding of power to faculty by the administration so that faculty can make decisions about the educational setting in which they work. Depending upon the degree of power granted to them, faculty may gain decision-making abilities in matters related to curriculum, governance, evaluation, salaries, tenure, promotion, and so forth. In settings with a high degree of faculty governance, faculty may control a school, program, or department through committee structure and may be responsible for virtually all decisions; in such settings, the administrators themselves serve at the pleasure of the faculty. In most settings, however, faculty members participate in decision making without having absolute authority; their decisions are subject to review and authorization by program or institutional administrators. Through elective or appointive procedures, faculty members contribute to discussions about or carry out functions related to programmatic matters, serving as advisors to the administrator (e.g., a school principal, ESL program director, or department head) who actually makes the final decisions.

This conceptualization of faculty empowerment is based on a philosophy of academic program management that stresses a sharing of authority for decision making, rather than the centralization of authority in which all decisions are made at the highest echelons of power and are imposed on people below. In settings characterized by some degree of faculty empowerment, faculty members are consulted by administrators—hence the term *consultive management*. Although the organizational structure may still be hierarchical, and the administrator may still retain responsibility and authority for the final say, the expectation in a consultive model is that many or all members of the faculty will participate in making decisions and in initiating change (Powers & Powers, 1983); hence the term *participatory decision making*. The consultive model proposes that success can be achieved when skilled, engaged faculty members are permitted to delve into areas in which they have a keen interest, and when they are assisted and encouraged by a skilled, trusting manager. In a sense, empowerment of faculty entails engaging, energizing, and enabling faculty to contribute to their schools, programs, or departments, and profession.

Faculty empowerment is also used to describe educational environments in which faculty members take charge of their own professional development. Here the term refers to the role of self-reflection and self-determination in professional growth. Richards and Lockhart (1994) cite the importance of a teacher's power in determining his or her effectiveness in teaching and other professional activities.

Whether referring to faculty decision-making powers or the ability to take charge of one's own professional development, faculty empowerment can denote collective empowerment or individual empowerment. Collective empowerment refers to granting authority for decision making to the faculty as a group and to the collective effect of that power on their professional lives, the program, its host institution, the larger community, and the profession. This concept of empowerment suggests that a faculty group which is encouraged and enabled to help determine and effect changes in the educational environment has greater power than one which simply carries out the ideas of an authoritarian leader. Individual empowerment refers to giving power to individuals and to the effects of that power on individuals' professional development and on the program, institution, community, and profession. Used in this sense, the term implies that empowered individuals, who are given the right and the resources to manage their own careers and to participate in decision making in their schools or programs, are more effective than those whose ideas are ignored.

Some degree of faculty empowerment is important in all educational settings. Because programs in which faculty contribute to rather than dominate decision making are more common, the focus here is on the nature and effects of participatory decision making. The term ESL faculty is used throughout to refer to any members of a language program who teach or conduct research regardless of their specific titles or the particular staffing configuration of the program.[1] The term language program administrator refers to principals, program directors, or department heads of ESL programs. It should be noted that the references cited in this chapter come from literature both within and beyond the field of ESL, revealing my belief that educational leaders from one setting can make use of ideas and strategies of leaders in other educational settings. Research is needed, however, to determine whether certain of these strategies work better at some levels of education than at others, or if certain strategies are more effective with ESL faculty than with faculty in other disciplines.

Why Empower Faculty?

There are many advantages to consultive management and participatory decision making. First, involving faculty in decision making enhances their sense of ownership of the language program, strengthening their bond with the program and their sense of responsibility for its successes and failures (see Garcia, 1986). Involving faculty in decision making also promotes teamwork by building group solidarity and a sense of camaraderie. It helps faculty members view their peers as colleagues, rather than competitors, as the focus is on the choices and initiatives of the group, rather than the status of individuals. It encourages faculty members as a group to sort through solutions carefully—as their own well-being is at stake—and to stand behind decisions.

Engagement in decision-making processes allows faculty members to play a role in controlling their own fate; this involvement is central to job satisfaction (Locke, Fitzpatrick, & White, 1983; Near & Sorcinelli, 1986) and to morale (Seldin & Associates, 1990). Enhanced job satisfaction and positive morale, in turn, contribute to a willingness to cooperate and to a long-term commitment to the program. As Fjortoft (1993) says, "feelings of personal importance to the organization and of having real influence are vital links to commitment" (p. 14). In addition to heightening the sense of ownership, commitment, and job satisfaction, involving faculty in decision making brings a greater number of ideas into consideration, enlarges the range of alternatives that the program can choose from, and makes innovation more likely (Stoller, 1994a). Faculty who are involved in decision making are more willing to accept change, since it is not imposed on them from above (Fullan, 1993; Nichols-Casebolt, 1993). The ability to accept change also contributes to the prevention of burnout (to be discussed later).

Even when the many benefits of faculty empowerment are pointed out to language program administrators, they are often reluctant to cede power to the faculty. This reluctance has multiple roots. First, some administrators see participatory decision making as threatening to their own power base and status. For them, power means prestige and security. Their erroneous belief is that power is finite and that giving away power has no reward. Second, sharing decision making requires some degree of flexibility when administrators find themselves in a position to agree to and enact other people's proposals. Some administrators prefer to hold on to their own rigid, perhaps safe and conservative line. Third, some administrators are not willing to take the blame for, or be held accountable for, failures derived from implementing others' decisions. They see their reputations as deriving solely from their own successful accomplishments and are unaware of the recognition that may come from the skillful management of cooperative processes. Fourth, some administrators do not want to change their management style. They reject change per se, preferring the status quo. Finally, some administrators fear the inefficiency of democracy, the slowness of group decision making, and the complexity and lack of clarity in discussions and decisions that accommodate divergent views. They may prefer to act quickly on their own, enacting only those solutions that are comfortable for them and under their absolute control.

In contrast, assuming the role of facilitator rather than dictator is in fact liberating for many language program administrators, as it lightens the burden of managing the entire program, allows them to rely on others' expertise and assistance, and builds strength in many pockets of the program, rather than isolating it in one place—the leader's office. One positive outcome of such an administrative posture is that progress—at the program level—does not depend solely on the strength or attentiveness of a single individual. Leaders who work as members of a team, rather than as lonely autocrats, recognize the energy and effectiveness resulting from collaboration and cooperation. They are relieved to know that every initiative does not hinge on their performance alone, and they are cheered to know that their colleagues support decisions for which the heads themselves are ultimately held accountable.

Some faculty members themselves may resist participating in decision making. They may prefer to accept a passive role, allowing the language program administrator to make all the choices, bear the burden of agonizing through the difficult ones, and take criticism for the unpopular ones. Some faculty members have little confidence in their own abilities to guide a program and fear that failure will result from their involvement. Or, these faculty members may suspect that the offer to share power is not honest, and that their decisions will later be overturned by a disingenuous leader, who first asks for their ideas and then criticizes, subverts, or ignores those ideas. As a result, they may be unwilling or unable to invest the time necessary to share in running the program, especially if they suspect that their participation is "an empty exercise" (Fjortoft, 1993). Finally, they may be resistant to change of any kind and may fear that the new role will impose impossible burdens on them (Fullan, 1993).

In participatory decision making, the program administrator must be sincere about sharing power, must accept the consequences of letting others' ideas come to the fore, and must reward rather than punish faculty members for their participation. Complementarily, faculty members must take their responsibilities seriously and must invest time and energy in helping make judicious decisions. Accepting shared power implies accepting shared responsibility and shared liability for the outcomes of decisions. Faculty involved in decision making need to know that they will share some of the blame for unpopular decisions, as well as credit for popular ones. Program administrators and faculty must view the benefits of participatory decision making as outweighing the disadvantages, if they decide to adopt such a model.

What Processes, Strategies, and Environments Help Empower Faculty?

Faculty can be empowered through the process of consultive management whereby program administrators involve members of the faculty—through consultation and consensus—in the development of policies and procedures that are meant to guide the program and faculty members' professional development. Powers and Powers (1983) cite several important elements in consultive processes that bring faculty members into institutional decision making: the importance of coalition building, to ensure support for decisions arrived at collectively; the acceptance of task orientation, a focus on the needs of the organization, rather than those of individuals; the movement of power from a single, central authority into the hands of the group; and the need for an exchange of information, so that all parties understand the issues, consider alternative solutions, and have the opportunity to present their views.

Building Consensus and Coalitions

Consensus decision making is a process through which a group examines available options and makes choices through negotiation and readjustment of priorities. Rule by consensus does not require that unanimity be achieved, but rather that ideas from the group be reviewed at length and that compromises be offered so that a majority accepts the choices made. Building consensus requires an investment of time, especially if opinions vary widely or if the task under discussion is complex (Soppelsa, in press); time is needed to consider all perspectives and to forge agreement. The time investment pays off in important ways because reaching consensus heightens the collective sense of ownership of the plan and promotes support for and cooperation in the new undertaking.

In some ESL faculty groups, it may be difficult to reach consensus because of subgroups that habitually disagree on matters substantial or insubstantial. In such an environment, the language program administrator—eager to build a consultive, participatory process—will need to initiate discussions about the benefits of adopting a participatory model and the requisites for its success. Providing concrete examples of actions taken by consultive groups and specifying participants' roles may help reluctant faculty members to develop an interest in participatory decision making.

In working toward a collegial exchange of ideas and group decision making, the program administrator may begin consideration of a new project or a perceived problem by talking informally with several members of the faculty prior to public discussion, to "test the water" and learn individuals' views on the matter. By consulting with individuals prior to large meetings, a leader may discover areas of agreement and may be able to forge coalitions among hitherto unallied individuals or groups, or uncover the roots of potential resistance. This process may help preclude resistance that can surface at meetings where new initiatives are sprung on the group with no warning.

In forming the agenda for subsequent large group meetings, the leader should address the opinions and underlying concerns that have surfaced in earlier conversations. For example, in planning for a faculty-designed performance appraisal process, the language program administrator may need to place on the table examples of fears expressed by faculty members who have had unhappy experiences in the past (no names attached), or who worry about peer review of teaching portfolios or student evaluations. In preparation for group discussions, the language program administrator may also ask small groups of interested faculty members to study the issues and report to the whole group. Such study groups or task forces may become the nucleus of consensus on a new undertaking and may help to persuade others to cooperate.

Refocusing Attention

Another feature of consultive decision making is task orientation, which focuses on outcomes of decisions to be made rather than the roles or status of individuals. In faculty groups in which individuals with strong personalities dominate discussions or seek to hold onto certain responsibilities, maintaining focus on the task at hand can help advance the process of decision making. Barwick (1990) suggests that leaders encourage the study of (and reward the exercise of) interdependence, cooperation, and collaboration in working toward group goals.

Redistributing Power

In addition to a refocus of attention on task, consultive decision making also requires a redistribution of power. Empowerment of ESL faculty requires that the language program administrator accept the role of facilitator rather than that of autonomous dictator, and assume responsibility for planning, organizing, and motivating, rather than just deciding and doing. The responsibility of the leader is to set processes and procedures in motion by which faculty members can exercise their creativity, enhance their skill in teaching, research, and service, and help build program quality. In organizations with high employee involvement, the leader is a "coach, facilitator, and encourager" (Rogers & Byham, 1994, p. 199).

For some language program administrators, moving from autocrat to facilitator may be a frightening prospect, as they may fear losing control of the program and the faculty. Some language program administrators have no experience or training with the consultive approach and no personal inclination to act as part of a team. Many simply do not know how to share power and authority. They may attempt to give the appearance of sharing power, but in fact they "second guess" their faculty members, reneging on offers to allow faculty to make decisions or reversing decisions when the faculty's choices do not meet with their approval. As Powers and Powers (1983) point out, such administrators use coercion "although their behavior may not ever be blatantly aggressive or explicit" (p. 25). In contrast, the success of participatory decision making depends on the willingness of the leader to accept others' ideas and choices and to acknowledge the ability of the faculty to debate issues and reach consensus.

Exchanging Information

Sharing power requires sharing information. While engaging ESL faculty in the decision-making process, the language program administrator must allow open access to information pertinent to the issue under consideration. The administrator must share information he or she has access to and allow members of the faculty to bring up ideas that they feel are relevant to the discussion. This open exchange of ideas is a requisite of participatory decision making because it allows for maximum participation among the discussants, the review of all opinions and facts related to the issue, and consideration of the widest possible range of alternatives.

These four elements—building consensus, refocusing attention, redistributing power, and sharing information—are the cornerstones of participatory decision making. In many ESL programs, both the leader and the faculty must learn the process of consultive governance. It would be wise to read about the approach first (see Harvey & Drolet, 1994; Powers & Powers, 1983), to discuss it with others who are already using it, and to agree as a group to adopt it, before simply plunging in. When the principles of the approach have been accepted, they must be practiced in order for participatory decision making to succeed.

What Are the Keys to Successful Participatory Decision Making?

Consultive governance requires skilled leadership as well as energetic participation by faculty. Skilled leadership associated with the consultive process requires respect for the persons consulted, a belief in their ability to effect positive change, a recognition of faculty potential for creativity, and a willingness to accept proposals advanced by others (Garcia, 1986). In addition, a number of personality variables and interpersonal skills are requisite for the leader of participatory decision making. These include a genuine interest in others' views and a willingness to accept others' perspectives on a problem; skill in listening, motivating, and delegating; tolerance for mistakes (Barwick, 1990); attention to the affective domain in helping create an environment conducive to clear thought and a free exchange of ideas (Pennington, 1985); promotion of open and active discussions by eliciting respectful behavior and attentive listening by all participants; skill in moderating discussions to ensure that all members have equal opportunity to present their ideas; acceptance of the different communication styles, pace of work, interests, and talents of individual faculty members; skill in ensuring that all participants feel included and that the contributions of all participants are acknowledged; trustworthiness and accountability in upholding decisions made in consultation (Kirby & Colbert, 1994; Reitzug, 1994); and a sense of humor to help relieve tension and add enjoyment to the process of reaching consensus (Barwick, 1990). The administrator's skill in leading the faculty depends in part on their respect for his or her abilities; Tack and Patitu (1992) point out that respect for the abilities of one's superior contributes to job satisfaction and promotes a willingness to cooperate.

Effective communication skills are crucial. Both in symbolic gestures, as in making sure to greet faculty members and inquire about their work, and in actual consultation on matters of import to the program, the language program administrator must pay attention to the faculty. Frequent contact between the language program administrator and individual faculty members is beneficial in furthering mutual understanding and support. Informal conversations with faculty are probably as important as formal meetings because they further mutual understanding and promote a sense of ease of communication, even where the parties may not always agree. A leader's interest in each faculty member as an individual fosters cooperative working relationships[2] (Tack & Patitu, 1992).

The role of an orchestra leader provides an apt metaphor for the empowering language program administrator. Like a conductor, the leader of an ESL program who empowers his or her faculty must know the work of the faculty very well. The leader must understand the roles of the individual members of the group and the standards of quality to which they aspire. The effective leader helps each member perfect his or her technique and teaches the group how to work together in harmony, despite their differences in talent and focus. The leader has a vision of the future and of the potential quality of the collective effort. Like a good conductor, the leader is skilled in motivating individual members to perform at their best and to contribute their finest effort to the undertaking of the group. The desired outcome is a harmonious, powerful performance, which educates and uplifts the community.

Following the metaphor of the language program administrator as conductor, faculty members are like the members of the orchestra. They must be skilled professionals. They must study and practice their roles. They must respect their colleagues and be committed to their colleagues' successful performance, as well as their own. They must be dedicated to the task at hand and trust the leader to bring their efforts together to accomplish the group goal. Although individual members should be skilled performers when they join the group, they are expected to continue to develop throughout their careers and to achieve higher levels of skill and involvement as they grow.

To participate actively in consultive governance, ESL faculty members need to be skilled in presenting their own views effectively, participating in group discussions, building consensus, working with others, problem solving, resolving conflicts, and so forth. Many faculty members begin their teaching careers weak in these skills, which are rarely taught or even mentioned in teacher-training programs. Sponsoring a workshop or other professional development opportunities for faculty to develop these skills is a wise investment for an ESL program.

In addition to building skills in group processes, faculty members may need to become better informed about the topic(s) under consideration. For example, in a program interested in developing a new test of listening proficiency, a group of faculty members may need to learn about such matters as statistical tests for item validity in order to develop reliable new tests for the program. The opportunity to study new areas and build new expertise enables faculty members to contribute new ideas to the decision-making process. This example points to the importance of professional development in the empowerment of faculty (to be discussed later).

Finally, faculty members need to accept responsibility for their role as participants in decision making. They must make a commitment to their colleagues to share in the tasks of decision making and make a commitment to the program to contribute their finest efforts in researching alternative choices and selecting the best possible solution for the good of the program.

How Does Participatory Decision Making Evolve?

In a setting with skilled leadership and committed faculty members, participatory decision making and consensus building require exploration of the question at hand, discussion of alternatives, and negotiation. Exploration of the topic begins when a problem is discovered or a desire for change arises. The impetus for change may come from any faculty member or from the program administrator, or it may, in fact, originate with a student or other member of the larger institution or community. (See Stoller, this volume, for a discussion of impetuses for change and innovation.) The faculty member or administrator who initiates the discussion begins by providing information on his or her understanding of the situation. If no immediate solution is found and the administrator and faculty find the problem compelling, plans are made to address it. The administrator may provide a timeline for study of the issues and for resolution of the problem, and may ask for volunteers or assign specific individuals—with particular expertise or interest in the area—to look into the issue on behalf of the larger group. The administrator might volunteer to conduct the study himself or herself.

It is critical that sufficient information be disclosed to the study group so that it can delineate the range of possible solutions to the question under consideration. Thus, the program administrator may need to share information not normally accessible to faculty members (e.g., resources that are available for the undertaking or constraints imposed by the host institution or community). It may be necessary for the leader to serve as interpreter of that information, educating faculty about issues or characteristics of the larger community about which faculty may have relatively little knowledge.

Communication is key in participatory decision making. Discussion may take place informally at first, enabling individual and small-group reflection to occur. Research may continue until it appears that the study group has the needed facts or that the time allotted for study has run out. At that time, a meeting is scheduled for formal discussion. Depending on the nature of the matter under consideration, all members of the faculty may be included, or a representative group may meet and propose a decision. Everyone involved should be given an opportunity to present his or her views, and everyone's questions should be answered. Members of the group must be willing to consider all sides of an issue and to suspend personal self-interest to work toward a solution that is in the best interests of the program.

Garcia (1986) provides several tips for overcoming barriers to decision making through consensus. If a large group has trouble reaching a decision, she suggests that smaller groups try to reach consensus and then return to the bargaining table. Or, if some individuals simply cannot agree with the group when general consensus has been reached, they may be asked to write a "minority report based on their logic" (p. 51), but the group will go forward with its decision. At the conclusion of the process, the language program administrator should express appreciation for the willingness of the group to work together toward a common solution and their success in doing so.

When a decision has been made, the language program administrator may need to carry the proposal forward to higher authorities for final approval. He or she may also propose a process and timetable for implementation or may ask the faculty to do so. The leader must also provide the necessary resources for undertaking the new task. As implementation begins, the leader should ask for periodic progress reports and should offer assistance to facilitate the process. After full implementation has occurred, it is appropriate for an evaluation of outcomes to be conducted. Faculty members should participate in the design of the evaluation process and collection and analysis of the data (Soppelsa, in press). The findings of the review process may lead to further discussion, consensus building, and decision making regarding continuation of the project. Table 1 summarizes the process of participatory decision making.

Table 1. Participatory Decision Making

Initiation of Decision Making	STEP 1	Problem or desire for change is identified.
	STEP 2	Information about the issue is provided.
	STEP 3	Discusson begins.

Alternative 1: Quick Fix

Immediate Solution and Implementation	STEP 4	An immediate solution is found; consensus is reached.
	STEP 5	The solution is implemented.

Alternative 2: Study and Discussion

Study and Negotiation	STEP 4	No immediate solution is found; plans are made to address the issue.
	STEP 5	The administrator sets a timeline for study of the problem.
	STEP 6	A task force is appointed to gather information, if necessary.
	STEP 7	New information is shared.
	STEP 8	Discussion begins again.
	STEP 9	Consideration of alternatives and negotiation take place.
Consensus and Implementation	STEP 10	Consensus is reached; teamwork is acknowledged.
	STEP 11	The decision is taken to higher authority for approval, if needed.
	STEP 12	Implementation plans are drawn up and begun.

How Can the Administration Involve Faculty in Program Administration and Research?

Members of the faculty may be consulted in as many areas of program administration as appropriate and desirable, given the structure of the program and the host institution. Many ESL programs have great latitude in administrative structure and decision making, working under only the broadest guidelines or limitations set by their host institutions or communities. These programs should make use of participatory decision making in virtually all areas in which faculty wish to play a role. Naturally, as Kirby and Colbert (1994) point out, there may be some areas, such as management of the physical plant or supervision of clerical staff, in which faculty do not wish to be involved, and in which their involvement would take time away from other duties in which they have greater expertise and a greater stake.

Faculty members may be asked to help make choices relating to the optimal administrative structure of the program; for example, what administrative tasks should be carried out by the language program administrator? In some programs, for example, hiring and supervision of clerical staff and recruitment of students is left to the program administrator. Faculty may also help identify those tasks which are best left to the assistant director and to faculty members themselves. Faculty should play a key role in shaping the curriculum, developing materials, and selecting textbooks for their courses (see Byrd, 1994). In addition, faculty members should take part in the following activities:

- Developing program handbooks, policy statements, and placement or proficiency tests

- Planning or sponsoring extracurricular activities and defining and overseeing student services

- Providing feedback on budget deliberations and allocation of resources

- Allocating time and money for professional development opportunities

- Conducting research regarding the effectiveness of the program and suggesting remedies for weaknesses

- Determining job responsibilities and program size

- Designing faculty evaluation processes and participating in the collection and review of data used in performance appraisals (Brown & Pennington, 1991; Soppelsa, in press)

The role of faculty in participatory decision making can only be defined in more specific terms after taking the following into consideration: the size and type of program in which they work; the type of administrative structure which exists; the skills, talents, and interests of all employees; and the resources available. In every setting, the actual degree of participation, the level of authority faculty members have, and the particular consultive structure developed will be unique.

What Is the Connection Between Empowerment and Professional Development?

The ability of faculty to participate in decision making derives not only from the ceding of power to them by the language program administrator, but also from their willingness and ability to assume responsibility, engage in study and reflection, and address the needs of the program and the professional issues of the day. The strength of a program derives from the intellectual power of its faculty and their capacity for effective teaching, research, and service. Members of the faculty should be asked to help define and develop a system by which both individual and collective growth are encouraged. The most important reason for sharing power in promoting professional growth is that individuals themselves have the greatest control over their own development. As Brighton (1965) says, "the best and only effective motive for change is one that comes from within" (p. 25). Faculty members value their right to intellectual autonomy and to independent learning (Tack & Patitu, 1992). Teachers as well as administrators should set goals for professional growth, choose opportunities appropriate within the particular framework of the program, and develop a system of rewards for participation and achievement.

The Leader's Role in Encouraging Professional Growth

The dedication of language program administrators to supporting professional development is a clear sign of their commitment to faculty empowerment, since it indicates an eagerness to give faculty members access to new knowledge, and a willingness to allow discoveries made by the faculty to affect the future of the program. What is required from leaders is a tolerance for new ideas. In addition, administrators should model good practice through their own active study and participation in professional organizations and events. They should encourage experimentation with new courses, teaching techniques, materials, and approaches. Administrators can guide faculty in professional development efforts by proposing a long-term plan of assignments that facilitates incremental development in teaching skills. Pennington (1989) suggests a model of staged teacher development in which teachers move from more supervised teaching of familiar courses to self-directed design and teaching of new courses.

Language program administrators have significant power to facilitate professional development. The most basic contribution they can make is to grant faculty members time to set goals for professional development, work toward improvement, evaluate outcomes, and revise or expand their goals. Administrators should endeavor to provide financial support for faculty members to attend courses, conferences, and workshops. If the program's level of funding does not permit payment of travel costs, faculty members should still be encouraged to participate in such activities by being permitted to take time off, ideally without loss of pay.

Program administrators can demonstrate their commitment to professional development and spur faculty on by offering incentives for faculty participation. The most obvious incentive is financial; raises in salary may be attached to achievement of specific levels of professional development, or monetary prizes may be given. Many other tangible incentives may be offered including grants for professional supplies, books, materials, or equipment. Release time for special projects or movement to preferred office or classroom space may be granted. Nonmonetary rewards may also be given in recognition of good teaching, research, or service.

Rewards for recognized success in teaching or research must be built into the performance appraisal system of the language program. Many programs use advancement in rank as a reward for success. A career ladder allows faculty to reach for specific goals and gain recognition for achievement of those goals. Higher rank, heightened status, and recognition by one's peers are powerful incentives for most people. Whenever possible, ESL faculty should be involved in defining incentives for professional development and deciding what rewards will be allocated to which people on the basis of what achievement.

Responsibilities of Empowered Faculty Members in Professional Development

Individuals are the strongest determiners of the direction of their own growth. ESL faculty members should play an active role in planning for their own professional development. They are most likely to invest time and energy in areas that interest them, rather than in areas of inquiry chosen for them by others. Allowing faculty members to map out their own courses of study is cost effective, in both time and energy expended.

Serious professionals do not sit and wait for opportunities to be handed to them from above; they take responsibility for seeking out opportunities and enlarging their repertoires independently. Faculty members have important resources close at hand that can assist in their professional development. One of the most important resources is colleagues within the program or in allied fields. Conferring with others and exchanging ideas about teaching, research, and service are important avenues for expanding one's horizons and sharpening one's thinking. Faculty members may also benefit from study groups that look into topics of shared interest; action research projects may be undertaken by pairs or groups of faculty members with the goal of enhancing instruction (Nunan, 1990; van Lier, 1994).

Faculty members can also look for opportunities for further study in local colleges or universities or by correspondence. They should make every effort to attend professional meetings and conferences, to meet with colleagues from other programs, and to hear about current research in the field. Faculty members should also try to keep up with publications in their field, perhaps focusing on a particular area of interest. Nowadays, one can join computer discussion groups to exchange ideas with professionals around the world from the comfort of one's own office. (See Morley, 1993, for further discussion on professional development.)

It should be acknowledged that all these measures take time and energy, and faculty members who are overworked have little desire to take on additional activities beyond their immediate teaching responsibilities. For professional growth to occur, workloads must be reasonable, and rewards for professional development must be worthwhile. Successful professional development plans require a partnership between language program administrators and faculty members. When faculty are faithful in working toward professional development, both individual and collective benefits arise (Barnes, 1992). On a faculty team where curiosity, study, and exchange of ideas are valued, everyone, including students, benefits.

What Are Some Strategies for Helping Faculty
Maintain Productivity and Avoid Burnout?

All administrators face the challenge of helping faculty members maintain or strengthen their productivity and commitment to growth over the course of their careers and avoid burnout, an all too common phenomenon that is accompanied by the gradual depletion of energy and loss of enthusiasm for work. Burnout is a threat in all teaching fields because of the wear and tear imposed by the intellectual and emotional challenges of teaching and the pressures of academic bureaucracy. In fields like ESL, additional stress stems from the desire to support students who are struggling to adjust to a new environment and to decipher an unfamiliar educational system.

Some ESL teachers must endure working conditions that take a large toll on their energy and commitment to the field. Many are underpaid, and many work at more than one job to make ends meet. They are called on to contribute to more than one program and to teach a variety of courses to possibly large numbers of students. Burnout is nearly inevitable under such conditions. Unless a process is developed to replenish emotional resources and renew personal energy sources, many ESL faculty will suffer from discouragement, with a sense of defeat, apathy, or disaffection toward their programs. In the worst case, such people become uncaring, unproductive, and uncooperative members of the faculty.

Bryne (1994) points out that because burnout is complex, attempts to explain its origins in single causes are futile. She identifies a number of factors involved in the etiology of burnout among elementary and secondary school teachers, including a low level of self-esteem, work overload, conflict among teachers' many roles, emotional exhaustion, and belief in an "external locus of control" (i.e., that one's fate is a consequence of forces outside one's own control). These factors, common in higher education as well, indicate a need for improved working conditions and faculty empowerment as keys to preventing burnout.

Improved Working Conditions As a Key to Burnout Prevention

Language program administrators have a responsibility to advocate for adequate salaries, benefits, and good working conditions for their faculty. Educational leaders know that teachers who feel that their pay and working conditions are at least adequate are more satisfied and more productive, in general, than those who feel underappreciated or exploited (Davidson, 1994; Tack & Patitu, 1992). It may be an uphill battle for ESL program administrators to ensure fair pay, adequate fringe benefits, decent workloads, high-quality working conditions, and institutional support for the members of their faculty. ESL programs are often accorded second-class status within their host institutions, and the working conditions and compensation of their faculty members may be inferior to those of peers in other departments (Staczek & Carkin, 1985; Vandrick, Hafernik, & Messerschmitt, 1994). Furthermore, many ESL programs at university and college levels are self-supporting, and they may teeter on the brink of insolvency from time to time. Administrators in such situations may be forced into awarding lower salaries than they would prefer or to reducing numbers of faculty at times in which student enrollments and resulting program income are low. Nevertheless, it is the ethical responsibility of every language program administrator to work for adequate compensation and working conditions for their faculty. Not only are fair working conditions ethical, but they also deter burnout and rapid turnover among faculty.

Faculty Empowerment As a Key to Burnout Prevention

Language programs need to empower faculty to work actively against burnout. To begin with, it is useful to talk about burnout and the responsibility of every individual to monitor his or her own personal and professional health and invest in work and study experiences that provide new challenges, reinforce good practice, and build self-confidence. Language program administrators should assist faculty members in working against burnout by sponsoring opportunities for renewal, such as group discussions, retreats, guest speakers, workshop attendance, conference participation, and other forums for an exchange of ideas. Other opportunities for enrichment come from travel to or exchanges with other programs to observe their practices, or to the countries from which overseas students come. It may be possible for programs to pay for such faculty travel as part of a student recruitment plan.

Bringing in new books and materials is another way to provide opportunities for personal growth and to prevent burnout. A specific budget allocation may be provided each year for the purchase of new materials, preferably to be selected by faculty members themselves. Encouraging faculty to teach new courses, undertake nonteaching responsibilities, write new materials, and engage in action research can also help faculty members avoid burnout (Jensen & Soppelsa, 1996). To keep intellectually alive and interested, it is important to expand one's repertoire, look for new approaches, and experiment with new strategies. Individual faculty members should be empowered to provide input regarding their own teaching, administrative, or research assignments, weighing the comfort of repeating an assignment against the challenge of tackling a new one.

Varying the assignments of faculty members is a significant tool in working against burnout. ESL faculty involvement in curriculum and materials development, financial management, faculty evaluation, and many other areas can prevent burnout. Involving faculty in the heart of program management promotes sustained energy and interest. Some language programs can afford to fund individual or group research projects by giving faculty members release time from teaching to, for example, analyze proficiency test items, determine student success rates in various courses or curricula, or develop program handbooks, policy statements, brochures, or teaching materials. Conducting research allows faculty members to explore new topics, enlarge their expertise, and build self-confidence. Some research opens new frontiers for the field at large, which brings faculty members recognition by their peers and enhancement of their status. Even where release time is not possible, ESL faculty may find the time to embark on action research projects focused on the improvement of their own classroom teaching.

Confronting Burnout

Sometimes, regardless of the commitment of the language program administrator to support enrichment opportunities for faculty, an individual may become discouraged, alienated, or unproductive. Often, the situation is a result of personal as well as professional hardships. Unknowingly, a program may hire an individual who has had a difficult career and who arrives with a lack of interest in professional development opportunities or a disinclination to participate in the full life of the program. In some cases, efforts to revive the individual's interest in his or her career are unsuccessful, and the individual may choose to leave the program or profession, or may be asked to leave.[3]

In the unfortunate event that a senior or tenured faculty member has grown stale, uninterested, or uncooperative, and does not choose to leave the program, the department head has a responsibility to try to re-energize the individual and to limit the potential negative impact on colleagues and the life of the program (see Lucas, 1990). Here are some suggestions for the educational leader working with disaffected faculty members:

1. Continue to expect the best of all faculty. Don't write off any individuals as beyond redemption. Assume that there is some "life" left in them. Keep feeding them new ideas, asking them to participate, giving them avenues for participation and renewal, and listening to their ideas and concerns. Continue to be clear in expressing what you expect of all faculty—encouraging and rewarding good practice and refusing to tolerate poor work.

2. Do not allow the discouraged member to dissuade you or other faculty from working toward your highest potential. Look for partnerships for the disaffected member of the faculty that might promote participation. Take note of personal or professional conflicts that impede effective collaboration. Offer tips for successful partnering with difficult individuals, and reward those who maintain positive relationships with them. (See Harvey & Drolet, 1994; and White, Martin, Stimson, & Hodge, 1991, for strategies for working with difficult individuals.)

3. Be trustworthy. Keep your word and do what you say you will do, even when it means you must confront a difficult individual with criticism or sanction. When praise is due, give it.

4. Stay cool. Do not sacrifice your professional demeanor by losing your temper or sniping. Do not "sink" to the level of the disaffected.

What Are Some Strategies for Empowering New Faculty?

New faculty are the future sustainers and future leaders of a program. Much time and money may be invested in hiring them, and it is in the program's best interests to ensure that successful and productive newcomers will stay on the faculty for a long time. Their longevity in the program is cost effective in programmatic as well as financial terms. Retention of newcomers obviates the need to spend money to recruit and hire others, and more importantly for most programs, it facilitates continuity of quality if opportunities for professional development are assured and active participation in the program is rewarded. (See Geddes & Marks, this volume, for information on the hiring process.)

Ensuring that new ESL faculty members will become empowered (and remain energized) requires care on the part of the language program administrator or mentors responsible for the orientation of new staff. As White, Martin, Stimson, and Hodge (1991) state, "the initial induction period can be crucial in setting the tone of the relationship between the individual and the organization" (p. 62). Orientation should take several forms and should begin as early as possible in the individual's association with the program. The first step is to provide access to information about the program (including its mission, faculty, students, curriculum, resources, student services and extracurricular activities), job expectations and performance standards, the host environment, and the larger community.

To accommodate newcomers' needs, the information should be provided in a variety of formats (e.g., handbooks, discussions, meetings, workshops, private conversations, and tours). It is helpful for the newcomer to receive information from a variety of sources and persons, to gain a well-rounded picture of the new work environment. Dissemination of information should also take place on several occasions, rather than at one sitting, to allow the newcomer to build a fuller view of the program. Describing the relationship of the newcomer's particular assignments to the program as a whole will help the newcomer see the big picture as well as help clarify his or her relationship to other faculty. The administrator and other members of the faculty should encourage questions, provide full answers, and repeat information as requested by the newcomer. Orientation takes time and requires patience, but it is more efficient than allowing a newcomer to learn by trial and error; in addition, it prevents many misunderstandings and avoids wasted effort.

The second step requires that the language program administrator smooth the way for the newcomer, introducing him or her to members of the faculty and to key personnel in the administration, rather than expecting fruitful meetings to occur spontaneously. In addition to informal meetings with colleagues, including the newcomer in regularly scheduled meetings will help cement his or her engagement in the program and acceptance by others.

Another way to assist newcomers in becoming successful participants in the program is to encourage collaboration with acclimatized faculty. Arrangements for teaching partners, mentors, and discussion networks allow for mutual stimulation and support and facilitate positive working relationships, as long as the parties participate willingly and are positively rewarded for their contributions. Newcomers may benefit from seeing demonstrations of what the program considers effective teaching, research, and service, so that program expectations will be clear, especially if the newcomers have just come from programs that are different in perspective or mission.

Finally, the newcomer should learn about the participatory decision-making process adopted by the program faculty. Opportunities to read about group processes, consensus building, and conflict resolution should be made available, and new faculty members should observe how group decisions are made. A peer coach may be appointed to assist the newcomer in practicing these skills as he or she enters the group decision-making process.

What Is the Role of Empowered Faculty in Program Relationships With the Outside World?

Empowered faculty can play a variety of roles not only within the walls of the language program, but also in relationships with the outside world. Within the larger institution, such as the school district or campus, ESL faculty members should represent the program in forums in which relevant issues are discussed. Faculty members may serve on institution-wide committees or task forces. They may represent their program in community organizations or projects. Beyond the local setting, faculty members may hold offices in professional organizations and present papers at professional conferences. And they may be active on state, regional, or national boards, making decisions about ESL curricula and standards for wider domains. These types of activities allow faculty to demonstrate their interest in and sense of responsibility for their community and profession. The resultant confidence in their abilities to serve ably in those settings is a reflection of their empowerment, their acceptance of responsibility as professionals.

Empowered faculty may also lend their strength to student advocacy, shouldering responsibility for building acceptance and appreciation for the students in their new academic and community environments. They may serve as mediators between students and the host community and as supporters of newcomers' rights in the new society (Diaz-Rico, 1995). By collaborating with ESL students in their exploration of their new surroundings, these faculty members help empower students to function more successfully. Beyond helping them learn English, they may teach students leadership skills and the nature of participatory decision making, to enable students to make positive contributions in school and societal settings.

Empowered faculty and their programs can become advocates for international and multicultural education, helping strengthen opportunities for students from around the world to join educational environments outside their home countries and cultures. Empowered ESL faculty members are part of a larger endeavor, which involves the sharing of knowledge and understanding between societies.

Conclusion

Empowerment of language program faculty through participatory decision making and ongoing professional development promotes effective program management, encourages and facilitates both individual and collective commitment to the program, leads to a shared sense of mission, allows for cooperation and collaboration, and wards off burnout. Involving faculty in decision making—in a climate of mutual respect built over time through successful collaboration—requires skillful leadership and a belief in the talents and effectiveness of faculty. Both leaders and faculty members must become skilled in negotiation, compromise, and consensus building and must be willing to allot time to attend to program needs, rather than to self-interest alone. The importance of participatory decision making in the ultimate success of a language program reveals the need to include training in interpersonal and leadership skills, collaboration, and consensus building in teacher education programs, to ensure that future teachers will become engaged, energetic, and effective contributors to the language programs in which they work and to the larger field of ESL.

Endnotes

1. Empowerment of clerical and support staff is also possible and in most settings desirable, but will not be dealt with here.

2. It is surprising that the majority of ESL college and university administrators studied by Reasor (1986) were rated as more task oriented than people oriented. Further

research is needed to determine whether that is an accurate representation of ESL administrators today and how such an orientation correlates with an ability to motivate and empower faculty members.

3. White, Martin, Stimson, and Hodge (1991) discuss disciplinary and dismissal measures, pp. 86–90.

Discussion Questions and Activities

1. What are some of the benefits of empowering faculty? What are some possible disadvantages?

2. How does empowerment of faculty relate to professional growth?

3. What characteristics and behaviors of language program administrators are conducive to faculty empowerment?

4. What are some strategies that an administrator can employ to prevent faculty burnout?

5. What are the major challenges that administrators face when attempting to empower faculty?

6. Imagine that you are the director of a university-based intensive English program. The university's central administration has decided that all salary increments for faculty will be merit based from now on, not need based or seniority based. Describe the steps that you would take to empower members of your faculty to devise a system for merit raise distribution.

Suggested Reading List

Powers, D. R., & Powers, M. F. (1983). *Making participatory management work: Leadership of consultive decision making in academic administration.* San Francisco: Jossey-Bass.

The authors present a broad review of patterns of decision making in institutions of higher education with specific recommendations about the use of participatory decision making. The book chronicles trends and realities of university governance against the backdrop of theories of organizational management.

Seldin, P., & Associates (Eds.). (1990). *How administrators can improve teaching: Moving from talk to action in higher education.* San Francisco: Jossey-Bass.

This collection of articles on the power of effective administration presents many ideas and strategies that will be useful to language program leaders in public and private programs, at elementary, secondary, and tertiary levels. The volume, which contains 11 articles, is divided into three sections: Key influences on teaching quality, The administrator's role in strengthening instructional quality, and Making teaching excellence an institutional priority.

White, R., Martin, M., Stimson, M., & Hodge, R. (1991). *Management in English language teaching*. New York: Cambridge University Press.

The authors present a well-rounded overview of management in English language programs and schools, from the British perspective. It contains three main sections: People and organizations, Marketing, and Finance. It provides an excellent introduction to the basics of school and program management, as well as stimulating follow-up activities for managers-in-training.

Chapter 10

THE L2 STUDENT ADVOCATE

Mary Ann Christison
University of Utah/Snow College

ebster's Third New International Dictionary defines an advocate as someone "who pleads the cause of another; who argues for, defends, maintains, or recommends a cause." This definition provides an adequate description of one of the major roles of language program administrators who advocate for and are advocates of the language program, the students it serves, and often other language minority students on their campuses and in their communities. Although this chapter focuses on the language program administrator as student advocate in university and college settings, the perspectives offered are valuable for any program administrator who must advocate on behalf of second language (L2) students, no matter what the setting.

The number of language minority students, both native and foreign born, on campuses in English-speaking countries increases annually. *Open Doors* (Davis, 1996), a publication of the Institute of International Education, indicates that the international student population in the United States has risen from 34,232 in 1954 to 454,787 in 1996. At the same time, the number of L2 students from immigrant and refugee families is increasing as well. As the number of non-native speakers increases in public schools, colleges, and universities, the need for intercultural understanding and intercultural communication skills becomes greater. Thus, the advocacy role of the language program administrator becomes even more important.

Because non language program faculty, staff, administrators, and students are sometimes unfamiliar with the cultures and languages of language minority students, frequent miscommunications arise. It is during these moments of misunderstanding that language program administrators are often called upon to serve as advocates for language minority students. There are four main ways that language program administrators can function as advocates for L2 students: They can serve as *classroom* advocates, *cultural* advocates, *language* advocates, and *academic* advocates. In these varied, yet often overlapping, advocacy roles, the language program administrator helps those who come into contact with L2 students understand the challenges that L2 students face while trying to succeed academically and socially in their communities. Simultaneously, administrators assist L2 students in adjusting to their new environments.

The Language Program Administrator As Classroom Advocate

Language program administrators are frequently called upon by mainstream faculty and language minority students to clarify student-teacher misunderstandings that occur in mainstream classrooms. Faculty often call language program administrators, who are viewed by many as experts in L2 issues on campus, about L2 students who are having difficulties in their classrooms. During these conversations, faculty often vent their frustrations that result from having non-native speakers in their classes and seek advice on how to deal with these students to help them succeed. Similarly, L2 students often return to the language program, seeking advice from language program faculty and administrators on how to deal with the frustrations that they are experiencing in mainstream classes.

These frustrations can often be attributed to the diverse cultural assumptions that faculty and students bring to class (see Fitch, 1986). When people from multiple cultural backgrounds experience events or behaviors together, such as events in a classroom, the groups will interpret the events differently. What follows are seven common classroom events or behaviors followed by a common U.S. interpretation of the event and a non-U.S. interpretation. The intention is not to stereotype behaviors in any way, but rather to provide clear and practical examples of how behaviors can have more than one interpretation. The job of a language program administrator as a classroom advocate is not to interpret classroom events for either students or academic faculty, but rather to provide concrete examples to show that more than one interpretation is possible.

Event/Behavior 1: The quiet student. When an L2 student does not interact during classroom discussions, a teacher often makes several assumptions consistent with his or her culture. A teacher from the United States might believe that the student who does not interact has not done the homework, is lazy, is unmotivated, or cannot handle the course content. An L2 student, however, may have a different set of interpretations. For example, in many cultures, silence is a sign of respect. Knowledge is respected and valued, and the teacher is seen as a person who has knowledge. When the teacher speaks, students listen. The students themselves are not seen as a source of knowledge, and therefore are not expected to contribute to class discussions.

Event/Behavior 2: The student who does not ask questions. When students do not ask questions before, during, or after class, a U.S. teacher assumes that students understand course assignments, content, tests, and general procedures. U.S. teachers may also believe that if students have questions or need clarification on any matter relating to the class, they will seek help from their teacher or peers taking the class. A non-U.S. student, on the other hand, may have an entirely different set of assumptions. Students in some cultures believe that the individual student must take full responsibility for not understanding. In other words, if students do not understand the content of the course, it is their own fault. To admit that they do not understand something and to draw attention to themselves in front of their peers would be extremely awkward. Some students would never think about seeking help in such circumstances from either the teacher or their peers. It would be embarrassing to do so.

Event/Behavior 3: The student who makes no eye contact. Some cultures avoid direct eye contact with other people, including teachers and elders. U.S. teachers often consider the behavior rude or believe the students are disinterested or unmotivated because the same behavior from U.S. students often means just that. Some L2 students, however, come from cultures in which it is considered impolite and disrespectful to look directly at a speaker.

Event/Behavior 4: The soft-spoken student. Many L2 students speak in soft voices if addressed publicly. They believe it is impolite to speak loudly. U.S. professors, on the other hand, believe that it is impolite to not adapt one's voice level when speaking to a group. Some professors become frustrated with L2 students because they will not speak up even when asked to do so.

Event/Behavior 5: The student who nods his head. When a U.S. teacher is lecturing, some L2 students nod their heads up and down. From a U.S. cultural perspective, the nodding signals understanding on the part of the students as well as agreement with the speaker. This is certainly not the case with all cultures. When nodding, many L2 students are simply signaling respect and active listening. This behavior does not mean "I understand" or "I agree."

Event/Behavior 6: The student who copies from written sources. Another common cultural difference occurs when a student copies word-for-word from written sources. The U.S. teacher reacts with charges of plagiarism. Some L2 students, however, have a different set of cultural assumptions. Relying on a knowledgeable expert for clarity of the written word is a much better alternative than choosing to write something poorly in one's own words.

Event/Behavior 7: The student who helps others during exams. Some cultures value group success over individual success. Being the best individual in a group is not as important as helping members of the group succeed. Knowing the answers and not helping others is considered cheating in those cultures. University faculty within the United States assume competitiveness among students. Helping each other on a test is considered cheating.

The different cultural assumptions highlighted here represent a sampling of classroom events and behaviors that can lead to teacher-student misunderstandings. When L2 students and faculty see the world in different ways, they often reach out to the language program administrator for assistance in bridging the gap of understanding. In such circumstances, the language program administrator functions as a classroom advocate, helping both students and faculty develop intercultural understanding and improved communication (Cochran, 1992).

When receiving calls from faculty about an L2 student or from an L2 student about a faculty member, the following steps can be taken to play the pivotal role of impartial listener, facilitator, and mediator:

1. Listen carefully to the complaint or problem. Restate the complaint as you understand it. Check to make certain that your understanding is correct.

2. Ask the student or faculty member if there may be another way to view the situation. The answer to the question will often be no. Tell the person that you are thinking of a past experience that reveals another way of interpreting the situation.

3. Give an example, similar to the ones just described, to illustrate diverse perspectives on the same classroom event.

4. Without being too directive, suggest that the faculty member or student consider classroom events and behaviors that cause misunderstandings and frustrations from multiple perspectives. The insights gained can facilitate a teacher-student conversation to remedy the situation.

The Language Program Administrator As Cultural Advocate

As a cultural advocate, the language program administrator can help students and those who communicate with L2 students on a regular basis (e.g., instructors, residence hall directors, advisors, counselors, cashiers, cafeteria personnel) understand the complexities of cultural adjustment and intercultural communication.

Dimensions of Cultural Adjustment

In the process of adjusting to being a student in a new educational environment (whether it be a language program, college, university, or public school), L2 students often experience culture shock, a cycle of events that have been interpreted in many different ways (see Brislin, 1981; Damen, 1987; Harris & Moran, 1975; Thomas & Harrell, 1994; Torbiörn, 1994). Most commonly, the term culture shock is used to describe the dynamics of adjustment and entry into a new culture (Brein & David, 1971). When students first enter a new culture, they react positively; they feel that everything about the new culture is wonderful. This period is often referred to as the honeymoon period (Seelye, 1968, 1974). Later on, everything seems wrong with the new culture, moving students into the hostility stage (McLeod, 1980). It is not that anything has really changed externally, but there are internal changes for the student. It is during this stage when students experience feelings of, for example, fatigue, sleeplessness, anxiety, depression, anger, malaise, and homesickness (Damen, 1987). Luckily, for most students the hostility stage does not last forever; it is assuaged by time. Gradually, students emerge from this stage with increased abilities in understanding not only the target culture, but their own as well. The language program administrator plays an important role in helping university personnel understand what culture shock is, and in providing information to L2 students to help them manage their adjustment.

It is important that the language program administrator impart a sympathetic but not defensive view of the target culture when dealing with students experiencing culture shock. This orientation establishes empathy and wins the student's confidence. During conversations about the stages of culture shock, the language program administrator can help students understand that their feelings of alienation will not last forever and that their feelings are a normal part of the process of cultural adjustment.

Not all university faculty and staff have traveled and lived in different cultural environments, so it makes sense that they may not be aware of the difficulties that L2 students experience in adjusting to a new environment. As Storti (1990) explains, "The old proverb notwithstanding, we cannot put ourselves in someone else's shoes. Or, rather, we can, but it's still our own feet we will feel" (p. 51). Students can experience difficulties of many types on campus (see Althen, 1994a) and their experiences will inevitably impact their ability to function well in their classes. Some of the areas in which L2 students experience the most difficulties are described below:

School environment. L2 students must adapt to a new school environment in which they must cope with different routines for registration, interaction with professors, classroom culture, and grading, just to name a few differences. Most of the students who study in language programs are used to being in top form academically. In their new surroundings, they do not know how to function very well because of new sets of institutional and cultural expectations. They are unable to make the kind of contribution academically to which they are accustomed.

Community adjustment. When one moves to a new community, one has to learn to get around for basic survival needs. L2 students must learn where to buy food and shop for things they need, which shops carry which goods, how to take public transportation, where it is safe and not safe. Until one becomes comfortable with daily routines, there will be discomfort and difficulties.

Climatic adjustment. One of the most immediate adjustments that newcomers must make can be to climate. Changes in weather and climate can cause havoc in the body. In cold climates, skin can dry and crack. In tropical climates, skin can break out in rashes or other irritations. In addition, many L2 students experience a marked loss of energy and need more sleep when they change climates. Low-grade fevers and headaches are also symptoms of climatic adjustment. These changes often result in modified physical activity, which can affect how students feel over the long run.

Poor communication. Initially communication is always a challenge for L2 students. Communicating on the telephone and interacting with native speakers while shopping are two difficulties that most students experience immediately. Establishing personal relationships is also difficult if communication skills are minimal. Yet developing friendships and support groups is an essential component in cultural adjustment. L2 students have left their close friends and families behind but want to feel at home where they are (Storti, 1990). Feeling at home is difficult. In the beginning, there are so many areas of adjustment. Almost every opportunity for communication provokes confusion and helplessness. Students cannot figure out what is happening in most communicative encounters at the university. The feeling of confusion is followed by the fear of not knowing what is expected of them. Feelings of anger, embarrassment, and irritation often follow. This communication pattern continues for weeks, often months, as students adjust.

Sacrifice: Having to do without. It may seem hard for someone who has been born and raised in a country like the United States, where so much is available, to believe that living here means having to do without. Yet, that is exactly what it means for many L2 students. They are unable to find the food and spices they are accustomed to, the bread they like, clothes and shoes that are comfortable, and the common medicines they are used to. No matter where they go, things are different.

In explaining the different dimensions of adjustment for international students to individuals who interact with these students, the language program administrator becomes a cultural advocate. The impact of so much that is new and unfamiliar seriously disrupts life and, in fact, can be debilitating. When individuals approach their interactions with L2 students from this point of view, they are often more successful in helping students move forward in their educational goals; as a result, these individuals are likely to feel more successful as educators and service personnel.

Intercultural Communication

In addition to helping university personnel appreciate the many dimensions of cultural adjustment, language program administrators can be cultural advocates by providing information on intercultural communication. L2 students are often considered by faculty and staff to be the ones with the difficult point of view. Language program administrators might find it helpful to introduce an adaptation of Storti's (1990) five-stage model that illustrates the roots of communication difficulties and possible solutions. This model is effective because it involves all parties in the communication and does not make any value judgments; it helps both university personnel and L2 students understand their behavior and attitudes. Storti's model—interpreted here for the language program administrator—basically charts two possible paths of communication between people of different cultures. (See Figure 1.)

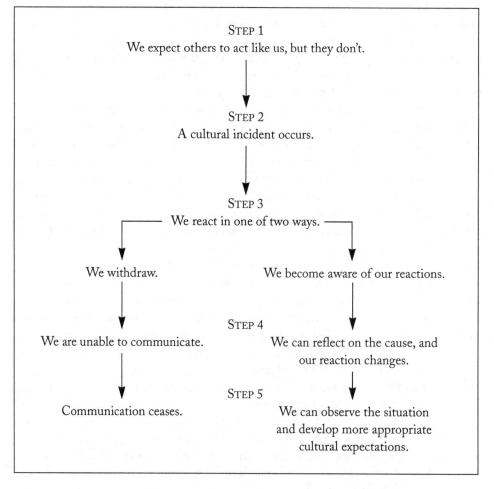

STEP 1
We expect others to act like us, but they don't.

STEP 2
A cultural incident occurs.

STEP 3
We react in one of two ways.

We withdraw.

We become aware of our reactions.

STEP 4

We are unable to communicate.

We can reflect on the cause, and our reaction changes.

STEP 5

Communication ceases.

We can observe the situation and develop more appropriate cultural expectations.

Figure 1.
Adaptation of Storti's (1990) five-stage model of intercultural communication.

The following example illustrates Storti's model with more specific detail. The teacher expects the L2 student to act like U.S. students in the classroom. The L2 student does not meet those expectations. Instead, he is very quiet. A cultural incident occurs. If the teacher complains about the student's behavior and judges the student as being unmotivated or unable to handle the material without attempting to obtain more information, the process of intercultural communication ceases. However, if the teacher becomes aware of her reaction, reflects on it, and comes to understand her own expectations, she will be in a position to see the student's point of view and can begin developing more appropriate expectations, such as realizing that the L2 student may be quiet to demonstrate respect. An outcome of this reflective behavior might include the teacher's talking to the student about classroom expectations and encouraging the student to develop alternative classroom behaviors.

One danger of being a cultural advocate is the possibility of oversimplification of an extremely complex phenomenon. For this reason, language program administrators should focus on the process of cultural adjustment and intercultural communication rather than on a list of do's and don'ts for the people involved.

> The classification of behavior as desirable or taboo endows it with misleading objectivity. Behavior is ambiguous: the same action may have different meanings in different situations, so that it is necessary to identify the context of behavior and the contingencies of action before the [sojourner] can be armed with prescriptions for specific acts. Fulfillment of this strategy is impossible since the [number] of possible events is [unlimited]. (Stewart, 1972, p. 20–21)

It goes without saying that a language program administrator should develop an intercultural perspective by learning as much about other cultures as possible. An administrator must be aware of ethnocentrism, prejudice, and the tendency to stereotype. The best way to combat these difficulties is to develop sensitivity to other cultures and learn to accept them as equal though different (Nayar, 1986). It helps to have the mindset that no culture is necessarily superior. The role of the language program administrator as an effective cultural advocate is as a mediator and an ambassador of culture, not as a purveyor or an imposer of culture.

The Language Program Administrator As Language Advocate

Language program administrators often find themselves serving the function of language advocate. It is not uncommon for administrators to be questioned about the "listening" classes the program offers or the reading lab space that is needed simply because those with whom they are dealing do not understand the nature of second language acquisition or the needs of second language learners. Language program administrators also receive phone calls from frustrated faculty members who are disturbed by grammatical errors in the written work of L2 students or students' inability to express themselves fluently in class. These faculty members sometimes question the effectiveness of the language program curriculum because of L2 students' persistent grammatical errors, even after successfully completing the language program. What non-language professionals do not realize is that often students' problems are not grammatical at all:

> more often, the problem of communicating successfully originates from the ESL student's limited or skewed perception of what is expected. Typically, [L2 students] ... resort to coping skills that have worked in their native languages and cultures but that are inappropriate for the expectations of the U.S. academic audience. (Reid, 1992, p. 211)

In such situations, misunderstandings abound. L2 students are unable to make themselves understood, and faculty cannot see beyond surface errors to evaluate the students' grasp of content.

Language program administrators often find themselves in the position of trying to explain to faculty and other personnel the challenges of learning a second language. It is sometimes difficult to get across the notion of what English language proficiency means to individuals who may have had little experience in learning another language for the purpose of completing academic studies in that language. Native speakers of any language take the knowledge that they have of their mother tongue for granted because the knowledge they have is tacit. Language program administrators can function as language advocates by raising linguistic awareness in at least three ways. First, they can help faculty (and others who come into contact with L2 students) understand the difficulties of learning a second language to the level required for mainstream classes. Second, they can help these individuals comprehend how the knowledge that L1 and L2 speakers have is different.[1] Third, they can help faculty see beyond surface errors to evaluate the students' grasp of content. Administrators can also function as language advocates by helping faculty understand possible areas of difficulty for L2 students in their classes. The following list is not meant to be exhaustive, but it represents a beginning in identifying areas of difficulty for L2 students:

1. L2 learners often find it difficult to handle the volume of reading and writing assigned in mainstream classes. One reason for student difficulties may be that students rely on word-for-word translations to enhance comprehension.

2. Many L2 learners are also new to studying in institutions of higher education. They do not fully understand how they learn, and they have insufficient study skills.

3. L2 learners often find it difficult to respond in writing to the wide range of assignments and question types on exams. Short essay answers that require stating a main idea and supporting it with facts are particularly problematic, especially with rigidly enforced time constraints.

4. L2 students may be unaware of standard academic writing conventions and expectations, especially if the students arrive in an English-speaking country having learned most of their English in their home country.

5. L2 students may have difficulty grasping new material that is presented orally (i.e., in a lecture format). They often rely on reading skills rather than listening skills to comprehend new information.

6. L2 students do not contribute orally to class discussions with ease. They rely on answers that they may have prepared in advance. Consequently, when called on in class, they cannot give quick answers.

7. L2 students will have difficulty giving formal presentations in class without practice.

The Language Program Administrator As Academic Advocate

In their role as academic advocates, language program administrators serve the needs of both L2 students and content-area faculty. They are often approached by L2 students who are experiencing difficulties in their mainstream courses but who want to be successful in their studies outside of the language program. Administrators also have contact with faculty who have a range of attitudes about L2 students,

> from those who are having trouble accepting the fact that [demographic] changes have profoundly affected the types of students coming into ... colleges and universities, to those so entrenched in their traditional roles that they refuse to change their instructional repertoire, to concerned faculty who recognize that accommodations are in order, but feel at a loss in terms of expertise and experience.
>
> While many faculty are skilled teachers, there is a growing, discernible mismatch between teaching strategies they have honed over the years for one type of student and approaches which will engage the linguistically and culturally diverse students presently enrolled in their classes. As increasing numbers of native-born and immigrant language minority students enter postsecondary education, faculty require assistance in dealing with the instructional demands of this burgeoning student population. (Snow & Kamhi-Stein, 1996, p. iv)

As an academic advocate, the language program administrator can assist both L2 students and faculty. Suggestions for L2 students most often focus on the kinds of activities that students might pursue to improve their academic performance. Suggestions for faculty emphasize the adjustments that faculty might make in their teaching to reach as many students as possible and to enable students to meet the conceptual and linguistic demands of their courses.

Suggestions for L2 Students

Language program administrators are often approached by L2 students who are finding it difficult to succeed in their regular classes. In these situations, language program administrators can refer students to a language program advisor or a faculty member who has responsibilities for counseling such students, or they can offer students advice themselves. Administrators can serve these students in a time-efficient and helpful manner by offering suggestions from a convenient checklist, as depicted in Figure 2.[2]

When meeting with L2 students who are experiencing difficulties in their academic classes, language program administrators should follow these procedures:

1. Try to understand the nature of the student's problems and determine the root(s) of the problems.

2. Go through items 1–6 on the checklist. (See Figure 2.)

3. Ask if the student is already following these sugggestions.

4. If the answer is no, encourage him or her to pursue the activities and report back to you in another week. If the answer is yes to most of the questions, then recommend number 7 on the list and help the student make the necessary contacts.

CHECKLIST (√) FOR ACADEMIC SUCCESS

√ 1. If you are having difficulty understanding the lectures in class, ask your teacher if you can tape-record the lectures so that you can listen to them at home.

√ 2. Edit and review your class lecture notes as soon as possible after class. The task is much easier when the material is fresh in your mind.

√ 3. Try to anticipate lecture material before class. Prepare for the lecture by studying the assigned readings, completing the homework assignments before class, and reviewing your notes. You will understand more of the material if you follow these suggestions.

√ 4. Find a study partner. Make sure your partner is committed. Agree on how you will study together. Exchange phone numbers and agree to notify one another of any change in plans. You might want to share notes or quiz each other before exams.

√ 5. Sit near the front of the class so that you can see the board and see and hear the teacher and other class presentations.

√ 6. When you don't understand something in class, ask for clarification from either your teacher or a peer. If you feel embarrassed to ask your questions in class, see your professors during their office hours. Chances are that if you don't understand the course material, there are others just like you. You are not alone.

√ 7. If you still feel unsuccessful in your classes and do not notice any improvement in your performance, consider hiring a tutor or enrolling in additional ESL courses to improve your English language abilities. Contact the campus language program, the English department, a campus learning assistance center, or a campus tutoring service for assistance.

Figure 2. **Student checklist for academic success.**

Suggestions for Faculty

Language program administrators can assist faculty to meet the academic needs of their language minority students in a number of ways (see Jenkins, 1997). Whatever approach one takes, however, it is important to work under the assumption that the faculty member is concerned about all students and wants to find ways to help them to be successful. To assist faculty, the language program administrator can create various checklists that address faculty concerns and answer regular faculty queries. The goal of the checklists should be to introduce faculty to strategies that enhance classroom teaching and conditions for learning for all students, but that are critical for L2 students.

A sampling of such checklists is included here: Figure 3 emphasizes general classroom strategies that support L2 students, Figure 4 highlights strategies for enhancing daily lessons, Figure 5 lists techniques for creating positive classroom affect, and Figure 6 includes strategies for improving lectures.[3] Other areas of concern (that are worthy of similar checklists) include making textbooks accessible, preparing students for exams, writing exams and quizzes, structuring syllabi, involving students actively in learning, assembling academic information, and modeling the research process. (See Snow, 1992, 1993, 1994; and Snow & Kamhi-Stein, 1996, for materials designed to assist content faculty to meet the needs of growing numbers of language minority students.) The checklists, once constructed, can be used in a variety of ways by language program administrators, who can do the following:

1. Send out checklists in response to phone inquiries from faculty who call to express concern or frustration about an L2 student's progress.

2. Be proactive. Send the packet of checklists, with a cover memo from you, to all faculty explaining the use of the checklists and offering assistance when needed.

3. Offer a free workshop for faculty. Work with one department at a time. If the workshops are interesting, educational, and informative, departments will request the workshop in future years.

4. Publish checklists, one at a time, in a faculty newsletter.

5. Ask to have the checklists included in new-faculty orientation materials.

6. Sponsor a bag-lunch series for interested faculty during which you can focus on different strategies for meeting the needs of language minority students.

Conclusion

The preceding discussion provides an overview of the different ways in which the language program administrator can be an advocate for L2 students. As a classroom advocate, the language program administrator offers advice on how students and faculty might deal with frustrations in the classroom, providing clear and practical examples of multiple interpretations of classroom behaviors. As a cultural advocate, the language program administrator helps students and those with whom they communicate to understand the complexities of cultural adjustment and intercultural communication. Language program administrators also function as language advocates, helping faculty understand possible areas of language difficulty for L2 students in their classes. In the role of an academic advocate, the language program administrator assists L2 students, focusing on the kinds of activities that students might pursue to improve academic achievement. They can also assist faculty by suggesting adjustments that faculty might make in their teaching to reach as many students as possible. By functioning as classroom, cultural, language, and academic advocates, the language program administrator plays an important role in promoting a successful intercultural dialog, breaking down intercultural barriers, minimizing miscommunication, and facilitating more successful interactions between L2 students and the individuals with whom they communicate.

GENERAL CLASSROOM STRATEGIES THAT SUPPORT L2 STUDENTS

√ 1. Be aware of your body language. It can be misinterpreted. Rather than avoid the quieter students, initiate conversation. After class, you might find out how comfortable they are in class and what activities they like best.

√ 2. Solicit informal, written feedback from students. Find out what they like, what they don't like, and what they would like to do differently. Do not rely on large-group discussion to obtain this feedback. The most vocal students will tend to dominate the discussion and will be the only ones to voice their opinions.

√ 3. Remind students about your office hours and encourage students to come to see you for individual help. If it is possible, schedule your office hours directly after class so that students can ask for clarification while questions are fresh in their minds.

√ 4. Develop multiple means for monitoring student progress during the term. Don't rely on a single final exam. Feedback to students should come early and often.

Figure 3.
Checklist of general classroom strategies that provide support for L2 students.

STRATEGIES FOR ENHANCING DAILY LESSONS

√ 1. Write all homework assignments on the board.

√ 2. Distribute handouts and announce reading assignments ahead of time (if appropriate) so that students can familiarize themselves with the material before class.

√ 3. Encourage students to form small study groups.

√ 4. Make a point of rephrasing the main points or more difficult concepts of each lecture.

√ 5. Be aware that idioms and slang expressions may hinder comprehension. Monitor your speech, know when you use slang, and be prepared to provide alternative explanations.

√ 6. Write legibly at all times.

√ 7. Assign specific homework tasks that relate to the coursework and tell the students why you are having them complete the task.

√ 8. Vary the pace of your lessons and break up content into accessible units.

√ 9. Be organized in your lectures; use clear transition markers to further comprehension.

√ 10. Write key words, phrases, and ideas on the blackboard.

Figure 4. **Checklist for enhancing daily lessons.**

TECHNIQUES FOR CREATING POSITIVE CLASSROOM AFFECT

√ 1. Encourage students to ask questions.

√ 2. Reward risk taking.

√ 3. Encourage collaborative efforts.

√ 4. Encourage respect and understanding among all students.

√ 5. Engage all students in classroom conversation, not just the verbal students.

√ 6. Avoid joking or teasing because of accent or ethnic background.

√ 7. Learn your students' names.

Figure 5. **Checklist for creating positive classroom affect for L2 learners.**

STRATEGIES FOR IMPROVING LECTURES

√ 1. Begin the day's lecture with a brief review of the points covered the previous day. This review gives L2 students an additional chance to check understanding. Another technique for reviewing that has been very helpful with L2 learners is having the entire class work in pairs and quickly summarize the previous day's lesson. Then, work as a unified class to clarify the main points. When you begin the new lecture, clarify the topic of the lecture for that day and state the key concepts and objectives. Summarizing and anticipatory strategies are essential for L2 students.

√ 2. At the beginning of the term, take time to review some key points about note-taking and offer some strategies that will work well for your lectures. Sharing examples of well-taken notes is helpful. After one of your lectures, provide a partially completed lecture outline by distributing it in class, placing it on reserve in the library, or putting it on a Web page. Ask the students to complete the outline using their notes. Emphasize the relationship between the outline and the notes they took. If you are aware of a few students who take good notes, privately encourage them to share notes periodically with the L2 students. This can be done formally as a tutorial or informally in partnerships.

√ 3. To assist students with note-taking strategies, identify key vocabulary and new terms on the board. Follow an outline and an orderly progression of ideas. Take steps to make certain that the essential lecture information is easily identified. Use illustrations, charts, graphic organizers, and demonstrations throughout the lecture.

√ 4. Encourage note-taking by allowing students to use their notes on some exams. This strategy works well when asking students to demonstrate an understanding of important concepts, rather than memorized facts. Because many L2 students suffer greatly from test anxiety, being able to use notes at times can be very useful. Consider collecting notes periodically and grading them to emphasize their importance.

√ 5. Concrete examples are necessary for L2 students. It is important to conceptualize main ideas for L2 students within more familiar contexts. Build in redundancy with anecdotes and examples that students can relate to.

√ 6. For longer, more complicated lectures, distribute a handout or put the information on an overhead transparency. Visual aids that illustrate the points being made are helpful for L2 learners. When you write on the board, it is important to write legibly. Many L2 students are not familiar with cursive writing and abbreviations. Check comprehension regularly rather than at the end of the lecture.   *Continued*

√ 7. Encourage L2 students to bring a small audio-cassette recorder to class and record the lectures. After class, they can listen to the lecture as many times as they need to in order to understand the contents of the class lecture.

√ 8. Relate your lecture material to reading assignments. Refer to page numbers in the reading so that there is an alternative source of information to which L2 students can refer for an expansion of the ideas.

√ 9. Modify your normal conversational speech for lectures to make it as comprehensible as possible. Use slower speech, emphasize key words, and enunciate clearly.

√ 10. Use body language to aid comprehension: Make eye contact with all students, emphasize main points through gestures and facial expressions, and highlight major transitions with broad gestures.

√ 11. Reserve time at the end of the lecture to clarify main points. Have the students compare notes in teams. Prepare questions to ask of the entire class.

Figure 6. **Checklist with strategies for more effecive lectures.**

Endnotes

1. This situation is very clearly demonstrated each quarter in an introductory linguistics course I teach. I write a sentence on the board, such as "John walk to the store every day to buy milk and bread." I ask the native English speakers if this sentence is okay. Almost before I finish writing, someone tells me that I have forgotten to put the "s" on the word "walk." They take it so much for granted, that they may not even be aware that leaving the "s" off was purposeful. Omitting the "s" is something native speakers don't often do. When I ask the native speakers why "walk" needs an "s," they usually cannot explain it. "You just do," they say. On the other hand, the second language speakers in the class can tell me the rule right away: a third-person singular subject in the present tense requires an "s" on the verb. The native speakers are not even aware of person or number, so those concepts also have to be explained before the native speakers can understand the rule.

   Because this type of language activity has always been useful in raising language awareness in native English speakers in my introductory linguistics course, it works with faculty and staff as well. A similar set of language problems can be developed to raise language awareness with faculty.

2. Similar checklists can be created for students who are having difficulties coping with heavy reading loads, group work, in-class exams, library research, and so forth.

3. Even though there has been much experimentation with alternative instructional techniques in recent years (Johnson, Johnson, & Holubec, 1994; Stevenson & Stigler, 1992), lectures remain the most popular method of delivering new information in colleges or universities.

Discussion Questions and Activities

1. Of the four student advocacy roles outlined in this chapter (classroom, cultural, language, and academic), which role do you think is most challenging? Why? What can an administrator do to minimize the challenge?

2. In what other ways can a language program administrator function as a student advocate?

3. In this chapter, the author highlights the different student advocacy roles that a language program administrator must play. Can you draw any parallels to the advocacy roles that the adminstrator must play for language program faculty?

4. Name two specific steps that a language program administrator could take to help a student who is experiencing the hostility stage of culture shock.

5. Imagine that you are a language program administrator. A faculty member from the history department calls you to complain about all of the L2 students in his class who cannot speak or write English. You know that all of the L2 students in his class must have scored at least 500 on the TOEFL. You also know that he is a new faculty member. What techniques and strategies would you employ in this situation?

6. Give one clear example of how you would use the classroom "events/behaviors" from this chapter to help an L2 student who is angry with a faculty member. The student has reported that the faculty member embarrassed her in front of the entire class by reprimanding her for never speaking up in class; the teacher made her repeat a response multiple times until she spoke loudly.

7. Create a checklist of strategies to disseminate to interested faculty in one of the following areas of common faculty concern: making textbooks accessible, preparing students for exams, writing exams and quizzes, structuring syllabi, involving students actively in learning, assembling academic information, or modeling the research process. Use what you know about learning in general, and the needs of L2 students in particular, to construct the checklist.

Suggested Readings

Cochran, E. (1992). (Ed.). *Into the academic mainstream: Guidelines for teaching language minority students.* Alexandria, VA: TESOL.

Cochran compiled this handbook with the assistance of an editorial committee from the City University of New York system, in response to numerous requests from faculty for guidance with language minority students who, despite having been declared language "qualified" by the system, still have difficulty academically. Practical suggestions for integrating L2 students into college courses are offered, along with checklists grouped according to pedagogical values.

Snow, M. A., & Kamhi-Stein, L. D. (Eds.). (1996). *Teaching academic literacy skills: Strategies for content faculty*. Los Angeles: California State University, Los Angeles.

This training manual, designed for content-area faculty, was developed with support from the Fund for the Improvement of Postsecondary Education (FIPSE). The exercises and activities presented in the manual were developed for mainstream faculty interested in enhancing their teaching and abilities to reach language minority students. The instructional enhancements provide faculty with means for integrating the teaching of language and critical analysis along with course content, the aim being "to make instruction accessible to language minority students while maintaining or increasing the academic rigor of the courses" (p. v).

Storti, C. (1990). *The art of crossing cultures*. Yarmouth, ME: Intercultural Press.

The author focuses on the basic psychological processes involved in encountering a foreign culture and adapting to it. He suggests a model for making cultural adjustment that language program administrators will find useful. Storti uses a superb sampling of excerpts in literature to make his points.

Chapter 11

OUTREACH ON AND OFF CAMPUS

Rebecca Smith Murdock
University of North Texas

nglish language teaching programs have an ethical, legal, and professional obligation to meet the academic, personal, and psychological needs of
the students they serve (see Althen, 1994a). In addition, they must also
serve the needs of their own communities. Responding to these diverse
needs in a responsible and professional manner involves more than carefully designed English language classroom instruction. ESL students
require a variety of special services, such as housing placement, advice on insurance and
medical services, counseling on immigration matters, help in setting up bank accounts
and securing postal services, information about matriculating into major departments,
and on-campus employment procedural information, to name just a few (Middlebrook,
1991). To address these needs, many language program administrators consider outreach
activities to be essential.

Outreach activities involve going beyond the obvious and visible boundaries of an
organization. English language program outreach may take on a variety of overlapping
functions, including establishing linkages, building bridges, creating partnerships, networking, undertaking collaborative efforts, liaisoning, creating connections, or establishing strategic alliances. However the actual activity is labeled, outreach activities should
arise out of the real needs of ESL students, the institution, and the broader community.

One important function of the language program administrator is to analyze, plan,
and lay the groundwork for outreach activities; establishing relationships and then
maintaining and modifying linkages with on-campus academic and nonacademic units
as well as off-campus contacts are additional responsibilities that are often administrative in scope.

Campus and community outreach opportunities for English language teaching programs are explored here with an initial focus on outreach activities toward academic units
on campus. Suggestions are made for linkages with nonacademic units on campus, along
with a discussion of off-campus community partnership possibilities.

Outreach Linkages With On-Campus Academic Units

The benefits derived from an ESL program's outreach to academic departments and
colleges can be significant, affecting the intellectual and critical thinking abilities of lan-

guage program students in addition to mainstream students and faculty. When ESL programs link up with other academic units on campus, everyone involved develops a more mature sense of self and others (see Bryd, 1986). Because ESL programs rarely have the opportunity to choose or negotiate their academic "home" (see Kaplan, this volume, for further information on the location of ESL programs within their home institutions), most language program administrators try to integrate the program into the academic community by initiating mutually beneficial outreach activities with traditional academic units. Through on-campus outreach, a language program can work toward accomplishing five principle goals:

1. Ensuring that the ESL program demonstrably participates in achieving the institution's mission and goals.

2. Increasing the credibility, viability, and stability of the ESL program.

3. Creating an environment on campus wherein ESL program students, faculty, and staff are seen as essential and valuable campus resources.

4. Making additional and improved resources available to the ESL program.

5. Becoming an integral part of efforts to internationalize the campus and the community in part by promoting culture learning (see Mark, 1994).

These goals can be achieved in a number of ways, including the following nine suggestions for outreach activities with on-campus academic units:

1. Encourage course-to-course linkages. These linkages work well between the ESL program and more traditional academic departments. In most cases, it is not necessary to seek official approval or be involved in too much administrative paper-pushing to create these linkages. Most often arrangements are made with individual faculty members who teach courses that lend themselves to such a liaison. Mainstream students enrolled in, for example, communication, education, and/or TESL programs may benefit from participating in an intercultural communication course offered by the language program itself. (See Maggio & Gay, 1986, for a description of such a course.) Linkages that send language students out into mainstream course settings give foreign language departments, for example, a ready source of native speakers for one-way or two-way conversation partnerships; two-way partnerships, of course, give both participating ESL students and foreign language learners opportunities to practice language outside of the classroom. (See Stoller, Hodges, & Kimbrough, 1995, for guidelines on setting up a conversation partner program.) ESL students might also be called on to give presentations about their home countries in geography, history, political science, and international education courses. This guest speakers concept can be extended to other fields, such as business and hotel restaurant management, with targeted topics.

2. Collaborate with academic departments to establish sheltered or adjunct courses for nonnative speakers. Invite academic departments to work with the ESL department in designing special sections of liberal studies/general education courses that pose extraordinary challenges for nonnative speakers (e.g., English Composition, American National Government, Art History, Introduction to Biology, and Business Law). Staffing may be assumed by the academic department with its own faculty, by the ESL

program, or by both cooperating departments. Because these credit-bearing courses will generate "full-time equivalencies," the cooperating academic department may gain monetarily from the liaison.

3. Negotiate foreign language credit for ESL classes. To obtain an associate or bachelor of arts degree in most U.S. institutions, students must complete a certain number of hours in a foreign language. An ESL program administrator can negotiate with key administrators in the university to have English language study satisfy the foreign language requirement for ESL students. Even though students may not actually receive credit hours toward their degree, when they satisfy the school's English language expectations, they will have also met the foreign language requirement to obtain the A.A. or B.A. degree. This provision gives ESL students greater flexibility in planning their long-term course of study.

4. Establish a campus-wide speakers bureau. The ESL program can publicize the expertise of its faculty so that other faculty members in more traditional departments understand the range of resources available to them. ESL faculty members might be invited to speak about adjusting to living in a foreign country in an anthropology course, about language teaching methodologies in an education class, about diverse educational systems and their impact on society in a sociology class, and about learning strategies in a cognitive psychology class. ESL faculty can also offer their expertise on diversity in the classroom, language-sensitive classrooms, and cross-cultural learning/teaching at orientation sessions for new faculty, new graduate teaching assistants, and new international students (see Byrd, 1988; Gamboa, 1988; Kuhlman, 1988; Sarles, 1988; Steglitz, 1988). Similarly, the ESL program can invite departmental faculty to make special presentations to ESL classes, providing its students with "authentic" listening and note-taking opportunities. Such linkages with regular faculty simultaneously showcase the curriculum, professional work, and expertise of language program faculty as resources available to others on campus.

5. Encourage joint projects with academic units. A variety of projects can be pursued that involve collaborative work with academic units on campus. Academic departments that are writing grants to bring in sponsored international students and scholars can strengthen their proposals by including a well-designed language support program or cultural orientation that will be offered by the ESL program when sponsored students arrive on campus. (See Mickelson, this volume, for more information on grant writing.) The ESL program may want to join forces with another department to produce a special publication or video; language program students can often provide translation services for such projects. In cases where the language program and another department (i.e., a foreign language department or a TESL program) can benefit from shared equipment (such as software, computers, books, or audio-tapes), working together and sharing expenses is an effective way to make limited dollars go further.

6. Become a research site for graduate students and faculty. The ESL program can be a valuable site for research in areas such as Teaching English as a Second Language, Educational Administration, Educational Studies, Bilingual Multicultural Education, Composition and Rhetoric, and Applied Linguistics. The ESL program will need to develop a reasonable and workable policy to receive, evaluate, and accept or reject research proposals that involve the ESL program's students, staff, and faculty so that instruction and the normal workings of the ESL program are not compromised.

7. Become a training site for teachers in training and interns. Practicing teachers in Bilingual Education, Education, Speech Communications, Teaching English as a Second Language, Foreign Languages, Applied Linguistics, and Counseling may need practical experience to supplement their theoretical training. The ESL program can arrange for carefully supervised classes, tutorials, and counseling sessions to enhance program offerings and internshps. Detailed guidelines for intern selection, work expectations, training, supervision, observation, and evaluation must be worked out in advance. ESL programs may also hire graduate assistants who are enrolled in relevant academic departments. Other forms of internships could also be developed with academic departments. For example, communications students might produce educational or promotional videos about the ESL program and its students; other students in the same area may interview and film ESL program personnel or students for a radio or television program. Business management students may wish to organize a recruitment campaign. Computer Science students could be involved in designing administrative or educational software or creating an ESL program homepage on the World Wide Web. Art students may be involved in designing a new language program brochure.

8. Become a campus-wide site for testing and training international teaching assistants (ITAs). Assuming authority and responsibility for designing and implementing a successful ITA program strongly and positively links the ESL program to every department on campus that hires international graduate assistants. (See Constantinides, this volume, for principles governing a successful ITA program and for suggested readings that can guide administrators in establishing and maintaining a practical, efficient, and helpful testing and training program for international teaching assistants; see also Landa, 1988.)

9. Establish a campus-wide language-referral program. The ESL program can make itself accessible to all departments on campus as a referral point for international students, faculty, visiting scholars, or staff who need English-language assistance or who are seeking information about the non-English languages represented in the program. When the ESL program is successful in helping departments solve language-related problems, academic departments will become strong allies of the ESL program and work on its behalf.

Linkages With On-Campus Nonacademic Units

In addition to establishing strong alliances with academic units for the mutual benefit of the language program and the academic units themselves, creating partnerships with nonacademic units is equally important and actually crucial to the physical, fiscal, and administrative survival of the language program. Through outreach to nonacademic units, the ESL program increases resources and problem-solving flexibility and language program students receive additional and improved assistance. Through services provided to nonacademic campus units, the ESL program and its students, faculty, and staff become important campus resources, gaining obvious value, and thus a measure of stability.

The most obvious connections to be made are to the nonacademic offices on campus that are already providing services to matriculated international students and other non-native speakers. This would include the international office and the foreign student advisor's office, if indeed they are separate. No matter how far apart the ESL program and the international office are administratively or physically, the ESL program administrator should try to establish a close relationship because the international office most likely provides services that are important to language program students; these could include issuing I-20s, providing immigration and naturalization counseling, arranging airport pickup, organizing campus orientations, and providing other crucial services to international students. On many campuses, these services are cooperatively managed by the language program and international office.

In addition to this strategic alliance with the international office and foreign student advisor, there are many other possibilities for outreach to nonacademic campus units. The list that follows represents a starting point.

1. Work closely with the public affairs office (PAO) to raise the recognition level of the ESL program on campus. Through the services of this office, announcements of the accomplishments of ESL students, faculty, and staff can be sent to campus and local newspapers as well as to students' home-country newspapers. When critical international events occur that affect students in the ESL program, the PAO can serve as an important disseminator of information. At the same time, ESL students, faculty, and staff comprise a valuable body of experts who can be used by the PAO for advice regarding protocol with foreign visitors, translation services, and valuable intercultural resources. When the PAO understands the important role that an English language program plays on campus, it will be certain to include information on the ESL program in all regular institutional publications, enhancing recruitment for both the college or university and the ESL program. When the PAO needs photos of international students (or a diverse student body) for institutional purposes, the ESL program can arrange for international students to participate in photo sessions.

2. Coordinate efforts with admissions offices. Oftentimes applications for international ESL admissions are processed not by the ESL program but by the campus admissions office; therefore, good communication between the ESL program and the admissions office is crucial. In order to enhance its marketability overseas and its credibility on campus, the ESL program should work with the admissions office to develop a single application form on which international students can choose one of several options: ESL only, ESL followed by college or university admission, or college or university admission only. The language program administrator might also suggest that the ESL program become part of all university admissions recruitment literature and presentations. To facilitate international admissions, the ESL program could provide on-site English language proficiency testing, allowing the university to admit more international students and the ESL program to expand. In other words, if students qualify for admission to the university in every way except for having satisfied the requirement for English language proficiency, they could be admitted conditionally, tested on arrival, provided with academic English language preparation courses, and mainstreamed when they have successfully completed the ESL program or passed a language proficiency exam.

3. Support the athletics office. The ESL program can promote campus athletic events by requesting free tickets to undersold athletic events. While filling empty stadium seats, ESL students benefit in many ways from participating in such campus activities. The ESL program can also support the athletics office by helping provisionally admitted international student athletes to improve their language skills and thereby maintain student status (F-1) and eligibility for sports.

4. Maintain contact with campus information centers. The ESL program needs to keep campus information centers—such as telephone operators, student union information desks, recorded campus events telephone lines, and on-line campus events directories—informed about activities concerning ESL students (e.g., international student orientation sessions, the institutional TOEFL, international food fairs, international club meetings). ESL students can misunderstand postings or face-to-face instructions and end up in the wrong place at the wrong time. Because these information centers are often the first contact for times, dates, and places for such activities, they are usually most appreciative when receiving this key information.

5. Work with computer-center personnel on campus. Most university computer centers provide free or inexpensive computer short courses for staff, faculty, and students. Because access to technology is important for ESL students, the ESL program can make arrangements for advanced ESL students to take these short courses. In addition, language programs that run their own computer labs may depend on computer-center expertise during initial setup or when lab crises occur.

6. Establish good relations with the business office. ESL students often arrive with a single, large bank draft made out to either themselves, the ESL program, or the university. An international bank draft can take up to 2 weeks to clear. In the meantime, the student is left with no available funds. Good relations with the business office can result in the student's receiving a partial cash advance for immediate living expenses. Because ESL students often experience delays receiving their tuition money and personal expense checks from their sponsors or families, cordial relations with the business office can also result in, for example, extensions for tuition payments and perhaps a partial cash advance for the student's most pressing needs.

7. Collaborate with the counseling center. ESL students are often in need of counseling for test anxiety, culture shock, roommate conflicts, and personal problems that they bring with them from home. Graduate students in counseling or clinical psychology can meet course and practicum requirements by organizing special counseling sessions for ESL students. In this way, ESL students can receive counseling free or for a minimal charge.

8. Negotiate with food services. Adjusting to food in a foreign country is difficult; adjusting to cafeteria food can be almost impossible for some students. It is important that the ESL program act as a liaison between the cafeteria and the students. Cafeteria personnel should understand the dietary needs of the international student body, many of whom live in campus housing facilities. Individual student complaints may not go far in making changes, but the ESL program administrator can be successful in negotiating for students. Asian students, for example, appreciate rice and fruit served three times daily. The university will want to meet the needs of international students to keep on-campus housing units full and to provide food services for as many clients as possible.

9. Cooperate with campus fitness facilities. Participating in campus fitness and sports activities is important for students' psychological and physical health. When students are happy and healthy, they are more successful academically. The ESL program can help students create intramural sports teams, such as soccer, baseball, volleyball, and tennis. Intramural teams also provide international students with an opportunity to interact with native speakers and to learn firsthand about the culture of playing sports in the United States.

10. Work with the grants and contracts development office. The development office regularly scans the congressional record for Requests for Proposals (RFPs). Development offices often have the impression that there is a lot of money out there that goes begging because faculty members are not willing to pursue it. If the ESL program administrator is willing to engage in grant writing, the program's reputation will immediately be enhanced. The knowledge and experience of professional staff in a development office can aid ESL programs in writing successful grant proposals and administering them correctly. Grants bring financial benefits to the ESL program and the campus at large.

11. Develop a relationship with the health center. Making major life changes can put anyone at a health risk. ESL students often experience more change than any other group of students. A wise language program administrator will develop a good relationship with the health center because more than likely, at some point during the year, one of the students will need the assistance of the health center and a medical doctor at an inconvenient time. The health center can be a valuable referral source, passing on the names of doctors who are experienced in working with nonnative speakers. In turn, the ESL program can assist the health center by contacting students and even placing holds on student records if, for example, a student has not bought the required health insurance or has not paid for medical services.

12. Collaborate with the on-campus housing office. A good relationship with the housing office is invaluable. Most international students request to have U.S. roommates so that they can practice their English. The housing office will need to coordinate these requests, keeping records of U.S. students who want international roommates. The housing office can also be asked to keep extra sets of blankets, sheets, and pillows for students who arrive late at night, after stores have closed, and without having brought their own bedding. The ESL program can act as a referral for campus dormitories by regularly including housing information in ESL program application packets. In addition, the language program can act as a sort of clearinghouse, benefiting both the ESL program and the housing office. Students are often required to sign a contract with an on-campus residence hall for an entire year, and there is a severe penalty for breaking the contract unless they are able to sell it to someone else. Because new ESL students are admitted at each intake date, they are candidates for buying midyear housing contracts.

13. Network with campus library personnel. It is important for the ESL program to work closely with campus library facilities. Nurture relationships with librarians who will be willing to conduct special introductory sessions for ESL students on how to use the library (e.g., operate the computer catalog, find books, check out materials, use microfiche and microfilm). ESL faculty can provide librarians with copies of the language-sensitive worksheets that they have created for library assignments as a guide to working with nonnative speakers. ESL program administrators can write letters to participating library personnel thanking them for their special attention (sending copies of the letters to senior level administrators). Such actions are much appreciated by the library staff, as their job is to provide library services for the entire campus.

14. Build linkages with the registrar's office. Establishing an excellent working relationship with the registrar is important. ESL students frequently need copies of important documents because obtaining a duplicate original in some countries is nearly impossible. The ESL program administrator can lay the groundwork for such requests, working

with the registrar to release original transcripts to a student who legitimately needs them. If the registrar's office is also in charge of space for the university, a cooperative working relationship is critical. As the ESL program changes and expands, additional classroom space may become critical. If personnel in this office understand the unique needs of the language program, they can often allocate space that is not appropriate for larger classes but might work for smaller ESL classes.

15. Maintain contact with campus media. The campus newspaper and radio and television stations can be used to educate mainstream faculty and staff and U.S. students about the goals and benefits of international education. Articles that promote culture learning and the value of diversity are essential. The campus newspaper might be willing to assign the ESL program a regular column. The column could feature articles about students, their home-country celebrations, holidays for the month, and international geography quizzes. Publicity for and stories about international activities on campus (or in the community) can be featured by the campus newspaper as well. Requests for home-stay families and announcements about conversation partner programs can be publicized for maximum outreach. The campus radio station may agree to a weekly spot sponsored by the ESL program. The program could feature popular music from different countries, as well as interviews with international students who have unique and interesting backgrounds. For its revenue-generating activities, such as an international festival and an international film series, the ESL program could also purchase advertising space from the newspaper. (See Jenks, this volume, for additional ideas for promoting the language program through campus media.)

16. Create a partnership with the campus testing center. An ESL program has many testing needs (e.g., TOEFL, TWE, TSE, SAT, ACT, GRE, GMAT). A good relationship with the campus testing center can lead to more flexible and effective student placement and registration procedures. Tests can often be administered and scored by testing office personnel, releasing ESL faculty from these responsibilities. The ESL program and the testing center can share exam fees so that the administration of tests is revenue generating for both. The ESL program needs to work closely with the testing center in posting the dates of relevant tests and making the information readily available to ESL students.

17. Work with the alumni office. In coordination with the alumni office, the ESL program can set up a useful database about international students with information solicited from graduating students. After asking for permission to access this database, the language program can use it to track former students and maintain contact with them. Language program alumni can be sent ESL program newsletters, college calendars, holiday cards, and yearly update letters. Alumni contacts such as these often result in contributions to the college. The ESL program might work with the alumni office to set up an ESL scholarship fund for these potential donations.

18. Network with the campus study abroad office. The ESL program can provide the office with a list of names of international students who might serve as contacts for U.S. students planning to study abroad. These same international students might be contacted to give an oral presentation or to present a slide show to interested study abroad applicants. Nurturing a cooperative relationship with the study abroad office might lead to new ESL students or new student groups for special language programs.

Off-Campus Outreach

Off-campus outreach can take many forms. Nowhere is this more aptly demonstrated than in NAFSA's (1994) *Model International Student Involvement Programs* and Popham's (1996) *The Resource Book: Sample Materials for Community Program Developers in International Education*. Off-campus outreach undertaken by an ESL program can enhance the experiences of ESL students with U.S. language and culture while also enhancing the multicultural experiences of participants from the community. In general, ESL students, faculty, and staff can contribute in three ways to the community. They can provide language services, they can supply cross-cultural resources, and they can raise local awareness about the positive financial impact of the ESL population on the community. These outreach activities, if structured with sensitivity and care, can lead to enhanced visibility for the language program in the community.

Language Services

Off-campus outreach can provide valuable language services to the community. Five possible language-related outreach activities are outlined below.

1. Offer translation services. The ESL program can coordinate important language translation services to the community, with an emphasis on providing translators when necessary to local hospitals, law enforcement agencies, and courts. The ESL program can also act as a broker for less urgent language translation needs, matching students to various translation jobs (at the chamber of commerce, popular tourist sites, local hotels, publishers), negotiating fees, setting deadlines, and following up. Translation services such as these not only serve important community needs but they also supply ESL students with experiential language learning opportunities and occasional supplemental income. (See Beck & Simpson, 1993, for a discussion of related voluntary community service and its relation to language learning.)

2. Arrange for tutorials in the public schools. Many K–12 schools with ESL students welcome tutors for their new students at the beginning levels. The tutors work with the new students for 1–2 hours a day for the first few weeks, explaining classroom procedures and processes in the native language. The young ESL students are able to ask questions and seek clarification in their native language. The native language tutor does not teach ESL but rather acts as a link between the public school teacher and the newcomer to the school. Students from a nearby college or university language program can volunteer for the tutorial project as a service to the community.

3. Develop continuing education courses. Advanced ESL students and graduates can teach courses in the college's Division of Continuing Education or in a local adult education center. Topics for the courses could be Japanese flower arranging, origami, martial arts, regional cooking, and survival language skills for the traveler. Such courses are normally popular, if well advertised. ESL students benefit from contact with native speakers from the community, gain confidence through sharing their expertise, and sometimes earn money for their efforts if federal regulations allow it.

4. Create a workplace ESL program. ESL programs can offer special workplace English courses for non-English-speaking community members. A special rate can be set to make the program affordable for individuals who want language training but cannot

afford it. The ESL program can contact local businesses, send out flyers, and create an easy system for registration. Such programs go a long way toward establishing positive visibility for the program.

5. Set up a pen pal program. Many elementary schools are interested in participating in an international pen pal program. Usually there are more teachers and classes who want to participate than the program can accommodate. Pen pal programs work best when they are short term and limited in scope. ESL students agree to participate for one quarter, for example, and write five letters to their young pen pals. The program works best when ESL students receive some general guidelines regarding giving information about one's home culture and asking questions of one's young pen pal, and suggestions for topics for the first letter (e.g., schools in your country, clothes, food, family life, and so forth).

Cross-Cultural Resources

ESL programs can create linkages with the community by providing cultural resources through a variety of activities:

1. Organize performance programs. Local clubs, civic and social groups, public schools, retirement centers, church groups, and other community organizations are always looking for interesting educational programs. Some ESL programs have created credit-bearing ESL courses in which ESL students prepare and later conduct presentations to the community about their customs and cultures. The quality of such programs improves when ESL faculty are assigned to provide oversight as part of their workload, scheduling presentations, organizing transportation, and arranging for music and technological support. Sponsoring groups are usually willing to write letters about student performances to senior level administrators or to local media, enhancing the reputation of the ESL program and the college at large.

2. Set up a homestay program. Many ESL students request homestay information when they apply for admission to a language program. In a homestay, ESL students live with a U.S. family and pay room and board. Homestay programs can be beneficial for everyone involved. They provide ESL students with opportunities for valuable interpersonal interactions, language practice, and insights into the host culture. Participating U.S. families benefit by learning firsthand about another language, culture, and country. The intercultural exchange that naturally occurs through a homestay program prepares U.S. children for the ever-changing world and global economy. Of course, the ESL program benefits from homestay programs as well if the program is well organized, with an ESL staff person assigned to oversee the program, place students with families, set fair amounts for room and board, and act as a mediator and facilitator. Because homestays are so popular, the ESL program is perceived as meeting student and community needs simultaneously.

3. Sponsor an international festival. Perhaps the most visible ESL program community event is an international festival, featuring food, games, and activities in a bazaar-type atmosphere. International fairs are usually extremely popular with the community, serving to whet the appetite and create a desire to learn more about other cultures and customs. The festival involves ESL students in a community-building opportunity. Students plan the menu, cook and serve the food, talk to people, make new friends, and

work together. For the festival to be successful, it is important for an ESL staff person to establish a budget and provide oversight for the festival.

4. Create networks with host families. Many U.S. families are interested in international students but feel they are not yet ready to act as homestay families. A host-family program provides U.S. families with opportunities to get to know ESL students and to include them in a variety of family activities. Host families can invite students to dinner, movies, and special events; to stay for the weekend; or to accompany them on short trips. The host family can be involved to a greater or lesser degree depending on their own comfort level. Many host families end up becoming homestays. Families, students, and the ESL program benefit in much the same way as with the homestay program.

5. Network with the local police department. The legal system and the culture of law enforcement offices in the United States confuse and frighten many international students. In addition, law enforcement officials often lack experience with the students' cultures and customs and can misinterpret students' actions and behavior. The ESL program can act as an important link between the police and the ESL students, explaining the culture and customs of each group to the other. The ESL program can introduce the police department to the NAFSA video *A Little Street Wisdom*[1] which can sensitize the police to the fears that international students have and which can be included in orientation sessions facilitated by the local or campus police.

Economic Impact on the Local Community

Another contribution of the ESL program to the community comes from the money spent by the international students in the area. ESL program administrators can inform the community of the economic impact made by international students by conducting a small study to determine approximately how much is spent by international students in the local area annually, or by using information provided in the NAFSA advocacy information packet (specifically the "Economic Impact at the State and Local Levels" statement, which reveals the collective financial contribution made by foreign students attending institutions of higher education).

Outreach by the ESL program administrator to local businesses can make their interactions with international students more efficient and more cordial. The ESL program administrator can negotiate for simplified forms, group advising, and designated personnel to handle international students at the Social Security office, police departments, hospitals, the driver's license office, local banks, doctors' offices, insurance companies, apartment complexes, furniture stores, rental agencies, telephone and utilities companies, car dealerships, and other local businesses that regularly receive ESL program students as customers. Obviously, these arrangements can be mutually beneficial. Cordial working relationships often lead to business sponsorship of ESL program activities, contribution of gifts and prizes for special events, and ESL program scholarships.

If the ESL program administrator is successful in publicizing the positive impact of international students on the local economy, the result will be increased goodwill and assistance from many community resources. The chamber of commerce, industrial development organizations, and city and state government offices may cooperate in creating and providing attractive brochures about local history, sights, activities, and special events for inclusion in language program recruitment mailings. ESL program students may be invited to participate in community celebrations and activities. Outreach to other service providers in the community can lead to easier access to services by ESL program students. Representatives from community agencies can be included in language program orientation sessions to formalize and institutionalize the linkages.

Conclusion

Klineberg and Hull's (1979) landmark study of international students' experiences documented the positive relationship between the students' contact with members of the host culture and their improved psychological adjustment, satisfaction, and general success. Outreach initiated by an ESL program administrator can increase students' contact with campus and community members, improve services provided to students, and promote campus and community opportunities for internationalization. As ESL student needs are met, campus and community needs for services, information, and a broader world view are also met. ESL program administrators must commit time and energy to creating linkages, bridges, partnerships, networks, collaboration, liaison, and alliances—whatever label is used—to undertake and accomplish successful outreach both on and off campus.

Endnotes

1. This video, written and directed by Gail Kellersberger, can be ordered through NAFSA: Association of International Educators, 1875 Connecticut Avenue, NW, Suite 1000, Washington, DC 20009-5728.

Discussion Questions and Activities

1. Language program administrators have many and varied responsibilities. Why should on-campus and off-campus outreach be considered a priority?

2. If a language program administrator has just now decided to make a commitment to creating on-campus linkages, should the administrator begin with establishing partnerships with academic units or nonacademic units? Provide a rationale for your answer.

3. What are some of the problems that a language program administrator should anticipate when undertaking collaborative efforts with off-campus community organizations? How can these potential problems be avoided?

4. The author has listed numerous strategies for creating partnerships on and off campus. Can you think of any other ways of creating strategic alliances that will be mutually beneficial?

5. Assume that you are an administrator of a new campus-based ESL program. Choose five on-campus linkages and five off-campus linkages to establish first and explain your rationale for selecting each one.

6. Imagine that you have just been hired as a new ESL program administrator. Design a half-page advertisement to promote your program. In this advertisement, the main focus and key selling point is to be the strong connection between the ESL program and the local community.

7. Imagine that as a director of a university-based ESL program, you have just successfully negotiated with the History Department to set up a sheltered ESL course in American National Government. The course is designed for graduates of the ESL program and will carry university credit. Note that some of the parties involved may see this sheltered course in a negative light. What concerns can you anticipate from the international students, the academic department, the ESL program, other departments on campus, and American students?

Suggested Readings

Althen, G. (Ed.). (1994b). *Learning across cultures.* Washington, DC: NAFSA: Association of International Educators.

This edited volume provides an overview of issues related to cross-cultural communication and explores cultural barriers, culture shock, and models of cultural adjustment. Of particular interest to language program administrators concerned with on- and off-campus outreach are two chapters: (a) the Althen chapter, "Cultural differences on campus," which provides detailed explanations of differences in culturally based assumptions that people from different countries bring into typical campus situations, and (b) the Mark chapter which describes a variety of approaches undertaken by Michigan State University to internationalize the campus experience of U.S. and international students.

NAFSA: Association of International Educators. (1994). *Model international student involvement programs.* Washington, DC: Author.

This volume encourages the development of innovative international and U.S. student involvement and linkage programs and their replication on other campuses. A variety of funded and completed projects are listed; detailed reports of the purpose, design, and evaluation of the projects are available from NAFSA. (The volume is available from the Cooperative Grants Program, NAFSA: Association of International Educators, 1875 Connecticut Avenue, NW, Suite 1000, Washington, DC 20009-5728.)

Popham, M. (1996). *The resource book: Sample materials for community program developers in international education.* Washington, DC: NAFSA: Association of International Educators.

In this useful handbook, the author compiles information, sample documents and forms, and resource suggestions collected from programs throughout the United States. Material is organized into four categories: recruitment and organization of volunteers; host family, homestay, speakers bureau, and spouse programs; receptions and dinners; and newsletters.

Part IV

THE LANGUAGE PROGRAM
ADMINISTRATOR AS ORGANIZER

Chapter 12
THEORY AND PRACTICE IN
LANGUAGE PROGRAM ORGANIZATION DESIGN
Joseph O. Davidson and Joy S. Tesh

Chapter 13
PERSONNEL MATTERS
Joann M. Geddes and Doris R. Marks

Chapter 14
THE LANGUAGE PROGRAM BUDGET:
FINANCIAL PLANNING AND MANAGEMENT OF RESOURCES
John J. Staczek

Chapter 15
TIME MANAGEMENT PRINCIPLES
FOR LANGUAGE PROGRAM ADMINISTRATORS
Mary Ann Christison and Fredricka L. Stoller

Chapter 12

THEORY AND PRACTICE IN LANGUAGE PROGRAM ORGANIZATION DESIGN

Joseph O. Davidson and Joy S. Tesh
University of Houston

ptimal organization design and proven organizing techniques are critical to the smooth operation of any language program. Seasoned program administrators know only too well the damaging consequences that can result from organizational breakdown—consequences that range from unpleasant (e.g., a heated exchange between an administrator and a faculty member who does not like the disorganized way the administrator runs meetings) to disastrous (e.g., a decision made by several sponsors to remove their students from the program because of organizational breakdowns that result in anticipated services not being provided).

As the administration and curricula of language programs have become more technologically sophisticated, as students and sponsors have become more discriminating, and as teacher training programs have begun introducing administrative concerns into their curricula, the need for organization design models and demonstrated organizational techniques relevant to language programs has grown. Two contrasting models of organization design are discussed here, as well as optimal parameters for the design of language programs and organizing techniques for tasks faced by program administrators.

Language Program Organization Design

Gibson, Ivancevich, and Donnelly (1991) define organization design as the superstructure within which the work of an organization occurs. That superstructure is built by managerial decisions that delineate the number and types of jobs in the organization and the processes that coordinate, control, and link them, such as authority relationships, communication networks, and specific planning and organizing techniques. The language program administrator is involved to one degree or another not only in (a) building or repairing such a superstructure (e.g., defining the program's organizational structure, writing job descriptions, rewriting job descriptions to meet changing realities, and establishing committees and specifying their charges), but also in (b) running the day-to-day administrative operations that require specific organizational techniques (e.g., keeping records, tracking students' progress, communicating program policies and goals to faculty and staff, chairing committees and running meetings, delegating tasks, making decisions,

managing faculty and staff, and building morale). Both tasks are key to the optimal management of a language program. It is important to note, however, that effective organizational techniques can flourish only when the superstructure is hospitable—that is, when
the program has an appropriate organization design.

In this century, managers and organization design theorists and researchers have contributed to a considerable body of literature that contains numerous and conflicting opinions on optimal superstructures (Lee, Luthans, & Olson, 1982; Likert, 1967; Weber,
1925/1947). The program administrator who faces the necessities of building a program
superstructure from the ground up, or repairing that superstructure periodically—to keep
up with new technology and new curricula, to keep pace with the shifting priorities of the
marketplace, or to confront the exigencies of a tighter budget or the luxuries of a more
plentiful budget—is certainly at no loss for ideas. Although research has been based on
optimal design structures for business, government, the military, and the church, there is
much that is applicable to the design of a language program, whether its administrative
setting is a university, community college, or private language school.

The two organization designs presented here have received considerable theoretical
and practical attention in the literature, but surprisingly, there is little agreement on the
terms used to designate them. Following Burns and Stalker (1961) and Gibson,
Ivancevich, and Donnelly (1991), the terms *mechanistic* and *organic* are used here. These
terms are descriptive of the variables in each model and are suggestive of the significant
differences between them.

Mechanistic Model

The mechanistic model, articulated by Weber (1925/1947) and others (Fayol,
1916/1949; Metcalf & Urwick, 1940; Mooney, 1947; Urwick, 1944), argues for the theoretical and practical advantages of a bureaucratic (mechanistic) organizational structure.
Weber refers to bureaucracy as a particular way to organize collective activities that stresses the need for authority, hierarchies of control, and an explicit chain of command. A
bureaucratic organization is one that operates with machine-like precision to accomplish
its objectives.

The mechanistic model of organization design is characterized by the following features: First, jobholders specialize in particular tasks and become experts at those tasks.
Management then holds the jobholders responsible for the effective performance of those
tasks. Second, the performance of all jobs is based on a system of rules to ensure uniformity and coordination among tasks. With such a system, managers eliminate uncertainty
in task performance resulting from individual differences. Third, each jobholder reports to
one, and only one, manager. Each manager is granted authority from the top of the organizational hierarchy. The chain of command, from top to bottom, is unbroken. Fourth,
jobholders relate to other jobholders and clients in an impersonal, formal manner; they
maintain a social distance with subordinates and clients. This eliminates personalities and
favoritism from the efficient accomplishment of organizational goals. Finally, hiring is
based on technical qualifications that are determined by examination or that are guaranteed by diplomas certifying the appropriate training, or both. Promotions are based on
seniority and achievement. Jobholders are protected against arbitrary dismissal.
Employment is viewed as a lifelong career and jobholders feel loyalty toward the organi-

zation. (See Weber, 1925/1947; and Gibson, Ivancevich, & Donnelly, 1991.) According to Weber (1925/1947),

> The bureaucratic type of administrative organization … is, from a purely technical point of view, capable of attaining the highest degree of efficiency and is in this sense formally the most rational known means of carrying out imperative control over human beings. It is superior to any other form in precision, in stability, in the stringency of its discipline, and in its reliability. It thus makes possible a particularly high degree of calculability of results for the heads of the organization and for those acting in relation to it. It is finally superior both in intensive efficiency and in the scope of its operations, and is formally capable of application to all kinds of administrative tasks. (p. 337)

The design of many U.S. language programs today contains aspects of the mechanistic model. Here are some examples:

1. Many programs value specialization; that is, they prefer that teachers specialize in one or two particular levels and skills. For example, a teacher may be assigned level-three reading and level-three writing, teaching those classes, and only those classes, each term, and becoming an expert in those areas.

2. Many programs provide teachers not only with a course curriculum, but also with a class syllabus outlining which pages and exercises are to be covered each day. The more detailed the syllabus, the more uniformity there will be across each level in the program. Administrators in large programs, in programs that make use of graduate teaching assistants, or in multiple-site programs may find this advantageous because it eliminates uncertainty in teaching performance resulting from individual differences, professional inexperience, or the absence of propinquity.

3. Some programs have explicit chains of command. All communication in such programs is vertical. If moving upward, the communication must pass through each superior in the chain of command until it reaches the appropriate level. If moving downward, it must pass through each subordinate in like manner.

4. Many programs have hiring, promotion, and dismissal policies that match those of the mechanistic model. They hire based on professional qualifications such as degree, field, length and type of professional experience, and letters of recommendation; they promote based on seniority, program contributions, and professional achievements; and they terminate only after due process has occurred.

Organic Model

The second organization design of interest to language program administrators is the organic model. This design, as explicated by Likert (1967), holds that the most productive organization is the one that maximizes flexibility and adaptability, encourages complete confidence and trust between superiors and subordinates, and taps a wide range of human motivations to achieve organizational goals. Communication flows in all directions, both vertically and laterally. Teamwork is substantial, and decision making and control functions are shared widely throughout the organization. Training resources provided by the organization are outstanding as they seek to build upon the value and worth of each employee. The organic organization seeks to provide a supportive environment in which human resources are valued and personal growth and responsibility are stressed. Such an organization ensures

> a maximum probability that in all interactions and in all relationships within the organization, each member, in the light of his background, values, desires, and expectations, will view the experience as supportive and one which builds and maintains his sense of personal worth and importance. (Likert, 1967, p. 47)

Aspects of the organic model of organization design are also found in many U.S. language programs. Here are some examples:

1. Numerous program administrators value flexibility and adaptability; they expect their teachers to teach most, if not all, skills in most, if not all, levels. Thus, they encourage a range of professional development activities for each faculty member. Level, skill, or content area specialization is viewed as an obstacle not only to the professional growth of the specialist, but also to other teachers who may wish to teach such classes, but cannot because they are not the "experts."

2. Many language programs provide opportunities for professional training that build up the value and worth of each faculty and staff member. They hold timely, well-organized, and appropriately focused in-service or residency meetings with internal or outside experts. They provide travel funding to relevant local, regional, and national professional meetings. They provide release time for materials development. They encourage research, publications, and grant proposal writing.

3. Numerous programs allow for communication not only vertically, but also laterally through cooperative teaching, peer coaching and observation, and joint writing and piloting of new materials.

4. A large number of programs value teamwork and have established a committee system so that decision making and control functions are shared widely throughout the program. Committee recommendations may be advisory or binding. Areas of concern include long-range planning, curricular and personnel matters, professional development, and program marketing, to name a few.

Likert (1967) profiles the organic organization using eight characteristics. Table 1 lists those characteristics and how they are realized in both the organic and the mechanistic language program.[1] It is Likert's view that administrators in organic programs focus on building and maintaining a highly effective and highly motivated human organization to achieve desired results, whereas those in mechanistic programs emphasize procedures and outcomes and closely monitor adherence to standard operating procedures and achievement of designated objectives. In Likert's view, Weber's vision of the ideal organization design—that of a smooth-running, machine-like bureaucracy—is fundamentally flawed because it downplays the significance of human motivation and employee attitudes. Where Weber wants to control human beings, Likert wants to motivate them. Where Weber favors job specialization to achieve organizational goals,

Likert urges flexibility and adaptability. Where Weber proposes the centralization of all decision making, Likert emphasizes the importance of employee input.

Optimal Model for Language Programs

How can these differing visions of optimal organization design be applied to the organization of language programs? Is one design ideal for all administrative settings and for all program sizes, or is the better design dependent on the setting and the size? Are the mechanistic and organic designs located on a continuum, or are they mutually exclusive? The information in Table 1 would seem to indicate that the models are mutually exclusive and that the organic model is the more desirable. Neither conclusion is justified.

Table 1. **Profile of Language Program Organizational Characteristics**

Characteristics	Organic model	Mechanistic model
1. Level of confidence and trust in program leadership by faculty/staff	Faculty/staff feel free to discuss problems with program administrators, who in turn seek faculty/staff input.	Faculty/staff, fearing sanctions, do not feel free to discuss problems with program administrators.
2. Range of motives tapped by program leadership to achieve program goals	Administrators tap a full range of motives including economic and noneconomic (desire for status, affiliation, and achievement; desire for new experiences; and motivations arising from group goals). Faculty/staff attitudes are strongly favorable toward the language program and its goals.	Administrators tap only physical security, economic needs, and, to a lesser degree, desire for status. Teacher attitudes toward the language program are generally not favorable.
3. Direction of communication flow; degree of information accuracy	The direction of flow is both vertical (up and down) and lateral. This multidirectional flow promotes openness and accuracy and discourages information distortion.	The direction of flow is down the chain of command. The information can end up distorted, inaccurate, and viewed with suspicion by faculty/staff.
4. Degree of centralization of decision making	Decision making is shared by administrators and faculty/staff. Both participate to affect program policies, curricula, and activities. Committee decisions may be advisory or binding.	Decision making is restricted to the administrator(s). Faculty/staff have little or no input into program policies, curricula, and activities.

Continued

Table 1. (Continued)

Characteristics	Organic model	Mechanistic model
5. Degree of faculty/ staff participation in goal setting	A range of participatory methods is used to solicit faculty/staff input on program goals: committees, surveys, informal interviews, and program self-studies. The input may be advisory or binding.	Program administrator or higher authority (department chair, college dean, or corporate CEO) sets program goals. Faculty/staff do not provide input.
6. Degree of control throughout the program	The control function is dispersed. Faculty/staff, along with program administrators, are involved in problem solving. Performance appraisals improve communication, generate mutually established goals, provide feedback, encourage development, and are the basis for fair rewards. Appraisals tend to be complete and accurate.	The control function is centralized with the administrator (or higher authority). Performance appraisals tend to be punitive and are used for "policing." They are usually incomplete and often inaccurate. Administrators emphasize the fixing of blame for mistakes.
7. Degree and nature of interactions between program leadership and faculty/staff	Extensive, collegial interaction exists between program administrators and faculty/staff. There is a high degree of confidence and trust.	Little interaction exists between the program administrators and faculty/ staff. There is a mutual lack of commitment and sometimes even fear and distrust on the part of faculty/ staff.
8. Degree of commitment by program administrators to provide for the professional development of faculty/staff through in-service training, workshops, conferences, release time, and so forth	Program administrators have a strong commitment to human resource development and actively pursue it.	Program administrators have a low commitment to human resource development.

(Adapted from Likert, 1967, pp. 197–211)

Most optimally designed language programs, if not all, have features of both the organic and the mechanistic models. The particular mix in each case depends on administrative setting and size. For example, administrators in programs that depend heavily on graduate teaching assistants or part-time, non-benefits-eligible instructors to staff classes are likely to use more mechanistic organizing techniques than organic. On the other hand, administrators who work only, or mostly, with full-time professionals with graduate degrees in hand are likely to employ more organic organizing techniques than mechanistic. If too many mechanistic techniques are used with degreed professionals, or if too many organic techniques are used in programs with mostly graduate teaching assistants or part-time, non-benefits-eligible staff, the program will have trouble. Graduate teaching assistants, for example, do not typically have the professional experience to share decision-making responsibility with the program administrator; part-time instructors do not typically have the time or the commitment to be so involved. On the other hand, most degreed professionals expect program governance to be shared. The administrator who cuts professional faculty/staff out of the decision-making loop, even if the input is only advisory, will inevitably create unrest, unfavorable attitudes, low morale, and unending confrontations.

Program size also affects program design. A small program may have a few part-time teachers with only one administrator who is involved with teaching as well as administrative responsibilities; in this scenario, specialization becomes infeasible, and flexibility is indispensable. It is axiomatic that the smaller the program, the fewer the design options.

Optimal language program organization design comes down to this: Consistent with administrative setting and program size, the program administrator makes use of a number of participatory methods with faculty and staff, provides a supportive environment in which human resources are valued and personal growth and responsibility are stressed, and employs, to the extent possible, organizing techniques that reflect these principles. When administrators focus on building and repairing program superstructures using these guidelines, faculty and staff attitudes generally will be favorable, organizational breakdowns should be minimal, and job satisfaction, especially the administrator's, will be remarkable.

Organizational Responsibilities

Language program administration encompasses three types of administrative tasks: technical, human, and conceptual. Examples of technical tasks might be computerizing the program's record keeping, creating program budgets, recruiting new students, or keeping in touch with national or international academic organizations; human tasks could include building faculty and staff morale or fostering a teamwork environment with careful hiring, orientation, and assignments; and conceptual tasks would be time management or planning and implementing a program self-study (Katz, 1974/1983; Pennington, 1985). Pennington (1985) concludes that the ability to handle technical tasks is most essential at lower levels of administration (administrative assistant, office manager, or information systems specialist), the ability to deal with conceptual tasks is more important at higher levels (associate director or director), and an understanding of organizational skills for human tasks is needed at all levels. In a survey of 28 directors of AAIEP (American Association of Intensive English Programs) member programs, Pennington & Xiao (1990) found that the administrative tasks considered most critical were either human or conceptual. The least important tasks were technical. The perceived importance of human and conceptual tasks squares nicely with characteristics of the organic design.

Language program administrators must have the skills to deal with a variety of tasks, including keeping records, running meetings, establishing committees, conducting a program self-study, and improving communication. The organizing techniques discussed here reflect many of the organization design principles mentioned above. Emphasis is placed on making use of a number of participatory methods to solicit faculty and staff input on program goals and policies, and providing a supportive environment for personal growth and responsibility.

Keeping Records

It would appear that record keeping is a purely technical task in which program personnel gather a large amount of data each term from application forms, immigration documents, placement and diagnostic tests, student progress reports, revenue reports, and a variety of other sources. Administrative assistants, office managers, information systems specialists, or student office assistants file the information or enter it into a computer, retrieve it when needed, and "massage" it to the specifications of a higher level administrator. Office personnel who are familiar with vendors' products and costs can make informed recommendations for the purchase of hardware and software appropriate to program record-keeping needs. All of these technical tasks, done properly, can result in timely and accurate reports for program managers (Davidson, 1984).

However, the reports are useful only if the program administrator understands the purpose and value of the data being collected, and knows how to use them to facilitate critical decision making. From this perspective, record keeping is partly a conceptual task. If data are collected and never used, employee effort is wasted. For example, why enter a student's high school or college transcript into a computer data base if grade point average is not a program admission requirement? Data can always be collected for future research purposes, but program administrators should weigh that possibility against program costs for data collection and storage.

Program directors should meet with office personnel on a regular basis to make sure that appropriate data are being collected and stored in approved ways. Such meetings should include updates on new federal, state, and institutional mandates that affect the language program and that require additional records or the submission of additional reports. As new legislation is passed, as new technologies come on the market, and as program priorities shift, program record keeping will need to keep pace. Staying abreast of these changes requires a dynamic programming environment in which computer software is periodically modified and enhanced to provide the requisite reports. Assembling a qualified and dependable office staff, accepting their input, and working together are essential to professional information management.

To be effective in critical decision making, program administrators must receive timely and useful reports that are based on up-to-date and accurate data. The diversity of language program administrative settings, the range of program offerings, and the differing levels of information management sophistication among language programs make it difficult to formulate a detailed list of records to be kept and reports to be generated that are common to all programs. A brief, sample list might include financial bookkeeping (revenue and expenditures), application counts, enrollment forecasts (Mead, Davidson, & Hanna, 1986), student placement, class schedules and rosters, registration no-shows and walk-ins, student demographic data, and student course evaluations.

Another matter of some concern is the confidentiality of records. The Family Educational Rights and Privacy Act (i.e., the Buckley Amendment) protects a student's records from disclosure without prior consent unless the information requested constitutes directory information, which includes, but is not limited to, name, address, telephone listing, date and place of birth, current class schedule, and dates of program attendance. Information concerning daily attendance, classroom behavior, academic progress, or personal problems may not be released to the public (including sponsors) unless the student agrees.

Students need to indicate whether or not they give permission to the program to (a) release only directory information, (b) release no information at all (including directory information), or (c) release all information. This can be accomplished by having students sign an "Authorization to Release Student Information" form indicating their preferences, and then placing the forms in a notebook conveniently located in the language program office. Program personnel should refer to that notebook before any directory information on a particular student is given out to the public. It should also be checked upon receipt of a sponsor's request for information concerning a student's academic progress, class attendance, and so forth. In all cases, a student's stated preference regarding the release of directory and personal information must be respected. If no signed form is on file for a given student, no directory information for that student should be released to the public.

Running Meetings

Teachers and administrators in most language programs bring outstanding backgrounds in education, travel, and teaching to the programs in which they work. They represent differing points of view and are most often articulate and quite willing to express strong opinions. They usually represent the best in human resources and deserve the opportunity to participate in program governance and decision making. Organizing adventurous people who are passionate about their work for an efficient meeting can be a challenging and exhilarating experience, but leading such a meeting is not an exercise for the faint-hearted. Keeping in mind the main functions of a meeting will help. Jay (1976/1983) identifies six such functions:

1. In the simplest and most basic way, a meeting defines the team, the group or the unit. Those present belong to it; those absent do not. Everyone is able to look around and perceive the whole group and sense the collective identity of which he or she forms a part.

2. A meeting is the place where the group revises, updates, and adds to what it knows *as a group.*

3. A meeting helps every individual understand both the collective aim of the group and the way in which his own and everyone else's work can contribute to the group's success.

4. A meeting creates in all present a commitment to the decisions it makes and the objectives it pursues. Once something has been decided, even if you originally argued against it, your membership in the group entails an obligation to accept the decision.... For most people on most issues, it is enough to know that their views were heard and considered. They may regret that they were not followed, but they accept the outcome.

5.   A meeting is very often the only occasion where the team or group actually exists and works as a group, and the only time when the supervisor, manager, or executive is actually perceived as the leader of the team, rather than as the official to whom individuals report.

6.   A meeting is a status arena. It is no good to pretend that people are not or should not be concerned with their status relative to the other members in a group. It is just another part of human nature that we have to live with.

> Despite the fact that a meeting can perform all of the foregoing main functions, there is no guarantee that it will do so in any given situation. It is all too possible that any single meeting may be a waste of time, an irritant, or a barrier to the achievement of the organization's objectives. (pp. 121–123)

Teachers and administrators in language programs may not subscribe to Jay's sixth meeting function, that of "status arena," but the first five are probably important for encouraging open communication in a language program. One highly desirable organizational skill for any program administrator is the ability to run an effective meeting that "creates in all present a commitment to the decisions it makes and the objectives it pursues" (Jay, 1976/1983, p. 121).

Because meetings are made up of people, whoever is running the meeting needs to deal carefully and sensitively with them. In this regard, Jay (1976/1983) offers sound advice:

Control the garrulous:
In most meetings someone takes a long time to say very little. As chairman, your sense of urgency should help indicate ... the need for brevity.

Draw out the silent:
In any properly run meeting, as simple arithmetic will show, most of the people will be silent most of the time. Silence can indicate general agreement, or no important contribution to make, or the need to wait and hear more before saying anything, or too good a lunch ... but there are two kinds of silence you must break: (1) The silence of diffidence. Someone may have a valuable contribution to make but be sufficiently nervous about its possible reception to keep it to himself. It is important that when you draw out such a contribution, you should express interest and pleasure (though not necessarily agreement) to encourage further contributions of that sort. (2) The silence of hostility. This is not hostility to ideas, but to you as the chairman, to the meeting, and to the process by which decisions are being reached. This sort of total detachment from the whole proceedings is usually the symptom of some feeling of affront. If you probe it, you will usually find that there is something bursting to come out and that it is better out than in.

Protect the weak:
Junior members of the meeting may provoke the disagreement of their seniors, which is perfectly reasonable. But if the disagreement escalates to the point of suggesting that they have no right to contribute, the meeting is weakened.

Encourage the clash of ideas:
But, at the same time, discourage the clash of personalities. A good meeting is not a series of dialogues between individual members and the chairman. Instead, it is a crossflow of discussion and debate, with the chairman occasionally guiding, mediating, probing, stimulating, and summarizing, but mostly letting the others thrash ideas out. However, the meeting must be a contention of *ideas*, not people.

Watch out for the suggestion-squashing reflex:
Students of meetings have reduced everything that can be said into questions, answers, positive reactions, and negative reactions. Questions can only seek, and answers only supply, three types of response: information, opinion, and suggestion. (p. 133)

How can we improve or even survive in our programs without the dynamic exchange of ideas? Suggestions that come from inclusive meetings where the free flow of ideas is encouraged may be somewhat unsettling to program administrators on occasion, but if we are to set up viable organizations, we have to value the contribution of ideas from everyone who works in the program.

In almost every modern organization, it is the suggestions that contain the seeds of future success.... The trouble is that suggestions are much easier to ridicule than facts or opinions. If people feel that making a suggestion will provoke the negative reaction of being laughed at or squashed, they will soon stop.... It is all too easy and a formula to ensure sterile meetings.... Take special notice and show special warmth when anyone makes a suggestion, and to discourage as sharply as you can the squashing-reflex. (Jay 1976/1983, pp. 133–134)

One might ask, why have meetings anyway? Administrators have no choice if they hope to promote positive working relationships and open communication in a healthy workplace. What kinds of meetings are necessary in language programs? Certainly, at a minimum, the entire group of teachers and administrators needs to meet at the beginning of the term, at mid-term, and at the end of the term. Other groups and subgroups need to meet more often and for more specific purposes throughout the term. Meetings need to be run so that maximum participation by all employees is assured and so that communication flows in all directions, both vertically and laterally.

Establishing Committees

Program governance is a major issue in many language programs. How are decisions made and how are policies implemented? In mostly organic language programs, committees with elected or appointed members are established to ensure the opportunity for program-wide participation by all professional employees in the decision-making process. A sampling of standard committees and their responsibilities follows:

1. A policy and planning committee or executive committee serves in an advisory capacity to the director in matters of policy and planning for the program and recommends action on such matters as program goals, new programs, new positions, new policies, budget, tuition, curriculum, and so forth. The program director usually serves as the committee chair.

2. A personnel and recruitment committee makes recommendations to the director on matters pertaining to the program's professional staff: hiring, reclassification, evaluation, leaves of absence, reduction in force, termination, merit, and so forth. The program director may serve as the committee chair.

3. A curriculum committee establishes and updates curriculum guidelines for the program. Members review textbooks and other teaching materials and recommend the adoption of student texts as well as the purchase of teacher resource materials for the program. The associate director, the academic coordinator, or a teacher in the program may serve as the committee chair.

4. A professional development committee promotes the professional growth of the faculty and staff by encouraging research, supporting attendance and presentations at professional conferences, organizing workshops, and inviting speakers to in-service sessions or program events. Members may help to establish a professional reference library that includes student texts, teacher-reference books, and relevant journals and publications. The associate director, the academic coordinator, or a teacher in the program may serve as the committee chair.

5. A student activities committee recommends appropriate field trips and program-wide activities for students and helps to plan and carry out those activities. The foreign student advisor or a teacher in the program may serve as the committee chair.

6. An elections and grievances committee conducts program elections for committee service and considers formal grievances from teachers or administrators. The committee, after hearing a grievance, may choose to write an opinion on the matter and forward that opinion to the appropriate person or body for disposition. The committee's purpose may be to determine whether proper procedure was followed and whether the grievance is justified. An elected faculty or staff member usually serves as the committee chair.

Although committee service and teachers' meetings represent important opportunities for participation in a program's decision-making process, these gatherings may also be time-consuming and may involve seemingly unending work. Committee service is usually reserved for full-time, benefits-eligible teachers in a language program, but what are the responsibilities of part-time personnel? The answer will vary from program to program, but one point is clear: All teachers need to understand which nonteaching responsibilities are expected by the administration. Written job descriptions should carefully delineate job responsibilities with regard to attendance at and participation in in-service training sessions, faculty meetings, and committee meetings.

Conducting a Program Self-Study

The program self-study, a project which combines all three administrative task types (technical, human, and conceptual), is another excellent way to encourage faculty and staff participation in program decision making. It brings together faculty, staff, administrators, and even students, every 3 to 5 years, to build on program strengths and to improve upon program weaknesses. This undertaking enhances openness between administrators, faculty, and staff; improves communication flow; and heightens group functioning.

Both TESOL and NAFSA: Association of International Educators have taken the lead in establishing standards and providing helpful suggestions for designing, organizing, and implementing the postsecondary program self-study (Kells, 1988; Marsh, 1994; TESOL, 1986a, 1986b). Several program administrators have documented the procedures and reported the results of their program self-studies in the literature (Frank, Bogen, & Dunlop, 1984; Wintergerst, 1995). In general, the profession strongly endorses periodic program self-evaluation. It subscribes to Kells's thesis that

> regardless of the particular leadership style, governance mix, or organizational arrangement, the program or institution involved will be able to function more effectively if its intentions are clearer, if the average professional's knowledge of how well the place functions is greater, if the distance between personal and institutional intentions is relatively narrow, and if more often than not the members of the group are inclined to face problems as practical matters to be solved together. (Kells, 1988, p. 146)

Improving Communication

A key human and conceptual task faced by all language program administrators is effective verbal and written communication. The able communicator speaks and writes clearly and accurately and takes care to document all important program policies, whether through memos, notes, and letters or through more formal vehicles such as program handbooks. Administrators should take care to put in writing only those policies and procedures that have been finalized and approved. Verbal understandings, in place of written policies and procedures, are justified only when the governing federal, state, or institutional policy is unclear (e.g., allowing a mental-health day to be counted as sick leave) or when the administrator has not determined the consequences or the ramifications of a policy but is willing to try it on a trial basis for a period of time (e.g., allowing all faculty to use the program fax machine for professional purposes only). Where feasible, administrators should work to bring resolution to verbal understandings as quickly as possible. The fewer the verbal understandings, the fewer the communication breakdowns, and ultimately, the fairer the workplace. The following sections provide information on proven techniques for effective verbal and written communication within a language program.

In-service training. Clear communication and professional development can best be encouraged when teachers are given paid release time from teaching to meet with their colleagues to discuss curricular concerns, to plan for the next term, or to reflect on the previous term. Days set aside for professional development and in-service meetings may be a luxury in some programs, but for those programs in which time and money can be allotted, the in-service experience can contribute to a positive environment and encourage personal and professional growth and responsibility.

In many programs, in-service meetings are the responsibility of an academic coordinator or a professional development committee. Whatever the design may be, it is best to involve as many teachers as possible in planning the meetings. In-services can become miniconferences modeled after TESOL or other professional conferences. The planning committee can encourage participation by inviting teachers to submit proposals for pre-sentations before a designated deadline. Members of the committee can then read the proposals and select those that are appropriate for the program being planned. Several suggestions can be offered to teachers to encourage them to participate:

1. The teacher has given a presentation at a professional conference and can adapt that presentation for an in-service.

2. The teacher has attended a professional conference or workshop and can share what was learned.

3. The teacher has read a current publication in the field and can tell colleagues about it.

4. The teacher has a practical teaching strategy to share.

5. The teacher has developed audio, video, or written materials relevant to the language program curriculum and can provide a demonstration.

6. The teacher has used one of the textbooks on the booklist for the coming semester and can share ideas about what works and what does not work.

7. The teacher would like to lead a discussion concerning a particular curricular or program issue.

In addition to teacher presentations, speakers can be invited, and publishers can come in with book displays and presentations. In-service time can be given to discussion and problem solving, and independent working groups can spend time on textbook recom-mendations, diagnostic testing, or other curricular concerns. If in-service meetings can be scheduled before the start of a term, teachers and administrators can discuss policies, pro-cedures, and program issues before students arrive and classes begin. Creative ideas can be heard and productive time can be spent in more ways than can be imagined if time and money are available to make in-service opportunities possible.

Program handbooks. In all language programs, regardless of size, the need exists for written guidelines, compiled in handbooks, to guide both students and employees through the maze of policies and procedures that evolve during any program's existence. Separate handbooks can be developed for students, teachers, and other employees.

Student handbooks might include information about immigration requirements as well as information about the program, such as levels of study, classes, labs, textbooks, computer services, campus activities, health care, refund policies, requirements for suc-cessful completion of the term, and policies concerning academic honesty, attendance, and academic progress. Student handbooks can be given to students at orientation or dur-ing the first week of classes; they may need translation into the students' first languages. The student handbook is an important source of information in clarifying the program's responsibilities to the student and the student's responsibilities to the program.

Faculty/staff handbooks are essential sources of information for all program employ-ees. While most handbooks are in a constant state of revision because of changing policies and procedures, to try to operate without a set of written guidelines would most likely be demoralizing to all who are trying to understand their roles in the organization. A well-written handbook can help employees understand their positions and their responsibilities to the program and can go a long way toward improving communication and ensuring fairness in the workplace.

Faculty/staff handbooks might include information regarding program policies such as hiring, pay schedules, pay increases, job classifications, time and work policies, classroom observation, evaluation, absences, substitute remuneration, sick leave, voluntary leave, leave without pay, and termination. Job descriptions, committee descriptions, and evaluation instruments are also important inclusions. Some handbooks include a section called "procedures" with information on how standard and regular tasks are accomplished (e.g., where to pick up a paycheck and how to report student attendance and grades). This section of any handbook can be extensive and may seem overwhelming, but program administrators will find it extremely useful to have as much information as possible in writing. Teachers and other employees can then use the handbook on an "as needed" basis (like a cookbook, if you will) to find out how to recommend a change of level for a student or what to do in case of a weather emergency. Some of these procedures will change as soon as the program puts them in writing, but that reality should not discourage writing them as they are understood at the time. When change occurs, as it certainly will, the administrator has a written point of reference, a benchmark, from which to work.

Developing a separate handbook of administrative procedures can be tedious, but it is vital to the efficient running of a language program and, indeed, may be required by the institution or company to which the program belongs. When writing administrative procedures, some program administrators have found it useful to record the date the written procedure was established and the date the procedure was revised. Written policy information on revenues, expenditures, budgets, account controls, check/cash handling procedures, check distribution policy, and spending reimbursement policy, to name only a few possibilities, can be invaluable to the administrative team of any program.

Calendars. A term calendar is basic to any language program organizational plan and is an important guide for students, teachers, and administrators. The calendar can be simple or elaborate but needs to contain dates of program beginnings and endings as well as notices of field trips, special events, deadlines, and holidays to be observed. Many programs find it useful to prepare separate calendars for teachers/administrators and students for beginning-of-term distribution. The teacher/administrator calendar might include all the student information plus notices of professional conference dates, in-service events, faculty meetings, committee meetings, and other information needed only by program personnel. The calendar becomes a master schedule for the program that contains essential information for teachers who are planning class events that should not collide with program events. Program administrators are well advised to seek as much input from teachers and program staff as possible before the final printing and distribution of the calendar. The program calendar is, after all, the blueprint from which everyone works.

Schedules. Class schedules are essential to peace and productivity in a language program, but creating schedules that make everyone happy may be a very complex administrative process. Students usually expect and receive reasonable schedules. Teachers also expect reasonable schedules, but because of the unknowns involved in new student enrollments and the impossibility of predicting the number of levels and sections in each new teaching term, many programs hire teachers with the understanding that the teachers may be asked to teach any skill at any level—from beginning to advanced—in any given term, at any hour. Daily schedules may remain consistent for teachers in some programs, while in others, daily schedules may vary from term to term. Probably there are as many configurations of teaching schedules as there are programs, but whatever the configuration may be, administrators need to clarify scheduling guidelines to those teachers whose lives and time are greatly affected by the schedules they receive. Written understandings are always in the best interest of everyone concerned. The following questions need to be answered when considering what to put in writing concerning teaching schedules:

1. How many hours of teaching are required daily/weekly in order to be considered full time and benefits eligible?

2. Does the program expect faculty members to be willing to teach any level or skill offered by the program during any term?

3. Are teachers required to rotate through all levels of the program or do teachers specialize in certain levels or skills?

4. Will teaching hours be consecutive or will there be a break for the teacher between scheduled classes?

5. Will teachers be able to specify time, level, or skills preferences or will these be assigned by the program without regard to teacher preference?

6. Are initial teaching assignments likely to change during the first weeks of the term?

7. Will classroom space be available at the time the teacher requests?

Conclusion

It is suggested here that the preferred organization design model for language programs lies closer to the organic end of the continuum than to the mechanistic. The more an administrator can encourage faculty and staff participation in program decision making, the higher their morale, and the more efficient the program. Committees, self-studies, handbooks, in-service time, and calendars all represent organizing techniques characteristic of the organic model. As Likert (1967) writes,

> the performance and output of any enterprise depend entirely upon the quality of the human organization and its capacity to function as a tightly knit, highly motivated, technically competent entity.... Successful organizations are those making the best use of competent personnel to perform well and efficiently all the tasks required by the enterprise. (p. 134)

An administrator who moves the program as far in the direction of the organic model as setting and size will allow, who focuses on human and conceptual tasks (leaving technical tasks to trained and qualified personnel), and who performs those organizational tasks with attention to participatory methods will build an exemplary superstructure in which human worth is valued and personal growth and responsibility are emphasized.

Endnote

1. In columns two and three of Table 1, the terminology referencing language programs is the authors'; the terminology describing general characteristics in the first column is Likert's. It is important to note that Likert's understanding of the negative consequences of the mechanistic design is based on the large corporation. The much smaller size of language programs may ameliorate these consequences in some instances.

Discussion Questions and Activities

1. Consider a language program (or other organization) that you know. What aspects, if any, of the mechanistic organization model and organic organization model best match the needs of the program?

2. Would it be easier to change a language program from a predominantly mechanistic model to a predominantly organic model or vice versa? Explain.

3a. Imagine a busy language program administrator. List 20 tasks required of that person.

3b. Then consider the following definitions of technical, human, and conceptual skills (Katz, 1974/1983):

Technical skill implies an understanding of, and proficiency in, a specific kind of activity, particularly one involving methods, processes, procedures, or techniques. [It] involves specialized knowledge, analytical ability within that specialty, and facility in the use of the tools and techniques of the specific discipline. (p. 24)

Human skill is the executive's ability to work effectively as a group member and to build cooperative effort within the team he leads. This skill is demonstrated in the way the individual perceives (and recognizes the perceptions of) his superiors, equals, and subordinates, and in the way he behaves subsequently. (p. 24)

Conceptual skill involves the ability to see the enterprise as a whole; it includes recognizing how the various functions of the organization depend on one another, and how changes in any one part affect all the others; ... Recognizing these relationships and perceiving the significant elements in any situation, the administrator should then be able to act in a way which advances the over-all welfare of the total organization. (p. 26)

3c. Now revisit your list of administrative responsibilities. Classify them as either technical, human, conceptual, or some combination of the three. Discuss how each task would be carried out in mostly organic, then mostly mechanistic programs.

4. Mead, Davidson, and Hanna (1986) provide a simple formula (see Figure 1) for predicting enrollment 1–2 months prior to registration. (Note that the formula does not claim to predict the exact number of students but to be within ±10 of the final count.)

TOTAL NUMBER OF STUDENTS = WI + (SU x TA)
TA = CA + (TIME x AVE APP)

WI = anticipated number of walk-in students (students who did not submit an application prior to the day of registration; an average of the last several corresponding semesters is used)

SU = the average show-up rate during the past several semesters (determined by dividing the number of students who enroll—excluding walk-ins—by the total number who apply)

TA = the total anticipated number of applications

CA = the current number of applications

TIME = the number of weeks remaining until registration

AVE APP = the average number of applications received per week (based on the numbers received per week in corresponding terms in previous years)

Figure 1. **Formula for predicting enrollment.**

Table 2 gives sample application and enrollment count data for fall semesters between 1987 and 1996. Blank cells indicate that no student registered on that day. An application count up to the fourth week preceding the Fall 1997 registration period is also provided. How many registered students (±10) should the program director expect for Fall 1997? How many will have applied? How many will be walk-ins?

Now, step back. What problems do you see with the formula? Should the current economic and political fortunes and misfortunes of nations be considered? How should recent trends (in the last 1–2 years) in the ebb and flow of language program students coming to the United States be treated? If the final enrollment count for Fall 1997 turned out to be 170 students, what should the trend in show-up percentages in Table 2 tell you about the show-up percentage for Fall 1997? Can other factors impact the final enrollment count? (For formula solution, see end of chapter.)

Table 2.

Language Program Fall Semester Cumulative Application and Enrollment Counts 1987–1996

	1987	1988	1989	1990	1991	1992	1993	1994	1995	1996	1997
APPLICATIONS RECEIVED											
Weeks before registration											
10	164	180	121	147	135	136	132	117	105	86	80
9	175	193	123	158	140	146	138	127	111	98	86
8	185	199	139	166	175	166	155	137	123	116	96
7	195	206	145	177	192	187	173	149	132	126	101
6	207	213	161	189	200	212	184	163	137	136	108
5	218	221	175	204	243	235	205	169	149	151	153
4	232	236	188	221	254	256	266	206	174	203	174
3	248	262	195	257	273	283	290	227	190	222	
2	265	271	211	268	289	308	301	249	225	241	
1	278	275	216	270	284	325	313	257	245	248	
0	282	274	217	266	289	328	341	272	250	259	
DAILY CUMULATIVE ENROLLMENT											
Day of registration											
1	117	99	84	99	100	108	148	141	124	127	
2	140	109	90	103	110	129	160	151	131	145	
3	146	118	90	104	113	133	169	156	138	153	
4	147	122	95	120	124	140	177	165	145	158	
5	151	126	97	122	132	—	183	169	151	164	
6	159	129	—	—	133	154	186	—	—	165	
7	—	—	—	123	—	156	187	172	153	—	
8	—	131	—	124	—	—	—	173	—	169	
9	—	—	98	128	135	—	190	174	158	—	
10	162	132	—	131	139	—	211	—	162	170	
11	—	—	100	—	—	—	—	—	165	—	
12	—	—	—	132	—	—	—	—	167	—	
*Walk-ins**	28	18	11	18	23	29	22	29	16	14	
New students	10	7	5	10	14	19	8	15	10	10	
Former students	18	11	6	8	9	10	14	14	6	4	
Final count	163	133	102	133	145	158	211	174	167	171	
New students	122	97	75	92	96	107	141	114	116	112	
Former students	41	36	27	41	49	51	70	60	51	59	
Percent to show up	48	42	42	43	41	39	55	53	60	61	

*Walk-ins are included in the daily cumulative enrollment counts.

Suggested Readings

Davidson, J. O. (1984). Record keeping for critical decision making. *American Language Journal, 2*(2), 77–85.

Davidson makes the case that the computerization of intensive English program offices is essential for informed administrative decision making. Computer-generated reports that are timely, accurate, and useful assist administrators at all levels to make the best decisions possible. Davidson illustrates this with three computer-generated reports and shows how they can be used to facilitate critical decision making (e.g., forecasting enrollments, detecting early signs of shifts in enrollment patterns, or monitoring the shifts and assessing their significance for long-range planning). The article concludes with a formula for predicting enrollment a month or more before registration occurs.

Kells, H. R. (1988). *Self-study processes: A guide for postsecondary and similar service-oriented institutions and programs* (3rd ed.). New York: American Council on Education/Macmillan.

This classic text on postsecondary self-study processes, in its earlier second edition, served as the basis for TESOL's and NAFSA's pilot programs in self-study and self-regulation. Kells elucidates, with the help of many examples, a method for ongoing institutional and programmatic self-assessment and change, and the relationship of accreditation to self-study. Detailed suggestions concerning motivation, preparation, leadership, design, organizational dimensions, study and planning cycles, and the like are furnished. The text is designed for use as a handbook for participants in self-study processes at postsecondary institutions and programs, a basic reference for administrators on the processes and uses of self-study, and a reader-manual for workshops and courses on self-study processes.

Pennington, M. C. (1985). Effective administration of an ESL program. In P. Larson, E. Judd, & D. S. Messerschmidt (Eds.), *On TESOL '84: A brave new world for TESOL* (pp. 301–316). Washington, DC: TESOL.

Pennington applies the administrative skills classification of Katz (1974/1983)—technical skills, human skills, and conceptual skills—to the ESL program context. She groups a selected number of language program administrative tasks under each skill heading, confirms Katz's contention that the relative importance of each skill type differs at different levels of administration, and discusses the creation of administrative teams with complementary skill repertoires. She concludes by calling for ESL programs to provide administrative traineeships through administrative practicums.

Solution to Discussion Question and Activity No. 4

How many registered students (±10) should the program director expect for Fall 1997?
Answer: 131. *How many will have applied?* Answer: 230. *How many will be walk-ins?*
Answer: 21 students. WI = 21, SU = 48%, TA = 230, CA = 174, TIME = 4, AVE APP = 14.

What problems do you see with this formula? Answer: The show-up percentage has been
rising over the last few years. This might indicate that instead of taking the average show-
up rate from the last 10 years (48%), an average of the last 3 years should be taken. That
show-up rate would be 58%, 10 percentage points above the 10-year average. Calculating
averages based on the last 10 years of data can distort the real picture. What happened 8,
9, or 10 years ago may not have relevance for projecting enrollment today.

Should the current economic and political fortunes and misfortunes of nations be considered?
Answer: Yes. If your language program receives a large number of applications from a
country that has recently suffered severe inflation, the chances are that relatively few of
the students from that country will have the money to attend the program that semester.
You need to revise your show-up percentage downward. If war breaks out in a region or
between or among countries, this might prevent students from leaving the area for the
United States. Again, your show-up rate would need to be revised downward.

*How should recent trends in the ebb and flow of language program students coming to the
United States be treated?* Answer: More attention should be paid to recent trends than to a
10-year average for the reasons mentioned above.

*If the final enrollment count for Fall 1997 turned out to be 170 students, what should the
trend in show-up percentages in Table 2 tell you about the show-up percentage for Fall 1997?*
Answer: If the final enrollment count was 170 students, one of the following would have
to have happened: (a) The show-up percentage jumped to approximately 65% and the
AVE APP remained at 14; or (b) the show-up percentage was less than 65%, but the
AVE APP increased.

Chapter 13

PERSONNEL MATTERS

Joann M. Geddes
Lewis and Clark College

Doris R. Marks
Beaver Acres Elementary School

he effective management of human resources is crucial to the success of a language program. By dedicating time and effort to researching, creating, and implementing personnel policies and procedures, the language program administrator greatly increases the program's ability to attract and retain quality faculty and staff. These employees, in turn, provide the instructional and support services that fulfill the program's mission.

An overview is provided here of some of the most basic human resource issues that administrators must address: staffing, supervision and evaluation, ongoing feedback and problem solving, changes in personnel, and professional enrichment. These issues are not presented in any particular order, as most personnel functions and activities are interrelated and interdependent, and may occur simultaneously. The checklists provided with each section are intended to assist the reader in reviewing main ideas, and to serve as guides for administrators as they plan, carry out, and supervise personnel-related activities at their institutions.

Staffing

Ultimately, the success of any language program is determined by the skills and commitment of its administrative, instructional, and support staff. One of an administrator's most important responsibilities is therefore to ensure that policies and procedures for hiring dedicated and qualified personnel are developed and implemented. To that end, administrative practices and procedural recommendations are presented here with regard to job analyses, recruitment and screening, interviewing, and hiring.

Job Analysis and Job Description

All language program staffing considerations must begin with a clear understanding of how each position contributes to the program as a whole. Administrators should be familiar with the duties and responsibilities of all positions. Together with faculty and support staff, administrators should periodically conduct job analyses and review job descriptions.

A job analysis should not result in a list of ideal behaviors or expectations; rather it should realistically describe what can and should be expected from a person in a particular position (i.e., reporting relationships; duties and responsibilities; required knowledge, skills, and abilities; degrees, specialized training, and educational background). Those responsible for job analyses should begin by reviewing the program's mission, outlining program needs, and comparing positions and job descriptions with those in similar programs and departments. One particularly effective job-analysis strategy involves identifying and prioritizing specific tasks, and then linking them to the knowledge, skills, and abilities necessary for successful performance in particular positions (Feild & Gatewood, 1989).

Program or institutional guidelines often dictate the format and language of job descriptions. Administrators should not take full responsibility for writing or revising job descriptions after job analyses. Rather, collaboration with other language program personnel, during job analyses and the subsequent development or revision of a job description, (re)introduces employees to the goals of the language program. At the same time, it gives them direct input into the staffing process. (See Figure 1 for a summary of procedures for job analysis and job description.)

____ Determine who will perform the job analysis.
____ Review the program and institutional mission.
____ Review program goals.
____ Determine how each position fulfills the mission and goals.
____ Review the existing job description.
____ Interview or survey employees currently in the targeted position.
____ Interview or survey other language program faculty and staff members.
____ Collect and review parallel job descriptions from other language programs or departments.
____ List duties performed and responsibilities required.
____ List knowledge, skills and abilities, educational background, and experience required.
____ Using a consensus-based activity, categorize and prioritize the requirements of the position.
____ Write or revise the job description.

Figure 1. **Recommended procedures for job analysis and job description.**

Recruitment and Screening

Recruitment is often seen as a periodic process that takes place only when positions need to be filled. Ongoing recruitment efforts, however, reflect a commitment to quality staffing. When an administrator adopts proactive strategies to develop relationships with teacher training institutions, to network with colleagues at other institutions, and to actively support and participate in professional organizations, the language program will benefit from positive external exposure.

Many factors can make staffing needs within a language program unpredictable, such as fluctuations in enrollment, unanticipated personnel changes, and sponsorship of special programs. Hence, it is advisable to screen all inquiries and to interview promising applicants periodically throughout the year. Program administrators should maintain active files that list prospective employees for short-term as well as long-term teaching assignments and support services.

Selectively granting "information interviews" is another beneficial, though indirect, recruiting practice. Individuals requesting such interviews may be seeking general job search advice, or they may be interested in a specific position within the program. While these interviews are generally viewed as beneficial to the people who seek them, establishing positive public relations through such interviews can ultimately benefit the language program as well.

When a position opens, a recruitment plan that attracts the largest pool of candidates must be developed. When publicizing a position, it is important to consider what to include in the job announcement, when and where to advertise, and whom to involve in the process. The basic qualifications of those responsible for recruiting and screening should include a fundamental understanding of specific job requirements and program goals, the ability to analyze and assess objectively the background and potential contributions of all candidates, and an awareness of institutional and program guidelines based on equal opportunity and affirmative action principles.

When hiring for part-time positions and short-term programs, it may be more efficient and practical for a program administrator to assume most of the responsibilities. However, when long-term positions open, a search committee or a team of interviewers should become involved in the hiring process. If the group represents all or most of the language program units, including administration, office management, support services, and instruction, it is more likely that all relevant needs and concerns will be considered. Team or committee members might also be appointed from other departments or programs within the institution; such collaboration could provide opportunities for greater language program integration into the institution, and could also promote a deeper understanding of the role of the language program among colleagues within the institution.

Effective recruitment and preliminary screening should result in a strong pool of applicants from which to make selections. After eliminating less-qualified individuals, it is advisable to choose three to five finalists. Ideally, each of these candidates will possess the knowledge, skills, and abilities outlined in the job description, as well as other attributes that reveal their potential for positive contributions to the language program. (See Figure 2 for recommended procedures for recruitment and screening.)

Interviewing

The selection interview is ordinarily one of the concluding steps taken in differentiating among finalists. During the interviewing process, interviewers confirm preliminary assumptions and further assess candidates' interpersonal, analytical, and communication skills. At the same time, interviewees have the opportunity to solicit more specific information about the job and working environment. When a site visit takes place, program representatives can introduce their program, institution, and community to the candi-

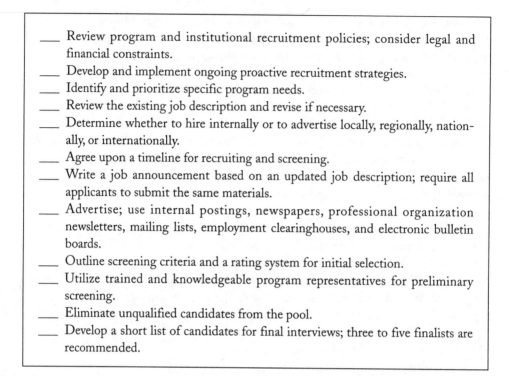

____ Review program and institutional recruitment policies; consider legal and financial constraints.

____ Develop and implement ongoing proactive recruitment strategies.

____ Identify and prioritize specific program needs.

____ Review the existing job description and revise if necessary.

____ Determine whether to hire internally or to advertise locally, regionally, nationally, or internationally.

____ Agree upon a timeline for recruiting and screening.

____ Write a job announcement based on an updated job description; require all applicants to submit the same materials.

____ Advertise; use internal postings, newspapers, professional organization newsletters, mailing lists, employment clearinghouses, and electronic bulletin boards.

____ Outline screening criteria and a rating system for initial selection.

____ Utilize trained and knowledgeable program representatives for preliminary screening.

____ Eliminate unqualified candidates from the pool.

____ Develop a short list of candidates for final interviews; three to five finalists are recommended.

Figure 2. **Recommended procedures for recruitment and screening.**

dates. While highlighting major attractions, an honest and objective overview will assist in preventing false expectations from forming. Interviewers and finalists alike must attempt to determine if there is a good match between the candidate and the program.

At some institutions, human resource specialists from outside the language program conduct initial applicant screening; the language program administrator, however, usually has final responsibility for establishing and implementing a fair, objective, and legal interview process. Careful preparation is a prerequisite to every interview. To develop a comprehensive and uniform procedure, the job description should be reviewed, interview strategies determined, and an interview format chosen.

Basic interview formats identified in the literature include the traditional unstructured interview, the situational interview, the experience description interview, and the patterned behavior description interview. During the initial planning process, individual interviewers may have different format preferences. Administrators should present the team of interviewers with viable options and should encourage collaborative planning and decision making. A well-informed choice of format, or a combination of formats, will enable interviewers to collect as much relevant information as possible about each candidate, in as consistent a manner as possible.

During a *traditional unstructured interview*, applicants are often asked to answer hypothetical and factual questions related to individual beliefs and perspectives (Coady, 1990). For example, candidates may be encouraged to discuss personal opinions and reflect on theories and practices in teaching and learning, intercultural communication, or office management. Interviewers generally want to know what the prospective employees know or what they have studied (see below for sample questions).

Sample Traditional Unstructured Interview Questions

1. Please discuss the role of the teacher in the second language classroom. In your opinion, how does second language learning theory relate to the work you do in the classroom?

2. Do you believe that computer-assisted learning is a valuable and necessary component of an ESL curriculum?

3. As office manager, what innovations could you bring to our language program?

4. What do you think are the most important qualities of a host family coordinator?

A *situational interview* (Feild & Gatewood, 1989; Latham, 1989) also includes hypothetical questions, but they are tied more closely to the requirements of the position. Interview questions, which are drafted after analysis of the position and associated responsibilities, are based on critical incidents, such as descriptions of effective and ineffective job behaviors, that have recently occurred within the program; and the knowledge, skills, and abilities that would allow applicants to respond appropriately to similar situations (see Feild & Gatewood, 1989). Preparation and planning for a situational interview demand an extensive initial time commitment because benchmark answers must be agreed upon and an appraisal instrument, with an objective scoring guide, must be developed ahead of time. When relevant program personnel provide input into the choice of questions, the acceptability of answers, and the appraisal instrument, the planning process can become one of consensus building and staff development for the entire program (see below for sample questions).

Sample Situational Interview Questions

1. If you joined a program whose faculty had agreed to use an instructional approach that was new to you, what would you do?

2. If you were asked to develop an ESL course that was based on a popular computer program, what steps would you take?

3. As office manager, if you were asked to develop a new data collection system, how would you proceed?

4. If you were asked to give a host family orientation, what activities would you schedule and what information would you provide to both new and experienced participants?

During an *experience description interview*, candidates are asked to describe actual experiences by reflecting on past responsibilities and practices. If candidates have had no related experiences, they may be asked to imagine that they have worked in the field or to describe a parallel situation (see below for sample questions).

Sample Experience Description Interview Questions

1. Please describe how theories of second language learning are reflected in your teaching.

2. Describe the role of computers in your classroom.

3. Describe an experience that you have had in developing and managing data collection systems.

4. Tell us about any of your prior experiences that would relate directly to the coordination of our host family program.

A *patterned behavior description interview* is a more structured extension of the experience description interview. Advocates suggest that it is important to ask questions that oblige interviewees to go beyond surface descriptions and explain how tasks associated with previous positions were performed and how responsibilities were fulfilled (Feild & Gatewood, 1989; Janz, 1989; McLaughlin, 1990). Janz has stated that behavior descriptions reveal

> specific choices applicants have made in the past, and the circumstances surrounding those choices. The interviewer probes the details of the situation and what the applicant did in that situation, or what the applicant did the next time the situation arose. (p. 159)

Concrete descriptions of prior work-related experiences are sought by interviewers to determine how a candidate actually fulfilled the responsibilities assigned (see below for sample questions). The use of such a format stems from the belief that past performance is an indicator of future behavior.

Sample Patterned Behavior Description Interview Questions

1. Please describe a typical lesson in which you have tied second language learning theory to practice in your ESL classroom. What did you do? How and why did you choose to use specific methods and techniques?

2. Describe how you have implemented innovative computer-assisted learning techniques into a course, or part of a course. If you have not yet done so within the classroom itself, how have you incorporated computers into your work?

3. Please describe any data collection systems or projects that you have already developed and tell us about the steps that you have taken to do so.

4. Please tell us about any volunteer training you have provided and how it would relate to the work done by our host family coordinator. Describe how you facilitated specific activities that took place during the training and why you chose to incorporate them.

When time and resources allow, it is beneficial to request that finalists for instructional positions *teach a model lesson* as part of the interview process. Language program students may be recruited for this exercise, and may even be asked to provide input on the candidates. Although a video of a past teaching experience may be submitted in place of a live lesson, asking all candidates to teach lessons—under the same conditions—facilitates more objective comparisons. Coady (1990), in describing such a strategy, has asserted that teaching simulations show us how well candidates relate to students, deliver information, and stimulate thinking. Poorly planned or executed lessons may indicate less than enthusiastic interest, weak organizational skills, or insufficient training. Site visits that require both an interview and classroom teaching will provide greater insights upon which to base selection decisions.

Throughout the entire interview process, interviewers should make every effort to maintain consistency and to follow legal guidelines. All applicants should be asked to submit the same information and fulfill the same requirements. When accurate and detailed notes are kept and all documentation is carefully reviewed, fair comparisons and objective recommendations can be made. (See Figure 3 for recommended procedures for interviewing.)

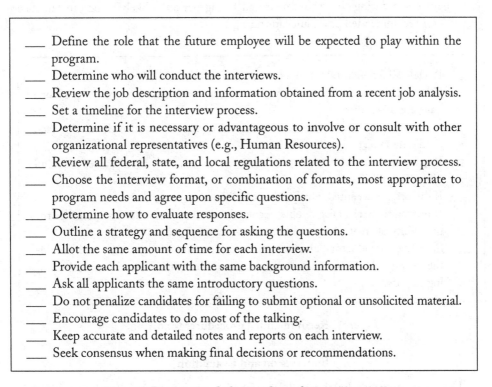

____ Define the role that the future employee will be expected to play within the program.

____ Determine who will conduct the interviews.

____ Review the job description and information obtained from a recent job analysis.

____ Set a timeline for the interview process.

____ Determine if it is necessary or advantageous to involve or consult with other organizational representatives (e.g., Human Resources).

____ Review all federal, state, and local regulations related to the interview process.

____ Choose the interview format, or combination of formats, most appropriate to program needs and agree upon specific questions.

____ Determine how to evaluate responses.

____ Outline a strategy and sequence for asking the questions.

____ Allot the same amount of time for each interview.

____ Provide each applicant with the same background information.

____ Ask all applicants the same introductory questions.

____ Do not penalize candidates for failing to submit optional or unsolicited material.

____ Encourage candidates to do most of the talking.

____ Keep accurate and detailed notes and reports on each interview.

____ Seek consensus when making final decisions or recommendations.

Figure 3. **Recommended procedures for interviewing.**

Hiring

Following the selection of one candidate or several finalists, thorough reference checks should always take place. No offer of employment should be made before prior work experiences have been verified and as much information as possible from past supervisors and colleagues has been obtained. It is important to ask all references the same general job-related questions and then to probe for specific details. Past and present employers may be willing to reveal poor work performance or to offer positive recommendations that confirm a good match between the candidate and the position. A standardized questionnaire will assist in maintaining objectivity and consistency (see the appendix for a sample reference check questionnaire).

When references support the recommendation of the interviewers, the candidate of choice should be notified as soon as possible, and all contractual information should be reviewed. Other finalists should not be contacted unless this individual has formally accepted the position and agreed upon a starting date. If no strong or suitable candidate is identified, the language program director or search committee should declare a failed search. It is far better to fill the position with a short-term employee or to temporarily reassign duties than to hire someone who cannot satisfactorily fulfill the responsibilities of the position.

Both introductory and long-term orientation sessions should be scheduled to maximize the possibility of a successful entry into the program. When a new employee is provided with extensive background information and practical training, the return on the investment made during the recruitment and hiring period is likely to be greater. (See Figure 4 for recommended procedures for hiring.)

____ Review all federal, state, and local legal constraints.

____ Conduct thorough reference checks using a standardized reference questionnaire for all finalists.

____ Summarize the information received from each source and include it in each candidate's file.

____ If reference checks confirm the selection committee's first choice, make an offer of employment.

____ If the offer is accepted, notify other candidates.

____ If reference checks raise doubts, reconsider ratings of candidates. Consider the possibility of an alternate candidate or declare a failed search.

____ Schedule introductory and long-term orientation sessions that will provide the new employee with as much background information and practical training as possible.

Figure 4. **Recommended procedures for hiring.**

Supervision and Evaluation

Language program administrators interact with support staff and faculty whose work styles, personalities, and commitment to the program differ dramatically. It is, nonetheless, the administrator's responsibility to oversee and assess objectively the job performance of each employee in a manner that will promote personal and program growth. Administrators must establish criteria and a formal plan for supervising and evaluating employee performance.

Supervision

Supervision—a process that is commonly linked to evaluation, staff development, and management—includes a variety of activities that assist administrators in gathering important program-related data and that establish channels of two-way communication between supervisors and employees. Clear supervisory guidelines must be established because supervisorial responsibilities are often assumed by a number of different employees, such as directors, office managers, curriculum specialists, and master teachers. Program components requiring supervision must initially be identified, possibly including instruction, support services and programs, maintenance, and security. Next, program administrators and staff should agree upon the most appropriate supervisorial model and corresponding procedures and techniques. Prior to doing so, however, a review of the current literature on supervision of administrative, support, and instructional personnel is recommended.

Supervision models are based on a range of distinct philosophical assumptions and management styles. Supervisors, for example, may adopt approaches that are directive, authoritarian, and top-down, or that are nondirective, interactive, and collaborative. A number of models have evolved during the past three decades from work done earlier on clinical supervision (Cogan, 1973; Goldhammer, 1969). According to Pajak (1993), clinical supervision models and approaches in the 1970s and early 1980s "generally emphasized the importance of positive collegial relationships between supervisors and teachers in promoting teacher growth and in facilitating the collaborative discovery of meaning in classroom events" (p. 9).

Recently, more technical and developmental clinically based approaches have been introduced. Technical/didactic models (Pajak, 1993) have added step-by-step procedures for planning, observation, and conferencing stages. In one such approach (Acheson & Gall, 1992) the focus is on a teacher's behavior in the classroom and on how instruction (course content and process, not an individual's personality) can be analyzed using one or more systematic procedures. With this approach, supervisors assist instructors—in a manner that is described as democratic, interactive, and objective—in gaining the skills necessary to meet performance goals.

In the developmental supervision model, supervisors match their approach with the teacher's current developmental level (Glickman, Gordon, & Ross-Gordon, 1995). In this way, supervisor behaviors are gradually modified to promote and accommodate long-range teacher development toward higher levels of reflection and problem-solving ability. Supervisors who adopt developmental approaches may choose to oversee, direct, and control the work done by a new and inexperienced instructor; however, when interacting with an experienced master teacher, the supervisor may be inclined to be nonjudgmental and may attempt to facilitate clarification and self-awareness experiences.

Approaches to supervision that have been applied to the field of second language teaching have been presented by Freeman (1982), Gebhard (1984), and Stoller (1996). Whereas Freeman and Gebhard outline a range of possibilities, Stoller offers an adaptation of a clinical supervision model through which she suggests that we can (a) provide objective feedback on instruction, (b) diagnose and solve instructional problems, (c) assist teachers in developing strategies for more effective instruction, and (d) help teachers develop a positive attitude towards continuous professional development.

It is the responsibility of all supervisors to identify a model of supervision that is congruent with the assumptions underlying the program's operating principles. The following questions, adapted from the work of Pajak (1993), may assist the language program administrator in guiding the selection process:

1. What does this model of supervision imply about supervisor and supervisee relations?

2. Would I feel comfortable with this model of supervision as either a new or an experienced staff member?

3. Do I feel comfortable using this model as a language program administrator or supervisor?

4. What might program personnel learn about themselves if this model were adopted?

5. Would this model assist in promoting personal and program growth through effective communication and objective feedback?

6. Does this model facilitate the successful implementation of evaluation policies and procedures?

7. Does this model assist in gathering the information required to make sound staff development and management decisions?

8. Would this model of supervision contribute to the successful delivery of services?

After identifying a model of choice, administrators are faced with the challenge of developing a realistic plan for implementing its procedures and techniques. All supervisors must understand the goals of the program and the roles and responsibilities assumed by staff members. In addition, adequate time and resources should be allotted not only for supervisory activities, but for the training necessary to provide supervisors with the managerial, technical, and interpersonal skills needed to fulfill their duties.

Effective supervision is a cornerstone upon which a strong program is built and maintained. When administrators establish supervisory guidelines that allow for (a) well-informed choices, (b) realistic implementation plans, (c) meaningful feedback, and (d) personal and professional growth, a positive and supportive work environment can be fostered. (See Figure 5 for recommended procedures for supervision.)

Evaluation

Evaluation should play a prominent role in the evolution of an employee's career. At any given time, the language program administrator, faculty, and staff may be involved in entry-level evaluations of new employees, periodic appraisals involving supervisors or review committees, or ongoing self-assessment. Formative evaluations are "designed and used to promote growth and improvement in a person's performance or in a program's development" (Joint Committee on Standards for Educational Evaluation, 1988, p. 184). They may be linked to ongoing professional enrichment activities, informal as well as formal review, peer interaction, and self-assessment. Summative evaluations, which are often tied directly to promotion, compensation, and other retention and reward decisions, are "designed to present conclusions about the merit or worth of a person's performance" (p. 187).

___ Identify program components, such as instruction, office support, or maintenance, in which supervision is required.

___ Review and assign supervisory responsibilities.

___ Examine current research and literature on supervision.

___ Select a model of supervision and identify related approaches, procedures, and
techniques.

___ Establish a plan for the implementation of formal and informal supervisory
activities.

___ Conduct supervisory activities.

___ Provide honest and meaningful feedback.

___ Determine when and how to link supervision, evaluation, and development
activities.

___ Periodically check for congruence between supervisory practices, program mission, and operating principles.

Figure 5. **Recommended procedures for effective supervision.**

In practice, an employee is first evaluated during the hiring process. At that time, those charged with the responsibility of recommending the most qualified and promising candidate will seriously evaluate the applicant on the personal attributes and competencies outlined in the job description. A new hire should always be placed on probation in order to assess performance and determine if there is indeed a proper match with the program. It is advisable to establish structured avenues through which systematic feedback and guidance can be provided during this period. A positive and supportive environment, one that facilitates communication between the employee and the supervisor, will enhance the possibility of a happy and successful career in the program.

Should concerns arise regarding a new hire, it is important to address them as soon as possible. On the basis of probationary evaluation guidelines, supervisors may recommend further orientation and training to address specific shortcomings; however, since major changes become more difficult for both the employer and the employee after the probationary period, nonrenewal of the short-term agreement should also be seriously considered at this time.

Employees who are issued long-term contracts, following probationary status, should expect periodic formative and summative evaluations. The relationship that a language program has with its host institution may dictate the guidelines and criteria for the appraisals; however, when a language program must develop or adapt an evaluation model independently, it is essential to return to the job description and program mission to establish performance standards and indicators tied to the duties and responsibilities outlined. A review of the research and recommendations made by the Joint Committee on Standards for Educational Evaluation (1988) might lead staff members to ask the following questions: Is our evaluation process ethical and legal? Is it informative, timely, and influential? Is it efficient, easy to use, and viable? Does it provide accurate and objective measures and outcomes?

Because language program personnel may have distinctly different job descriptions and contractual agreements, evaluations will be based on a variety of measures, instruments, and sources of information. Faculty members, for example, may be asked to demonstrate teaching effectiveness and scholarship, as well as to provide evidence of valuable service to the program, institution, and profession. Evaluations of instructional personnel frequently include a combination of supervisor and peer classroom observations, structured observations by trained observers (Medley, Coker, & Soar, 1984), student evaluations, self-assessment reports, standardized or holistically rated student achievement results, and documentation of scholarship and program contributions (Arreola, 1995; Harris, Monk, McIntyre, & Long, 1992; Pennington & Young, 1991).

Appraisals of administrative and support personnel may focus on communication, organization, productivity, motivation, attendance, management, supervision, planning, leadership, and other functions specific to the position (Bouchard, 1992; Fox, 1991; Matthies, 1991). Observations and ratings of noninstructional personnel by higher level supervisors should be supplemented by input from colleagues within the program and institution. Other constituents, such as students, parents, educational advisors, or embassy representatives, might also contribute to the process.

Clarifying specific objectives and defining the criteria upon which the evaluation is to be based will assist administrators in selecting appropriate measures, strategies, and techniques. Each approach to evaluating personnel requires the accurate, objective, and unbiased collection of relevant information by well-trained personnel who are aware of the many options available for fulfilling these responsibilities. The administrator must guarantee proper documentation and meaningful feedback during all stages of the process. (See Figure 6 for recommended procedures for evaluation.)

Ongoing Feedback and Problem Solving

While systematic supervision and evaluation normally provide the framework through which recommendations for recognition, remediation, staff development, or personnel changes are addressed, incidents that positively or negatively impact program services may arise at any time. Administrators may become aware of outstanding contributions, steadfast commitment, or irregular performance via (a) informal observation; (b) discussion with other staff members, students, and institutional employees; (c) self-disclosure by the individual; or (d) other unanticipated sources.

A key factor in the successful management of personnel is open and honest communication. Ongoing dialogue that takes place in an atmosphere of mutual trust and respect will assist the administrator in motivating employees and in exercising leadership. Supervisors who consistently recognize achievement and provide positive feedback to dedicated and effective employees will do much to encourage still greater efforts and stronger commitments.

Unfortunately, there will occasionally be a subtle or dramatic change in the performance of a valued employee, resulting in the employee's inability to meet program expectations. The first step in resolving substandard performance is to identify problematic behaviors, such as excessive absences, consistent tardiness, or verbal abuse, and the pro-

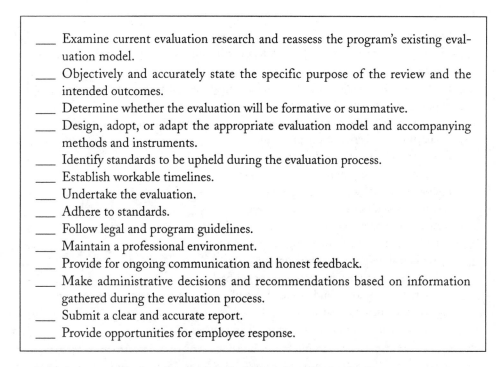

___ Examine current evaluation research and reassess the program's existing evaluation model.

___ Objectively and accurately state the specific purpose of the review and the intended outcomes.

___ Determine whether the evaluation will be formative or summative.

___ Design, adopt, or adapt the appropriate evaluation model and accompanying methods and instruments.

___ Identify standards to be upheld during the evaluation process.

___ Establish workable timelines.

___ Undertake the evaluation.

___ Adhere to standards.

___ Follow legal and program guidelines.

___ Maintain a professional environment.

___ Provide for ongoing communication and honest feedback.

___ Make administrative decisions and recommendations based on information gathered during the evaluation process.

___ Submit a clear and accurate report.

___ Provide opportunities for employee response.

Figure 6. **Recommended procedures for evaluation.**

gram rules or expectations that are being violated. Next, the supervisor must determine the severity of the problem and a course of action.

Because one troubled employee can seriously impact staff and student morale as well as the ability of the program to provide acceptable services, early intervention on the part of the supervisor is usually crucial to the long-term effectiveness of the employee and the program. First, the supervisor should review institutional guidelines to determine when and how to document interactions and communication with the employee. Human resource specialists (Personnel Services, 1993) suggest that administrators (a) guarantee a process that is fair to the employee, (b) consider the employee's reaction to corrective action, (c) ensure that the plan of action fits the severity of the problem, and (d) execute proper follow-up to corrective action. When working with marginal performers (see Bridges, 1990), supervisors will be most effective if they focus on assisting individuals to fulfill program expectations, rather than attempting to diagnose personal problems or counsel.

Supervisors must recognize the value of sustained interaction with all employees. It is equally important to observe, monitor, and interact with highly effective personnel as it is with marginal performers. To maintain open communication and respond to individual as well as program needs, ongoing feedback and problem-solving strategies should be developed and implemented. (See Figure 7 for recommended procedures for ongoing feedback and problem solving.)

____ Objectively observe and monitor all employees regularly.
____ Identify and recognize significant contributions and commitment to the program.
____ Regularly acknowledge and, if possible, reward exemplary performance.
____ Support and encourage competent employees.
____ Identify problematic behaviors when substandard performance is observed.
____ Ascertain the severity of the problem.
____ Determine the source of the problem.
____ Determine the course of action to be taken.
____ Follow institutional and legal guidelines.
____ Discuss expectations with the employee.
____ Initiate corrective intervention or move to dismiss as soon as possible.
____ Establish a timeline for meeting expectations.
____ Complete all required documentation.
____ Do not diagnose personal problems or counsel.
____ Support the employee and all other members of the program when corrective measures are being pursued.
____ Maintain open communication with all employees.

Figure 7. **Recommended procedures for ongoing feedback and problem solving.**

Changes in Personnel

Short- and long-term personnel changes occur for a variety of reasons in a language program. Some changes in personnel are internally motivated and are initiated to support personal and program growth. Experienced employees may be encouraged to assume new responsibilities or to become involved in innovative projects. For example, curriculum revision efforts may be assigned to faculty members with release time. Sabbaticals and professional leaves of absence may be granted, and in-house or institutional promotions may take place. Such vertical and horizontal movements within an organization often provide incentives that result in renewed commitment and dedication to the program and profession.

Other changes in personnel are tied to the economic well-being of the organization. When a program operates in a profit-making environment and administrators find themselves in a growth cycle, additional hiring may take place; however, when a program experiences an economic downturn, financial constraints and budgetary concerns may have a serious impact on the retention of personnel. A reduction in language program staff is often due to a decline in enrollment or organizationally mandated budget cuts. When nonrenewal of some contracts is anticipated, the program administrator should be prepared to support all faculty and staff. Periods of reduction, transition, redistribution of workloads, and reorganization may be marked by the pain of losing valued colleagues and the fear of further reductions.

Cutbacks require special efforts to assist both those exiting and those remaining. Individuals who must depart will appreciate assistance and direction in searching for alternative employment and planning for the future. Program members who remain may require assistance with stress management, morale building, and reorganization challenges. Green (1992) suggests that effective communication is key to reducing organizational dysfunction. Rumors and negativism must be countered, and honest and open sharing of information must take place.

Occasionally dismissal or forced resignation is unavoidable because of poor performance. This drastic course of action should be pursued only after all options to support a troubled employee and to provide remediation have been explored. Dismissal should always be the final step taken in the corrective or disciplinary process. In most working environments, immediate termination or suspension of duties can result only from major acts of misconduct or a serious dereliction of duty (Fortunato & Elliott, 1988).

When disciplinary or corrective action takes place, it is critical that employees have access to grievance procedures and that due process be guaranteed. Procedures outlined by the institution should be strictly adhered to. Management must seek to remain fair and objective while fulfilling supervisory responsibilities. Administrators must also establish a framework that will facilitate the short-term redistribution of duties and support ongoing program services.

The personnel implications of forced resignation, dismissal, or a reduction in staff should not be underestimated; during this time, the administrator, faculty, and staff of the language program will be greatly challenged to fulfill their responsibilities. Conversely, personnel changes that promote opportunities for growth may allow programs to maintain or recapture the energy, vitality, interest, and expertise necessary to achieve program goals and objectives. (See Figure 8 for recommended procedures for making changes in personnel.)

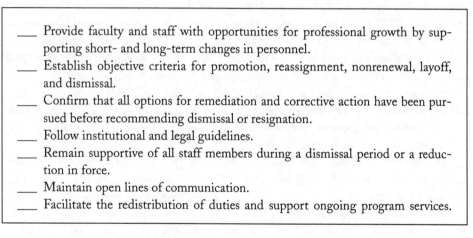

_____ Provide faculty and staff with opportunities for professional growth by supporting short- and long-term changes in personnel.

_____ Establish objective criteria for promotion, reassignment, nonrenewal, layoff, and dismissal.

_____ Confirm that all options for remediation and corrective action have been pursued before recommending dismissal or resignation.

_____ Follow institutional and legal guidelines.

_____ Remain supportive of all staff members during a dismissal period or a reduction in force.

_____ Maintain open lines of communication.

_____ Facilitate the redistribution of duties and support ongoing program services.

Figure 8. **Recommended procedures for making changes in personnel.**

Professional Enrichment

Management research in business and academia has begun to focus increasingly on employees as valued assets, and to stress that human resources are the essential capital upon which we rely for quality education and services. Administrators must acknowledge the important role played by faculty and staff, and determine how best to invest in developing and retaining employees with the highest possible skill, performance, and motivation levels.

Training and development (see Freeman, 1982) should begin during the probationary period and should be maintained throughout an employee's tenure. All program members will benefit from training to improve basic skills and acquire new ones, and from development activities that offer opportunities to engage in inquiry, exploration, contemplation, and reevaluation of job performance and career goals. It is also beneficial, as pointed out by Harris, Monk, McIntyre, and Long (1992), to support training as advanced preparation for new responsibilities or assignments. Promotion from within and options for career advancement are examples of incentives and rewards that should be incorporated into the language program's long-term personnel goals. Planning that links periodic job analyses, program assessment, and personnel evaluation to enrichment objectives is one of many interdependent management functions. Both employee and program needs should form the basis for activities related to continuing education, in-service training, and staff or professional development (Harris, Monk, McIntyre & Long, 1992; Hayes, 1995; Stoller & Christison, 1994).

When undertaking realistic goal setting, employees should work to identify and prioritize individual and program target areas for professional enrichment. During this process, the administrator should address financial and scheduling implications, and promote fair and equitable policies for the allocation and distribution of resources. Conference attendance, workshop participation, independent study, research, and enrollment in professional courses are traditional avenues to enrichment. As noted by Stoller and Christison (1994), in-house activities such as inviting guest speakers, sponsoring faculty brown-bag lunches to share ideas and materials, and scheduling yearly retreats for more in-depth collaboration must also be recognized as integral components of professional development. Furthermore, all program personnel should be encouraged to pursue involvement in peer coaching, mentoring, networking, teamwork, joint planning, teaching exchanges, observations, cooperative learning, or reflective teaching. Opportunities such as these—within the program, institution, or local community—offer affordable, practical, and effective options for all employees.

Professional enrichment activities should provide program personnel with the tools and insights they need to fulfill current and future responsibilities and to counteract burnout. Ultimately, all administrators should strive to develop a supportive working environment that offers a variety of enrichment and advancement opportunities. A workplace that encourages growth and rewards positive contributions will not only retain, but will also attract, qualified and dedicated employees. (See Figure 9 for recommended procedures for professional enrichment.)

___ Commit to an ongoing professional enrichment program.

___ Seek input from all members of the language program.

___ Prioritize based on recent needs assessments, evaluations, and long-term individual, program, and institutional goals.

___ Identify and target internal and external resources.

___ Commit internal resources to professional enrichment early in the fiscal year.

___ Take advantage of opportunities within the program, institution, and community.

___ Provide appropriate incentives and rewards.

Figure 9. **Recommended procedures for professional enrichment.**

Conclusion

Although language programs differ greatly in the scope and variety of services offered to students, almost all programs share one characteristic. They are labor-intensive operations, and as such, the faculty and staff constitute the most important program resource. It is therefore incumbent upon administrators to dedicate significant time and energy to (a) the implementation of personnel practices that establish and promote an atmosphere of mutual trust and respect, (b) the hiring and retention of loyal and motivated personnel, and (c) the development of an infrastructure that maximizes the potential of each individual. Effective management and leadership strategies that result in proactive human resource policies and procedures are essential to the long-term success of language programs.

Discussion Questions and Activities

1. Identify one instructional or support position within a language program. If you were responsible for doing a job analysis and writing a job description for that position, what knowledge, skills, and abilities would you require? What duties and responsibilities would you include in the job description?

2. You are planning to interview finalists for the position described above or for an instructional or support position in your language program. Which interview format or combination of formats would you use and why? List five questions that you would use during the interview. Discuss the rationale for your choices.

3. What is the relationship between the supervision and evaluation of personnel, and the development of professional enrichment plans? Provide examples.

4. If your language program were transitioning from a skills-based curriculum to a content-based curriculum next year, what professional enrichment activities would you include in the program's long-term plans?

5. How can language program administrators improve their human resource management skills? Suggest a professional enrichment plan for an active language program administrator.

6. As director of a language program, imagine that you hired a new instructor one month ago. You have already received complaints from students and other staff members about the instructor's interpersonal skills. How did you respond to those with whom you spoke? What course of action will you now pursue?

Suggested Readings

Bridges, E. M. (1990). *Managing the incompetent teacher* (2nd ed.). Eugene, OR: ERIC Clearinghouse on Educational Management, University of Oregon.

This book is written for administrators who supervise and evaluate teachers. It provides well-researched guidance for working with marginal or incompetent educators. Bridges outlines procedures for determining whether instructors are meeting evaluation criteria and suggests how to provide appropriate remediation. In the final section of the book, the author addresses issues related to the dismissal and forced resignation of an employee.

Eder, R. W., & Ferris, G. R. (Eds.). (1989). *The employment interview: Theory, research, and practice.* Newbury Park, CA: Sage.

This text brings together and compares a variety of theories and related research underlying different interviewing strategies. The editors provide a comprehensive review of the literature, while multiple contributors offer fundamental background information, application suggestions, and commentary that can assist in designing more valid and reliable interview formats.

Harris, B. M., Monk, B. J., McIntyre, K. E., & Long, D. F. (1992). *Personnel administration in education: Leadership for instructional development* (3rd ed.). Boston: Allyn & Bacon.

Although this text does not focus specifically on language programs, it could serve as a valuable resource for administrators who are interested in an overview of the many issues and challenges faced in human resource management. Of particular interest are the chapters on recruitment, selection, evaluation, management, development, and training. Extensive appendixes include sample forms, lists, profiles, and other tools for completing the administrative functions described in the text.

Pennington, M. C. (Ed.). (1991). *Building better English programs: Perspectives on evaluation in ESL.* Washington, D. C. NAFSA: Association of International Educators.

Three articles from Part IV of the Pennington volume (written by Fox, Matthies, and Pennington and Young) impart important information about performance reviews of language program instructors and administrators. The Pennington and Young chapter, entitled "Procedures and instruments for faculty evaluation in ESL" (pp. 191-227), provides an in-depth discussion of instruments and procedures used in faculty evaluation. Useful appendixes give the reader samples of rating scales and forms, as well as lists of faculty standards and categories for evaluation. The chapters by Fox, entitled "Evaluating the ESL program director" (pp. 228-240), and Matthies, entitled "Administrative evaluation in ESL programs: How'm I doin'?" (pp. 241-256), introduce the rationale behind administrative evaluations and identify related procedures and approaches. In her appendixes, Matthies provides a checklist for evaluating a language program director and an evaluation form for students.

Appendix
Sample Telephone Reference Check Questionnaire*

Candidate _____ Position _____

Reference _____ Date _____

Company/Institution _____ Phone _____

My name is _____ and I work in the _____

language program. We are filling a position and would like to verify employment information on

(applicant's name), one of your former/current employees.

1. Can you verify her/his title and dates of employment?

2. What is/was the nature of her/his job?

3. Would you please comment on her/his:
   a. Attendance
   b. Dependability
   c. Ability/willingness to assume responsibility
   d. Ability/willingness to follow directions
   e. Degree of supervision required
   f. Quality of work
   g. Quantity of work
   h. Interpersonal/intercultural communication skills
   i. Overall attitude

4. How would you summarize her/his strengths?

5. How would you summarize her/his weaknesses?

6. Why did she/he leave the position?

7. Would you re-employ? Why/Why not?

8. I'd like to describe the position that we are going to fill, and ask if you think there would be a match.

9. Is there anything else that you would like to comment on regarding the applicant's employment or job performance?

Comments:

*Adapted from "Exhibit F—Sample Reference Check," by Personnel Services (1993), *Supervisor's Manual*, Recruitment and Selection Section, Portland, OR: Lewis and Clark College

Chapter 14

THE LANGUAGE PROGRAM BUDGET: FINANCIAL PLANNING AND MANAGEMENT OF RESOURCES

John J. Staczek
American Graduate School of International Management

or the language program administrator, resources are key to successful program development and delivery. The two principal resources available to language program administrators are (a) the cadre of professionals who provide academic services through instruction, administration, information management, curriculum development, student advisement, evaluation, and research and (b) the money to provide these academic services. As a budgetary entity, the language program places certain demands on its home institution (Staczek & Carkin, 1985) because each of these services, together with many others, has associated *direct* and *indirect costs;*[1] these costs must be covered by program *income* if we accept a principle of resource management that affirms that *expenses* cannot exceed income over the period of a calendar year. It is this principle that establishes a framework for a discussion of the academic budget and its management. To facilitate the discussion of language program budget management, the definitions of budgets and management from Szilagyi (1988) will be adopted:

> [Budgets] are formal statements of future expenditures, revenues, and expected profits developed to control the use of an organization's financial resources. Budgets form the last link in the management chain that began with goals and strategies. Thus, they are the most detailed management practice used to ensure that an organization's goals are achieved. (p. 563)

> [Management is] the process of integrating resources and tasks toward the achievement of stated organizational goals. Managers—those who practice management—are responsible for giving direction to the organizations they manage. They must translate organizational goals into unit objects, organize resources (people, finances, and equipment) in a manner to achieve results, and see to it that the stated goals are met. (p. 5)

Within colleges and universities, the language program should be expected to operate from a budgetary and management perspective as any other academic program on campus. That its income may be derived differently (i.e., that it is not allocated by way of a public legislative process in the case of public institutions and is established on a *cost-for-services basis*) should make no difference to the process of management. Ultimately, sound business practice must underlie the academic language program enterprise.

The above discussion of budget and management provides a framework for referring to the following matters of importance:

1. The language program as a budgetary entity.

2. Its reporting relationships within a larger institutional setting.

3. Strategic planning with regard to goals, *expenditures*, income, and other *revenue* expectations.

4. Budget features and processes.

5. Monitoring and auditing procedures.

The budgetary management principles and practices discussed here are expected to have universal application and are, of course, interpretable according to local institutional expectations and regulations. The guidelines presented should be viewed as sound budgetary practices to which a language program administrator (who usually serves as budgetary manager as well) must be responsibly committed.

The Language Program in the Institution

Across U.S. colleges and universities, it is not unusual to find a variety of placements of the intensive English program. (See Kaplan, this volume, for more information on program placement.) Whatever the setting, most often the language program is expected to be self-sufficient financially, to be able to manage its own financial affairs, and to be responsible for the sound investment of its resources. While these expectations may have been different in the 1980s and early 1990s, because of the willingness of universities and colleges to launch such programs and make *front-end investments*, the fiscal restraints and budgetary cutbacks at the same institutions in the mid-1990s have been the motivation for a shifting of risk away from the institutional parent to the program itself. During the 1990s, higher education has found itself unable to cope with (a) limited growth in tuition income, federal funding for instruction and research, endowments, and even investments; and (b) increases in expenditures that have resulted from increases in salaries, *fringe benefits*, costs of materials and services, and a general change in the national and global economic environment. Sound fiscal practice has indicated that any risk has to be the responsibility of the language program and not the institution. And, as we shall see later, the risk now faced by language programs can be managed.

Success in the management of a language program is not solely dependent on managing fiscal resources. It also requires that administrators[2] work with other language program professionals (e.g., instructors) and skilled staff in the overall organization and management of human and financial resources (see Staczek, 1991). The successful language program, as is well known in professional and academic circles, has often become a source of revenue for other offices in its institutional setting. That this occurs ex post facto and is not part of any early and principled planning is unfortunate. In my opinion, if the language program, whatever its institutional home, is able to bear some shared costs of services, it is within its best interests to do so provided that there has been appropriate consultation and negotiation.

Programs As Budgetary Entities

In the introduction to this chapter, as well as elsewhere in this volume, language programs are referred to as academic units within institutions; they are located budgetarily within those institutions for accounting and auditing purposes. As institutional budgetary entities, language programs are part of a system that can be monitored with regard to the sound use of fiscal resources. Language program income may not come from the same sources as other institutional income, yet program budgets are held to the same accounting and auditing practices as other units. That language program budgets are trackable entities whose activities are budgetarily similar to those of other academic programs is important for program administrators to keep in mind.

The role of the budget and budgeting process is quite complex and multidimensional. Budgets are important to language program administrators for a number of reasons:

First, they aid in planning in that they force management to develop achievable goals and basic plans and policies associated with these goals. In other words, budgets set a standard of production (the budgeted amount of output). From an organizing point of view, budgets help clarify responsibilities among organizational members. This is particularly important in coordinating the activities of the organization. The interaction between managers and subordinates that occurs during budget development helps define and integrate performance-related activities. By specifying what resources are to be used, budgets help achieve goals through the successful implementation of the organization's strategies. This is an important part of the leading function. Finally, from a control view, budgets lead to the efficient use of resources, assist in preserving valuable resources, and establish a mechanism for periodic organizational analysis.

More than anything, budgets are important and universally read "money." Dollar figures are a common denominator among managers across a wide variety of organizational activities, including the purchase of raw materials and equipment ..., selling and advertising expenses in marketing, hiring and training of [personnel], and so on. Since profits are expressed in monetary terms, budgets are used by profit-oriented firms in estimating and guiding activities. (Szilagyi, 1988, pp. 563–564)

As Szilagyi refers to *profits*, it is important to digress for just a moment and to keep in mind at this point that universities, colleges, and academic programs often think of profits euphemistically, thus calling them *surpluses*, even *variances*. Such excess of income (or increase in net *assets*) is often unanticipated, given the nature of language programs as we know them. Profits (or whatever terminology is used) do appear in monthly statements that are monitored by accounting offices. And, when they do appear, they must be explained (perhaps more so in public than in private institutions). What is important when defending surpluses is to demonstrate a plan, a *strategic plan*, that connects achievable goals, strategies for achieving those goals, and the program's ability to invest in itself with regard to the acquisition of materials, equipment, furniture, even space, and the development of its professionals. Surpluses, as with all resources, can be managed effectively provided there is a plan.

Reporting Relationships

With the variety of placements of a language program within an institution comes a variety of reporting relationships, not only to the next higher level of academic administration (such as a department chair, dean, associate dean, or vice president) but also to a fiscal administrator (or budget officer) in the institution. This fiscal administrator—often in the office of the chief financial officer or treasurer, or the office of the administrative vice president—is the individual (or office) responsible for monitoring and auditing accounts, to ensure sound accounting practice.

If the language program has an agreed-upon strategic plan for the effective use of its resources, the academic and fiscal officers overseeing the language program can be helpful in implementing the plan. Their offices are often the source of information about policies and practices within the institution. Language program administrators should turn to them not only to seek their advice but also to trumpet the successes of the program in terms of such matters as student advancement through degree and certificate programs of the institution, acquisition of materials and equipment, and investment in the institution through contributions to other units in lieu of services and goods. In this way, programs demonstrate their integration into a system, into an organization that works for mutual benefit.

Strategic Planning

As part of the budgetary process, it is important for the language program administrator (in consultation with faculty and staff) to take the initiative to establish budget-related goals and objectives, with methods for accomplishing them—essentially a strategic plan. Strategic planning has been defined as "a set of activities that lead to the definition of objectives for the entire organization and to the determination of appropriate strategies for achieving those objectives" (Szilazyi, 1988, p. 869). (See Klinghammer, this volume, for a more extended discussion of the strategic planning process.) Essentially, a budget without a plan is no more than an idea without a way to implement it. The plan becomes a statement of incremental academic and professional development and, like ongoing curricular reform (the so-called unfinished curriculum which is a curriculum undergoing development, evaluation, and adjustment or change), is the statement that builds the reputation of the program.

The statement of goals and objectives needs to be realistic and suited to the individual language program. The goals (long-range as they are) and objectives (short-term achievables) are to be established by the program director, in consultation with faculty and staff. Each of the goals and objectives can be costed; that is, a cost for each can be determined within established institutional and professional guidelines.

The process of establishing goals and objectives is a time-consuming one because it necessarily must involve people in its development. Involvement in the process becomes a way for language program personnel to invest themselves in the growth and development of the program. This kind of investment represents a form of engagement, and engagement is empowerment through knowledge and participation. (See Soppelsa, this volume, for further insights on empowerment.)

Figure 1 illustrates the important relationship between fiscal goals and objectives and related strategies for accomplishing them. The goals/objectives for a given *fiscal year* could include the acquisition of income (box 1) through regular student enrollments (box A) and special, short-term language programs (box B) that will support salaries, fringe benefits, and expenses consonant with program delivery and faculty/staff development within the program and institution for that year. Program planning ideally and practically should also include some long-range goals for which (a) accumulated capital (in the form of planned and managed surpluses) will be set aside for future development activities such as the purchase of additional services, materials, equipment, and space rental, and/or (b) *overhead* expenses as might be appropriate to the institution. Such surpluses, if they are to be realized, can be planned and managed within an institutional framework that allows a budgetary *carry-over* of surplus from one year to the next, or trades of capital with another unit (e.g., a dean's office, through which advanced purchases can be made from one or another account to be paid back in kind in the next fiscal budget). A trade of capital might take the form of purchase of equipment from a budget external to the program with payback to come the following year in terms of an equivalent dollar amount in travel reimbursement. Often called a form of creative budgeting, this system of trade or, more euphemistically, organized integrated budgeting requires careful planning and consultation.

Achievable fiscal goals and objectives (1–3)

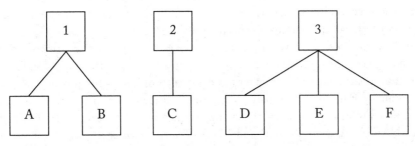

Strategies (A–F) for accomplishing goals and objectives

Figure 1. **Relationship between fiscal goals/objectives and strategies.**

Budget

With a plan to provide academic instructional services—given all its attendant needs for personnel, materials, equipment, space, curricular and professional development, research, travel, and promotion (through advertising and publicity)—a first budget that eventually becomes a framework for subsequent budgets is prepared. With some adaptation, language program budgets can be formatted to complement generic designs for sections of the budget that ought already to be available in the institution. Thus, the language program begins to fit into an established system for proposing a budget statement of (a) projected and actual income and (b) projected and actual expenditures. If prepared properly and if consonant with a plan for delivery of instructional services, the budget is the statement—when reviewed, adjusted, and approved—of planned activities for a fiscal period of 12 months.

The proposed budget plan of income and expenditures, accompanied by a narrative justifying both, consists of a number of categories of income sources and resource expenditures, as outlined in Table 1. Activity in each of these categories has budgetary consequences that can be planned and managed.

Table 1. Budget Categories

Income/Revenue Sources	Resource Expenditures
Instructional fees	Salaries
Other contributions and transfers	Current expenses
	Capital equipment
	Overhead

Expenditures

Among the guiding principles in determining a budget from the expenditure side of the ledger is the notion that every activity in a program has a cost, whether direct (salaries), indirect (fringe benefits), or even hidden (some food and beverages for visitors, petty cash reimbursements). The prudent administrator, in the preparation of a budget, is the one who successfully predicts these activities and projects an appropriate cost based on local, institutional, and national norms or available formulae.

The director does not have to rely on wit alone to determine the costs of program goods and services; the director should look to the institution and the profession for guidance. Institutional sources of information include such offices as the treasurer, the registrar, Continuing Education, International Programs, academic departments, deans offices, and the like. Professional sources of information include associations such as TESOL, AAAL, NAFSA, AAIEP, UCIEP, and MLA; *The Chronicle of Higher Education;* electronic lists, bulletin boards, electronic mail, and the World Wide Web of the Internet; and colleagues around the world. Unlike the situation of 10 or 15 years ago when very little information seemed to be available, there is now more information than a single individual can profitably digest and use. Now one's unwillingness to seek information, solicit advice, and network represents a pitfall of organizational planning.

Salaries. As in most other organizations, salaries usually represent the largest expenditure of a language program budget. Salaries must be determined within existing institutional and professional guidelines. Consistent with criteria for academic preparation and rank (e.g., instructor, assistant professor, associate professor, professor, adjunct or part-time instructor), information is readily available. In my opinion, language program instructional salaries must be set at a rate consonant with equivalent appointments in cognate departments within the institution such as English and foreign languages. Others in this volume will have argued for professional salaries for professional services. I would only echo their calls for professional compensation.

This category will include a salary for the program director or for a portion of that individual's effort throughout the fiscal year. This may be done on the basis of a full-time equivalent (FTE) position; that is, if the individual has a faculty salary of $36,000—at a particular rank—for a 9- or 10-month contract period, during which the individual is expected to teach six courses, for the sake of argument, release from teaching or reassignment from teaching to administration might take the form of a .50 FTE for instruction and a .50 FTE for administration. The remaining 2- or 3-month summer contract needs to be a percentage of the regular academic year contract, let's say an additional .33 FTE. If that is not workable, there may already be existing guidelines or formulae within the institution for annualizing the 9- or 10-month contract. None of this means that program directors should be expected to teach .50 FTE. This is a principle to be determined within the program itself.

Other instructional salaries will be either full time or part time. All full-time salaries will necessarily require an additional percentage contribution for fringe benefits available within the institution; these include employer-related contributions to, for example, social security, disability insurance, worker's compensation, and retirement. The percentage contribution is predetermined and is not subject to negotiation; fringe benefit contributions can range from 18% to 34% of full-time salaries, which means that, at a fringe benefit rate of 25%, a $30,000 FTE salary will cost the program an additional $7,500. If, for example, that same faculty member is on loan from another department to teach .50 FTE in the language program, the program director would calculate the same $30,000 position at $15,000 plus $3,750 for fringe benefits. This is just one example of a possibility within the program.

Adjunct or part-time instructors' salaries are managed differently. Part-time instructors are often paid on a per-course basis, without fringe benefits. Another instructional category might be that of a student in training who could be paid at an hourly rate rather than on a per-course basis. The director would need to determine, given institutional and professional guidelines, an appropriate salary rate for this type of instruction.

All of the same can be said for the nonacademic or secretarial and clerical staff of a program. Institutional and professional guidelines are useful sources of information when determining salaries for nonacademic personnel. In addition, student assistants who qualify for work-study might also be employed as nonacademic personnel. Their cost to the program is not budgeted at full-time rates but rather at shared contributing rates according to federal guidelines.

A final salary item is the honorarium, which provides the program with an opportunity to invite individuals to serve as visiting consultants for curriculum, materials, and program development or to present specialized lectures or workshops for students and faculty. (Any other expenses billed by the consultant would fall under the next category of Current Expense.)

The salary category might resemble the following in a budget:

SALARIES
 Academic
  Director (administration and instruction)
  Faculty (full time)
  Faculty (part time)
  Hourly instruction
  Honoraria
 Nonacademic
  Secretarial (full time)
  Secretarial (part time)
  Student assistants
  Work-study students
  Fringe benefits @ x % of total full-time salaries

Current expense. As a budgetary category, the current expense portion of the budget is perhaps the longest because of the potential number of subcategories; and while it may be long, it is certainly one of the most straightforward for the variety of goods and services it contains. A listing of the subitems (nonsalary items, or what might be called consumables in the sense of purchasable and tangible items) is more revealing than any explanation. These subitems include, but are not limited to, the following:

1. Communications (telephone lines and sets, long distance, telex, facsimile)

2. Office supplies (audio tapes for duplication, computer diskettes, other office and laboratory disposables)

3. Duplication and copying (photocopying, both internal and external)

4. Educational materials (shelf-test kits, bluebooks, maps, class sets of books)

5. Library materials (program-internal library and university or college library contributions in the form of print resources and other media such as commercial tapes, videos, CD-ROMs)

6. Promotional materials (brochures, videos, posters, advertisements)

7. Computer software (instructional and managerial)

8. Travel (professional development, conference participation, educational field trips, program development/student recruitment)

9. Concession (program-related receptions and representation, food and beverages)

10. Equipment maintenance contracts and equipment replacement

According to local institutional guidelines, much of the above can be purchased within the institution; some may also be "outsourced" (that is, purchased outside the institution at more competitive rates and without the usual and customary built-in overhead charges) based on competitive bidding. There is no magic number for items in the current expenses category. However, there is one caution, namely, that photocopying and long distance communication can add up over the period of an annual budget. Both areas need to be appropriately budgeted and carefully monitored.

The most important consideration in the current expense category is that faculty and staff have sufficient support for instruction and for reasonable professional development (e.g., attendance and participation at local, regional, and national conferences). The allocation of travel funds (for professional development and other program activities) has to be made on a principled basis, as does every other decision in budget management; travel guidelines need to be established with regard to the purpose and extent of funded travel for program development, promotion, and recruitment; faculty professional development; and other program-related travel such as educational field trips.

Capital equipment. This budgetary category includes major purchases of office furniture and equipment (e.g., duplicating machines), computers, and laboratory equipment that represent significant outlays of dollars initially but not regularly. Often these items require narrative justifications within the institution and must be open to competitive bidding for purchase and possibly creative cost sharing. Two examples may suffice:

1. The purchase of specialized computer video terminals for the media lab on a cost-share basis, in which, for example, the language program offers to purchase certain equipment that may also be used in the lab by other students, providing, of course, that the lab would also provide service for the equipment.

2. Video camera upgrades that will facilitate recording oral language interviews; the camera could be used by other language programs on a shared basis.

Both types of purchases would require service maintenance contracts and replacement costs budgeted under the current expense category.

Overhead. This category may or may not have expense implications for a language program budget depending on the institutional commitment and relationship to the language program. However, it must be borne in mind that general university or college budgets do contain an overhead category that is budgeted as a percentage of the total of such items as space and utilities. If the language program is required to make a percentage contribution for its use of space and utilities, this can also be accomplished on a contribution basis to other offices with which the program interacts, namely, the registrar, International Programs, purchasing, the dean's office, or other institutional offices. This contribution may take the form of an assignment of a percentage of FTE for positions in those offices because the workload of the individual has increased as a result of program activity. This is only one example, among many, of an approach to the issue of institutional overhead charges.

Income/Revenue Sources

There are two approaches to take for the income or revenue side of the budget. The first assumes a proposed initial budget for a new language program; in the case of a new program, where income is zero, a budget has to be projected on the basis of projected enrollment. Projected income in the form of fees may be "costed" according to an existing fee structure for similar instruction in the institution, an alternate fee structure (cost for services), or a combination of the two. Projected enrollments will help to establish instructional staffing needs on the basis of class sizes and teaching loads. These figures are initially helpful in determining the costs of instruction and may in fact be calculated estimates. Of course, these estimates are approximate calculations of direct instructional costs and would not normally include other administrative and expense costs related to the program. In other words, for an initial budget, a lot of costing has to be estimated. It is prudent to overestimate costs in order to ensure a necessary minimum level of income to cover program expenses. If, however, there is a contribution of *start-up* or *seed money* for the program, this becomes an effective cushion against risk. Nonetheless, it should be borne in mind that these funds eventually may have to be repaid or reimbursed.

The second approach is based on the principle that the program is not a new one but an established one with a pattern of enrollments, revenues, and expenses. In this approach, the budget needs to be an anticipating statement of revenues and expenses, a statement against which progress can be measured. Income *projections* are made on the basis of historical figures with the surplus from the previous year (in the form of carry-over revenue that is not dependent on a pattern of enrollments or expenses) or the previous year's budget deficit that is taken as a loss against anticipated revenues. Over time, programs develop an information database on student enrollments, fees, and expenditures that permit program administrators to project future income. (See Davidson and Tesh, this volume, for a formula to predict student enrollments.) This historical information is useful for analyzing budget fluctuations which can later be planned for and managed only if historical data are accurately recorded and maintained. White, Martin, Stimson, and Hodge (1991) present a set of practical perspectives, albeit somewhat abstract for those not familiar with budgets and budget statistical analyses, on how changes over time in budget variables (e.g., enrollment, peak demand for teachers) can affect income and profit projections.

Instructional fees. An established structure is used to determine student fees, possibly based on institutional formulae such as credit or noncredit course tuition, nonresident and resident tuition, or cost-for-services. These fees are determined by considering the costs of full-time study; following established guidelines for the issuance of F-1 visa status (a student visa), this normally means 20–30 hours of instructional contact per week. Some greater portion of this is direct instructional contact, and some smaller portion of it is conducted outside the classroom (in, for example, language, computer, or writing laboratories). If the program authorizes part-time study, contact hours have to be costed not on the basis of percentages of full-time study but on the basis of actual costs. This would mean, using hypothetical figures, a rate structure of the following type for a 15-week semester program:

1.0 FTE study (25 hours/week)	$5,000
.75 FTE study (20 hours/week)	$4,500
.50 FTE study (15 hours/week)	$3,500
.25 FTE study (10 hours/week)	$2,500

The instructional and administrative costs referred to earlier are built in to such a rate structure under the categories of salary, current expense, capital equipment, and overhead. The fee structure must also include a formalized refund policy for students who withdraw from the program. Such a refund policy can be established within institutional guidelines and must be made known to all potential applicants through promotional materials.

Instructional fees are the major source of revenue for language programs. Fees for other services might well include the following:

1. Program application fee (covering costs incidental to registration and subsequent communication)

2. Testing administration fee (covering costs associated with the Institutional TOEFL, for example, or prescreening tests conducted abroad during a recruitment trip)

3. Accent or dialect reduction clinic fee (a fee for hourly referrals for specific instruction on pronunciation)

4. Activity fees (covering costs associated with field trips, including admissions fees, vehicle rental, and mileage)

5. Lab fees (covering materials required for the smooth operation of a lab and contributing to replacement costs)

Although these fees can be discrete budget items, the first two can easily be folded into a single fee, much like the general application fee that accompanies university or college admissions applications. Generally, none of these fees should be considered refundable, either in whole or in part.

Other contributions or transfers. In this revenue category, if such revenue is available, would be found the seed money (reimbursable or nonreimbursable) referred to earlier, any funds generated through specific contracts for services (e.g., with foreign governments, universities, businesses, corporations, or other such offices), competitive grants to provide specific services, or gifts from alumni or international, national, and local organizations. In the case of grants and contracts, it is expected that the institution will charge an overhead rate on all direct costs. It is not uncommon, however, for language programs that have generated grants or contracts to negotiate a whole or partial return of overhead costs to the program. In effect, the return to the program becomes an in-kind contribution from the institution itself. (See Mickelson, this volume, for more detailed information on grants and contracts.)

Monitoring and Accounting

Budgets, as statements of fiscal activity associated with the delivery of a program, are predictable because revenues coincide with periodic startups (e.g., quarters or semesters) and because expenditures continue through entire budget cycles (salaries and expenses are monthly costs). The expectation is that revenues are available to cover anticipated expenditures. Borrowing or deficit spending is not a sound business or accounting practice.

Monitoring Income and Expenditures

With the knowledge that there is banked revenue in a program budget, the director, aware of monthly costs to the program, is able periodically to monitor the flow of the budget. Generally, an institutional accounting office has an established reporting mechanism for monthly budget sheets. On the basis of sound accounting practices, information is available in these budget statements that demonstrates monthly rates of expenditures by category in relation to monthly allocations of revenue. That is to say, if the program operates on a quarterly budget, expenditures can nonetheless be tracked by intervals of one month. If expenses, for example, for the first month exceed a third of revenues, and for the second month also exceed a third of revenues, that would leave less than a third of revenues for the remaining month, assuming expenses for the third month would be roughly equivalent to the first and second. Monitoring devices such as this one are already built into general accounting and reporting procedures. Moreover, they are built into each of the budgeted categories. These devices become referential guides to patterns of expenditures and are thus helpful to the planning and monitoring process.

These monthly statements are useful for monitoring accounting procedures. However, it should be remembered that the issuance of such monthly statements in institutions and organizations is not usually as timely as program administrators would like. Thus, administrators need to develop similar internal systems that can help in the monitoring process. Not knowing the pattern of expenditures to revenue is no excuse for over-spending. Resources need to be monitored carefully. When patterns have been established, they become benchmarks by which administrators are guided further in the accounting process. Monthly forecasting of expenditures, given a history of expenditures, becomes important to the process.

Finally, with regard to periodic budget statements, the language program administrator should make certain to understand accounting and reporting procedures and review the books with some regularity to ensure that revenues and expenditures are accurately and properly posted. If they are not, a significant amount of labor is involved in the tracking process, and additional labor, as all labor, has its costs in the normal operation of a program.

Justification of Expenditures

The need to justify expenditures may seem like a minor point in the budgetary process, yet it is one worth mentioning. Many program expenditures require no more authorization than the signature of the program director or designee. Some, mostly larger purchases, often require a next-level approval. It is prudent to understand the requirements and policies of the home organization, including the need to provide written justification for large expenditures. Nothing is more awkward in an organizational setting than to miss a step in a formalized process and thus slow down the purchase of goods and services. Imagine ordering replacement computer equipment for the writing laboratory only to learn 2 months after submitting the purchase order that another level of approval, with written justification, was required. The acquisition process is stopped, and instruction is impaired.

Proposed Budget Increases

A budget is not static; thus, it is subject to fluctuations. Normally there are more increases than decreases because goods and services are subject to external inflationary increase. Therefore, from one year to the next, consistent with institutional and program goals, adjustments should be made to revenues and to the cost of goods and services. The director needs to understand the position of the program with regard to the institution and its revenues. If an institutional plan includes a budget increase or decrease, the language program should expect to follow suit. However, if language program revenues are not tied to public funding, the program would not be expected to decrease its revenues and expenses. If it is tied to public funding, then commensurate adjustments must be made.

Unforeseen Expenses

Unforeseen expenses can result in hidden program costs. Take, for example, the loss (through natural disaster or pilferage) of computer equipment or of instructional materials. The program or the institution may have insurance to cover this loss, but insurance reimbursements are usually never for full value. Thus, the program will have to make up the difference. These are unforeseen, often unavoidable hidden costs that can be planned for over time as patterns of expenditures are developed in the form of, for example, equipment or materials replacement, and as surpluses are produced.

Fund Transfers Between Categories

In the course of a budget period, it is not unusual to discover that expenditures in certain budget categories have been either over- or underestimated. This may not seem to present a problem, as the categories are all part of the same overall budget. After all, if the money is available in one category, it is logical to assume that it is just as spendable in another. However, that may not universally be the case. Depending on institutional guidelines and accounting practices, it may be possible to convert salary to current expense but not current expense to salary; or salary may not be convertible into capital expenditures. Or institutional guidelines may permit such transfers only within certain limits, of perhaps 5%. Transfers between categories may require some form of justification and an appropriate authorization at another level. For this reason, it is most important that the program administrator be familiar with institutional guidelines to manage effectively a contingency such as unforeseen expenses or fund transfers by category.

Conclusion

This chapter has provided an overview, with a number of examples and some detail, of language program resource planning and management. The resources were described in terms of a budget statement of activities to be accomplished and paid for, all within a larger context of instructional and support services. The magic, if there is any, in the management of a budget is the magic that knowledge, understanding, and creativity bring to the organization and management of resources. In its development and implementation, the budget is the organizing device that allows professionals in a language program to provide their instructional services. In the hands of a skilled language program administrator working with a cadre of professionals, the budget is the silent partner in a successful enterprise.

Endnotes

1. Italicized terms are defined in a glossary at the end of the chapter.

2. Language programs have been managed skillfully by academic and nonacademic directors. That there are differences between corporate and professional managers is not a matter to be ignored. For a perspective on the cultures of corporate and professional management, the research by Raelin (1986) is quite useful.

Discussion Questions and Activities

1. Why is it important for a language program to have a strategic plan? How does a strategic plan relate to resource management?

2. How should a language program administrator develop strategies for determining salaries for instructional and support staff?

3. To what extent does a program administrator have a responsibility to involve program faculty and staff in the development and implementation of a budget? How can faculty and staff benefit from becoming involved in the process? How can the language program benefit from faculty and staff participation in budget planning?

4. Language program budgets are normally crafted to follow the general format of the home institution. In this chapter, Staczek identifies commonly used income and expenditure categories. What categories are required by an institution with which you are familiar? Is the terminology used the same or different from the model proposed in this chapter?

5. Propose a programmatic budget for a language program of 42 FTE students. What are the preliminary considerations with regard to income and expense? Compare a program of this size with one of 63 students.

Suggested Readings

Raelin, J. A. (1986). *The clash of cultures: Managers and professionals.* Boston: Harvard Business School Press.

Although not directly applicable to language program contexts, Raelin provides an excellent analysis of the cultural differences in organizations between corporate managers and salaried professionals.

Szilagyi, A. (1988). *Management and performance*. Glenview, IL: Scott Foresman.

In this text, Szilagyi provides a comprehensive overview of organizational management and performance based on a case study approach to ansalysis and problem solving.

White, R., Martin, M., Stimson, M., & Hodge, R. (1991). *Management in English language teaching*. New York: Cambridge University Press.

The authors of this guide, the only of its kind, discuss the organization and management of English language teaching programs. The perspective is largely applicable to private proprietary programs.

Glossary

assets. In financial accounting, assets are tangible and intangible property items that can be made liquid or turned into cash. Such tangible items may be equipment and supplies; intangible items are services that can be provided.

carry-over. In accounting practice, a carry-over is a sum of money that can be transferred within the same account.

cost-for-services basis. The price set by a vendor for the purchase of a service, such as an hourly or daily rate.

deficit. A shortage of money attributed to expenses exceeding income.

direct cost. The price of services or goods, including salaries, equipment, and supplies.

encumbrance. A financial obligation or responsibility, such as continuing monthly basic telephone costs.

expenditure. An amount or outlay of money for the purchase of services or goods. Often used interchangeably with the term expense.

expense. The cost of an item of services or goods. Often used interchangeably with the term expenditure.

fiscal year/period. An accounting or budget cycle of 12 months during which income and expenses are tracked. A typical academic institution cycle is July 1 through June 30.

fringe benefit. An employment benefit or enhancement, such as health, dental, or life insurance, provided to an employee in addition to salary. A type of indirect cost that may be shared between employer and employee.

front-end investment. An initial commitment of funds not usually generated by a unit itself to establish a program or to make a purchase of some significance (e.g., language laboratory equipment). A front-end investment may take the form of a no-cost loan—to be repaid over an agreed-upon period of time—or a direct grant.

income. The amount of money received during a fiscal period for the purchase of services and goods. Income may come in the form of program fees, no-cost loans, or grants. Also referred to as revenue.

indirect cost. A category of expense, contrasted with direct costs, that is established by an entity (usually the institutional budget office) to cover fringe benefits and overhead.

overhead. Operating expenses related to the cost of space use, utilities, maintenance, and fringe benefits, all exclusive of the costs of direct purchases of goods and services.

profit. An overage of money after all expenses have been paid.

projections. Anticipated income or expenses based on enrollment or spending patterns.

revenue. Money collected from all sources, including registration and fees, loans, grants, and sale of goods and services. Also referred to as income.

seed money. Financial contributions from other units or entities to initiate a program or to purchase goods and services, before program income from registration and fees is available. Like front-end investments, seed money may take the form of loans or grants.

start-up money. Also known as seed money.

strategic plan. A set of activities that lead to the definition of objectives for the entire organization and to the determination of appropriate strategies for achieving those objectives.

surplus. A euphemism for profit, referring to the excess of funds after expenses have been paid.

variance. The difference between income and expenses. May be positive (i.e., profit, surplus) or negative (i.e., deficit). Also a euphemism for profit, loss, or deficit.

Chapter 15

TIME MANAGEMENT PRINCIPLES FOR LANGUAGE PROGRAM ADMINISTRATORS

Mary Ann Christison
University of Utah/Snow College

Fredricka L. Stoller
Northern Arizona University

For what is Time? Who is able easily and briefly to explain it? Who is able so much as in thought to comprehend it so as to express himself concerning it? And yet what in our usual discourse do we more familiarly and knowingly make more mention of than Time? And surely we understand it well enough when we speak of it, we understand it also when in speaking with another we hear it named. What then is Time? If nobody asks me I know; but if I were desirous to explain it to someone that should ask me, plainly I know not.—*St. Augustine*

anguage program administrators are busy people. Whether they administer small programs by themselves, or administer large programs with assistance, their multifaceted jobs require that they manage their time wisely. The job of a language program administrator is complex, making time management a formidable challenge. Kaplan (this volume) compares the responsibilities of a language program director to a divisional dean, in a college or university setting, rather than a departmental chair because of the scope of responsibilities so often associated with language program administration. Although specific administrative duties differ at every institution, language program administrators are often partially or fully responsible for overseeing student admissions, designing curricula, administering placement exams, managing budgets, scheduling classes, supervising faculty, hiring and firing faculty and staff, running meetings and orientation sessions, building linkages with campus and community entities, advocating for students and faculty, and providing immigration and academic advising. In addition to these so-called standard duties are the unforeseen tasks that surface in response to sudden requests for information, unanticipated student and faculty crises, abrupt breakdowns in technology, unexpected personnel illnesses, and disruptive computer viruses, to name just a few unanticipated but predictable occurrences. As indicated elsewhere in this volume, language program administrators must also be skilled communicators, leaders, negotiators, decision makers, innovators, strategic planners, and grant writers.

To accomplish all of this successfully, language program administrators must prioritize strategically, plan effectively, delegate sufficiently, and avoid procrastination. When language program administrators manage their time wisely, both the manager and the program will benefit in many ways. One of the greatest challenges associated with time management is that language program administrators, like other managers, are not in total control of their time. Their time is partly controlled by their superiors and partly by the program itself; thus, a manager's own time is quite restricted (Schilit, 1983). Given the limited time available, how can language program administrators best fulfill their responsibilities? Some principles of time management are explored here that can assist language program administrators in their jobs and in their private lives as well.

The Concept of Time

Many different English expressions are associated with time. "Time flies" is used when one has not accomplished expected outcomes within the time available. "Time will take care of it" is stated when one feels that, given enough time, a particular condition will rectify itself. "Sorry, I just don't have time" is asserted rather than admitting that a request or proposal is not sufficiently important to warrant taking the time or finding the time.

People talk about time as if it were something physical, but time is only a theoretical construct. Time cannot be physically experienced by seeing, hearing, feeling, or tasting it. Time is measured by a clock and calendar. Many language program administrators feel that they are victimized by clock time. There is a conflict between time as it is measured and time as it is lived. In the busy lives of program administrators, there is no rhetorical question asked more often than "Where has the time gone?" To be sure, time does not depart the scene. The real question is "How could I have planned so poorly and have left so much to be done in so little time?"

Considering the fact that each day has the same number of minutes and hours, how is it that some people seem to accomplish so much and others so little? As an example of someone who is struggling with time, let's take a look at Janice.

> Janice tumbles out of bed at 7:45 a.m. Her stomach is churning; she's in a panic. She has an extremely important meeting with the academic vice president set for 9:15 a.m., and her alarm didn't go off. She has a 45-minute commute to work, but this morning because she'll be leaving during rush hour, it will take her an hour at least. Janice dashes out of the house after a meager breakfast of coffee and toast. Naturally she has no time for a real meal. And anyway, breakfast is always a nuisance; she can never find anything convenient, tasty, and quick to eat.
>
> Janice arrives late at the office, barely in time to meet the vice president. The meeting does not go well. She feels hassled, hungry, and inarticulate. The rest of the day assumes the same disjointed pattern. Janice loses an important memo and almost misses another meeting. Distractions abound; students drop by every few minutes with questions or problems, preventing

any solid accomplishments. She tries all day to find time to skim a recently arrived journal, review possible textbooks for adoption, and create new instructional materials for her own class. She ends up going to her one class inadequately prepared, with papers only half corrected. She misses lunch, and by the time 5:00 p.m. rolls around, she has a headache and is exhausted.

Her drive home is complicated by traffic. In addition, she gets pulled over by a highway patrolman because her registration has expired. She's too tired to cook when she gets home, so she orders a pizza. By the time she is ready for bed, her nerves are shot. She has a sinking feeling.

Hopefully, Janice's story does not sound too familiar. If it does sound familiar, even some of the time, you are definitely a candidate for a few principles on time management. If it does not sound familiar, perhaps you have already mastered many of the time management principles presented here. Whether you feel that you manage time well or not, we hope that all language program administrators benefit from the following discussion. Life does not have to control us as it is controlling Janice. With a few purposeful changes, we can all control and manage our own time more wisely.

Before you continue, please turn to Appendix A and complete the brief inventory on Time Management for Language Program Administrators. This inventory is designed to help you determine what your time management needs are. Your score on this inventory will help you decide how to handle the material in this chapter.

A Key Time Management Principle

The productive use of time is ultimately a personal judgment call. Through your daily, weekly, and yearly actions, you are choosing whether or not you will achieve a successful professional life and the personal life that you desire with your close friends and families. How you feel about your ability to manage time is based on one basic principle.

Before this principle is introduced, please turn to Appendix B and complete the activity. Please do not read the next section until you have completed the activity in Appendix B.

If you are like most language program administrators who have not taken courses in time management, there may be little relationship between the two lists that you generated in Appendix B. Most likely you are not using the bulk of your professional time to pursue activities that you value. This fact plays itself out in how you manage your professional time.

The effort that one expends on any given task finds its true reward not in pay but from personal fulfillment (Engstrom & Mackenzie, 1988). If most of your time is spent pursuing activities that you do not value, you cannot possibly expect to feel motivated toward the task or to be organized and productive. To be successful time managers, it is imperative to cease to regard work as a means to an end—a chore to be disposed of so that enjoyment can be found. Productive, result-oriented work should be viewed in its proper perspective as an integrated, essential, and pleasant part of living (Batten, 1963; Covey, Merrill, & Merrill, 1996).

At the core of Janice's problem was the fact that her workday was filled with tasks and activities that were not at the core of her value system. She wanted to read over a recently arrived journal, create new activities for her class, and review textbooks that had just arrived. She did not get to these tasks, nor had she for months. Because she did not purposefully structure her life to allow time to pursue the activities that she valued, she did not approach the other activities in her life in a purposeful and organized way. Disorganization added considerable stress to her life.

To create a professional work life that allows time to pursue the activities that matter, this basic principle of time management should be observed: *Your values and how you use your time must be connected* (Winwood, 1990). This approach to time management could be called "personal strategic planning." In program-level strategic planning, a program administrator matches program goals and objectives, as reflected in the program mission statement, to strategies for accomplishing those goals and objectives. (See Klinghammer, this volume, for more information on strategic planning.) In personal strategic planning, parallel actions must be taken.

> *What is your personal professional mission statement? Write it down. Post it where you can see it often. How do the professional activities that you pursue in any given day complement your mission statement? Train yourself to consider this question continually.*

The basic objective of time management is not to become super-efficient, super-productive, or super-busy, but to use time in ways to achieve important personal goals. As you manage your time, keep asking yourself, "Is this activity advancing my priority goals?" or "Is this really what I want to be doing with my time?" (Ferner, 1980, p. 204).

You may be asking yourself, "What does making a list of the activities that I value and my general goals have to do with finding time in my life and getting organized?" The connection is actually quite clear. In essence, if a certain amount of your time is not spent pursuing your goals and moving forward with activities that matter in your life, you will sabotage your own time management and organizational efforts (see Schofield, 1981; Winston, 1978).

> *Look at the list of professional activities that you value in Appendix B. Circle the three most important activities. These are the activities that you will want to make a first priority.*

Priority activities may be ongoing, such as reading journals, or time limited, such as completing a paper, report, or project. Language program administrators must decide what percent of their work time will be spent pursuing these activities. Ten percent, 15, 20, 25, or higher? Making time for valued professional activities, before planning and organizing the remainder of one's time, is an important step in time management.

> *How many hours will you allot to high-priority professional activities? For example, if you normally put in a 40-hour work week, and you have decided to spend 25% of your time pursuing certain valued activities, you will need to set aside 10 hours a week to work on them.*

Reasons for Organizing and Managing Time

Language program administrators often bemoan the fact that they do not have time to get organized. Despite the fact that everyone has 24 hours in each day, many colleagues seem to pack a whole lot more into their day. How do they do it? More importantly, why do they do it? What motivates people to get organized? Culp (1986) highlights five important reasons for organizing and managing time:

1. You can reduce stress. Being disorganized adds stress to life. How often do you have to look for misplaced items? How often are you hurried or late? How often do you not have enough time to get everything done that needs to be done? Moments such as these are stressful. Certain aspects of your life (such as traffic, mishaps, other peoples' reactions, children, and spouses) may not necessarily be within your control. Yet, applying better time management strategies and organizational skills are within your control and will help reduce overall stress.

2. You can increase productivity. If you are disorganized, you are not as productive as you could be. It does not matter that you somehow get the work done. If you are organized, you not only accomplish your objectives but also do a better job. Your surroundings at home and at work say a lot about you. If everything in your office is disorganized and you cannot find anything, your colleagues notice. They adapt their behavior toward you. As a language program administrator, your job is to lead. Coworkers will take their cue from you. Being organized means increased productivity, and increased productivity means success.

3. You can retain control. Being organized and managing your time allow you to control your life to some extent. When no conscious effort is made to manage time, time will control you. Not managing your time or organizing your life guarantees that there will be important items (e.g., reports, contracts, syllabi, fee schedules) that you cannot find when you need them and tasks that you cannot complete that need to be finished. A life without time management is a life without control.

4. You can gain perspective. Managing your time and developing organizational skills can heighten awareness and change your perspective on issues. When you are not managing your time, it is impossible to see where you are and where you are going. Without time management, you are likely to react without thoughtful consideration of the issues.

5. You can add time to your life. When you manage your time well, you will have enough time to pursue your personal goals and dreams. It will feel as though you have more time because your plan will include time to think, organize, and create. After actively engaging in time management, you will feel strongly motivated and productive. You will feel in control; you will have a sense that it is possible to achieve your goals.

Understanding the benefits of time management is motivating, but just exactly how can a language program administrator get organized? With an endorsement of the most basic time management principle (*your values and how you use your time must be connected*) and a concerted effort to decide how much work time should be spent pursuing highly valued professional activities, language program administrators can begin to plan for successful time management.

A Plan for Successful Time Management

Language program administrators can manage their time successfully by incorporating time management into their daily routine, by dealing with unfinished business and incomplete tasks, and by avoiding crisis management whenever possible. When combined into regular and systematic practice, these three approaches coalesce into a coherent plan for successful time management.

Incorporating Time Management into the Daily Routine

Language program administrators can manage each day more efficiently by setting aside just 5 minutes a day (either at the end of a work day or at the *very* beginning of a new day) to organize their time and activities. Initially, it may take more than 5 minutes but when it becomes a routine practice, less time is needed to manage one's time. Organizing one's daily routine is essentially a four-step process:

- Step one. Make a list of the "to dos" for the day. Be sure to include your valued activities, old business, routine appointments, and office hours in your list. Consider the sample list that appears in Figure 1.

- Step two. Prioritize daily tasks. Assign a number to each task depending on its urgency and importance. How you prioritize daily tasks (perhaps with a number system like the one outlined in Figure 2) is purely subjective, based on your own evaluation of the tasks on the list. A prioritized "to do" list may look like the one in Figure 3.

January 31, 1997

Set up an appointment with the VP
Call admissions on KS
Evaluate the three new student files and dictate letters
Keep office hours
Write memo about the plan for quarter-semester conversion
Type up tentative teaching schedules and distribute
Draft invitations for the International Club party
Get a birthday card for J
Pick up dry cleaning on the way home from work
Clear e-mail
Clear phone mail
Respond to today's mail
Work on my book for an hour
Return phone calls from yesterday afternoon
Read journal for 30 minutes

Figure 1. A "to do" list.

 # 1: High priority
These tasks must be worked on or completed today. They include valued activities as well as others that are viewed as very important and urgent.

 # 2: Priority
These activities should be completed within the week.
They are important but not urgent.

 # 3: Low priority
These activities are less important and less urgent and may have to wait.
They should be completed within 2 weeks.

Figure 2. **A rating system for a "to do" list.**

January 31, 1997

#1	Set up an appointment with the VP
#1	Call admissions on KS
#2	Evaluate the three new student files and dictate letters
#1	Keep office hours
#2	Write memo about the plan for quarter-semester conversion
#1	Type up tentative teaching schedules and distribute
#2	Draft invitations for the International Club party
#2	Get a birthday card for J
#3	Pick up dry cleaning on the way home from work
#1	Clear e-mail
#1	Clear phone mail
#1	Respond to today's mail
#1	Work on my book for an hour
#1	Return phone calls from yesterday afternoon
#1	Read journal for 30 minutes

Figure 3. **A prioritized "to do" list.**

- Step three. Assign an approximate completion time to each task. If high-priority tasks require more time than you have, cross out one or two of them and move them to another day. Priority and low-priority tasks may have to be scheduled later in the month. This approach to time management will provide you with insights into what you can and cannot accomplish. It will also help you set limits for yourself. The goal, of course, is to eventually be able to attend to all high-priority tasks each day.

- Step four. Evaluate your ability to accomplish designated tasks by rating them as completed, scheduled for another day, delegated (with a checkup time established), in process, or deemed unnecessary (and consequently deleted from the list).

It is not uncommon, however, for language program administrators to receive urgent requests for information from senior-level administrators, sponsoring agencies, colleagues, faculty, and staff that require a change in one's schedule and priorities. It is important to determine what percentage of time will be spent on tasks that are someone else's priorities. For example, the dean or vice president may ask for information about language program enrollment trends that will take time and effort to collect. It would not be prudent to deny the request, but one's response should be framed in a way that demonstrates one's time management principles and programmatic priorities. You can respond to such a request by letting the senior person know that you would be happy to complete the task, how much time it will take, and when you can have it finished. If there is pressure to complete the task immediately, state your willingness to comply but inform the senior official of the tasks that you will be unable to complete as a result of your immediate compliance. This technique places responsibility for changing your time management plans into the hands of the requestor.

Dealing With Unfinished Business and Incomplete Tasks

Newcomers to time management often have lists of unfinished business or tasks that have piled up. How can language program administrators handle unfinished business and incomplete tasks in an efficient manner?

> *Write down all of your unfinished business in a list. You may be able to compile the list immediately. Sometimes, after you have thought about unfinished business for a few days, other tasks will come to mind. Prioritize the list. Put the tasks or projects that seem most urgent or most important first. Then, decide how much time is needed to finish up each responsibility. Finally, ask yourself how much of your day you want to devote to these tasks. (For example, let's say you have a list of 10 unfinished tasks that will take you 25 hours to complete. If you are willing to devote 2 hours a day to these tasks, it will take you about 2.5 weeks to complete them.)*

Engaging in an exercise like this can help language program administrators see just how much time they have; it also gives them a better sense of when they are in a position to accept new tasks and responsibilities.

Avoiding Crisis Management Whenever Possible

In the life of every language program administrator, there are tasks that are urgent but not important; tasks such as these often require some form of crisis management, a less than effective time management approach. Consider the following crisis management scenario:

> Janice arrives at the office. Her secretary hands her a note stating that two former students are waiting to see her. They each need letters of recommendation today. The students drove 2 hours to talk to Janice and to get the letters. The Dean called and needs some statistics for a 10 a.m. meeting with the president. In addition, a teacher has called in sick, asking Janice to substitute in her 10:30 a.m. class.

Janice spends the next 2 hours working on statistics for the Dean. She compiles them just in the nick of time and takes them to the dean's office. To her dismay, she finds that the meeting was canceled, but no one had bothered to tell her. She returns to her office, quickly throws some tried and true class activities together, and then substitutes for an hour. She returns to her office at 11:30 and spends the next hour and a half writing letters for the two students who have been waiting since 8:00 a.m. At 1:00 p.m. she looks at her own "to do" list and realizes that she is behind. She has not corrected papers for her own class, completed next semester's class schedule for faculty review, or responded to the two recruitment agencies that are sending students to the program for the next class cycle.

Had Janice been more attuned to the principles of time management, she might have approached the day in a different manner. Let's take another view of Janice's morning to see how time management principles are applied effectively.

By the time Janice arrives at work, she has already evaluated her work day and knows that it is full. She knows that responding to the three unanticipated requests essentially would mean that these new tasks would be considered more important than the ones she had previously scheduled. She has to ask herself if this is true. Is she willing to remove some previously designated "high-priority" tasks from her list to attend to these new requests? Janice decides that these new tasks are urgent and important for the people who are making the requests, but they are neither urgent nor particularly important for the overall program nor for her own personal goals.

Janice meets briefly with the two students, giving them the proper forms to complete for requesting letters of recommendation from her. She directs their attention to her policy statement at the end of the form which explains that students should allow at least a week for letters to be sent. Janice tells the students that while she is happy to write the letters for them, she cannot do it today. It is hard for Janice to say no to students at any time, but it is easier when she understands the consequences of making such a decision. What would she change or give up to be able to write those letters today?

Janice asks her secretary to call the dean's office to tell him that the statistics he has requested can be available Thursday by noon. Does he still want them if he cannot get them today?

Janice is on call as a substitute teacher this week, so she has already planned how she will revise her schedule should the need arise.

Twelve Additional Time Management Strategies

Language program administrators can manage their busy lives and multiple responsibilities by following the time management plan outlined above. In addition to these basic time management principles, there are 12 additional strategies that may help language program administrators manage their time.

1. Delegate. Learning how to delegate is important for one's health, sanity, and language program. Although it may be true that no one can accomplish the task just as you can, it is better to get the job done even if it may not be completed exactly as you would have liked it.

2. Just say no. Of all the time-saving techniques ever developed, perhaps the most effective is the frequent use of the word "no" (Bliss, 1976). Language program administrators are conditioned to say yes to requests relating to professional work. We are trained to provide a social service under time constraints and a host of institutional directives (Drawbaugh, 1984). Saying no to a request is difficult. Having a system helps. Learn to say no to requests when any of the following conditions exist:

   • The request does not move you closer to your personal goals.
   • The request does not move the program closer to its goals.
   • Unreasonable pressure is exerted for an immediate answer when the request is made.
   • You are not sure that you can deliver.

3. Handle papers only once. When you go through your daily mail, handle each piece of paper a single time. Throw junk mail directly in the trash (or better yet, the recycling bin) as soon as it is received. Open all other mail and make a decision about what to do with each piece of correspondence or take care of it immediately.

4. Develop a system for returning and taking calls. If you do not have a phone answering system or machine, get one. Clear your phone messages once in the morning and once in the afternoon rather than each time a message is left. When you return calls and the person is not available, leave messages asking that they call you, rather than call back again. If you are working on other tasks, let the answering machine pick up your calls.

5. Post regular office hours and keep them. During your office hours, keep your office door open. Be accessible to students, faculty, and staff during these times. Knowing that you are truly available during office hours makes it easier for students and co-workers to accept a closed and locked door later on. If you want to be organized and productive, you will need to have times when you are not interrupted.

6. Keep interruptions polite, brief, and to the point. Constant interruptions are typical for most language program administrators. These interruptions, while often necessary, can drain your energy and keep you from being as productive as you can be. Set aside time for no interruptions—shut your office door, lock it, and let the answering machine pick up your calls. At other times, keep interruptions focused; the goal is to keep the total time that you spend on interruptions to a minimum.

7. Develop a good filing system. Being organized and able to find important documents in a timely fashion requires a good filing system. If it frequently takes more than 30 seconds to find the piece of paper you need, you should rethink your system. If necessary, consult with other language program administrators to find out how they organize their files. Remember that you should only file items that you will need at a future date. Don't clutter your files with unnecessary items.

8. Develop strategies to assist you in managing time.

- Organize colleague's business cards, instead of scraps of paper, for contact information. Buy a small holder for the cards that you collect.
- Use computer form letters to answer the most frequently asked questions. With a simple change of address and salutation, they can still appear to be personalized.
- Have program-related resources (e.g., stationary, program stamp, brochures) at home and at work. No matter how hard you try to separate your home life from your life as a language program administrator, you may still have to attend to language program business while at home.
- Make certain that language program faculty and staff know when you are available and when you need uninterrupted time.

9. Plan for rest periods and vacations. When you formalize your daily plan, schedule a short morning and afternoon break, in addition to time for lunch. When you engage in long-term planning, plan for vacation days.

10. Keep co-workers informed. You can save time in the long run if you write short memos to faculty and staff and convene frequent and brief faculty and staff meetings. Keep your colleagues apprised of upcoming events, policy changes, problems, and future plans. Your co-workers will eventually learn to trust this procedure. In this way, personnel will not need to stop by your office individually to solicit information about routine matters.

11. Repeat presentations. Prepare standardized presentations, with handouts, to introduce new employees to the language program. The presentations can be repeated over and over again, with adjustments when necessary. When a new administrator joins the institution, schedule a time to make the presentation. In this way, misunderstandings and miscommunications can be avoided.

12. Deal with problems when they arise. Language program administrators encounter problems of some sort every day. Collect the necessary information to make a sound decision. Whenever possible, try to solve the problem on the day that the problem arises.

Procrastination

Procrastination has been singled out for special attention because it is the most costly of all internally generated time wasters. The practice of procrastination, that is, postponing until later what is uncomfortable to do at the moment, is so common that it is often referred to as a disease, a bad habit, or laziness. Everyone procrastinates on occasion. But when language program administrators procrastinate, faculty, staff, and students can be adversely affected. The basic rule to follow is to delay only if moving forward keeps you from a higher-priority activity.

It is important for language program administrators to become familiar with the underlying reasons for procrastination. Most people procrastinate to escape an overwhelming or unpleasant task, camouflage poor work, gain sympathy, get someone else to do the job, protect a weak self-image, or avoid change (LeBoeuf, 1979). These reasons are not normally accepted as legitimate. The only readily accepted reasons for procrastination

(Knaus, 1979) are physical incapacitation, ignorance (i.e., when a person does not realize that a deed needs doing), or delay that is part of an overall plan.

Procrastination adversely affects one's language program, and it creates emotional wear and tear on the individual. Procrastinators usually feel nagging guilt, self-disgust, worry, and hopelessness. For individuals who have the tendency to procrastinate, Drawbaugh (1984) offers these suggestions:

1. Assess your health. Eat wholesome food, get adequate sleep and rest, and exercise.

2. Observe your emotions. Notice how often you are angry, frustrated, or worried.

3. Review your work load. Delegate and manage your time. Learn to say no.

4. Analyze your habits. Are you chronically late in arriving at school, meetings, or appointments?

5. Consider the value of the activities that you are engaged in. Are there any activities that you can give up?

6. Manage your time well.

7. Follow through with tasks that need to be done.

8. Keep a list of what you accomplish. Focus on what you have done, not on what you have to do.

Conclusion

Time, in essence, measures the length of our lives; time management, however, determines the quality of our lives. Our abilities to manage time and to use it effectively and efficiently can move us to greater heights professionally and greater happiness and contentment in other parts of our lives. The challenge for language program administrators is to seize the opportunity to invest in time in the best possible way. And there is no better time to act than now.

> Eventually, you will find that you have mastered time. No longer will it be your master. You will know what your purposes are; you will have a priorities list; and you will guide your activities by those things that contribute most to your objectives. You will also know clearly what you want to do.... When you are master of your time, you will feel good about it. You will want to share your time mastery secrets with others—and you will have time to do it! (Love, 1981, pp. 273–274)

Discussion Questions and Activities

1. Why is it important to connect your values to how you manage your time?

2. Share the results of your Preliminary Inventory on Time Management (Appendix A) with a partner. What did you learn about yourself? What are you committed to changing?

3. What are the advantages to being organized? How do these advantages apply to you personally?

4. Think of all the administrative responsibilities that you have. Which responsibilities can be delegated to others in your language program?

5. Imagine that you direct a language program with about 150 students. You supervise a faculty and staff of 13. One of your greatest frustrations is that you are continually interrupted throughout the day. You find it impossible to get anything done. What steps can you take to change this situation?

6. Imagine that you are attending a faculty meeting in your college and have been unexpectedly nominated from the floor for the position of chair of an important committee. Although you are flattered, you realize that you must say no. How will you say no gracefully but forcefully to your peers?

Suggested Readings

Culp, S. (1986). *How to get organized when you don't have the time.* Cincinnati, OH: Writer's Digest Books.

The author offers practical suggestions for getting organized and finding time in all areas of one's life, including establishing priorities, making schedules, and redesigning space. Her chapter on procrastination is particularly useful, offering clear explanations about reasons for procrastination.

Drawbaugh, C. C. (1984). *Time and its use: A self-management guide for teachers.* New York: Teacher's College Press.

With regard to educators and other professionals, Drawbaugh focuses on increasing the reader's consciousness and awareness of time as a human resource. He offers educators procedures, practices, and tips for making better use of time. The book is designed to serve its readers as a practical self-management resource for learning about time. It is a "how to" book liberally sprinkled with "whys."

Robbins, A. (1996). *Personal power, II: The driving force.* San Diego, CA: Robbins Research International.

In this 30-day audiotape program, Robbins offers a system for creating change and expanding one's appreciation of personal progress. The program focuses heavily on managing one's life and making positive changes. Several lectures are devoted specifically to values clarification, goal setting, and managing time. The program is unique, motivating, and particularly relevant for chronic procrastinators.

Appendix A

PRELIMINARY INVENTORY ON TIME MANAGEMENT
FOR LANGUAGE PROGRAM ADMINISTRATORS

DIRECTIONS: Read each of the following questions below. Check yes if the statement is true for you 25% or more of the time. Check no if the statement is true less than 25% of the time.

1. Do you sometimes reach the point where you find yourself deliberately not opening your mail, reading your e-mail, and clearing phone messages for a few days?
       ❑ YES   ❑ NO

2. Is the top of your desk often so cluttered with piles of paper that you don't have any space left to do your work?
       ❑ YES   ❑ NO

3. Does it sometimes take you more than 10 minutes to unearth an important piece of paper from your files, desk, etc.?
       ❑ YES   ❑ NO

4. Are there papers on your desk, other than reference papers, that you haven't looked through for a week or more because you've been too busy to deal with them?
       ❑ YES   ❑ NO

5. Within the last 2 months, have you forgotten any scheduled appointment, anniversary, or specific date that you wanted to acknowledge?
       ❑ YES   ❑ NO

6. Do you tell co-workers not to touch anything in your office because, even though there's a good deal of mess, you know exactly where everything is located?
       ❑ YES   ❑ NO

7. Do you have some friends and family who get annoyed with you because you don't have time to return calls, answer letters, and spend time with them?
       ❑ YES   ❑ NO

8. Do you have stacks of articles and professional journals piling up because there's something important in each one, but so far you haven't had time to read them?
       ❑ YES   ❑ NO

9. Do you find yourself avoiding phone calls and socializing because you just don't have the time to deal with people or you just don't feel like dealing with them?
       ❑ YES   ❑ NO

10. Do you frequently procrastinate so long on a work assignment that it becomes an emergency or panic situation?
       ❑ YES   ❑ NO

11. Do you often misplace keys, glasses, gloves, handbags, briefcases, and other items?
❑ YES   ❑ NO

12. Do you have piles of papers in closets, in corners, or on the floor because you can't decide where to put them or what to do with them?
❑ YES   ❑ NO

13. Do you feel that your storage problems in your office could be solved if you had more space?
❑ YES   ❑ NO

14. Do you want to get everything organized in your office but it's such a mess that you don't know where to begin?
❑ YES   ❑ NO

15. Does your work day usually start with a crisis of some sort?
❑ YES   ❑ NO

16. Do you put off making decisions until the situation becomes an emergency?
❑ YES   ❑ NO

17. Do you make "to do" lists for the day and never make it through the lists?
❑ YES   ❑ NO

18. Do you have a difficult time keeping regular office hours?
❑ YES   ❑ NO

19. Are you constantly plagued by interruptions and as a result never seem to get anything done?
❑ YES   ❑ NO

20. Do you often find yourself agreeing to do something just because you don't know how to say no?
❑ YES   ❑ NO

SCORING: Give yourself one point for each yes.

1–4   You are relatively well organized and manage your time quite well. The additional organizational and time management principles in this chapter will be a helpful review. Congratulations!

5–7   You have a little problem with time management and organization. You should begin implementing the strategies outlined in this chapter.

8–10   You probably feel that you are about to lose control. You should begin following the time management suggestions outlined in this chapter.

11–20   You are disorganized and do not manage your time well. It's time for an organizational overhaul. Follow the program outlined in this chapter, get additional resource materials, implement plans, and make time management the most important event in your life until you get back on track.

Appendix B

TWO PERSPECTIVES ON PROFESSIONAL ACTIVITY

PART I: Make a list of 10 professional activities that you consider most important. In a perfect world where you had no other professional distractions or obligations, these are the activities that you would pursue and value above all other activities.

1.

2.

3.

4.

5.

6.

7.

8.

9.

10.

PART II: How do you spend your time? List the 10 activities that occupy the bulk of your time in a normal professional working day.

1.

2.

3.

4.

5.

6.

7.

8.

9.

10.

Part III: Put your two lists side by side. How do they compare? How many of the activities that you value (Part I) appear in the second list (Part II)?

Part V

THE LANGUAGE PROGRAM
ADMINISTRATOR AS VISIONARY

Chapter 16

TECHNOLOGY AND THE LANGUAGE PROGRAM ADMINISTRATOR

Michael Witbeck and Deborah Healey
Oregon State University

 hose involved in language teaching programs over the past few years will have certainly noted the increasing importance of technology, both in the delivery of instruction and in the administration of instructional programs. Changes in the cost and availability of electronic technologies—coupled with widespread enthusiasm for technological experimentation and for the implementation of technological solutions—have made real changes in the way teachers and administrators do their jobs. Most now believe that such technology-driven change will continue and perhaps even accelerate in the foreseeable future. But each incremental change, however exciting it may be, carries with it its own special set of problems; the effective management of the changes that technology brings represents one of the major challenges facing language program administrators. Sometimes, the mere pace of change seems daunting. New technology-based materials and methods appear constantly, while others become obsolete seemingly overnight. No one person can become expert in all these methods and materials, but a broad understanding of technology issues coupled with more in-depth knowledge of one or two technology-based techniques, such as file serving, electronic mail, or computer-assisted language learning, will be an indispensable asset to language program administrators.

Such knowledge is important for teachers too, but administrators have the additional responsibility of guiding the general direction of change and of establishing the evolved administrative structures and policies that change requires. The promises and challenges of technology in several areas of language program administration are discussed here. First, and most fundamental, is an examination of how the influence of technology on learning will bring about a revision—though not a wholesale rewriting—of the accepted definition of a language program, of what is expected from program employees, and of what students expect to receive from it. Next is a discussion concerning some of the consequences of choices about technology—the implications for office automation, instructional technology, personnel management, and staff development. Third is a look at the impact that technology tends to have on budgetary matters and how administrators must prioritize among competing interests. Finally, the *Internet*[1] and other distance technologies are surveyed in an attempt to assess their impact on instruction—both on site and at distances long or short—as well as their impact on program promotion, registration, and advising. While many of the examples will be drawn from personal experience in university-based intensive English programs, the concepts discussed here apply to a broad range of language teaching settings.

Evolving Definitions, Evolving Roles

Changes brought on by technology form a major component in the current evolution of a number of common teaching paradigms. Within one of these basic paradigms both the role of a language teacher and the definition of a language program have often been expressed in terms of classroom contact hours. Language program descriptions using contact hours are often seen in accreditation or recognition standards. A recognized intensive English program, for instance, is a program that offers a certain minimum number of hours per week of English as a second language (ESL) instruction, delivered by teachers of a certain level of qualification (University and College Intensive English Programs, 1993). Individual institutions and school systems also use this paradigm whenever they, in their turn, define instructor positions primarily in terms of classroom contact hours per week. The specification of number of hours is usually not considered sufficient in and of itself to define either a language program or a teacher's job, as most program standards and work agreements contain many other important expectations. Still, for most of us, these numbers, however they have been established, traditionally serve as the basic benchmarks for how our work is defined.

How the Language Program Has Been Redefined

Although contact hours of language instruction still form the basis of a language program, the current trend in many programs is toward the expanding importance of other nonclassroom services that affect student language learning and the program's overall strategies, including homestays, conversant programs, airport pickups, and technological opportunities and services. Learning centers—filled with audio, video, and computer equipment, as well as associated content materials—are growing more common and competitively necessary. Besides their language learning function, such technologies arguably have additional value in preparing students for the technology-based learning and working systems that they will inevitably face in other educational efforts or the workplace. But such changes have consequences that go beyond their effects on how learners learn. As materials and equipment become "smarter," for example, they become more amenable to self-access learning. As self-access increases in importance, new definitions of language instruction and of language programs must evolve. New definitions of language programs may be based on how they provide access to a variety of resources. Programs may focus on instruction in teacher-led group meetings, on individual self-access study, or possibly on access to technology training.

What the Program Expects From Teachers

The teacher's role in this changed program also must evolve. A common fear among teachers is that machines (and a few elite programmers) will take over the business of language teaching, putting masses of language teachers onto unemployment rolls. While such reactions are understandable, the fact is that wholesale job elimination by automation is highly unlikely. Teacher-led group activities of some kind—if not the central and privileged mode of service—will continue to be critical to student learning and to program offerings. At the same time, however, teachers will need to adapt, at the very least, to new techniques for using technology in their redefined classrooms. New rooms or refurbished old rooms with built-in video and computer displays are appearing as fast as the money can be found to equip them. The grain of truth in the teaching machine bogeyman is that teachers who cannot make effective use of this new equipment will indeed find themselves less in demand, at least to some degree. This issue is revisited in the discussion of staff development, but the point is made here that any change in the teacher's role will have consequences for the language program administrator not only in the area of staff training, but also in employee recruitment, compensation, and evaluation.

If the instructor's role is seen more and more as that of a facilitator, guiding students to the proper tools and resources for learning, then teachers must be able to perform this function. A teacher's ability to guide students in this way must also be the object of careful evaluation with the goal of recognizing and rewarding strong performance. This kind of teaching is not simple; and because it often occurs outside the traditional classroom, existing systems of measuring performance may not be adequate. Most people realize that for an instructor merely to point a student at a piece of equipment is insufficient. Proper guidance also involves training the student to use the learning tool and, better yet, adapting the learning tool to particular student needs.

In the past, the teacher may have been expected during the course of instruction (or in the teacher's spare time) to orient students to the use of technology or to delegate the task to learning center assistants, but this is becoming less and less an option. Enabling students to use learning technology effectively is time-consuming work that requires real commitment and expertise. Lab assistants can develop these skills, but only after they themselves have undergone considerable training and practice. Given even a moderate level of turnover, such training efforts are inefficient. There is no substitute for committed, long-term employees who are comfortable with technology or who can be trained to become so. It is wise to remember that the program's most adept computer user—the guru if you will—is not solely by virtue of computer expertise the best facilitator of computer-based learning, but it is inescapably true that instructors who have had significant experience in using technological tools and in guiding students in their use have a significant advantage over those without that experience.

Technology also creates some entirely new roles in the language program in the areas of setup and support. One of the lessons of computer programming is that the easier the program is for the *end user* to use, the harder it was for the creator to create. Similarly, the relative ease with which one language program student or instructor can reply to an electronic mail (*e-mail*) message from another country is a direct function of how much investment the institutions in both countries have made, not only in terms of *hardware* and *software* but also in terms of support personnel devoted to providing seamless and *transparent* e-mail service. At each local network level, somebody has to be in charge of adding and deleting e-mail users, of backing up the system regularly, of fixing the internal system when it breaks, of upgrading the system when the need arises (which it surely will), and of making certain that the system's *gateway* to the outside world stays open. The same is true of other services such as storage of shared files on a *server* or access to networked equipment such as *scanners*, printers, and *modems*. The person who does this general work of updating and maintaining a system may be a language program employee or may work for an outside provider. But whatever arrangements are made, administrators are often closely involved with choosing the providers, monitoring and evaluating their work, and responding to their suggestions.

Furthermore, this sort of general system maintenance must be distinguished from yet another technology-related task, that of data library management. If we compare a computer data library of electronic resources to an old-fashioned public library full of books, the network maintenance tasks mentioned above are analogous to the jobs of custodians, roofers, plumbers, and carpenters; they are necessary to keep the physical system functioning. But another highly important job at the public library is that of librarian. Some of a librarian's chief responsibilities are organizing and cataloging resources, acquiring new high-value resources, purging old low-value resources, developing systems to guide and assist user access, and providing outreach programs to make users more aware of what resources are available. For different sorts of information resources—such as books, microfiche, or CD-ROMs—librarians use different resource management tools, but no matter what the medium, the goals are the same.

After a language program obtains access to digital storage space on a network server, that space will begin to fill rapidly almost as soon as users become aware of how to use it, simply because the process of *file sharing* is so easy. As the volume of information rises, however, so does the difficulty of navigating through it to find anything useful. Just as a bulging file cabinet with no section dividers or folder labels would be almost useless, no matter what gems of materials might be buried somewhere inside it, a single crowded and disorganized server directory called "Teaching Materials" will reward only the most determined miner. Administrators need to make sure that the data are being managed effectively in accord with the basic goals of librarianship. Further, when determining who will perform this work, administrators should keep in mind the distinction we are making here between system maintenance and data library management. These are different kinds of tasks that will often require different employee training and ability. Because system maintenance is essentially content independent, it can usually be provided effectively by information system specialists who are not language teaching experts. Effective data management, on the other hand, is best provided by an accomplished language teacher who ideally has broad knowledge of the field, in-depth knowledge of the curriculum, and familiarity with the individual styles and abilities of the instructors who will use the resources.

One current approach to these technology demands is for a language program administrator to offer a reduced class load to an instructor with technology expertise in return for providing technological assistance to students and staff. This approach at least recognizes and seeks to compensate fairly an individual instructor for the time and effort that such support requires. At the same time, however, when one person is very visibly involved with technology, others may feel that they need not bother developing any level of technological expertise. It is essential, therefore, to establish the limitations and priorities of the position from the start by specifying in some detail not only the job holder's responsibilities but also the responsibilities of that person's colleagues in actively supporting the institution's technology goals. One product of such an approach might be a new and more widespread realization that technology responsibilities within a language program are now so large and varied that no one person can possibly handle them all. In general, it is probably best to see such highly idiosyncratic positions as transitional. As the field of technology in education expands, increasing specialization is inevitable, and future language programs will need many instructors who are highly proficient in digital technology—not just one or two. These instructors will have their own areas of expertise within the broader field.

What Students Expect From the Language Program

A final point here is that we can expect ever-increasing technological awareness among potential students, parents, and sponsors. As recently as 3 years ago, the average student enrolling at our ESL program had little or no keyboarding ability and very little confidence with any sort of software. We had to focus our training efforts at that entry level. Today, many students advance almost immediately from turning on the computer to questions on how particular word processing programs perform specific formatting functions. How much—or even whether—this kind of change in the nature and preparation of potential students results in specific differences in the language program's public relations or recruiting strategies depends on leadership decisions about what the overall strategy is and upon the context in which the school operates. We suggest, however, that a language program that is able to give its students access to a wide variety of cutting-edge technologies will probably wish to leverage this investment by giving its use of technology a prominent place in promotional and outreach efforts.

A natural and probably necessary part of such an effort will be to make sure that promotional content is itself delivered through state-of-the-art channels. But promotional focus on technology will not be for everyone, and language programs that cannot afford the very latest gizmos can take comfort from the fact that relative levels of available technology will probably not be an overriding factor in most students' choices of which language program to attend. All language programs will need to provide some level of technology to both students and teachers, and this will require periodic investment in upgrades and renovations. This will be necessary simply because the increasing use of technology worldwide will continually raise the expectations of students and others. But for most programs, technology by itself will not be the chief drawing card.

Choices About Technology

Language program administrators may make choices about technology in two major areas: office automation and instructional technology. These are not completely separate areas, since budget and personnel issues will affect both. Faster delivery of class lists and better mechanisms for grade input and recording will enhance what teachers do; more technologically skilled teachers will be able to adapt better to changes in administrative procedures that come about as a result of technology.

Office Automation

Administrators of language programs within other institutions may not be able to control how office automation is implemented within the larger institution they belong to. They may find themselves with no more and no less control than any other departmental supervisor has. Still, they must be aware of the possibilities and issues in order to influence the technology decisions that are made.

For independent language programs with more than a handful of students, however, office automation is not a question of "whether" but of "how much" and "how fast." Higher expectations drive a lot of the movement to automate. For administrators there is an increasing recognition of the value of timely and accurate information, especially when budgetary decisions have to be made. Better tracking of where students come from makes it more likely that promotion dollars will be appropriately spent. Clerical workers know what a difference good tools can make, be they receptionists who can let automated fax machines do the mechanical part of their jobs, secretaries who can generate updated class lists at a moment's notice to placate a teacher, or data input people who can let software create new term files and automatically copy repeated items. Students recognize the value of an accurate schedule and quick test-result reporting, and they and their parents or sponsors appreciate professional-looking grade reports and other correspondence. Teachers like to know who their students are before classes start, and they like to have a convenient way to enter grades. There is less patience now for having to guess how much money is left in the budget, for typing or writing various lists by hand, for dealing with hard-to-read grade reports, or for being surprised with half or twice as many students as one had expected at the beginning of term.

Administrators embarking upon office automation must keep in mind that perceived needs will change over time in largely unpredictable ways. As people realize what is possible, expectations are raised further. Office dynamics shift as one person or another moves ahead (or lags behind) in dealing with new technology and the changes it produces in language program operations. As systems become more complex, whether as a result of automation or of other factors, the people responsible for maintaining those systems become more critical to the program's success, and changes in personnel become more disruptive. The needs and desires of the people who implement the automation should be given special consideration as part of the design process.

One question that often arises is whether to use *off-the-shelf software* or whether to create *custom applications* to track information and to generate program reports. Custom software may fit current needs well, but may be more difficult to maintain and change when adapting to new program needs. Off-the-shelf software will require changes in the program to fit the software rather than the other way around. The following points are useful for reflection when making decisions about office automation:

- How well established and useful are current procedures?
  If the program will be making a lot of changes in procedures, it may be easier and less expensive to start with ready-to-use software until needs are more certain.

- How close a match is there between what ready-to-use software will provide and the information and report formats that the language program uses now?
  If it is close, ready-to-use software is probably a better choice.

- What, if anything, does the ready-to-use software not provide that the program deems essential now or envisions needing in the future?

    If the ready-to-use software is missing something that the program feels it must have, custom software is in order.

- How much training time is needed to use the new software? How much is provided by the vendor? How thorough and easy to use is the documentation?

    These are important questions to ask of both off-the-shelf and custom software providers.

- How easy is it to adapt the software? What happens if the size of the language program doubles, or drops dramatically? What happens if the curriculum changes so that classes meet more/fewer hours or more/fewer days than before?

    If the software cannot change to meet likely future needs, it is a short-term solution, and the cost should be evaluated accordingly.

Instructional Technology

With instructional technology as with office automation, those who are expected to implement the changes should be part of the decision-making process. It is a rare institution that can decree a change from above and have it implemented effectively by unwilling subordinates. Most teachers are concerned and dedicated professionals who will accept innovations when they see the value to their students. When teachers are reluctant to change, administrators should (a) make a good case for the benefits of the suggested innovations for the curriculum and students, and (b) back up the rhetoric with paid training time.

There are some myths about instructional technology that can get in the way of teachers' acceptance of change. The first is that instructional technology, most notably computers, will replace teachers. An institution that moves into instructional technology is adding a resource, not replacing one. Instructional technology can complement the curriculum, but it does not provide the human contact associated with personalized, meaningful, and motivating teacher-guided instruction. That said, having 2 hours of individual instruction on the computer—with good software that meets the student's individual needs—is probably better than choral recitation in a "devil take the hindmost" class of 50. Teachers in large classes can be more effective if they rotate most of the class off to computer-based instruction two-thirds of the time, freeing the teachers to work individually with a smaller group. The teacher in this situation would be facilitating learning for two-thirds of the group by setting tasks and checking student progress.

The second myth is that the computer is nothing more than a tool that helps teachers do what they do now, only better. Adding computers to a course changes the dynamics of the class. It will often shift the role of the teacher from leader to facilitator, a qualitative difference in instruction. If students are sitting at computer *monitors* in a lab setting, their attention will be not on the teacher at the front of the room, but on the monitors in front of their faces. Computers add both a public and a private dimension to learning. The computer screen is a much more public space than a workbook on a student's desk; passers-by may comment on what is happening on the screen in ways they do not with books. A networked room where students can share writing electronically and anonymously can make writing more public and peer correction more private than it would be in a nonelectronic setting. Hierarchies among students also disappear with electronic mail; those who are quick to speak have no advantage in this setting.[2]

The third and perhaps most inaccurate myth is that using technology saves money. The purchase cost, large or small, is just the beginning of the expenses when institutions decide to invest in technology. Computers and software depreciate rapidly and must be updated at least every few years. Just as it can be difficult to use the same book year after year, term after term, without students and teachers getting bored, software can become so thoroughly familiar that it loses effectiveness. With new equipment and new software, teachers need additional training. As teachers become more technologically proficient, they are able to take advantage of a wider range of technological resources—and will ask for them in their classrooms. More complex equipment also tends to have things go wrong in more complex ways, requiring specialists to maintain and repair it.

Given the cost and uncertainties involved in educational technology, administrators may question whether it is a worthwhile investment (see Rothstein & McKnight, 1996; and Warden, 1997). The answer will depend on a number of factors, including the following:

- What is the competition doing?

- What do students, parents, and sponsors expect and demand?

- What do teachers know how to exploit?

- How much of an investment is the institution willing to make in training as well as in hardware and software?[3]

Educational technology designed to enhance the curriculum is a powerful tool in the hands of a knowledgeable teacher. Teachers and administrators should work together to add technology to the curriculum and to prepare teachers to implement it effectively. It will cause changes in the interaction of teachers, students, and curriculum; thus, administrators need to be prepared to make sure the changes are channeled appropriately.

Personnel Management/Staff Development

Another area of change with a close connection to emerging technology is that of instructors' relations with one another. The administrator needs to anticipate the effect of such changes to minimize friction and encourage growth. The operating assumption at most language programs is that student learning is best facilitated by a team of professionals who work fairly closely together but who, because they are professionals, have developed individual and unique working styles and abilities. Of the many ways in which instructors may differ, one parameter is that some instructors prefer to work very closely with colleagues, while others are of a more independent persuasion. Technology, especially computer technology, has the potential to empower both individualists and working groups. An individual instructor with access to a computer, a scanner, a laser printer, and a photocopier, for example, now has materials-development capabilities that a few years ago were available only to large collaborating groups such as publishers. In the future this same individual may routinely have access to enough technology to choose to create *interactive video* lessons without any assistance or collaboration.

To groups of collaborators, however, computer technology offers all this and more. It provides simple methods by which groups of teachers can share their materials with the touch of a mouse. The same technology can make collaboration with other colleagues halfway around the world almost as easy. The consequence is that information sharers in a language program (or any other organization) may receive a disproportionate benefit when information technologies are introduced. The institutional value systems of most programs are based on a careful balance between recognition of individual effort and encouragement of collaboration. New information technology has the potential to change this balance, sometimes in ways that prove highly stressful, especially in the case of instructors who have long had a preference for and been successful with individual accomplishment. In a world that seems to favor sharing, they may begin to feel exiled and unappreciated. Administrative leadership in this area requires that the program be proactive in consciously and explicitly determining just what its values are. Rather than allowing the acceptance of technologically inspired values by default, the responsibility of the program administrator is to ensure that questions of institutional values are answered on the basis of principles and strategies rather than on the basis of available technology, which is—or should be—merely a tool for implementing strategies.

A point to remember here is that although the machines in themselves seem value-independent, most technologies lend themselves better to some modes of living and working than to others (see Bowers, 1988). One institution may believe that its survival is dependent on a very great degree of technology-based collaboration among staff, whereas another may expect better results from a diverse array of individuals. In either case, it is the belief itself, independent of working tools, that should guide the administration's work.

Budgeting for Technology

Technology is expensive and will continue to be an important factor in language program budgeting. As a percentage of overall spending, technology purchases may not seem nearly as large as some other cost areas. But most of these other costs—teachers' salaries, for example—are to some degree fixed and allow the administrator little room to move. As a percentage of the program's real discretionary budget, technology costs loom far larger, so large perhaps that in some cases even basic technology costs exceed the administrator's discretionary authority and purchases thus require time-consuming proposal and approval processes. But whether writing a proposal to obtain resources or deciding how to spend those already obtained, the challenge for the language program administrator is to sort through all the available technologies and try to ensure that the program chooses projects and equipment that really make a difference in teaching and learning.

The worst case, of course, is that a program may commit a large portion of scarce resources to the purchase of new technology only to see it gather dust, unused. This can happen partly because both technology vendors and in-house partisans of particular technologies will naturally emphasize the upside of proposed products or services and may try to downplay costs and drawbacks. Administrators generally recognize that if a number of teachers are excited and enthusiastic about a product, that excitement itself bodes very well for success. This enthusiasm factor, while very difficult to quantify, must have its place in the administrator's cost/benefit analysis. But so too must a clear understanding of all the associated costs and of the other difficulties in implementing technological systems. It is easy to see the price of technology in the cost of purchasing and installing new equipment. Less obvious are the costs of maintaining the new system and of managing the data within it, with an eye toward making it as easy as possible to use.

Budget Basics

Cost analysis should begin with the two basic categories of costs: Up-front costs include acquisition and setup of equipment, purchase of materials, and initial training of users, whereas downstream costs include maintenance, upgrades, and future training of additional users. Up-front equipment costs are the most obvious ones and are usually the easiest to establish. They include the purchase cost of computers, printers, projector/display systems, CD-ROM and hard drives, and so forth. Somewhat less obvious are the up-front costs of materials such as software licenses, reference works, and data banks as well as the initial cost of supplies such as printer paper and toner. Many technological systems resemble home music systems in that the acquisition cost of the materials library (e.g., compact audio disks) meets or exceeds the cost of the playback equipment.

Early training costs are also important. These vary according to the complexity and ease of use of the technology involved, and there is a natural tendency to underestimate them or even eliminate this line from the budget entirely. To some degree the excitement and enthusiasm generated by new equipment can lead to self-training and volunteer mentoring. It is also true that some systems are so easy to use—some voice mail systems, for example—that they can be implemented successfully with minimal initial training. But this approach can prove very costly in the long run. Whenever the worst case occurs and expensive new equipment does sit gathering dust, the difficulty can almost always be traced to a failure to provide for the needed materials, the needed training, or both.

And of course this is not all. Over the life of the system, downstream costs often far exceed initial setup costs. In businesses where computer workstations play a vital role, for example, one survey reports up to $40,000 in maintenance, upgrade, and training costs over the life of a typical $2,500 personal computer system (see Norton, 1995). While it is unlikely that any language program will be able to spend this much to support a workstation, the long-term costs of maintenance, management, and training are still significant. Thus, whenever an investment in technology is contemplated, the impact of downstream costs must be carefully weighed. Tradeoffs abound in this area. If a new database is needed, for example, should it be easy to use or full featured? If its use requires special training, will a real increase in productivity justify the expense of training? How many people will have to be trained to start with? How many will need to be trained in the future? If an expensive software package costs 10 times as much as the cheap package but requires only half the training, which is the better deal? Similar questions must be answered in acquiring almost any technology, from hand-held video cameras to new wiring schemes. New network-dependent services such as shared files and *net navigators* have a special set of downstream or infrastructure questions related to the number of simultaneous users the network can support. A new network service might be cheap to install and require little training but might still be a poor idea if the result is an overloaded network with all services slowed to a crawl.

Suggested Budgeting Guidelines

Language programs can help themselves answer such questions by developing broad technology acquisition strategies or guidelines. One simple guideline is that no proposal for technology acquisition should be considered if it does not include specific projections regarding initial materials costs, initial training costs, and downstream infrastructure costs as well as a clear explanation of how it furthers curricular aims. We might think of this as something akin to an environmental impact statement where the language program itself is the environment to be protected or enhanced. Where will equipment be stored? Who will keep the keys? Who will need training? Who will do the training? Has a current data librarian agreed to take on the maintenance of the new files or will that person have to give up something else to take this on? Clear answers to such questions during the early stages of the process will do much to smooth the way later. More important, if clear answers cannot be found, then the administrator has a good indication that resources might be better spent elsewhere.

Another acquisition guideline is that the very newest, cutting-edge commercial hardware always carries a significant price premium and should probably be avoided. It is unlikely that the performance benefits of having the very newest gadgets will ever be worth the premium paid. The opposite, however, is also true. The purchase of near obsolete technologies will quickly bring downstream performance penalties that are usually more than sufficient to negate the favorable initial pricing. For commercial hardware products in the mainstream market, most language programs will want to look for the nearly newest. As soon as this month's hot new technology comes out, last season's hot new technology tends to get a little cheaper while still offering a relatively long projected service life.

The situation in computer software is somewhat similar. Language programs hardly ever need the very latest software version; in fact, older programs can continue to give good service. There will come a time, however, when older software—while still doing its basic job—becomes dysfunctional from lack of compatibility with a changing network and/or *operating system* environment. When the day comes that a word processing program no longer prints, for example, it will not be on some random day when its printer function wears out; rather it will most likely be the day after the installation of a new operating system or printer to which the old program is not able to link properly. But this is usually far down the road in the software's life span.

In the meantime, software makers will be offering upgrades frequently and marketing them aggressively. Some language program users will be highly attuned to these offers and eager to try the new versions, whereas other users will be less concerned. Purchasing one or two copies of the upgrade can boost the morale and productivity of the former group while also allowing an in-depth evaluation of the software. As part of the evaluation, one needs to look carefully at the promised "new" features to determine if they are really needed, and also at any additional hardware requirements because they represent one of the large hidden costs of a software upgrade. Training must also be considered. If the new version is very different from the old version, there will be a period of lowered productivity while users adjust. The good news about computer software is that costs are controllable to some degree. Language programs in universities or other large organizations can often find favorable prices on commercial software by participating in volume purchase agreements. Other software needs can be met effectively by noncommercial products (i.e., *shareware* and *freeware*) with even lower prices.

Campus/Community Resources

It is also worth noting that language programs can serve their students well by pointing them toward other campus and community technology resources. As of this writing, for example, color laser printers are beyond the means of most language programs, but this need not stop a student who wants to use one to jazz up an overhead for a class presentation. Color printing of files from various standard programs is almost certainly available somewhere nearby, and what the student really needs are good instructions about how to find and use these services. The benefits of making local services known and accessible extend both to expensive equipment (printers, scanners, and video editors) and to specialized software such as *computer-assisted design* (*CAD*) or *molecular modeling programs*. By laying good groundwork, the language program can provide students with many such services without directly incurring the heavy expenses involved.

Taking available local resources into account can form an important part of the language program's overall technology strategy. Language programs cannot afford to respond to all of the potential demands for technology from its teachers and students and certainly should not try to do so. A better strategy is to provide a basic set of high-quality services and make a continuous commitment to maintaining that quality. In practice this may mean purchasing one quality piece of equipment rather than two or three cheaper ones, or perhaps foregoing new equipment completely for a time so as to devote resources to rewiring or expanding software and materials choices. Although some users, both students and teachers, will eventually have use for services beyond this basic set, even the most grandiose projects can often be initiated on or adapted for the basic equipment at hand.

Here we should also mention one case where locally available technology services can be more enemy than friend. This occurs when other *service providers* choose to upgrade software or hardware and the language program suddenly needs to catch up whether it wishes to or not. This happens most notably with word processing software. Most language programs wish to give their students access to word processing, and many do so in their own labs or learning centers. When other providers—such as libraries and computer centers which may offer similar services—upgrade to new versions of software, the language program will generally have to follow suit to provide users with a seamless way to use files that they create in other locations. In a similar vein, a language program may one day find that its own computer learning center—filled with oldish but still perfectly serviceable computers—has become the object of derision by language program students who have test-driven the newer models elsewhere.

Impact of New Communication Technologies

Hardly a day passes without some mention in the news of the Internet and other new communication technologies. Business cards now routinely carry the holder's e-mail address, along with telephone and fax numbers. Wireless, cable, and satellite communication can also be part of a language program, but the focus here is on the Internet and its impact on language program administrators.

Virtual Community of Administrators

Time is rarely a plentiful resource for administrators. Teachers, support staff, students, and their own supervisors make demands on administrators' time. Conferences have often provided the only opportunity for administrators to take a moment to talk with one another about the problems and issues they have in common or simply to commiserate. The explosive growth of e-mail, both at work and at home, has changed that. With e-mail, administrators can now have nearly instantaneous communication with other administrators around the globe. They can also benefit from a form of e-mail known as a *mailing list* where messages can be sent automatically to a large group of people. The mailing list TESL-L has a sublist, TESLIE-L, for language program administrators. There is also a list for NAFSA: Association of International Educators.[4]

One of the advantages of e-mail and mailing lists over telephoning is that communication does not need to be between 8 am and 5 pm in the respective time zones. As with a fax, sending and reading e-mail can be scheduled to take place at a relatively convenient time. E-mail messages normally contain the sender's name and a brief subject header, and so can be quickly scanned to identify those that need a timely answer. A professional network can be built around personal correspondence, even with people one has never met. The administrator with on-line access is no longer alone.

One of the disadvantages of e-mail, particularly of mailing lists, is that they can be too much of a good thing. The speed of communication possible with e-mail means that there may be an expectation of a quick response, much as there is with fax communication. It also can be easier to post a query on a mailing list than to research the answer oneself, which means that many messages on mailing lists are frivolous, unnecessarily loading the mailboxes of their recipients. The seductiveness of e-mail may mean that the administrator spends far more time on e-mail than is necessary or even wise. As the medium becomes more familiar over time, these drawbacks may disappear.

The Internet As a Teacher and Student Resource

Administrators are not the only ones who benefit from on-line communication. Teachers and students can use *on-line sources* (such as service providers like America Online) or a direct connection to the Internet to be in touch with a mind-boggling array of resources. Using on-line sources raises certain issues for administrators, including infringement of copyright, plagiarism, and misuse of Internet access and e-mail. Privacy and security issues, also germane here, are addressed later.

On-line sources can provide more current information than any printed document. The Internet in particular is updated with new information every moment of every day, from places all around the world. The *World Wide Web* offers text, graphics, sound, and video as its information mix, along with powerful search tools that help students and teachers find the topics they are interested in. A wide range of perspectives on any topic is generally possible because so many different people are information providers. On the other hand, there is no guarantee of accuracy; the Internet is not a refereed journal.

Language teaching makes much these days of "authentic" communication—using language not just for a classroom-related purpose, but to achieve a real-world end. Using e-mail for pen-pal exchanges is one way to make English language use authentic. In addition, as more places around the world have e-mail access, international students in particular can use it as a way to keep in touch with people at home. This reduces some of the anxiety for those who are far away, encouraging retention and making adjustment easier.

While the advantages of *on-line resources* and e-mail for students and teachers are considerable, administrators must take the drawbacks into account as well. For good and for bad, it is easy to download information. Teachers may use copyrighted information from on-line sources. Students may be tempted to plagiarize on-line sources, hoping their teachers will not recognize the work as someone else's. Teachers and students need to be aware of copyright regulations and realize that they cannot download information and pass it off as their own.

Another current topic is access to "adult" areas on the Internet. On-line, fee-based services have mechanisms to prevent access by unauthorized people; administrators who are concerned should make sure these protections are in effect. Those with direct Internet connections can purchase software that restricts access to known adult areas. The loophole in the software is that new sites come on-line constantly, and the software may not be able to keep up with all of them. Still, it makes it difficult for the normal student *net browser* to access these areas.

A related area of concern for administrators is misuse of e-mail—specifically, sending unsolicited and unwelcome messages to others. There is little administrators can do to prevent this except for educating e-mail users as to appropriate electronic behavior (i.e., *netiquette*) and imposing strong penalties on those who abuse their e-mail privileges. Administrators should keep in mind that the use of language program equipment, including mail servers, is not a guaranteed right. While monitoring individual messages would be both tremendously costly and potentially troublesome legally, mail users can be held to standards of behavior. All e-mail users should be warned never to leave a computer unattended with their personal e-mail account open, as this is an invitation to pranksters or others to misuse the account for their own purposes. All users of e-mail should be required to sign some sort of document that sets out expected standards of behavior.

New Communication Technologies for Providing Instruction

On-line sources are useful for on-site instruction. The Internet and audio and video teleconferencing can also be used for distance learning. Distance learning has been the subject of a number of books (Keegan, 1993; Rossman, 1992; Rossman & Rossman, 1995; Rumble, 1986; Schrum, 1991), so the issues that administrators should be aware of when considering it as a means of providing instruction are given only a cursory look here. With distance learning, *bandwidth*—the amount of information that can be sent over a line simultaneously—and cost are large concerns. The first question to address is whether communication should be *synchronous*, with both sides communicating directly to each other at the same time, as in a telephone call, or *asynchronous*, like e-mail, where time zone differences do not matter. The latter is much easier logistically and generally far cheaper, since transmission can be at whatever time is most inexpensive via the relatively inexpensive medium of the Internet or a service provider. In both cases, care should be taken to fit the instruction to the medium.

Issues related to synchronous communication include finding an appropriate time, choosing the transmission mode, making sure both sides have the equipment needed, and planning for technical difficulties. When the teacher and learners are in different time zones, finding an appropriate time for both parties may be difficult. The choice of transmission mode will depend on cost, bandwidth, and available equipment. Two-way video is the Cadillac of distance learning. It requires sophisticated equipment on both ends and a high-bandwidth connection, but the teacher-student interaction can be quite similar to that in regular classroom-based teaching. The Internet has an experimental transmission method called the *MBONE* that allows video, graphics, and sound as well as text in *real time*. This requires a very good quality, high-speed connection and a video and audio digitizer, and the resulting video is mediocre at best. A two-way audio connection is much easier and cheaper, requiring just a phone line and speakerphone, but does not provide visual contact. One-way video and two-way audio is another option, which falls in the middle in difficulty and cost.

As time goes on, ease should increase and prices should drop for distance learning with video. Cable companies are doing more in the area of education, and interactive cable is being tested now in a few areas in the United States. Computer, telephone, and cable companies continue to work more closely together to provide a seamless integration of data, voice, and video. This will likely prove to be a major growth area in education that language program administrators should be aware of.

Marketing the Language Program, Electronic Registration, and Advising

Whatever the future may bring in distance education, electronic media are increasingly important now in marketing, registration, and advising, particularly for intensive English programs. The World Wide Web's ability to display graphics, video, and sound as well as text have made it the medium of choice for advertising and promotion in many small businesses. Independent language programs can purchase space on existing Web sites, such as *Study in the USA*, or they can set up their own on-line Web location, known as a *home page*. While the Web is largely a noninteractive information provider, it allows users to send e-mail messages and to fill out on-line forms. The Web has begun to provide a risk-free way to send credit card numbers on-line, making it possible for students to send in an application and the corresponding fees electronically.

Registration is another area where change is occurring rapidly. Students in many colleges and universities can register by telephone or computer, and some school districts are experimenting with this option. When initial problems have been worked out, institutions have found this to be a cost-effective form of registration. Language program students may register the same way, but low-proficiency students, in particular, generally need more help in registering than native speakers. The language program should have advisors on hand to assist students. In this case, face-to-face contact is appropriate.

In other situations where technology itself is not the problem, some advising can also take place electronically. Language programs should offer students e-mail access to advisors so that students do not need to wait to see an advisor in person to get simple questions answered. The language program can also provide electronic access to the information itself. Many sources of information about visa requirements and life in English-speaking countries, for example, already exist on-line to help international students. The language program can provide instructions for retrieving that information. The language program's *Web page* can also be set up to link students directly to frequently requested on-line information.

Privacy and Security Issues

Technology can make it easier for people to communicate with each other and connect to information, but that ease comes at a price—the possible loss of privacy and data security. Any e-mail message is potentially public unless the user takes steps to encrypt the message so that only the intended receiver can decrypt and read it. For most messages, this is an unnecessary bother. It is rarely worth the trouble for message writers to send a decryption key by nonelectronic means to everyone they might e-mail. On the other hand, administrators should be sure to inform e-mail users of the possibility that their messages may be preserved for posterity with a mail server's routine *backup*, and they should clearly delineate language program policy about use of its mail server.

Language programs that have file servers or remote access to individual machines on a network have a larger issue in data security. The electronic links that add convenience to accessing information also make it possible for that information to be corrupted or destroyed. Even off the network, important data should be backed up regularly and stored elsewhere to protect from equipment failure, theft, and damage due to fire or flood. With the Internet, the risk can come from across the world almost as easily as from the next room. The precautions that administrators must take include password protection for access to any machine on the network, making sure that staff and students do not share their passwords with others. Sensitive information such as student grades should have a second level of password protection with a password different from that used to access the machine. If the network is large, there should be a network administrator responsible for security issues as well as maintenance and troubleshooting. The added expense of security precautions is like insurance—you only realize its value if you do not have it when you need it.

Conclusion

It is safe to predict that the new and evolving technologies described here will continue to create both headaches and opportunities for language program administrators well into the future. But technology is not the only area of change and evolution in the language program. Such matters as curriculum and program offerings, relationship to host institutions, and internal management structure will also continue to evolve and renew themselves. Arguably, the management of growth and renewal is or should be an administrator's chief preoccupation. Technology can appear intimidating and frustrating for administrators who rarely have the time to delve too deeply into the arcana of *T1 lines* or programming code. We believe that administrators who have had experience applying technological tools in real learning situations are better prepared than those who have not, but we do not assert that technical knowledge—no matter how extensive—is itself sufficient. We would like to suggest, instead, that effective technology leadership at the level of the language program administrator depends less on such detailed knowledge than on the same principles and strategies that guide the administrator in other areas. Just as the resolution of curriculum issues depends on a vision of how best to aid individual students and teachers in the creation of learning, many of the questions raised by the evolution of technology must also be answered in human rather than technical terms.

Endnotes

1. Because technology tends to be rich in jargon, a glossary of technical terms is included at the end of the chapter. Terms appearing throughout the chapter in italics are defined in the glossary.

2. Warschauer (1995) touches on these and other advantages to using e-mail in language teaching.

3. These and other computer lab–related issues are addressed in Hanson-Smith (1991).

4. To subscribe to the TESL-L mailing list, send a message to listserv@cunyvm. cuny.edu and in the message say: Subscribe TESL-L <your first name> <your last name>. The TESLIE-L sublist is especially useful for IEP administrators.

   To subscribe to the NAFSA net mailing list, send a message to listserv@vtm1.cc.vt. edu and in the message say: Subscribe INTER-L <your first name> <your last name>.

Discussion Questions and Activities

1. Why might the increased use of technology in a language program require changes in how the program evaluates the performance of instructors?

2. What kinds of support personnel are necessary to maintain an electronic network of digital communication and shared resources?

3. What are the advantages of making sure that language program students in a university setting have access to other computer labs on campus? What are the drawbacks?

4. In what ways can computerized record keeping and office automation change the needs and perceptions of administrators and staff?

5. What main points need to be covered in a language program's policy in regard to the proper use of electronic mail?

6. What are some potential problems related to the ease of information access made possible by the Internet?

7. Imagine that a school in the United States wishes to establish a distance learning arrangement with an institution overseas. What technology-related factors need to be considered?

8. Imagine that the president of a small college has decided to set up an intensive English program. The program staff will consist of a director, two instructors, and one full-time clerical person. The director has already been appointed and has been given a startup budget. One line of this budget makes $14,000 available for the purpose of acquiring four staff workstations at $3,500 each. A fax machine and a photocopier will also be provided, but no other lines in the budget relate in any way to the staff's use of technology. The new director is concerned about this area of the budget and has arranged a meeting with the president to discuss it. How should the director prepare for this meeting? What arguments might be used in support of increasing the technology allocation? What items are missing from the spending plan? If an increase is not possible and $14,000 is the maximum amount available, how should the director modify the plan?

Suggested Readings

Barlow, M., & Kemmer, S. (Eds.). (1995). *Technology and language learning yearbook* (Vol. 5). Houston: Athelstan.

This volume includes an annotated listing of organizations and publishers involved in technology-enhanced language learning.

Healey, D., & Johnson, N. (Eds.). (1997). *1997 TESOL CALL interest section software list*. Alexandria, VA: TESOL.

This is a comprehensive listing of software for English language teaching. Updated annually, it includes brief descriptions of each program and the types of students and proficiency levels each is designed for.

Leading and Learning With Technology.

This monthly magazine (in essence a combination of *The Computing Teacher* and *IRM Quarterly*) from the International Society for Technology in Education (ISTE) provides information for computer-using administrators and teachers with a focus on elementary and secondary schools.

Technological Horizons in Education (T.H.E.) Journal.

This free monthly publication includes articles about educational technology use, mostly geared toward administrators and developers, and short descriptions of new educational technology products and services.

U.S. Congress, Office of Technology Assessment. (1988). *Power on! New tools for teaching and learning*. Washington, DC: U.S. Government Printing Office.

This well-documented report surveyed the use of different types of technology in U.S. classrooms in the mid-1980s and made recommendations for technology use in schools. Most of the recommendations are still valuable.

U.S. Congress, Office of Technology Assessment. (1993). *Adult literacy and the new technologies: Tools for a lifetime.* Washington, DC: U.S. Government Printing Office.

This well-researched report examines methods of providing adult literacy training through technology. The comments about distance education and networking are helpful to those in language teaching, as well.

Warschauer, M. (1995). *E-mail in language teaching.* Alexandria, VA: TESOL.

This easy-to-read guide includes a collection of suggestions about ways to use e-mail in language teaching. The ideas are helpful for both teachers and administrators.

Glossary

asynchronous communication. Communication that can be delayed; both parties do not have to be present at the same time. Electronic mail is an example of asynchronous communication (cf. synchronous communication).

backup/to back up. A copy of data/to protect data by making a copy, which is usually kept in a separate location.

bandwidth. The amount of free space available on a transmission line; more is better, since the more there is, the larger the number of people who can be communicating over the same physical medium simultaneously.

computer-assisted design (CAD). Also known as computer-aided design; usually used for industrial or architectural drafting and three-dimensional modeling on the computer.

custom application. A computer program written to the specifications of a business (cf. off the shelf).

e-mail/electronic mail. A means of sending messages electronically.

end user. The person for whom programs are designed, as opposed to the programmer who writes the software.

file sharing. A means of allowing more than one person to look at the same electronic information easily.

freeware. Software that is free of charge; it is usually still copyrighted, but can be used and distributed freely.

gateway. A place where two networks come together and where messages can pass between them.

Gopher. A text-based type of information provider wherein users can search for a particular topic, and then read about it on Gopher. This has been largely superseded by the World Wide Web.

hardware. Equipment—the physical stuff—as opposed to software (computer programs).

home page. The starting point for a specific individual or institution on the World Wide Web.

interactive video. A combination of computer and videotape or videodisc where the computer can control what is displayed, when, and for how long on the video.

Internet. A very large scale interconnected network of networks. Institutions of higher education generally pay the Internet fee and provide access free to their faculty. Full access to the Internet allows users to send and receive electronic mail, send and receive files, read information on Gopher, and read and respond to information on the World Wide Web.

mailing list. An electronic system whereby those who have subscribed to the system (subscribing usually just entails sending an e-mail message) can create an e-mail message that is distributed to all those who subscribe to the list and can read all the messages posted by all other members to the list.

MBONE. The Multimedia backBONE is a transmission system that runs over the Internet and allows real-time transmission of voice and video as well as of text.

modem. A device that allows computer data to be sent over phone lines.

molecular modeling program. Very sophisticated software that allows users to see and manipulate on the screen models of molecules.

monitor. The screen (also known as a video display terminal, or VDT, or a cathode ray tube, or CRT).

net navigators/net browsers. These are software programs that make it possible for people to read and share video, graphical, and sound information as well as text over the Internet. They are used with the World Wide Web.

netiquette. Proper behavior on electronic mail and newsgroups (network etiquette).

off-the-shelf software. Software, usually for business, that can be purchased at a computer store and used as it is (cf. custom application).

on-line resources/on-line sources. Information that is available electronically, usually via CD-ROM, over the Internet, or through a service provider such as America Online or CompuServe.

operating system. The fundamental rules by which personal computers collect, organize, store, and present data; Windows 95 and Windows 3.1 are examples of operating systems.

real-time. Right now, as opposed to in a delayed way (as with e-mail). With real-time communication, I can type directly from my computer to you at your computer (cf. synchronous communication).

scanner. A machine that creates an electronic image of text or graphics.

server. The computer that is used to store shared information.

service provider. A company that provides electronic information, e-mail, and often Internet access.

shareware. A computer program that you can try before you buy. If you like and use it, you are expected to pay the author directly.

software. Computer programs that make the machine do things.

synchronous communication. Communication between people who are in some way connected to each other at the same time; the telephone is an example of synchronous communication.

T1 line. A very high speed voice and data transmission line that can be shared by a large number of people without making anyone's computer slow down.

transparent. Easy to use.

Web page. A place to go on the World Wide Web; Web documents are made up of pages.

World Wide Web (WWW, The Web). A system of communicating over the Internet that allows users to display graphics as well as text and to play sounds and video clips.

Chapter 17

GRANTS AND PROJECTS
(As if you don't have enough to do already)

Charles Mickelson
Ohio University

 nglish language programs rarely place much emphasis on grant and project activity because program directors (and the higher administration) often feel that such activity would be inappropriate to the mission of language programs or beyond their capabilities. Although there may be cases in which this is true, the reluctance to pursue grants and projects is more often due to a lack of awareness of existing opportunities and a lack of understanding about how those opportunities can be handled to strengthen the ability of language programs to meet their principal functions.

The mystique associated with grants and projects has led to misperceptions that have created barriers to language program involvement in these activities. Some grants and projects are limited to degree-granting units and tenure-track faculty, but language programs still have many grant and project opportunities available to them. It is simply not true that applicants have to be insiders to be considered for funding or that major funding agencies are not interested in second language instruction. Nor is it a fact that grants and projects always require extensive new curriculum design, heavy up-front costs for promotion and marketing, or new administrative hierarchies.

Numerous language programs have become involved in grants and projects without sacrificing traditional roles, neglecting regular course offerings, or straining their resources. In these cases, administrators have understood the benefits of involvement and have taken the necessary steps to avoid or overcome problems. (Appendix A lists some possible language program grants and projects.)

The overview of grants and projects provided here includes discussion of some key terminology, the benefits and risks associated with grant and project activity, and the steps that language program administrators must take to ensure success in such activities. Appendix B outlines the steps of the process with an abbreviated commentary.

Key Terminology

The terms *grant* and *project* have a large degree of overlap in common parlance. It would not be surprising, for example, to hear the director of a language program refer to "being awarded a grant for the implementation of a project" to teach ESL to prison inmates. However, the terms will be used here to distinguish between two different types of activities.

Grant refers to funding from an institution, organization, or agency for a specified activity that has been determined and publicized by the funding source. Potential grant recipients must convince the team reviewing proposals that they are the best choice to develop a plan to meet the grantor's specified objectives, or to implement a plan that the grantor has already developed. Grants, generally sought in competition with other programs, require that applicants follow rigid, nonnegotiable application procedures and absolute deadlines. An example that could be of interest to a language program might be a state Department of Education grant to provide in-service ESL workshops to secondary school teachers during a set period of time and for a specified amount of money.

Project refers to funding from an institution, organization, agency, or individual for special services initially proposed and later offered by the language program. In this case, the language program project developer must convince the funding source that the proposed services meet an existing need. Procedures and timelines are generally worked out as interest in the project develops. An example of a project might be funding for a 5-week summer workshop combining practical teacher training and language-skills enhancement; participants are funded by a teacher-training college in Country X, with whom the project was designed.

In the following discussion, when these distinctions are not of consequence, the term *grant* will be used to cover both types of activity.

Benefits and Risks Associated With Grants and Projects

Wise program administrators determine what types of grants to pursue by considering the potential benefits and risks and by evaluating their own program's strengths. With this firm base from which to write a proposal, they can then build on language program strengths and meet their own program's objectives as well as those of grant participants.

The benefit that initially attracts most language programs to grants and projects is enhanced revenue, and "taking a financial bath" is the risk that scares many away. More subtle benefits include faculty development and renewal, enrollment stability, program and faculty recognition, and language program integration into the larger institution.

Revenue Enhancement

The most obvious reward from a special grant is the monetary balance that remains after all costs are covered. Securing a surplus in funds, however, is not always straightforward. Some funding organizations insist on an accounting of every dollar spent on implementation; U.S. government grants routinely have this stipulation. In these cases, payments only cover documented expenses, leaving no surplus. If the sponsor pays projected expenses in full, the monetary surplus, if one remains, must then survive the scrutiny of the home institution. Often, the first instinct of an institution is to scoop all or most of a surplus into a general fund, taking possible revenue away from the participating program.

Grants may also produce financial benefits through *indirect cost return*, commonly known as *overhead*. An indirect cost rate, included in grant budgets, covers institutional costs that are difficult to itemize, such as equipment maintenance, utilities, facilities not paid for through usage fees, and services from institutional offices such as housing, accounting, and personnel. Most institutions have a set of overhead rates, negotiated with the federal government, that is dependent on the type of work to be done and whether it is to be conducted on or off campus. Overhead can be financially beneficial to language programs when parent institutions have an overhead distribution system that returns a portion of the overhead to the program, department, or college that generates the income (see Staczek, this volume, for more on overhead).

The ability to write off costs that would normally be handled within the regular language program budget represents another financial benefit of a special grant. For example, if a program has its own photocopier, computers, phones, and fax machines, the costs associated with their use can be included in the grant budget. It is reasonable to include a percentage of maintenance and depreciation costs in proposed budgets if the overhead assessment does not already cover them. If equipment must be purchased for the grant, that equipment may revert to the program for its own use when the grant is completed. If the grant involves travel to areas where the language program would like to recruit students or develop contacts, it may be possible to share travel costs between special grant and regular program budgets.

Financial Risks

One financial risk associated with grant activity is the possibility that it will never get off the ground. Program directors must be prepared to absorb costs for grant development and planning as they will not be covered by funding agencies unless the activity is approved for funding and is implemented. Because it is unlikely that all submitted proposals will be accepted, language program administrators must accept occasional rejections—and the associated planning costs—as part of the process. The possibility of rejection and the associated financial risks can be minimized by careful selection of grant activities. It is also wise to start small by, for example, selecting grants that require only slight modifications to existing program offerings, thereby minimizing the need for specialized program development. Obtaining assistance in preparing aspects of the proposal from one's home institution, for example from the Office of Grants and Contracts, can also cut down costs.

Risks and Rewards for Faculty

A financial benefit that does not bring increased revenue to the program, but that is felt more directly by program faculty, is the potential to supplement salaries through work on grants and projects. If grant activity is timed so that it will not interfere with the completion of an individual faculty member's contractual obligations, it may be possible to offer faculty supplemental contracts from the grant budget. If involvement requires a reduction in an individual's regular teaching or administrative load and an increase in grant activity, it may be possible to reduce normal contract amounts accordingly and write a new grant contract for a larger total sum. If the language program employs part-time faculty who would like to have additional work, grants are a natural way to increase their income.

The risks here are linked to expectations and perceptions. Since it is unlikely that everyone in a program will be involved in grant activity, it is important that the selection criteria for participation be clearly established and open to all. Even then it is naive to think that some individuals will not resent being left out. Nonetheless, grant and project activity may offer tangible rewards for everyone if enhanced revenue allows for benefits such as increased travel or equipment allocations. Such increases, however, can lead to unrealistic faculty expectations. Increased salaries, extra travel money, and equipment upgrades, which begin as bonuses brought in by grant activity, can quickly be assumed to be a standard part of faculty benefits. Clear and regularly repeated explanations of revenue sources and their transitory nature will help alleviate unrealistic expectations.

Faculty development and renewal are additional benefits derived from grant and project activity. Because grants normally diverge in focus, objectives, and intensity from regular language program offerings, participating faculty are stimulated by new challenges and responsibilities. For example, rather than focusing on the development of academic language skills, which is the standard focus of many language programs, grants may give faculty the opportunity to work with diverse students (e.g., businessmen/women, teachers, or other professionals who may be near beginners or quite advanced). In addition, faculty may have the chance to use their expertise to develop new courses, focusing on, for example, specific content areas, nonacademic communication skills, American culture, teacher training, and technology.

Grant and project activity also allows faculty members to branch out into other professional areas, developing new skills and expertise. For example, faculty may become involved in writing grant proposals or administering funded activities. Some faculty will thrive in their new jobs and will look forward to similar professional growth opportunities in the future. Others will be content to return to their full-time teaching positions, but with a greater appreciation for the demands of grant-related activity and administration.

One challenge for program administrators is to equalize opportunities to prevent faculty from becoming territorial about short-term assignments that may be better rotated to others. In addition, administrators must recognize the potential for overcommitting the faculty. Participating faculty who are overextended inevitably leave tasks to be picked up by program faculty who are not involved in the project. The ripple effect may leave a whole faculty suffering from stress and poor performance. Moreover, even in cases of short-term grants, where an adrenaline rush carries faculty through the implementation period, there may well be a post-grant letdown that is detrimental to the ongoing program.

Enrollment Stability

Although direct financial benefit is the most obvious reward of grant and project activity, nonmonetary benefits, including enrollment stability, program and faculty recognition, and program integration, are likely to have a long-range impact on the language program. Enrollment stability is of concern to language programs whose enrollment peaks when the new academic year begins and declines steadily until the next academic year. This cycle can create staffing problems, especially for programs that have a commitment to supporting as many full-time positions as possible. An emphasis on grant work during down periods can provide a more stable demand for faculty throughout the year. Even if this stability has no impact on annual budgetary figures, it is likely to pay great dividends in faculty morale.

There is, of course, some risk involved in enrollment stability based on *soft money* (i.e., money that is dependent on the continuation of grant contracts). The best hedge against this risk is to diversify grant activity in one of two ways. First, involvement in diverse activities protects against sudden losses when a certain type of grant or project dries up due to the loss of traditional funding sources, a decrease in student interest, or increased competition. Second, involving students from a variety of countries lessens the impact of sudden economic or political changes in a particular country or geographic region.

Program and Faculty Recognition

A language program's overall reputation can be enhanced through the careful design and successful implementation of grants, although the type of activity will determine where the impact is most strongly felt. For example, bringing in groups of professionals or high-quality graduate students raises awareness and support from the academic community, particularly if the program integrates faculty from other units into the grant activity through lectures and consultations. Success with grants funded by the government, businesses, or private foundations will be noticed by offices that are responsible for supporting institutional grant activity. Intensive language and cultural experience grants are likely to catch the attention of individuals interested in study abroad opportunities or continuing education.

Grants and projects are apt to increase the visibility of language programs because they often attract the attention of campus and community publications, television, and radio. This publicity is generally considered highly positive by senior administrators and funding agencies, especially if the grant is deemed financially productive or politically attractive. Often senior administrators are invited to grant-related receptions and activities; this involvement heightens their awareness of the language program. Whether the senior administrator participates in these activities or not, future discussions about the grant may provide opportunities for the language program administrator to reinforce the strengths and importance of regular program offerings.

In addition to on-campus recognition, language programs can attract positive attention from other institutions, potential students, and funding agencies as a result of successful grant activity. Participating students who have a positive experience carry those memories with them when they go home or to other institutions for further study. They become excellent word-of-mouth recruiters. In addition, language programs that can refer to successfully completed grants, especially if they demonstrate the confidence of major funding agencies, are well positioned to establish credibility with new contacts in the search for new grants.

Successful grant activity may also allow faculty to develop professional connections, consulting opportunities, presentations, or publications. Such activities enhance the individual faculty member's reputation and, at the same time, the reputation of the program. The cyclical effect (see Figure 1) of successful grant activity, increased numbers of program contacts, and an enhanced reputation can lead to even greater exposure and opportunities for future grants.

Gaining recognition, however, has its potential risks. Most obvious is the fact that a highly visible program is equally visible when it fails. To minimize the possibility of failure, language program directors are advised not to draft proposals by themselves, in isolation. They are well served by enlisting the support of others who can point out weaknesses and pitfalls in the initial proposal. Such support is particularly useful with *grant* proposals as the speed with which they must be produced can easily blind the writer to key elements that have been overlooked.

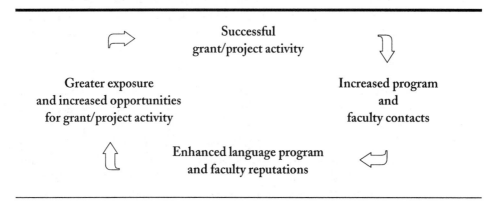

Figure 1. **The cyclical effect of grant and project activity.**

A second risk associated with visibility is that a highly visible program can be an attractive target for a take-over bid. A language program that engages in many short-term grants on its own may find that another office on campus, for example the Office of Continuing Education, is moving at a higher level to take over all grant activity. The only real defense in such a situation is to have built strong support from the administrative hierarchy under which the program has been operating.

Language Program Integration

As individuals from the university and community become involved in language program grants, they learn about the language program and receive firsthand exposure to the abilities of the language program faculty and staff. When language program administrators and faculty have established credibility in this way, they are more likely to be asked to participate in other institutional grants or on committees, resulting in increased language program integration into the academic community. They are then more likely to receive a good reception when issues of importance to the language program arise. To secure this integration, it is essential that grants be designed to run without placing undue stress on other units and that adequate compensation is provided for the involvement of other units.

Assessment of Strengths

Having determined what the language program can gain from grant involvement, directors can now turn their attention to determining what types of activities the program is capable of implementing successfully. The first step is to consider the strengths of the language program, its home institution, and the surrounding community.

To ensure success, the grant must be relevant to the abilities and interests of the existing program and its faculty. Favorable outcomes in grant activity generally require building on an existing record of success in areas related to the objectives of the grant; success also requires administrators and faculty who understand how to fulfill objectives and carry out implementation plans and who are interested in doing so. For example, a language program with a long history of excellent support services and instruction of university-level students may be totally unprepared to run a summer language program for junior high school students. On the other hand, a similar program using faculty with previous experience teaching in junior high schools and running summer sports camps may be well equipped to handle such a program—but only if those experienced individuals are enthusiastic about the grant.

It is equally critical for language program administrators to know their institution well. In determining the actual contents of a proposal, successful grant writers and project developers consider what the institution does well and who is responsible for doing it. They recognize the wisdom of including other institutional departments or offices in the proposal to tap their expertise and to establish credibility with higher level administrators and potential funding sources. In addition, they recognize that to gain institutional approval and support, the proposal must complement the stated mission of the institution and the working priorities of the administration and relevant faculty groups.

Language program administrators must also know what formal and informal support services exist for grant writers on campus, and which people have established a record of gaining grants in related areas. Even language program administrators who have confidence in their proposal writing ability will benefit from acknowledging and utilizing the expertise of others, some of whom may ultimately be consulted in the approval process.

Finally, language program directors who are considering a locally run grant must know the community well. When contemplating a grant, the director must determine whether the surrounding community can accommodate the number of students—of the background, age group, and interests—that will be brought on campus. In addition, they must ascertain if, for example, homestay families are available and if there are sufficient community resources to complement language program and institutional offerings.

Search for Grant and Project Opportunities

The next step is to begin searching for opportunities. Grant and project funding may originate from many sources, including the home institution, the local area, professional organizations, governmental agencies, nonprofit foundations, and major companies. (See Appendix C for a listing of World Wide Web information sources.)

Many educational institutions fund curricular innovations, instructional enhancement, equipment upgrades, and research projects through competitive in-house grant opportunities. Although many of these grants are restricted to tenure-track faculty or degree-granting units (often excluding language programs), there are often opportunities open for language programs. Commonly, language program administrators and instructors work together with faculty from qualifying academic departments or other offices, such as admissions or the international student support office, to draft joint proposals.

To gain access to this funding, language program administrators must show potential partners how collaboration is in their best interest. A willingness to write the grant proposal is often seen as a substantial benefit by harried academic department chairs. Language program faculty expertise in areas such as cross-cultural communication, orientation programs, or innovative uses of technology provides additional incentives for collaboration. Language program participation may also expand the scope of a proposal by including more diverse students or by providing an international experience for all participants. In seeking cooperative efforts, the language program director must keep in mind that few institutions are free of a power hierarchy; language programs rarely enter discussions with academic departments on an equal footing. Thus, the language program director must negotiate on the basis of service, knowledge, expertise, and experience that is essential to the success of the proposal.

There may also be opportunities within the community or region. For example, school districts impacted by immigrant populations may have grant money or project opportunities for teacher-training seminars or cultural sensitivity workshops. Local corporations might appreciate language enhancement tutorials for foreign associates visiting the area. Local businesses with non-native employees might desire Survival English or English for Specific Purpose classes to enhance employee confidence, performance, and promotion possibilities. To benefit from such opportunities, it behooves the language program director to know the community well enough to be aware of what special needs are likely to exist, what funds are available, and who to contact about ways language program faculty or administrators might be of help.

Professional organizations often offer project funding to their members. Organizations such as TESOL, NAFSA, and UCIEP fund research projects, community activities, travel, and study. Organizations outside the field also provide grants for language-related activities. Rotary International, for example, has supported EFL teachers in developing countries. While this type of activity is not likely to produce any income for language programs, it can result in increased program recognition and professional development opportunities for faculty.

State and national governments have been prime sources of grants for language programs. The United States Agency for International Development (USAID) and the United States Information Agency (USIA) have been major funding sources over the years, although the political climate at the time of this writing makes it uncertain whether that will continue. (To find out more about USAID and USIA funding opportunities, consult Appendix C.) In general, grants at this level can be divided into two types. A very small number can be bid for by a language program and delivered with its own resources. A far greater number require cooperation with other units, such as other departments within the university or organizations outside the university. In some situations, the combined resources of several language programs may be able to produce a much stronger proposal than an individual program could on its own. Many large development grants require second language teaching as part of the total package. A resourceful language program director may be able to contract for this part of the overall grant.

Funding from nonprofit foundations and major companies is also available to language programs. Most often, the onus is on the language program developer to lay out objectives that the foundation finds worthy of support and then to convince the foundation that the language program is able to meet those objectives. When a project is designed in cooperation with representatives of the group that is going to receive the services, the developer is more likely to convince the foundation that there is a strong chance for success.

Unlike grants, finding projects typically does not require directors to scan information services for notices of available funding. Rather, projects are developed by directors who notice student, university, or community needs that their language program can meet. Directors then develop a plan and approach the group who needs the service or those who might fund the project. A special project may be as simple as running trips to regional attractions for international students in the area. Or it may be as complex as setting up a combined English instruction, English teacher training, and English teacher-trainer training program in conjunction with a foreign university.

Project participants may be recruited in two ways. By far the easiest way is to work with one sponsoring agency or institution to provide a tailored service for a group of participants. The sponsor then selects the participants and sends them as a group. The alternative is to establish the project and advertise for participants just as language programs advertise for regular students. The advantage of the first method is that a contract can be written with the sponsor for a set number of participants who are handled with one transaction. Paperwork on the students all comes together, documents are handled through one person, the participants arrive and leave together, and an institutional representative often accompanies the group for all or part of the stay. The shorter the project, the greater this advantage becomes. If all applications must be handled individually, the administrative effort can become unmanageable for large-scale, short-term projects.

Development of a Proposal

When an interesting project has been identified, the developer must learn as much as possible about the potential participants, their backgrounds, interests, and motivation for participation. Because there is commonly a discrepancy between the objectives of the sponsoring agency and the participants themselves, it is critical to ascertain the participants' objectives and try to accommodate them.

Developers must also be adept at soliciting input from all affected local parties, such as housing, food services, recreational facilities, and academic departments during the initial stages of proposal development. As the proposal takes shape, dialogs should develop that recognize areas of expertise or lack of expertise. In the junior high school project example used earlier, the office that normally handles support services, housing, and activities for American summer camp participants should be consulted about procedures and pitfalls, but not about how to adapt their procedures to a group of Thai students.

Successful proposal writers must also maintain close contact with the funding agency or client group. Approaches for establishing and maintaining contact differ depending on whether the language program is the sole source for a project or part of a competitive grant selection process.

Sole Source Projects

Sole source projects, which come in many configurations, do not require competitive bids. (See Appendix D for an extended example of a sole source project.) Despite the fact that no other program is competing for the project, acceptance of the project is not guaranteed. Acceptance is more likely if language programs work with the client as a partner in designing the project. Language program project developers often make the common mistake, in this situation, of asking the client to specify exactly what they want, implying that the language program can deliver whatever is requested. This approach is misguided for the following reasons: (a) Clients rarely know exactly what they want because they are rarely experts in the field. Most commonly they have some general objectives and expectations in mind based on what they have read, heard, or seen. (b) Clients become disillusioned because they expect the language program to demonstrate its expertise during project planning.

Successful developers must hone the ability to learn what a client's general objectives are without committing themselves to meeting initial client requests. Such an ability allows developers to shape a project so that it takes advantage of strengths in their programs, institutions, and communities. An ideal approach is to present clients with several alternative plans. Discussing the strengths and weaknesses of each—in relation to targeted participants—can then lead to shared decisions about the final proposal. In this way, the developer solidifies the position of expert while acquiring additional credibility for demonstrating flexibility and willingness to adjust to the special needs of future participants, and clients gain a sense of project ownership and have an incentive to do whatever they can to make it work.

A great deal of diplomacy is required when shaping a project with clients; the key is to establish camaraderie and partnership. Ideas from the client can never be dismissed lightly, and certainly not with any sense of condescension. Client suggestions should be included whenever possible, or shown to already exist in the proposal albeit in a somewhat altered form, or given careful consideration before being dismissed on grounds specific to the realities of the situation and not to the general inappropriateness of the ideas.

Competitive Bids

Competitive bids are those for which a number of programs are submitting grant proposals. Often they are a response to a request for proposal (RFP) from an institution or a governmental agency. Here the ground rules are quite different due to more stringent guidelines regarding what activities must be performed to reach specified objectives and how the institution demonstrates its credentials.

In a competitive bid, there is less chance of creating an atmosphere of partnership in developing the proposal. Most commonly the contact person is required to release identical information to all who inquire. This does not diminish the importance of establishing a relationship with the contact person; a proposal writer who does not have the information being given to everyone else has incurred an unnecessary handicap as the information may well expand on or clarify the details of the RFP. In addition, discussions with the contact person can provide insights into how clearly the developers of the RFP understand the realities of implementing what they have outlined and the relative importance being attached to different objectives. The proposal writer should also determine if the writers of the RFP are going to evaluate the proposals or be involved in its implementation. While it is rarely permitted to contact those who will evaluate proposals, it is sometimes permissible to reach those who are involved in its implementation. They may be able to provide a much clearer picture of potential participants.

A more detailed discussion of grant writing is beyond the scope of this chapter. Interested readers should consult knowledgeable colleagues and support personnel at their institutions as well as Bauer (1995), Bowman and Branchaw (1992), Conrad (1980), Gilpatrick (1989), Krathwohl (1988), Lock, Spirduso, and Silverman (1993), Schumacher (1992), and Steiner (1988).

Development of a Budget

Whether a language program administrator is pursing a sole source project or a competitive grant, developing a budget to accompany the proposal is an important part of the process. There are several key points to consider when drafting a budget and figuring out how much to include for overhead:

1. A working budget should account for all costs. Many budgets omit the costs of development and marketing—such as communication costs, equipment and materials use, travel, and time expended by the director, the curriculum designer, and the support staff—because funding sources rarely pay for them as a line item. Nonetheless, these costs should be included in a column marked "nonbillable expenses" or "in-kind contributions," at least for the purpose of calculating an actual net balance when the grant is completed.

2. Budgets must be formatted to fit the sponsor's specifications. Because budget formatting requirements often differ from one institution to another, and from one sponsoring agency to another, two budgets may be necessary—one that complements the home institution's accounting system and one for the sponsor's. Linking the two in a computerized spreadsheet allows program directors to enter data and make changes, guaranteeing that the two are always matched. If institutional review or negotiations with the sponsor result in the need to make adjustments, changes can be tested quickly with the effects showing up clearly on each budget format.

3. The use of constants, such as the number of participants, can ease the budgeting process. Because constants reoccur in many cost calculations, they should be included in a separate section of the budget and then be referenced each time they are used in the spreadsheet. In this way, when a constant changes, new calculations can be made in the spreadsheet more easily.

4. Before finalizing a budget, program designers must determine what the sponsor requires for final accounting, how the home institution handles monetary surpluses at the completion of the grant, what the home institution sets as an indirect cost rate (overhead), and how the institution distributes overhead return. If either the sponsor or home institution plans to take unspent funds when the grant is finished, the budget should be written and watched carefully to see that all money is spent. What makes this tricky is that any sizable budget written well in advance of performance should include a contingency fund to handle unexpected expenses. One way to provide for this need is to budget for slightly increased percentages of salaries, communications, transportation, and other costs that are difficult to estimate. This approach allows for unexpected increases in each budget area, if needed, and covers some development costs, if it is not needed. A second way to respond is to include an

"administrative costs" line item in the budget; this approach may not be possible if the institution charges overhead for administrative costs. Yet, if institutional overhead does not cover the administrative costs of a self-supporting language program, a sponsor may accept the line item.

In terms of overhead, a language program should present its strongest case for low rates. How much flexibility an institution is willing to allow in setting the rate for a particular grant varies tremendously. However, there are at least three potential issues worth exploring. The first is whether the grant is attractive enough to warrant a reduction in normal amounts. A reduction may be justified due to the status of the grant, its potential as an entree to more extensive activities, or its fit with the institution's current emphasis. For example, if a grant involves a country with which the institution is attempting to create closer ties or if it is a pilot effort to develop a much larger endeavor in future years, administrators in charge of overhead may be willing to reduce the rate.

The second issue to explore is the fit between the basis for a particular rate and the actual demand of the project on institutional resources. For example, if project participants do not live in dormitories, register through normal channels, or make extensive use of libraries, labs, or recreational facilities, and if the language program is generally self-supporting in terms of equipment, materials, development, and promotion, a strong argument can be made for lower overhead rates because there are few institutional costs incurred.

Closely related is the question of which expenses should be assessed as overhead. Items for which participants are already paying identical rates as other students, such as dormitory fees, health coverage, or facilities charges, may sometimes be exempted from overhead assessment. Bear in mind that this argument has little chance of success if those facilities are subsidized by general institutional funds.

Collateral to the discussion of overhead rate should be the discussion of overhead fund distribution. Many institutions return a part of the overhead to the program(s), department(s), or college(s) responsible for the grant based on a fixed percentage or negotiated arrangements. In either case, it is important for language program directors to know how overhead will be distributed before the budget is finalized. A higher overhead is easier to live with if a substantial portion will be returned to the program for its own use. If overhead is returned to the home institution, language program administrators might want to view the budgetary "loss" as a way for the language program to strengthen its relations and recognition within the institution.

Maintaining the Long-Term View

Because no grant or project is an end in itself, language program administrators should plan with an eye for how the grant activity fits into the ongoing development of the language program. They should assume that the program will depend on the same or similar faculty, support staff, sponsoring agencies, institutional personnel, and clients long after a specific grant is completed. At the completion of the grant, faculty and staff may be tired but they should feel appropriately rewarded for their efforts—both financially and in quality of experience. Participants and sponsors should be satisfied and feel that the program was well worth the time and expense. Higher level administrators at the home institution should view the activity as a contribution to and not a drain on the various departments involved. In order to sustain such positive feelings, the language administrator should be able to justify all aspects of the program as necessary and reasonable.

Discussion Questions and Activities

1. Weigh the pros and cons of grant and project activity for language programs.

2. What are the challenges faced by a busy language program administrator when developing a grant proposal?

3. Imagine that you are the director of an intensive English program at a small college in the southeastern United States. You have received a request from a faculty member who has just returned from Korea to arrange a program for 30 16-year-old Korean students at your college. What do you need to determine about your language program, institution, and community before deciding whether to pursue the opportunity?

4. Assuming you have decided to go forward with the Korean project (see question 3 above), write a letter to the contact person in Korea requesting information that is key to developing a preliminary proposal. Refer to several aspects of your program that establish your qualifications and provide examples that might give direction to their response.

5. Identify a language program that you know well. From the list of project examples in Appendix A, select three that you think would be appropriate for the program and three that would not. Explain your selections with reference to specific factors that justify your choices.

6. You have determined that to implement one of the projects in Appendix A, a minimum of $100,000 is required to cover the direct costs of salaries, benefits, supplies, materials, transportation, activities, communication, and room and board. What costs remain to be considered? Determine how each would best be handled based on the approaches taken by your institution and by the sponsor. If possible, find out exactly what the institutional policy is.

Suggested Readings

Bowman, J. P., & Branchaw, B. P. (1992). *How to write proposals that produce*. Phoenix, AZ: Oryx Press.

Bowman and Branchaw provide an extensive review of the affective factors involved in proposal writing. Of particular interest is their treatment of how to determine the personality and perspective of the client and then shape writing style, layout, and graphics to best meet the client's expectations.

Conrad, D. L. (1980). *The quick proposal workbook*. San Francisco: Public Management Institute.

Although this volume is somewhat dated, Conrad's hands-on approach, with an emphasis on identifying needs, offers many practical suggestions that are applicable to language program contexts.

Krathwohl, D. R. (1988). *How to prepare a research proposal: Guidelines for funding and dissertations in the social and behavioral sciences* (3rd ed.). Syracuse, NY: Syracuse University Press.

Krathwohl's discussion of funding sources has great relevance to language program administrators. The excellent annotated bibliography can also be useful for language program administrators seeking more information on grant and project activity.

Schumacher, D. (1992). *Get funded! A practical guide for scholars seeking research support from business.* Newbury Park, CA: Sage.

Schumacher focuses most of his attention on proposals for research support from business. Regardless of the type of proposal, his suggestions on how to approach businesses and corporations can guide language program administrators in such ventures.

Appendix A

A Sampling of Successful Language Program Grant and Project Activities

Location	*Nature of grant and project activities*
On or near campus	• Short-term language and culture programs (noncredit) • Language and sheltered academic content programs (noncredit for language program institution; credit for participants' home institution) • ESP programs for targeted groups of students (e.g., police, economists, businessmen and women, bankers, athletes, musicians, journalists, engineers) • Practical teacher training workshops focusing on technology training, methodology, application of theory to specific teaching environments, networking, and materials development • Workshops and cultural orientation for teacher trainers from abroad • A language enhancement program at a local company worksite • Cultural and academic orientation programs for international students

Abroad	• Evaluation of a language training program
	• Design and implementation of a language training program
	   Community-based language center
	   Language program within or affiliated with a host country institution
	   Language program at an American institution branch campus
	   Independent language center
	   Government-funded language center
	   Language training program for executives or workers in a foreign company

Appendix B

Steps for Grant and Project Development and Implementation

These examples are intended to help readers see the potential breadth of each step; they are neither obligatory nor all-inclusive.

A. Determine the purpose.
- Consider the possibility of stabilizing the financial base of the language program, equalizing staffing needs throughout the year, providing faculty with opportunities for professional growth, creating stronger links with other departments throughout the home institution, and increasing the visibility of the program.

B. Determine the strengths.
- Evaluate the language program and home institution faculty, facilities, and existing programs.
- Assess existing international activities and agreements.
- Evaluate the support of the community.
- Evaluate attractive aspects of geographic location.
- Contact potential partners at other language programs or institutions.

C. Become familiar with grant and project activities taken on by other language programs.

D. Establish acceptable parameters for short- and long-term activities.
- Define the focus of activity (academic preparation, conversation, English for Specific Purposes, content with ESL support, teacher training workshops, teacher training degree programs, student/faculty exchange, academic orientation, travel tours with ESL support, American cultural experience with ESL support).
- Determine a funding source (home university; community; domestic or foreign business, foundation, or educational institution; individual participants; local, state, federal, or foreign government; or some combination of the above).
- Choose a location (on campus, off campus but within the community or region, outside the region, outside of the United States, or some combination of the above).
- Consider staffing concerns (internal to the language program, internal to the home institution, outside hires, qualifications, type of contract).
- Determine what resources are needed (space, equipment, support staff, administration, development and marketing time and costs).
- Evaluate ethical, political, and legal considerations; adhere to TESOL core standards, NAFSA code of ethics, NAFSA principles of international education, equal opportunity/affirmative action requirements, home institution mission and priorities.

E. Develop contacts and determine an appropriate grant or project to pursue.

F. Learn the procedural requirements.
- Review relevant institutional policies (offices to notify, forms to complete, approvals required, timeline for all of the above, a system for determining overhead).
- Determine the funding source's requirements (timelines, deadlines, appropriate contacts, allowable expenses, in-kind contributions, accounting system).

G. Write the proposal and budget.
- Keep the audience in mind with regard to their objectives and priorities, restrictions, decision makers, and successes and failures in past experiences with this type of activity.
- Respond to participants' backgrounds and needs, including objectives and priorities, level of preparation for content and language, and orientation possibilities prior to arrival.
- Collaborate with program faculty, home institution faculty and offices, the community, and grant or sponsor contacts in a manner that makes them feel like knowledgeable contributors without requiring extensive work or abdicating responsibility for the final project.
- Be thorough and cautious in budgeting; include all expenses, provide contingency funds for unforeseen expenses, understand the institutional and sponsor positions on positive balances and overhead rates/distribution, and make use of spreadsheet power with constants and linked formats.
- Anticipate areas of concern; be ready with explanations and options based on everything learned about the audience and participants.
- Be detailed in scheduling.

H. Implement the project.
- Orient the faculty and staff; include a discussion about sponsor expectations; participant expectations, backgrounds, and preparation; overall program components and integration; specific responsibilities; general responsibilities/expectations regarding activities, receptions, and so forth.
- Orient the students in the same way.
- Maintain ongoing communication; use the regular faculty/staff reporting system, sustain an ongoing participant feedback system, identify people for participants to go to with concerns, and so forth.
- Make any necessary adjustments. Note that, in general, minor adjustments are perceived by sponsors and participants as demonstrations of flexibility and sensitivity to participant interests; major adjustments are perceived as demonstrations of a lack of adequate planning. Adjustments that violate the sponsor's objectives should be avoided.

I. Evaluate and follow-up.
- Make contact with evaluation sources (participants, faculty, administration, and sponsor).
- Conduct immediate follow-up with participants (send them photographs, an address list of other participants, and an evaluation form).
- Contact participants with more long-term concerns, such as updates, reminders, or requests for suggestions on future programs.
- Submit a final report to the sponsor with an executive summary, table of contents, and complete evaluation with a section on suggestions for improvement of the same project and extensions to other projects.

Appendix C

Funding Sources

Most language program grants and projects develop through faculty contacts, relations with sponsors, university ties, and recruitment trips. Several works cited in the reference section provide extended lists of funding sources. Other funding sources can be located via the World Wide Web. The WWW sites noted below lead to most major resource locations. All are free; the first three are run through universities, and the last is run by a commercial enterprise.

http://infoserv.rttonet.psu.edu/gweb.htm (Grants Web)

http://www-unix.oit.umass.edu/~vladb/funds.html (Links to Foundations and Grants for Education)

http://pegasus.uthct.edu/OtherUsefulSites/Govt.html (United States Government and Grant Resources)

http://fdncenter.org/index.html (The Foundation Center)

An alternative to web surfing is a targeted database, for example the Sponsored Programs Information Network (SPIN), a private source to which many universities subscribe. It compiles data on a daily basis from major print media including the *Commerce Business Daily*, the *Federal Register*, and *The Chronicle of Higher Education*. It searches for grant opportunities by using key words and phrases, such as "English as a second language."

Appendix D

An Extended Example of a Sole Source Project

Location: In the United States on a university campus.

Focus: Language enhancement, dance history and criticism, dance instruction, and extracurricular activities.

College X runs a 5-week summer language and dance institute for students both from area colleges and from a Taiwanese Academy of Arts. U.S. students take 3 hours of dance history and criticism in the late morning while the Taiwanese students take 3 hours of English. Half of the time in English is devoted to general conversational fluency; the other half is devoted to understanding English specifically related to dance. U.S. and Taiwanese students meet together for 3 hours of dance instruction, half in the morning and half in the afternoon. Each Taiwanese student has a U.S. roommate. Evening and weekend activities include general interest movies, sports, and social gatherings, and live and filmed dance performances. The group spends one weekend in New York, highlighted by a major dance event. The culminating activity of the program is an afternoon of participant dance recitals and an evening banquet.

All participants pay standard tuition plus an activity fee that is set at the actual cost of the activities plus a 25% overhead charge. The host university keeps all tuition and fees received from the U.S. students. Tuition and fees from the Taiwanese students are placed in a project account that is managed by the language program director. The language program is responsible for overall project management; it plans and covers expenses for language instruction, room and board for the Taiwanese students, and all activities. It also makes a fixed contribution to dance studio expenses.

The host university assesses a 25% overhead charge on all expenses paid out of the project account, except for room and board. If there is money left in the budget at the end of the program, the university assesses a 25% overhead charge and transfers the rest to the language program's development account.

Part VI

PRINCIPLES AND RESOURCES FOR LANGUAGE PROGRAM ADMINISTRATORS

GENDER ISSUES
FOR THE LANGUAGE PROGRAM ADMINISTRATOR
Marian E. Blaber

IMMIGRATION PRINCIPLES
FOR THE LANGUAGE PROGRAM ADMINISTRATOR
Peter S. Levitov

INTERNATIONAL TEACHING ASSISTANT TRAINING PRINCIPLES
FOR THE LANGUAGE PROGRAM ADMINISTRATOR
Janet C. Constantinides

MARKETING PRINCIPLES
FOR THE LANGUAGE PROGRAM ADMINISTRATOR
Bradley D. Miller

GENDER ISSUES FOR THE LANGUAGE PROGRAM ADMINISTRATOR

Marian E. Blaber
Independent Consultant

Important Principles

1. Understand how gender distinctions in communication and management styles can influence your role as a program administrator. Learn how men and women generally differ in their approaches to communicating with individuals and in groups. Also, discover how men and women generally differ in delegating work, negotiating political situations, and gaining recognition.

2. Discover your management style and determine your career goals. Understand how your personality suits and does not suit your job description. Uncover ways to hone your management strengths and overcome your weaknesses. Engage in career mapping activities and ask yourself what you hope to accomplish in your position as program administrator.

3. Balance your personal and professional life. The message in the 1990s seems to be that all work and no play makes Jack or Jill all stressed out, less productive, and dull, dull, dull.

4. Find mentors and be part of a network. Don't go it alone. A mentor can provide guidance and inside information that may be critical for getting things done well. Networks include groups at your institution and professional organizations. Join both.

5. Understand your institution's culture and combat sexual discrimination. Learn about how women are viewed by your institution and become knowledgeable about sexual harassment guidelines. Make certain that language program personnel are aware of the guidelines.

6. Become political. Learn about the value system at your institution and find out what the institution expects of your language program. Become aware of the subtle and overt forms of prejudice within the institution.

Annotated Bibliography on Gender

Bravo, E., & Cassedy, E. (1992). *The 9 to 5 guide to combating sexual harassment.* New York: John Wiley & Sons.

This guide offers clear and concise information about what constitutes sexual harassment, how to safeguard against it, and how to confront it when it occurs. It is a guide, designed for both men and women, that outlines workplace policies that should be in effect to protect against sexual harassment; it explains procedures that managers and other employers should follow if presented with a case of sexual harassment, and provides references such as government agencies, support groups, and legal associations for information regarding sexual harassment.

Caplan, P. J. (1993). *Lifting a ton of feathers: A woman's guide for surviving the academic world.* Toronto: University of Toronto.

This book cautions us about the climate for women in higher education. It offers a helpful checklist to determine if one's institution is "women positive." It also provides recent data on gender discrimination. Caplan asserts that higher education is a male-dominated institution, slow to change, and often unfair to women. She warns of overt and subtle forms of prejudice against women, exploding the myths of collegiality, meritocracy, and liberalism which mislead women into feeling that discrimination is not present when, in fact, a double standard exists.

Feuer, D. (1988). How women manage. *Training, 34,* 23–31.

This article offers an overview of female managers, especially at lower and middle management levels. In this short piece, Feuer highlights a host of crucial issues that can distinguish male and female managers; these include communication styles, the ability to delegate work, the design of career goals, the necessity to find a mentor and to be a mentor, and the need to understand the politics of the workplace. With respect to gaining recognition, Feuer asks if women sabotage themselves with a myopic view of day-to-day tasks while men get ahead by learning to negotiate the political system.

Hunsaker, J., & Hunsaker, P. (1986). Working effectively in groups. In J. Hunsaker & P. Hunsaker (Eds.), *Strategies and skills for managerial women* (pp. 182–207). Cincinnati, OH: South Western Publishing.

This chapter discusses ways that men and women work differently in groups. It focuses on (a) improving the ability to delegate, (b) making group decisions, (c) recognizing how emotions play a role in group behavior, (d) identifying the pros and cons of making a group decision, and (e) conducting effective meetings. At the close of the chapter, action guidelines provide tips for working in groups.

Keele, R. (1986). Mentoring or networking? Strong and weak ties in career development. In L. Moore (Ed.), *Not as far as you think: The realities of working women* (pp. 53–68). Lexington, MA: Lexington Books.

In addition to explaining the importance of having a mentor, Keele discusses the power of networking. In this chapter, Keele provides examples of how strong ties and weak ties can strengthen career development, and she points out that a focus on both kinds of relationships can be more responsive to a variety of career needs. Keele questions how many workers actually attain a true mentor-protégé relationship—a relationship in which a person higher in the organization acts as a facilitator, coach, teacher, exemplar, counselor, and provider of moral support for the protégé.

Kofodimos, J. (1993). *Balancing act: How managers can integrate successful careers and fulfilling personal lives.* San Francisco: Jossey-Bass.

This text provides tools for men and women who need a greater balance between personal lives and work lives. The author's chief premise is that managers who maintain a balance in work, family, friendships, play, and self are happier individuals and more productive workers. The author identifies the root causes of imbalance as cultural, social, and psychological. Exercises in the book encourage individual self-awareness as well as providing practical solutions for those who spend a disproportionate amount of time at work. Suggestions for changing workplace policies are also provided.

Sander, B. R. (1993). The campus climate revisited: Chilly for women faculty, administrators, and graduate students. In J. S. Glazer, E. M. Bensimon, & B. K. Townsend (Eds.), *Women in higher education: A feminist perspective* (pp. 175–203). Needham Heights, MA: Ginn Press.

This chapter provides examples of the many ways that women feel subtle and not-so-subtle forms of discrimination (micro-inequities) on college campuses. Of special interest are findings that females still lag behind their male counterparts in rank, salary, and status. Sander's findings indicate that women's contributions are downplayed, making women appear less competent than men. With respect to women administrators, Sander asserts that problems of isolation and access are caused by the fact that too few women hold positions of power.

Tannen, D. (1994). *Talking from 9 to 5: How men's and women's conversational styles affect who gets heard, who gets credit, and what gets done at work.* New York: William Morrow.

The third book in a series on men's and women's communication styles, *Talking from 9 to 5* concentrates on communication in work situations and provides examples of how women and men can be interpreted differently because of communication styles. Topics include conversational rituals, indirectness, the glass ceiling, authority, status, sexual harassment, hierarchy, women as bosses, and talk at meetings. Tannen maintains that women should not need to adopt men's communication styles to be heard, but at the same time, she points out the necessity to understand how each style can affect outcomes.

Thuesen, J. M., & Kroeger, O. (1992). *Type talk at work.* New York: Delacorte Press.

Based on the theories of psychologist Carl Jung, *Type talk at work* helps readers identify personality types and describes how personality types can impact work performance. Using the Myers-Briggs Type Indicator of Personality, 16 personality types are presented. Readers can discover how their own personality types may influence work with respect to time management, conflict resolution, team building, stress reduction, and goal setting. Readers can also determine if their chosen careers are well suited to their personality types.

Tinsley, A. (1984). Career mapping and the professional development process. In A. Tinsley, C. Secor, & S. Kaplan (Eds.), *Women in higher education administration* (pp. 17–24). San Francisco: Jossey-Bass.

In this chapter, Tinsley poses questions so that the reader can reflect on personal values and professional goals. The author urges the reader to evaluate her (or his) work environment—in terms of the institution's values, mission, resources, and problems—to determine if the goals of the individual and that of the institution are compatible. Tinsley maintains that such planning can help clarify career goals and prospects for achieving them.

IMMIGRATION PRINCIPLES FOR THE LANGUAGE PROGRAM ADMINISTRATOR

Peter S. Levitov
University of Nebraska Lincoln

Important Principles

1. Learn the basic immigration terminology that foreign students encounter from the time of their admission to an academic program through the completion of their studies—for example, I-20 forms, visa, consulate, transfer of schools, extension of stay, and so forth.

2. Recognize that the U.S. Immigration and Naturalization Service (INS) is an enforcement agency, and, consequently, it will offer a perspective different from the student advocate perspective offered by a foreign/international student advisor.

3. Develop a broad understanding of the regulations that will be encountered. Regulations governing the responsibilities of institutions that enroll foreign students might cover such areas as admissions, record keeping, and reporting. Regulations that govern employment opportunities and re-entry into the United States after a temporary absence are of particular importance to foreign students. Some regulations have special relevance for language programs, for example the definition of a full course of study, a change of nonimmigrant classification, or an annual vacation. Familiarity with these regulations makes it easier to explain them to students, faculty, and staff.

4. Because regulations change from time to time, consult continually with the foreign/international student advisor at your institution. English language programs that are not based on a college campus should employ their own professional advisor.

5. Be aware that noncompliance with immigration regulations not only renders a student in violation of status but also places the program (and, where it is a unit of a larger institution, the institution itself) in jeopardy of losing its approval to issue I-20 forms and enroll F-1 students.

Annotated Bibliography on Immigration

Althen, G. (1995). *The handbook of foreign student advising* (2nd ed.). Yarmouth, ME: Intercultural Press.

While this volume dedicates only a few pages to immigration, it truly is the handbook for professionals working with foreign students in the United States. As such, it belongs on the bookshelf and in the hands of every English program administrator. Topics covered include the nature and role of the advisor's position, characteristics deemed important for advisors, knowledge and skills needed for the position, and excellent discussions of intercultural communication and problem solving in the foreign student context. Observations and suggestions on immigration advising complement the general text.

Gooding, M. (1995). *Faculty member's guide to immigration law*. Washington, DC: NAFSA: Association of International Educators.

This handy booklet is self-styled as a painless introduction to immigration law for faculty members and others who work with foreign students and scholars. It begins with a very useful section on basic immigration terminology and an explanation of documents commonly encountered by foreign students and their program administrators and advisors. The chapter on foreign students is clearly written in a style oriented to those who do not want to be mired in the technicalities of the regulatory world. This publication is expected to be updated every few years.

Leonard, J. G., & Yenkin, A. (Eds.). (1994). *F-1 GRAC pack*. Washington, DC: NAFSA: Association of International Educators.

This is an informative collection of handouts prepared by NAFSA' s Government Regulations Advisory Committee. Each document in the pack offers either a succinct explanation of an aspect of the foreign student experience in a regulatory context or a clear set of guidelines to enable the foreign student and the administrator or advisor to obtain a benefit accorded under immigration law. Programs are able to copy the handouts for students, staff, and faculty colleagues. The pack is revised periodically by NAFSA as major regulatory changes are promulgated.

The NAFSA ethics program. (1995). Washington, DC: NAFSA: Association of International Educators.

This booklet includes NAFSA's code of ethics and its principles for international educational exchange. The code, to which all NAFSA members subscribe as a condition of membership, sets forth standards for professional preparation and conduct. Sections address professional preparation, responsibilities in relationships with foreign students, professional relationships, administration of programs, ethical recruitment, admission of students, and teaching English as a second language, among others. The effective practice of international educational exchange is embodied in NAFSA's principles. Specific principles address the determination of English proficiency, English support courses, and intensive English programs.

Yenkin, A. (Ed.). (1995). *Adviser's manual of federal regulations affecting foreign students and scholars.* Washington, DC: NAFSA: Association of International Educators.

This loose-leaf volume is absolutely essential for every program or institution enrolling foreign students. It offers guidance to individuals working with foreign students through a general introduction to immigration law with chapters on (a) the legal status of nonimmigrants in the United States, (b) the responsibilities of institutions enrolling F-1 students, and (c) the F-1 status itself. Well documented with references to regulations, the manual combines an exposition of the basic rules governing foreign students with a hands-on, how-to approach to critical processes and procedures for both students and administrators/advisors. It is updated annually and is also offered in a Windows version, which includes key-word searching and the full text of pertinent regulations cross-referenced throughout the manual.

INTERNATIONAL TEACHING ASSISTANT TRAINING PRINCIPLES FOR THE LANGUAGE PROGRAM ADMINISTRATOR

Janet C. Constantinides
University of Wyoming

Important Principles

1. International Teaching Assistant (ITA) programs offer significant challenges to the language program administrator because they involve a struggle between units within a research institution for control of resources and power.

2. The proficiency levels needed by ITAs, especially in the area of oral skills, are often greater than those addressed in the most advanced language courses, thus requiring language programs to create specialized classes.

3. Proficiency for ITAs must include appropriate sociolinguistic expertise in addition to oral and aural skills. However, sociolinguistic expertise, without the necessary level of comprehensibility, is not adequate.

4. An ITA curriculum includes not just language instruction but also pedagogical skills, cross-cultural issues, and microteaching practice. Issues of assessment are equally important.

5. Not all ESL teachers are qualified to design an ITA curriculum and courses, teach all of the items in the curriculum described in 4 above, or assess the performance of students in an ITA program. To be qualified, teachers need to be ESL professionals in addition to having a thorough knowledge of postsecondary education systems and multicultural communication theory and practice.

Annotated Bibliography on International Teaching Assistants

This annotated bibliography on ITAs is divided into four sections: books, collections of articles, textbooks, and research reports.

Books

Madden, C. G., & Myers, C. L. (Eds.). (1994). *Discourse and performance of international teaching assistants.* Alexandria, VA: TESOL.

> This ITA volume, the first devoted entirely to language and teaching research, provides insights into contexts for ITA language use, discourse, interaction, and performance. The book is based on a theoretical framework of communicative competence, and each study included offers information that is useful for designing a curriculum, and, in some cases, for planning class activities.

Smith, R., Byrd, P., Constantinides, J., & Barrett, R. P. (1991). Instructional development programs for international TAs: A systems analysis approach. In K. J. Zahorski (Ed.), *To improve the academy: Resources for student, faculty, and institutional development 10* (pp. 151–168). The Professional and Organizational Development Network in Higher Education. Stillwater, OK: New Forums Press.

> Addressed to the ITA program administrator, this chapter explains how to use "the culture audit and environmental scan as effective methods for institutional analysis" (p. 152) in order to design an effective ITA program. The section titled "Issues in ITA Assessment" provides a good overview of assessment issues and methods.

Smith, R., Byrd, P., Nelson, G. L., Barrett, R. P., & Constantinides, J. C. (1992). *Crossing pedagogical oceans: International teaching assistants in U.S. undergraduate education.* ASHE-ERIC Higher Education Report No. 8. Washington, DC: The George Washington University, School of Education and Human Development.

> This monograph presents the history of teaching assistantships in U.S. universities. It highlights the public reaction to ITAs in the 1980s that led to the establishment of ITA programs in many institutions and states, sometimes voluntarily and sometimes by mandates. It also provides a guide to different types of ITA programs and discusses assessment issues for each program type. In addition, it gives a brief review of research in the field to 1991. Written primarily for university administrators, it provides suggestions for establishing and maintaining a high-quality ITA program.

Collections of Articles Related to ITAs

The volumes listed below were published after various national conferences on teaching assistants. Each volume has a section on ITA programs. Equally important are the more general discussions highlighting critical issues related to the training of teaching assistants. These discussions allow language program administrators to situate ITA issues within the larger research university context.

Chisum, N. V. N., & Warner, S. B. (Eds.). (1987). *Institutional responsibilities and responses in the employment and education of teaching assistants: Readings from a national conference.* Columbus, OH: The Ohio State University Center for Teaching Excellence.

Nyquist, J. D., Abbott, R. D., Wulff, D. H., & Sprague, J. (Eds.). (1991). *Preparing the professoriate of tomorrow to teach: Selected readings in TA training.* Dubuque, IA: Kendall/Hunt Publishing.

Lewis, K. G. (Ed.). (1993). *The TA experience: Preparing for multiple roles (Selected readings from a national conference).* Stillwater, OK: New Forums Press.

Textbooks

Byrd, P., Constantinides, J. C., & Pennington, M. C. (1989). *The foreign teaching assistant manual.* New York: Collier Macmillan.

This textbook, the first one published for ITA courses, focuses on the cultural and pedagogical components of an ITA course, including (a) an overview of the U.S. education system and profiles of teachers and students in U.S. colleges and universities; (b) classroom management and class preparation; (c) presentation skills, including assignments for microteaching exercises; and (d) structured observations of classes in a postsecondary institution. There is also a section on pronunciation with general strategies for improving the student's ability to speak and to comprehend American English. The book is designed to help potential ITAs develop strategies for learning about teaching which they can continue to use after the course is finished.

Pica, T., Barnes, G., & Finger, A. (1990). *Teaching matters: Skills and strategies for international teaching assistants.* New York: Newbury House.

Each chapter of this textbook focuses on a specific aspect of teaching, for example preparing for class or meeting students for the first time. Each chapter has a reading selection, followed by a comprehension check, discussion questions, and activities. Key terms for each chapter are provided, as are objectives for the chapter.

Smith, J., Meyers, C., & Burkhalter, A. (1992). *Communicate: Strategies for international teaching assistants.* Englewood Cliffs, NJ: Prentice-Hall Regents.

This text includes sections on language learning, including grammar. One interesting innovation is an appendix with lists of key terms associated with various academic disciplines. Prospective ITAs can use the lists to work on the pronunciation of vocabulary for their academic fields. Each chapter, divided among teaching skills, language skills, and cultural awareness, includes assignments for microteaching.

Research Reports

A number of articles related to ITAs have been published in the *TESOL Quarterly*. The first one listed, which is annotated, may be of special interest to the language program administrator.

Halleck, G. B., & Moder, C. L. (1995). Testing language and teaching skills of international teaching assistants. *TESOL Quarterly, 29*(4), 733–758.

The implications of this research project are that ITAs need to have attained a certain level of English proficiency before they will benefit from an ITA course. This is significant for curriculum development and raises important assessment issues.

Hoekje, B., & Linnell, K. (1994). "Authenticity" in language testing: Evaluating spoken language tests for international teaching assistants. *TESOL Quarterly, 28*(1), 103–126.

Hoekje, B., & Williams, J. (1992). Communicative competence and the dilemma of international teaching assistant education. *TESOL Quarterly, 26*(2), 243–269.

Tyler, A. (1992). Discourse structure and the perception of incoherence in international teaching assistants' spoken discourse. *TESOL Quarterly, 26*(4), 713–729.

Williams, J. (1992). Planning, discourse marking, and the comprehensibility of international teaching assistants. *TESOL Quarterly, 26*(4), 693–711.

MARKETING PRINCIPLES FOR THE LANGUAGE PROGRAM ADMINISTRATOR

Bradley D. Miller

Center for Quality Assurance in International Education/
Global Alliance for Transnational Education

Important Principles

1. Understand that marketing a language program is a multidimensional endeavor with interactions among variables associated with student recruitment, student retention, and administrative operations. Administrators can improve language program marketing by examining the relationships among these variables and their outcomes.

2. Fix language program marketing expenditures at 10–20% of program operating costs. Language program marketing efforts merit a fixed annual budget allocation because they drive a program's enrollment and provide the conduit through which students initiate inquiries to learn more about the program and its fit with their needs.

3. Recognize that student recruitment efforts fall into four major categories: *Collateral materials* such as brochures, videos, applications, flyers, or posters; *advertisements*, for example in study guides, advising manuals, newspapers, professional organization publications, and directories, or on television; *public relations activities*, such as recruitment fairs, exhibits, presentations, publications, speakers' bureaus, and visitors; and *Internet and World Wide Web* (WWW) *site development*.

4. With your collateral materials and advertisements, present a unified graphic image, convey a positive impression of the program, and be oriented towards students who are likely to flourish at your program site. Keep the narrative short and concise. Use a "frequently asked questions" format, while always striving to answer this question: How will the student benefit by attending your program? Link your narrative contextually to photograph placement. Highlight program attributes that will both attract potential students and inspire students to initiate contact for more information.

5. Create a database and maintain information on contacts emerging from public relations and outreach activities. Organize contact information so that it is retrievable by name, affiliation, address, telephone number, fax number, e-mail address, WWW site, and contact date and location, such as a conference, recruitment fair, or speaking engagement. Cultivate new sources from the Internet. Track and follow up on referrals that may come from language program alumni, on-campus linkages, and business contacts.

6. Regularly evaluate the timeliness and efficiency of the language program's administrative processing of student inquiries and applications. Print applications with a sequential alpha-numeric code that can be used to track the distribution of materials (e.g., walk-in inquiry, mail-in inquiry, direct mail campaigns, on-campus mailings, or recruitment fairs). Set up your computer database to sort, index, and report student application data in a variety of formats, such as by country, city, birth date, gender, received date, data entry date, I-20 mail date, or enrollment date.

7. Regularly convene focus groups of currently enrolled and departing students to determine student needs, program perceptions, and impacts of your collateral materials, advertisements, public relations activities, and Internet outreach marketing efforts. Ascertain what the students' expectations were before arrival and whether or not their expectations were fulfilled. This process will help you determine if the program is delivering everything that is promised in marketing efforts, which is an important ethical issue.

8. Ease barriers to student application and enrollment processes by not imposing penalties for late registration or cancellations, accepting credit cards, and allowing registration through multiple sources, such as mail, faxes, e-mail, or WWW sites.

9. Recognize the difference between peddling and marketing a language program. A peddling orientation views language program services as merchandise for sale. A marketing orientation endeavors to align prospective students' short-term and long-term needs and goals with language program strengths, and helps students obtain the information that they need to make informed decisions.

10. Develop a 5-year, data-driven marketing plan that addresses recruitment, retention, and administrative procedures. Identify performance indicators to ensure that the plan is on track; evaluate and amend the plan every year.

Annotated Bibliography on Language Program Marketing

Agar, M., & MacDonald, J. (1995). Focus groups and ethnography. *Human Organization, 54*(1), 78–86.

This article is an excellent resource for conducting focus group inquiries in educational settings. It provides guidelines for focus group data collection, analysis, and reporting methodologies. The methods are appropriate for use with international students.

Davis, T. M. (Ed.). (1995). *Open Doors 1994/1995: Report on international educational exchange.* New York: Institute of International Education.

Published yearly, *Open Doors* compiles and interprets statistical data on international student and scholar activity in U.S. higher education. It can be used as a baseline to develop a marketing plan or to amend an existing plan from year to year.

Jenks, F. L. (1991). Designing and assessing the efficacy of ESL promotional materials. In M. C. Pennington (Ed.), *Building better English language programs: Perspectives on evaluation in ESL* (pp. 172–188). Washington, DC: NAFSA: Association of International Educators.

This article, part of an edited volume on ESL program administration and evaluation, addresses the need for a client-service orientation when developing and assessing promotional materials in an intensive English program context. The author focuses on the fundamental aspects of print and nonprint promotional material production and provides useful guidelines for their evaluation.

National Association of College Admissions Counsellors. (1995). *Statement of principles of good practice.* Alexandria, Virginia: Author.

This statement sets forth practical guidelines for the promotion of educational programs and the ethical recruitment of students. Of particular relevance to language program marketing efforts are discussions of (a) marketing staff compensation; (b) the development of publications, written communications, and presentations at, for example, recruitment fairs; and (c) third-party recruitment agencies.

Usunier, C. (1993). *International marketing: A cultural approach.* Englewood Cliffs, NJ: Prentice Hall.

This volume provides information on the sociocultural aspects of international marketing and communication. It can serve as a particularly relevant reference tool for language program personnel who are traveling abroad to work with prospective partners and student advising agencies.

World Education Series: PIER Reports. Annapolis Junction, MD: PIER Publications.

This series of more than 40 volumes describes the educational systems of 80+ countries. Some of the PIER (Projects for International Education Research) reports include directories and profiles of educational institutions in the targeted country or region. The detailed and current information provided in the volumes is critical for sound and ethical student recruitment, placement, and advising. Reviewing select PIER reports before planning and then staffing an exhibit booth at recruitment fairs abroad is an absolute must.

REFERENCES CITED

Acheson, K. A., & Gall, M. D. (1992). *Techniques in the clinical supervision of teachers: Preservice and inservice applications* (3rd ed.). White Plains, NY: Longman.

Agar, M., & MacDonald, J. (1995). Focus groups and ethnography. *Human Organization, 54*(1), 78–86.

Alatis, J. E., with C. Le Clair. (1993). Building an association: TESOL's first quarter century. In S. Silberstein (Ed.), *State of the art TESOL essays: Celebrating 25 years of the discipline* (pp. 382–414). Alexandria, VA: TESOL.

Alderson, J. C., Krahnke, K. J., & Stansfield, C. W. (Eds.). (1987). *Reviews of English language proficiency tests*. Washington, DC: TESOL.

Althen, G. (1994a). Cultural differences on campus. In G. Althen (Ed.), *Learning across cultures* (pp. 57–71). Washington, DC: NAFSA: Association of International Educators.

Althen, G. (Ed.). (1994b). *Learning across cultures*. Washington, DC: NAFSA: Association of International Educators.

Althen, G. (1995). *The handbook of foreign student advising* (2nd ed.). Yarmouth, ME: Intercultural Press.

American Council on Education: Committee on Foreign Students and Institutional Policy. (1982). *Foreign students and institutional policy: Toward an agenda for action.* Washington, DC: American Council on Education.

Angelis, P. (1987). *Applied linguistics: Realities and projections.* Paper presented at the 1987 American Association for Applied Linguistics Conference, San Francisco, CA.

Arreola, R. A. (1995). *Developing a comprehensive faculty evaluation system: A handbook for college faculty and administrators on designing and operating a comprehensive faculty evaluation system.* Bolton, MA: Anker Publishing.

Baldridge, J. V., & Deal, T. E. (Eds.). (1983). *The dynamics of organizational change in education.* Berkeley, CA: McCutchan Publishing.

Ballard, B., & Clanchy, J. (1984). *Study abroad: A manual for Asian students.* Kuala Lumpur: Longman Malaysia.

Ballard, B., & Clanchy, J. (1991). *Teaching students from overseas.* Melbourne: Longman Cheshire.

Bame, J. (1995). *Designing strategy-based lecture listening materials.* Paper presented at the TESOL conference, Long Beach, CA.

Barak, R. J., & Breier, B. E. (1990). *Successful program review: A practical guide to evaluating programs in academic settings.* San Francisco: Jossey-Bass.

Barber, E. G., Altbach, P. G., & Myers, R. G. (Eds.). (1985). *Bridges to knowledge: Foreign students in comparative perspective.* Chicago: University of Chicago Press.

Barlow, M., & Kemmer, S. (Eds.). (1995). *Technology and language learning yearbook* (Vol. 5). Houston: Athelstan.

Barnes, G. A. (1992). A model for effective staff development. Paper presented at the annual TESOL conference, Vancouver, B.C., Canada. (ERIC Document Reproduction Service No. ED 347 829)

Barrett, R. P. (Ed.). (1982). *The administration of intensive English programs.* Washington, DC: NAFSA.

Barrett, R., & Parsons, A. (1985). Quality components of IEPs. *TESOL Newsletter, 19*(3), 15–16.

Barsi, L. M., & Kaebnick, G. W. (1989, February). Innovative universities. *AAHE Bulletin,* 10–13.

Barwick, J. T. (1990). Team building: A faculty perspective. *Community College Review, 17,* 33–39.

Batten, J. D. (1963). *Tough-minded management.* New York: American Management Association.

Bauer, D. G. (1995). *The "how to" grants manual* (American Council on Education/Macmillan Series on Higher Education). New York: Macmillan.

Bean, W. C. (Ed.). (1993). *Strategic planning that makes things happen: Getting from where you are to where you want to be.* Amherst, MA: Human Resources Development Press.

Beck, D. J., & Simpson, C. (1993). Community service and experiential language learning. *TESL Canada, 11*(1), 112–121.

Bennett, J. M. (1993). Cultural marginality: Identity issues in intercultural training. In M. Paige (Ed.), *Education for the intercultural experience* (pp. 109–135). Yarmouth, ME: Intercultural Press.

Bennett, J. M. (1995). *On being different: A new perspective on cultural marginality.* Plenary presented at the TESOL conference, Long Beach, CA.

Berg, B., & Ostergren, B. (1979). Innovation processes in higher education. *Studies in Higher Education, 4*(2), 261–268.

Biber, D., Conrad, S., & Reppen, R. (1996). Corpus-based investigations of language use. In W. Grabe et al. (Eds.), *Annual Review of Applied Linguistics, 16* (pp. 115–136). New York: Cambridge University Press.

Billson, J. M. (1988). No owner of soil: The concept of marginality revisited on its sixtieth birthday. *International Review of Modern Sociology, 18* (Autumn), 183–204.

Birnbaum, R. (1988). *How colleges work: The cybernetics of academic organization and leadership.* San Francisco: Jossey-Bass.

Bliss, E. C. (1976). *Getting things done: The ABC's of time management.* New York: Charles Scribner's Sons.

Bolman, L. G., & Deal, T. E. (1991). *Reframing organizations: Artistry, choice, and leadership.* San Francisco: Jossey-Bass.

Bottomley, Y., Dalton, J., & Corbel, C. (1994). *From proficiency to competencies: A collaborative approach to curriculum innovation.* Sydney, Australia: National Centre for English Language Teaching and Research.

Bouchard, R. A. (1992). *Human resource practices for small colleges*. Washington, DC: National Association of College and University Business Officers.

Bowers, C. (1988). *The cultural dimensions of educational computing: Understanding the non-neutrality of technology*. New York: Teachers College Press.

Bowers, R. (1983). Project planning and performance: Some thoughts on the efficiency and effectiveness of curriculum development projects; with a case study of the Centre for Developing English Language Teaching, Ain Shams University, Cairo. In C. J. Brumfit (Ed.), *Language teaching projects for the third world: ELT Documents 116* (pp. 99–120). New York: Pergamon Press.

Bowman, J. P., & Branchaw, B. P. (1992). *How to write proposals that produce*. Phoenix, AZ: Oryx Press.

Bravo, E., & Cassedy, E. (1992). *The 9 to 5 guide to combating sexual harassment*. New York: John Wiley & Sons.

Bray, R. (1995). ATESL series on the administration of intensive English programs: Realities and responses for new administrators. Workshop presented at NAFSA: Association of International Educators, New Orleans, LA.

Brein, M., & David, K. H. (1971). Intercultural communication and adjustment of the sojourner. *Psychological Bulletin, 76*, 215–230.

Bridges, E. M. (1990). *Managing the incompetent teacher* (2nd ed.). Eugene, OR: ERIC Clearinghouse on Educational Management, University of Oregon.

Bright, W., et al. (Eds.). (1992). *International encyclopedia of linguistics*. New York: Oxford University Press.

Brighton, S. (1965). *Increasing your accuracy in teacher evaluation*. Englewood Cliffs, NJ: Prentice Hall.

Brindley, G., & Hood, S. (1990). Curriculum innovation in adult ESL. In G. Brindley (Ed.), *The second language curriculum in action* (pp. 232–248). Sydney, Australia: National Centre for English Language Teaching and Research.

Brislin, R. W. (1981). *Cross-cultural encounters*. New York: Pergamon Press.

Brown, J. D. (1995). *The elements of language program curriculum: A systematic approach to program development*. Boston, MA: Newbury House.

Brown, J. D., & Pennington, M. C. (1991). Developing effective evaluation systems for language programs. In M. C. Pennington (Ed.), *Building better English language programs: Perspectives on evaluation in ESL* (pp. 3–18). Washington, DC: NAFSA: Association of International Educators.

Brumfit, C. J. (Ed.). (1988). *Annual Review of Applied Linguistics, 8*. New York: Cambridge University Press.

Bryne, B. M. (1994). Burnout: Testing for validity, replication, and invariance of causal structure across elementary, intermediate, and secondary teachers. *American Educational Research Journal, 31*, 645–673.

Burkhart, P. J., & Reuss, S. (1993). *Successful strategic planning: A guide for nonprofit agencies and organizations*. Newbury Park, CA: Sage.

Burns, T., & Stalker, G. M. (1961). *The management of innovation*. London: Tavistock Publications.

Burton, E. J., & McBride, W. B. (1991). *Total business planning*. New York: John Wiley & Sons.

Buttjes, D. (1991). Mediating language and cultures: The social and intercultural dimension restored. In D. Buttjes & M. Bryam (Eds.), *Mediating languages and cultures* (pp. 3–16). Clevedon, England: Multilingual Matters.

Byrd, P. (Ed.). (1986). *Teaching across cultures in university ESL programs.* Washington, DC: NAFSA.

Byrd, P. (1988). Cross-cultural half-way houses: Orientation within intensive English programs. In J. A. Mestenhauser, G. Marty, & I. Steglitz (Eds.), *Culture, learning, and the disciplines: Theory and practice in cross-cultural orientation* (pp. 45–49). Washington, DC: NAFSA.

Byrd, P. (1994). Faculty involvement in defining and sustaining the mission and standing of IEPs in U.S. higher education. *Journal of Intensive English Studies, 8,* 27–35.

Byrd, P., & Constantinides, J. C. (1991). Self-study and self-regulation for ESL programs: Issues arising from the associational approach. In M. C. Pennington (Ed.), *Building better English language programs: Perspectives on evaluation in ESL* (pp. 19–35). Washington, DC: NAFSA: Association of International Educators.

Byrd, P., Constantinides, J. C., & Pennington, M. C. (1989). *The foreign teaching assistant manual.* New York: Collier Macmillan.

Byrd, P., & Fox, L. (1988). Survey of college ESL credit: A report from a subcommittee of the Committee on Professional Standards. *TESOL Newsletter, 22*(2),11–12.

Caplan, P. J. (1993). *Lifting a ton of feathers: A woman's guide for surviving the academic world.* Toronto: University of Toronto.

Carkin, S. (1988). The granting of credit in an IEP: A case study. Paper presented at the TESOL Conference, Chicago, IL.

Carkin, S. (1995). Anatomy of a self-study: The use of on-site consultants at Utah State University. In A. Wintergerst (Ed.) *Focus on self-study* (pp. 63–77). Alexandria, VA: TESOL.

Chisum, N. V. N., & Warner, S. B. (Eds.). (1987). *Institutional responsibilities and responses in the employment and education of teaching assistants: Readings from a national conference.* Columbus, OH: The Ohio State University Center for Teaching Excellence.

Christison, M. A. (1997). *Becoming a language teacher.* Burlingame, CA: Alta Book Center.

Coady, S. (1990). Hiring faculty: A system for making good decisions. *CUPA Journal, 41*(3), 5–8.

Cochran, E. P. (Ed.). (1992). *Into the academic mainstream: Guidelines for teaching language minority students.* Alexandria, VA: TESOL.

Cogan, M. L. (1973). *Clinical supervision.* Boston: Houghton Mifflin.

Collins, J. C., & Lazier, W. C. (1992). *Beyond entrepreneurship: Turning your business into an enduring great company.* Englewood Cliffs, NJ: Prentice Hall.

Conrad, D. L. (1980). *The quick proposal workbook.* San Francisco: Public Management Institute.

Cook, K. J. (1994). *AMA complete guide to strategic planning for small businesses.* Lincolnwood, IL: NTC Business Books.

Covey, S. L., Merrill, A. R., & Merrill, R. R. (1996). *First things first.* New York: Simon & Schuster.

Culp, S. (1986). *How to get organized when you don't have the time.* Cincinnati, OH: Writer's Digest Books.

Cumming, A. (1993). Teachers' curriculum planning and accommodations of innovation: Three case studies of adult ESL instruction. *TESL Canada Journal, 11*(1), 30–52.

Damen, L. (1987). *Culture learning: The fifth dimension in the language classroom.* Reading, MA: Addison-Wesley.

Davidson, J. O. (1984). Record keeping for critical decision making. *American Language Journal, 2*(2), 77–85.

Davidson, J. O. (1994). Boosting faculty/staff morale at a university-based intensive English program. *Intensive English Program Newsletter, 11,* 6–7.

Davis, T. M. (Ed.). (1994). *Open doors 1993/1994: Report on international educational exchange.* New York: Institute of International Education.

Davis, T. M. (Ed.). (1995). *Open Doors 1994/1995: Report on international educational exchange.* New York: Institute of International Education.

Davis, T. M. (Ed.). (1996). *Open Doors 1995/1996: Report on international educational exchange.* New York: Institute of International Education.

De Lano, L., Riley, L., & Crookes, G. (1994). The meaning of innovation for ESL teachers. *System, 22*(4), 487–496.

Diaz-Rico, L. (1995). The role of teacher educators in language policy and planning. *TESOL Matters, 5*(2), 11.

Domb, E. (1993). Total quality management: Strategy for success through continuous improvement. In W. C. Bean (Ed.), *Strategic planning that makes things happen: Getting from where you are to where you want to be* (pp. 247–268). Amherst, MA: Human Resources Development Press.

Drawbaugh, C. C. (1984). *Time and its use: A self-management guide for teachers.* New York: Teachers College Press.

Drucker, P. F. (1973). Managing the public service institution. *Public Interest, 33*(3), 43–60.

Drucker, P. F. (1991). The discipline of innovation. In J. Henry & D. Walker (Eds.), *Managing innovation* (pp. 9–17). Newbury Park, CA: Sage.

Drucker, P. F. (1994). *Innovation and entrepreneurship.* Boston: Butterworth-Heinemann.

Eder, R. W., & Ferris, G. R. (Eds.). (1989). *The employment interview: Theory, research, and practice.* Newbury Park, CA: Sage.

Engstrom T. W., & Mackenzie, R. A. (1988). *Managing your time: Practical guidelines on the effective use of time.* Grand Rapids, MI: Pyranee Books.

Fayol, H. (1949). *General and industrial management.* (C. Storrs, Trans.). London: Pitman. (Original work published 1916)

Feild, H. S., & Gatewood, R. D. (1989). Development of a selection interview: A job content strategy. In R. W. Eder & G. R. Ferris (Eds.), *The employment interview: Theory, research, and practice* (pp. 143–157). Newbury Park, CA: Sage.

Ferner, J. (1980). *Successful time management: A self-teaching guide.* New York: John Wiley & Sons.

Feuer, D. (1988). How women manage. *Training, 34,* 23–31.

Fitch, K. L. (1986). Cultural conflicts in the classroom: Major issues and strategies for coping. In P. Byrd (Ed.), *Teaching across cultures in the university ESL program* (pp. 51–62). Washington, DC: NAFSA.

Fjortoft, N. (1993). Factors predicting faculty commitment to the university. Paper presented at the Annual Forum of the Association for Institutional Research, Chicago, IL. (ERIC Document Reproduction Service No. ED 367 268)

Fortunato, R., & Elliott, J. M. (1988). *A handbook for developing higher education personnel policies.* Washington, DC: College and University Personnel Association.

Fox, R. P. (1991). Evaluating the ESL program director. In M. C. Pennington (Ed.), *Building better English programs: Perspectives on evaluation in ESL* (pp. 228–240). Washington, DC: NAFSA: Association of International Educators.

Frank, T. S., Bogen, J. M., & Dunlop, P. C. (1984). … And one institution's experience. *TESOL Newsletter, 18*(3), 15.

Freeman, D. (1982). Observing teachers: Three approaches to in-service training and development. *TESOL Quarterly, 16*(1), 21–28.

Freeman, G. (1995). *Judging oral proficiency: Can the naive judge determine standardized test scores (Test of Spoken English) through an interview process?* Unpublished doctoral dissertation, Florida State University, Tallahassee.

Fry, M. E. (1986). *Selected perceptions of English-as-a-second-language programs in postsecondary institutions in the United States.* Unpublished doctoral dissertation (2 vols.), University of Southern California, Los Angeles.

Fullan, M. G. (1993). Why teachers must become change agents. *Educational Leadership, 50,* 12–17.

Fullan, M. G., & Miles, M. B. (1992, June). Getting reform right: What works and what doesn't. *Phi Delta Kappan,* 745–754.

Gamboa, D. (1988). The experiential approach to international student orientation. In J. A. Mestenhauser, G. Marty, & I. Steglitz (Eds.), *Culture, learning, and the disciplines: Theory and practice in cross-cultural orientation* (pp. 58–65). Washington, DC: NAFSA.

Garcia, A. (1986). Consensus decision making promotes involvement, ownership, satisfaction. *NASSP Bulletin, 70,* 50–52.

Gebhard, J. C. (1984). Models of supervision: Choices. *TESOL Quarterly, 18*(3), 501–514.

Gee, J. P. (1990). *Social linguistics and literacies: Ideology in discourses.* Bristol, PA: Falmer Press.

Gibson, J. L., Ivancevich, J. M., & Donnelly, J. H. (1991). *Organizations: Behavior, structure, processes.* Homewood, IL: Irwin.

Gilpatrick, E. (1989). *Grants for nonprofit organizations.* New York: Praeger.

Glickman, C. D., Gordon, S. P., & Ross-Gordon, J. M. (1995). *Supervision of instruction: A developmental approach* (3rd ed.). Boston: Allyn & Bacon.

Goldberg, M. (1941). A qualification of the marginal man theory. *American Sociological Review, 6,* 52–58.

Goldhammer, R. (1969). *Clinical supervision: Special methods for the supervision of teachers.* New York: Holt, Rinehart & Winston.

Gooding, M. (1995). *Faculty member's guide to immigration law.* Washington, DC: NAFSA: Association of International Educators.

Goodwin, C. D., & Nacht, M. (1983). *Absence of decision: Foreign students in American colleges and universities.* New York: Institute for International Education.

Grabe, W., & Kaplan, R. B. (Eds.). (1992). *Introduction to applied linguistics*. Reading, MA: Addison-Wesley.

Green, M. A. (1992). Personnel implications of "cutback" management at public colleges and universities. *CUPA Journal, 43*(3), 19–26.

Grey, M. A. (1991). The context for marginal secondary ESL programs: Contributing factors and the need for further research. *Journal of Educational Issues of Language Minority Students, 9*, 75–89.

Halleck, G. B., & Moder, C. L. (1995). Testing language and teaching skills of international teaching assistants. *TESOL Quarterly, 29*(4), 733–758.

Hamilton, J. (1996). *Inspiring innovations in language teaching*. Bristol, PA: Multilingual Matters.

Hanson-Smith, E. (1991). *How to set up a computer lab: Advice for the beginner*. Houston: Athelstan.

Harris, B. M., Monk, B. J., McIntyre, K. E., & Long, D. F. (1992). *Personnel administration in education: Leadership for instructional development* (3rd ed.). Boston: Allyn & Bacon.

Harris, P. R., & Moran, R. T. (1975). *Managing cultural differences*. Houston, TX: Gulf Publishing.

Harshbarger, B. (1994). TESOL task force urges accreditation of intensive English programs. *NAFSA Newsletter, 45*(6), 1, 28–31.

Harvey, T. R., & Drolet, B. (1994). *Building teams, building people: Expanding the fifth resource*. Lancaster, PA: Technomic Publishing.

Hayes, D. (1995). In-service teacher development: Some basic principles. *ELT Journal, 49*(3), 252–261.

Healey, D., & Johnson, N. (Eds.). (1997). *1997 TESOL CALL interest section software list*. Alexandria, VA: TESOL.

Henning, G. (1987). *A guide to language testing*. Cambridge, MA: Newbury House.

Henrichsen, L. E. (1989). *Diffusion of innovations in English language teaching: The ELEC effort in Japan, 1956–1968*. New York: Greenwood Press.

Henry, A. R. (1994). Immigrating to administration: Denativization and acculturation. Paper presented at TESOL conference, Baltimore, MD.

Henry, A. R. (1995). Gender differences in administrative styles. Paper presented at TESOL conference, Long Beach, CA.

Henry, A. R., Hamrick, J., & Porter, K. (1995). Taking on the challenges of self-study. In A. Wintergerst (Ed.), *Focus on self-study* (pp. 37–51). Alexandria, VA: TESOL.

Hoekje, B., & Linnell, K. (1994). "Authenticity" in language testing: Evaluating spoken language tests for international teaching assistants. *TESOL Quarterly, 28*(1), 103–126.

Hoekje, B., & Williams, J. (1992). Communicative competence and the dilemma of international teaching assistant education. *TESOL Quarterly, 26*(2), 243–269.

Holliday, A. (1992). Tissue rejection and informal orders in ELT projects: Collecting the right information. *Applied Linguistics, 13*(4), 403–424.

Holloway, C. (1986). *Strategic planning*. Chicago: Nelson-Hall.

Horowitz, D. M. (1986). What professors actually require: Academic tasks for the ESL classroom. *TESOL Quarterly, 20*(3), 445–462.

Hradesky, J. (1995). *Total quality management handbook*. New York: McGraw-Hill.

Hunsaker, J., & Hunsaker, P. (1986). Working effectively in groups. In J. Hunsaker & P. Hunsaker (Eds.), *Strategies and skills for managerial women* (pp. 182–207). Cincinnati, OH: South Western Publishing.

Hyson, R. J. (1991). Point seven: Institute leadership. In R. I. Miller (Ed.), *Applying the Deming method to higher education for more effective human resource management* (pp. 65–73). Washington, DC: College and Personnel Association.

Janz, T. (1989). The patterned behavior description interview: The best prophet of the future is the past. In R. W. Eder & G. R. Ferris (Eds.), *The employment interview: Theory, research, and practice* (pp. 158–168). Newbury Park, CA: Sage.

Jay, A. (1976). How to run a meeting. *Harvard Business Review, 54*(2), 43–57. (Reprinted in *Paths toward personal progress: Leaders are made, not born*, pp. 120–134, 1983, Boston: President and Fellows of Harvard College)

Jenkins, H. M. (Ed.). (1983). *Educating students from other nations*. San Francisco: Jossey-Bass.

Jenkins, J. (1997). Teaching international populations successfully: Things your faculty should know. *NAFSA Newsletter, 48*(5), 13.

Jenks, F. L. (1991). Designing and assessing the efficacy of ESL promotional materials. In M. C. Pennington (Ed.), *Building better English language programs: Perspectives on evaluation in ESL* (pp. 172–188). Washington, DC: NAFSA: Association of International Educators.

Jensen, C., & Soppelsa, E. F. (1996). Strategies for research in intensive English programs. *Journal of Intensive English Studies, 10*, 1–18.

Johnson, D. W., Johnson, R. T., & Holubec, E. J. (1994). *Cooperative learning in the classroom*. Alexandria, VA: Association for Supervision and Curriculum Development.

Johnson, J. P. (1996). *Strategic decision-making, commitment, and organizational justice: Implications for the control and performance of international joint ventures*. Unpublished doctoral dissertation, University of South Carolina, Columbia.

Johnstone, D. B. (1990). The challenge of self-renewal in the innovative college. *Innovative Higher Education, 14*(2), 107–122.

Joint Committee on Standards for Educational Evaluation. (1988). *The personnel evaluation standards: How to assess systems for evaluating educators*. Newbury Park, CA: Sage.

Jones, P., & Lewis, J. (1991). Implementing a strategy for collective change in higher education. *Studies in Higher Education, 16*(1), 51–61.

Kane, L. (1991). The acquisition of cultural competence: An ethnographic framework for cultural studies curricula. In D. Buttjes & M. Bryam (Eds.), *Mediating languages and cultures* (pp. 230–247). Clevedon, England: Multilingual Matters.

Kaplan, R. B. (1987). On ESL program administration. *Communique: An Occasional Publication of Interest to University and College Intensive English Programs, 3*, 2–4.

Kaplan, R. B. (1989). The life and times of ITA programs. *English for Specific Purposes, 8*(2), 109–124.

Katz, R. L. (1974). Skills of an effective administrator. *Harvard Business Review, 52*(5), 143–151. (Reprinted in *Paths toward personal progress: Leaders are made, not born*, pp. 23–35, 1983, Boston: President and Fellows of Harvard College)

Keegan, D. (Ed.). (1993). *Theoretical principles of distance education*. New York: Routledge.

Keele, R. (1986). Mentoring or networking? Strong and weak ties in career development. In L. Moore (Ed.), *Not as far as you think: The realities of working women* (pp. 53–68). Lexington, MA: Lexington Books.

Kells, H. R. (1988). *Self-study processes: A guide for postsecondary and similar service-oriented institutions and programs* (3rd ed.). New York: American Council on Education/Macmillan.

Kelly, P. (1980). From innovation to adaptability: The changing perspective of curriculum development. In M. Galton (Ed.), *Curriculum change* (pp. 65–80). Leicester, England: Leicester University Press.

Kennedy, C. (1987). Innovating for a change: Teacher development and innovation. *ELT Journal, 41*(3), 163–170.

Kennedy, C. (1988). Evaluation of the management of change in ELT projects. *Applied Linguistics, 9*(4), 329–342.

Kennedy, M. M. (1984). How evidence alters understanding and decisions. *Educational Evaluation and Policy Analysis, 6*(3), 207–226.

Kirby, P. C., & Colbert, R. (1994). Principals who empower teachers. *Journal of School Leadership, 4*, 39–51.

Klineberg, O., & Hull. W. F. (1979). *At a foreign university: An international study of adaptation and coping.* New York: Praeger.

Knaus, W. J. (1979). *Do it now.* Englewood Cliffs, NJ: Prentice-Hall.

Kofodimos, J. (1993). *Balancing act: How managers can integrate successful careers and fulfilling personal lives.* San Francisco: Jossey-Bass.

Kotter, J. P. (1995, March-April). Leading change: Why transformation efforts fail. *Harvard Business Review, 73*(2), 59–67.

Krathwohl, D. R. (1988). *How to prepare a research proposal: Guidelines for funding and dissertations in the social and behavioral sciences* (3rd ed.). Syracuse, NY: Syracuse University Press.

Kuhlman, A. (1988). Foreign student orientation at the University of Pennsylvania. In J. A. Mestenhauser, G. Marty, & I. Steglitz (Eds.), *Culture, learning, and the disciplines: Theory and practice in cross-cultural orientation* (pp. 35–38). Washington, DC: NAFSA.

Landa, M. (1988). Training international students as teaching assistants. In J. A. Mestenhauser, G. Marty, & I. Steglitz (Eds.), *Culture, learning, and the disciplines: Theory and practice in cross-cultural orientation* (pp. 50–57). Washington, DC: NAFSA.

Latham, G. P. (1989). The reliability, validity, and practicality of the situational interview. In R. W. Eder & G. R. Ferris (Eds.), *The employment interview: Theory, research, and practice* (pp.169–182). Newbury Park, CA: Sage.

LeBoeuf, M. (1979). *Working smart: How to accomplish more in half the time.* New York: McGraw-Hill.

Lee, M. Y., Abd-Ella, M., & Burks, L. A. (1981). *Needs of foreign students from developing nations at U.S. colleges and universities.* Washington, DC: NAFSA.

Lee, S. M., Luthans, F., & Olson, D. L. (1982). A management science approach to contingency models of organizational structure. *Academy of Management Journal, 25*(3), 553–566.

Leidecker, J. K., & Bruno, A. V. (1987). Critical success factor analysis and the strategy development process. In W. R. King & D. I. Cleland (Eds.), *Strategic planning and management handbook* (pp. 333–351). New York: Van Nostrand Reinhold.

Leonard, J. G., & Yenkin, A. (Eds.). (1994). *F-1 GRAC pack*. Washington, DC: NAFSA: Association of International Educators.

Levine, A. (1980). *Why innovation fails*. Albany, NY: State University of New York Press.

Lewis, K. G. (Ed.). (1993). *The TA experience: Preparing for multiple roles (Selected readings from a national conference)*. Stillwater, OK: New Forums Press.

Likert, R. (1967). *The human organization: Its management and value*. New York: McGraw-Hill.

Lock, L. F., Spirduso, W. W., & Silverman, S. J. (1993). *Proposals that work: A guide for planning dissertations and grant proposals* (3rd ed.). Newbury Park, CA: Sage.

Locke, E. A., Fitzpatrick, W., & White, F. M. (1983). Job satisfaction and role clarity among university and college faculty. *Review of Higher Education, 6,* 343–365.

Love, S. F. (1981). *Mastery and management of time*. Englewood Cliffs, NJ: Prentice-Hall.

Lucas, A. (1990). The department chair as change agent. In P. Seldin & Associates (Eds.), *How administrators can improve teaching: Moving from talk to action in higher education* (pp. 63–88). San Francisco: Jossey-Bass.

Mackey, W. F. (1966). Applied linguistics: Its meaning and use. *English Language Teaching, 20*(3), 197–206.

Madden, C. G., & Myers, C. L. (Eds.). (1994). *Discourse and performance of international teaching assistants*. Alexandria, VA: TESOL.

Maggio, M., & Gay, C. W. (1986). Intercultural communication as an integral part of an ESL program: The University of Southern California experience. In P. Byrd (Ed.), *Teaching across cultures in the university ESL program* (pp. 93–98). Washington, DC: NAFSA.

Makridakis, S., & Héau, D. (1987). The evolution of strategic planning and management. In W. R. King & D. I. Cleland (Eds.), *Strategic planning and management handbook* (pp. 3–20). New York: Van Nostrand Reinhold.

Mark, N. (1994). Promoting culture learning on campus: Internationalizing student life at Michigan State University. In G. Althen (Ed.), *Learning across cultures* (pp. 173–183). Washington, DC: NAFSA: Association of International Educators.

Markee, N. (1993). The diffusion of innovation in language teaching. In W. Grabe et al. (Eds.), *Annual Review of Applied Linguistics, 13: Issues in Second Language Teaching and Learning* (pp. 229–243). New York: Cambridge University Press.

Markee, N. (1994). Using electronic mail to manage the implementation of educational innovations. *System, 22*(3), 379–389.

Markee, N. (1997). *Managing curricular innovation in second and foreign language education*. New York: Cambridge University Press.

Marsh, H. L. (1994). *NAFSA's self-study guide: Assessment of programs and services for international educational exchange at postsecondary institutions*. Washington, DC: NAFSA: Association of International Educators.

Matthies, B. F. (1983). *A study of characteristics, qualifications, and perceived roles of the directors of ESL programs*. Unpublished doctoral dissertation, University of Illinois, Urbana.

Matthies, B. F. (1991). Administrative evaluation in ESL programs: "How'm I doin'?" In M. C. Pennington (Ed.), *Building better English programs: Perspectives on evaluation in ESL* (pp. 241–256). Washington, DC: NAFSA: Association of International Educators.

McLaughlin, D. (1992). Power and the politics of knowledge: Transformative schooling for minority language learners. In D. E. Murray (Ed.), *Diversity as resource: Redefining cultural literacy* (pp. 235–256). Washington, DC: TESOL.

McLaughlin, M. B. (1990). Searching. *CUPA Journal, 41*(3), 1–3.

McLeod, B. (1980). The relevance of anthropology to language teaching. In K. Croft (Ed.), *Readings on English as a second language* (pp. 539–549). Boston: Little, Brown and Company.

McWhinney, W. (1992). *Paths of change: Strategic choices for organizations and society.* Newbury Park, CA: Sage.

Mead, L., Davidson, J., & Hanna, M. (1986). Forecasting enrollment in intensive English programs. *TESOL Newsletter, 20*(3), 14, 16.

Medley, D. M., Coker, H., & Soar, M. (1984). *Measurement-based evaluation of teacher performance.* New York: Longman.

Merson, J. C., & Qualls, R. L. (1979). *Strategic planning for colleges and universities: A systems approach to planning and resource allocation.* San Antonio, TX: Trinity University Press.

Metcalf, H. C., & Urwick, L. (Eds.). (1940). *Dynamic administration: The collected papers of May Parker Follett.* New York: Harper & Row.

Middlebrook, G. C. (1991). Evaluation of student services in ESL programs. In M. C. Pennington (Ed.), *Building better English language programs: Perspectives on evaluation in ESL* (pp. 135–154). Washington, DC: NAFSA: Association of International Educators.

Mintzberg, H. (1987, July-August). Crafting strategy. *Harvard Business Review, 65*(4), 66–75.

Mitchell, R. (1995). International students: Steady hands on the looking glass. *Teaching Sociology, 23*, 396–400.

Mooney, J. D. (1947). *The principles of organization.* New York: Harper & Row.

Morley, J. (1993). The challenges and rewards of being an ESOL professional. *TESOL Matters, 3*, 18.

Munro, M. C. (1987). Identifying critical information for strategic management. In W. R. King & D. I. Cleland (Eds.), *Strategic planning and management handbook* (pp. 401–421). New York: Van Nostrand Reinhold.

Murray, D. E. (1992). Unlimited resources: Tapping into learners' language, culture, and thought. In D. E. Murray (Ed.), *Diversity as resource: Redefining cultural literacy* (pp. 259–274). Washington, DC: TESOL.

NAFSA. (1983). *NAFSA self-study guide: A guide for the self-assessment of programs and services with international educational exchange at postsecondary institutions.* Washington, DC: Author.

NAFSA: Association of International Educators. (1994). *Model international student involvement programs.* Washington, DC: Author.

The NAFSA ethics program. (1995). Washington, DC: NAFSA: Association of International Educators.

National Association of College Admissions Counsellors. (1995). *Statement of principles of good practice.* Alexandria, VA: Author.

Nayar, P. B. (1986). Acculturation or enculturation: Foreign students in the United States. In P. Byrd (Ed.), *Teaching across cultures in the university ESL program* (pp. 1–13). Washington, DC: NAFSA.

Near, J. P., & Sorcinelli, M. D. (1986). Work and life away from work: Predictors of faculty satisfaction. *Research in Higher Education, 25,* 377–394.

Nicholls, A. (1983). *Managing educational innovation.* London: Allen and Unwin.

Nichols-Casebolt, A. M. (1993). Competing with the market: Salary adjustments and faculty input. *Research in Higher Education, 34,* 583–601.

Niendorf, K. (1994). *A comparative study of non-native speaker performance on culture-fair and biased essay topics.* Unpublished doctoral dissertation, Florida State University, Tallahassee.

Norton, P. (1995). *Inside the PC* (6th ed.). Indianapolis: Sams Publishing.

Nunan, D. (1990). Action research in the language classroom. In J. C. Richards & D. Nunan (Eds.), *Second language teacher education* (pp. 62–81). New York: Cambridge University Press.

Nyquist, J. D., Abbott, R. D., Wulff, D. H., & Sprague, J. (Eds.). (1991). *Preparing the professoriate of tomorrow to teach: Selected readings in TA training.* Dubuque, IA: Kendall/Hunt Publishing.

Paiva, J. (1996). Accreditation activities underway. *TESOL Matters, 6*(1), 1.

Pajak, E. (1993). *Approaches to clinical supervision: Alternatives for improving instruction.* Norwood, MA: Christopher-Gordon.

Palmer, I. (1995). Present and future tense: Intensive English in the U.S.A. In T. M. Davis (Ed.), *Open doors 1994/95: Report on international educational exchange* (pp. 148–149). New York: Institute of International Education.

Palmer, J. D. (1980). Linguistics *in medias res.* In R. B. Kaplan (Ed.), *On the scope of applied linguistics* (pp. 21–27). Rowley, MA: Newbury House.

Pennington, M. C. (1985). Effective administration of an ESL program. In P. Larsen, E. Judd, & D. S. Messerschmitt (Eds.), *On TESOL '84: A brave new world for TESOL* (pp. 301–316). Washington, DC: TESOL.

Pennington, M. C. (1989). Faculty development for language programs. In R. K. Johnson (Ed.), *The second language curriculum* (pp. 91–110). New York: Cambridge University Press.

Pennington, M. C., & Xiao, Y. (1990). Defining the job of the ESL program administrator: Results of a national survey. *University of Hawaii Working Papers in ESL, 9*(2), 1–30.

Pennington, M. C., & Young, A. L. (1991). Procedures and instruments for faculty evaluation in ESL. In M. C. Pennington (Ed.), *Building better English programs: Perspectives on evaluation in ESL* (pp. 191–227). Washington, DC: NAFSA: Association of International Educators.

Personnel Services. (1993). *Supervisor's manual.* Portland, OR: Lewis and Clark College.

Pica, T., Barnes, G., & Finger, A. (1990). *Teaching matters: Skills and strategies for international teaching assistants*. New York: Newbury House.

Pistole, M. C., & Cogdal, P. A. (1993). Empowering women: Taking charge of our university careers. *Initiatives, 55*, 1–8.

Popham, M. (1996). *The resource book: Sample materials for community program developers in international education*. Washington, DC: NAFSA: Association of International Educators.

Powers, D. R., & Powers, M. F. (1983). *Making participatory management work: Leadership of consultive decision making in academic administration*. San Francisco: Jossey-Bass.

Price, J. J. (1995). Meet the TESOL accreditation advisory committee. *TESOL Matters, 5*(5), 15.

Raelin, J. A. (1986). *The clash of cultures: Managers and professionals*. Boston: Harvard Business School Press.

Reasor, A. W. (1986). Dominant administrative styles of ESL administrators. *TESOL Quarterly, 20*, 338–343.

Reid, J. M. (1992). Helping students write for an academic audience. In P. A. Richard-Amato & M. A. Snow (Eds.), *The multicultural classroom: Readings for content-area teachers* (pp. 210–221). White Plains, NY: Longman.

Reitzug, U. C. (1994). A case study of empowering principal behavior. *American Educational Research Journal, 31*, 283–307.

Richards, J. C., & Lockhart, C. (1994). *Reflective teaching in second language classrooms*. New York: Cambridge University Press.

Robbins, A. (1996). *Personal power, II: The driving force*. San Diego, CA: Robbins Research International.

Rogers, E. M. (1983). *Diffusion of innovations* (3rd ed.). New York: Free Press.

Rogers, E. M., & Shoemaker, F. F. (1971). *Communication of innovations: A cross-cultural approach* (2nd ed.). New York: Free Press.

Rogers, J. (1995, March). *University writing tasks: Survey results*. Paper presented at the TESOL conference, Long Beach, CA.

Rogers, R. W., & Byham, W. C. (1994). Diagnosing organization cultures for realignment. In A. Howard & Associates (Eds.), *Diagnosis for organizational change: Methods and models* (pp. 170–209). New York: Guilford Press.

Rossman, M. H., & Rossman, M. E. (1995). *Facilitating distance education*. San Francisco: Jossey-Bass.

Rossman, P. (1992). *The emerging worldwide electronic university: Information age global higher education*. Westport, CN: Greenwood Press.

Rothstein, R., & McKnight, L. (1996). Technology and cost models of K–12 schools on the national information infrastructure. *Computers in the Schools, 12*(1/2), 31–57.

Rumble, G. (1986). *The planning and management of distance education*. New York: St. Martin's Press.

Samovar, L., & Porter, R. (1991). *Communication between cultures*. Belmont, CA: Wadsworth.

Sander, B. R. (1993). The campus climate revisited: Chilly for women faculty, administrators, and graduate students. In J. S. Glazer, E. M. Bensimon, & B. K. Townsend (Eds.), *Women in higher education: A feminist perspective* (pp. 175–203). Needham Heights, MA: Ginn Press.

Santos, T. (1992). Ideology in composition: L1 and ESL. *Journal of Second Language Writing, 1,* 1–5.

Sarles, H. (1988). Brief course on America: An orientation to the study of American culture. In J. A. Mestenhauser, G. Marty, & I. Steglitz (Eds.), *Culture, learning, and the disciplines: Theory and practice in cross-cultural orientation* (pp. 25–34). Washington, DC: NAFSA.

Sashkin, M. (1993). *Putting total quality management to work: What TQM means, how to use it, and how to sustain it over the long run.* San Francisco: Berrett-Koehler.

Schilit, W. K. (1983). A manager's guide to efficient time management. *Personnel Journal, 62*(9), 736–742.

Schofield, D. (1981). *Confessions of an organized housewife.* Cincinnati, OH: Writer's Digest Books.

Schrum, L. (1991). *Distance education: A primer for administrators.* Eugene, OR: Oregon School Study Council.

Schumacher, D. (1992). *Get funded! A practical guide for scholars seeking research support from business.* Newbury Park, CA: Sage.

Scollon, R., & Scollon, S. (1995). *Intercultural communication.* Cambridge, MA: Basil Blackwell.

Seelye, H. N. (1968). Analysis and teaching of cross-cultural context. In *Britannica Review of Foreign Language Education* (Vol. 1). Chicago: Encyclopedia Britannica.

Seelye, H. N. (1974). *Teaching culture: Strategies for foreign language educators.* Skokie, IL: National Textbook.

Seldin, P., & Associates (Eds.). (1990). *How administrators can improve teaching: Moving from talk to action in higher education.* San Francisco: Jossey-Bass.

Simerly, R. (1993). *Strategic financial management for conferences, workshops, and meetings.* San Francisco: Jossey-Bass.

Smith, J., Meyers, C., & Burkhalter, A. (1992). *Communicate: Strategies for international teaching assistants.* Englewood Cliffs, NJ: Prentice-Hall Regents.

Smith, R., Byrd, P., Constantinides, J., & Barrett, R. P. (1991). Instructional development programs for international TAs: A systems analysis approach. In K. J. Zahorski (Ed.), *To improve the academy: Resources for student, faculty, and institutional development 10* (pp. 151–168). The Professional and Organizational Development Network in Higher Education. Stillwater, OK: New Forums Press.

Smith, R., Byrd, P., Nelson, G. L., Barrett, R. P., & Constantinides, J. C. (1992). *Crossing pedagogical oceans: International teaching assistants in U.S. undergraduate education.* ASHE-ERIC Higher Education Report No. 8. Washington, DC: The George Washington University, School of Education and Human Development.

Snow, M. A. (Ed.). (1992). *Project LEAP: Learning English-for-Academic-Purposes. Training manual—Year One.* Los Angeles: California State University, Los Angeles.

Snow, M. A. (Ed.). (1993). *Project LEAP: Learning English-for-Academic-Purposes. Training manual—Year Two.* Los Angeles: California State University, Los Angeles.

Snow, M. A. (Ed.). (1994). *Project LEAP: Learning English-for-Academic-Purposes. Training manual—Year Three.* Los Angeles: California State University, Los Angeles.

Snow, M. A., & Kamhi-Stein, L. D. (Eds.). (1996). *Teaching academic literacy skills: Strategies for content faculty.* Los Angeles: California State University, Los Angeles.

Solomon, L., & Young, B. (1987). *The foreign student factor: Impact on American higher education* (IIE Research Series No. 12). New York: Institute of International Education. (ERIC Document Reproduction Service No. ED 311 836)

Soppelsa, E. F. (in press). Evaluation principles and procedures. In F. Pialorsi (Ed.), *The Administration of English Language Programs*. Washington, DC: NAFSA: Association of International Educators.

Staczek, J. J. (1991). Professional development and program administration. *TESOL Journal, 1*(1), 21–22, 27–28.

Staczek, J. J., & Carkin, S. (1985). Intensive English program fit in traditional academic settings: Practices and promise. In P. Larson, E. Judd, & D. S. Messerschmitt (Eds.), *On TESOL '84: A brave new world for TESOL* (pp. 289–300). Washington, DC: TESOL.

Steglitz, I. (1988). Survey of university orientation programs for international students and scholars. In J. A. Mestenhauser, G. Marty, & I. Steglitz (Eds.), *Culture, learning, and the disciplines: Theory and practice in cross-cultural orientation* (pp. 5–15). Washington, DC: NAFSA.

Steiner, R. (1988). *Total proposal building* (2nd ed.). Albany, NY: Thistletree.

Stevenson, H., & Stigler, J. (1992). *The learning gap*. New York: Summit Publishing.

Stewart, E. (1972). *American cultural patterns: A cross-cultural perspective*. Yarmouth, ME: Intercultural Press.

Stoller, F. L. (1992a). *Analysis of innovations in selected higher education intensive English programs: A focus on administrators' perceptions*. Unpublished doctoral dissertation, Northern Arizona University, Flagstaff.

Stoller, F. L. (1992b). Taxonomy of intensive English program innovations. *Journal of Intensive English Studies, 6*, 1–25.

Stoller, F. L. (1994a). Change is inevitable, but innovation is desirable in intensive English programs. *TESOL Matters, 4*(4), 9.

Stoller, F. L. (1994b). The diffusion of innovations in intensive ESL programs. *Applied Linguistics, 15*(3), 300–327.

Stoller, F. L. (1995a). Innovation in a non-traditional academic unit: The intensive English program. *Innovative Higher Education, 19*(3), 177–195.

Stoller, F. L. (1995b). *Managing intensive English program innovations*. (NAFSA Working Paper No. 56). Washington, DC: NAFSA: Association of International Educators.

Stoller, F. L. (1996). Teacher supervision: Moving towards an interactive approach. *English Teaching Forum, 34*(2), 2–9.

Stoller, F. L., & Christison, M. A. (1994). Challenges for IEP administrators: Liaisons with senior-level administrators and faculty development. *TESOL Journal, 3*(3), 16–20.

Stoller, F. L., Hodges, R., & Kimbrough, J. (1995). Examining the value of conversation partner programs. *Applied Language Learning, 6*(1/2), 1–12.

Storti, C. (1990). *The art of crossing cultures*. Yarmouth, ME: Intercultural Press.

Stoynoff, S. (1989). Successfully implementing educational change and innovation. *ORTESOL Journal, X*, 17–33.

Stoynoff, S. (1991). Curriculum change and programming innovations in ESOL programs: Making it happen. *TESL Reporter, 24*(1), 9–15.

Swidler, A. (1986). Culture in action. *American Sociological Review, 50,* 273–286.

Szilagyi, A. (1988). *Management and performance.* Glenview, IL: Scott Foresman.

Tack, M. W., & Patitu, C. L. (1992). *Faculty job satisfaction: Women and minorities in peril.* ASHE-ERIC Higher Education Report No. 4. Washington, DC: The George Washington University, School of Education and Human Development.

Tannen, D. (1994). *Talking from 9 to 5: How men's and women's conversational styles affect who gets heard, who gets credit, and what gets done at work.* New York: William Morrow.

Taylor, B. (1987). An overview of strategic planning styles. In W. R. King & D. I. Cleland (Eds.), *Strategic planning and management handbook* (pp. 21–35). New York: Van Nostrand Reinhold.

TESOL. (n.d.). *Standards and self-study questions for postsecondary programs.* Washington, DC: Author.

TESOL. (1984). *Statement of core standards for language and professional preparation programs.* Washington, DC: Author.

TESOL. (1986a). *TESOL's manual for self study.* Washington, DC: Author.

TESOL. (1986b). *The TESOL core standards for language and professional preparation programs.* Washington, DC: Author.

Thomas, K., & Harrell, T. (1994). Counseling student sojourners: Revisiting the U-curve of adjustment. In G. Althen (Ed.), *Learning across cultures* (pp. 89–107). Washington, DC: NAFSA: Association of International Educators.

Thuesen, J. M., & Kroeger, O. (1992). *Type talk at work.* New York: Delacorte Press.

Tichy, N. M., & Charan, R. (1995, March-April). The CEO as coach: An interview with AlliedSignal's Lawrence A. Bossidy. *Harvard Business Review, 73*(2), 69–78.

Tinsley, A. (1984). Career mapping and the professional development process. In A. Tinsley, C. Secor, & S. Kaplan (Eds.), *Women in higher education administration* (pp. 17–24). San Francisco: Jossey-Bass.

Tomlinson, B. (1990, January). Managing change in Indonesian high schools. *ELT Journal, 44*(1), 25–37.

Torbiörn, I. (1994). Dynamics of cross-cultural adaptation. In G. Althen (Ed.), *Learning across cultures* (pp. 31–55). Washington, DC: NAFSA: Association of International Educators.

Tyler, A. (1992). Discourse structure and the perception of incoherence in international teaching assistants' spoken discourse. *TESOL Quarterly, 26*(4), 713–729.

University and College Intensive English Programs. (1993). *UCIEP guidelines.* Stillwater, OK: Oklahoma State University.

Urwick, L. (1944). *The elements of administration.* New York: Harper & Row.

U.S. Congress, Office of Technology Assessment. (1988). *Power on! New tools for teaching and learning.* Washington, DC: U.S. Government Printing Office.

U.S. Congress, Office of Technology Assessment. (1993). *Adult literacy and the new technologies: Tools for a lifetime.* Washington, DC: U.S. Government Printing Office.

Usunier, C. (1993). *International marketing: A cultural approach.* Englewood Cliffs, NJ: Prentice Hall.

Valdes, J. M. (1986). *Culture bound: Bridging the culture gap in language teaching.* New York: Cambridge University Press.

Vandrick, S., Hafernik, J. J., & Messerschmitt, D. S. (1994). Outsiders in academe: Women ESL faculty and their students. *Journal of Intensive English Studies, 8,* 37–55.

van Lier, L. (1994). Action research. *Sintagma, 6,* 31–37.

Wadden, P. (1994, August-September). The serfs and the gentry: ESL teachers in the academic fiefdom. *TESOL Matters,* 17.

Wall, S. J., & Wall, S. R. (1995, Autumn). The evolution (not the death) of strategy. *Organizational Dynamics, 24*(2), 7–19.

Warden, C. A. (1997). Price of progress. *TESOL Matters, 7*(1), 9.

Warschauer, M. (1995). *E-mail in language teaching.* Alexandria, VA: TESOL.

Weber, M. (1947). *The theory of social and economic organization.* (A. M. Henderson & T. Parsons, Trans.). New York: Oxford. (Original work published in 1925)

Wernick, A. (1992). *The international student handbook: A legal guide to studying, working, and living in the United States.* Washington, DC: American Immigration Law Foundation.

White, R. V. (1987, July). Managing innovation. *ELT Journal, 41*(3), 211–218.

White, R. V. (1988). *The ELT curriculum: Design, innovation and management.* New York: Basil Blackwell.

White, R. V. (1993). Innovation in curriculum planning and program development. In W. Grabe et al. (Eds.), *Annual Review of Applied Linguistics, 13: Issues in Second Language Teaching and Learning* (pp. 244–259). New York: Cambridge University Press.

White, R., Martin, M., Stimson, M., & Hodge, R. (1991). *Management in English language teaching.* New York: Cambridge University Press.

Williams, J. (1992). Planning, discourse marking, and the comprehensibility of international teaching assistants. *TESOL Quarterly, 26*(4), 693–711.

Williams, T. (1994). *An investigation into factors influencing student selection of intensive English programs in the southeastern United States.* Unpublished doctoral dissertation, Florida State University, Tallahassee.

Willis, S. (1996, Winter). Foreign languages: Learning to communicate in the real world. *Curriculum Update,* 1–6.

Winston, S. (1978). *Getting organized.* New York: Warner Communications.

Wintergerst, A. (Ed.). (1995). *Focus on self-study.* Alexandria, VA: TESOL.

Winwood, R. (1990). *Time management: An introduction to the Franklin System.* Salt Lake City, Utah: Franklin International Institute.

World Education Series: PIER Reports. Annapolis Junction, MD: PIER Publications.

Yalden, J. (1983). *The communicative syllabus: Evolution, design and implementation.* Oxford: Pergamon.

Yenkin, A. (Ed.). (1995). *Adviser's manual of federal regulations affecting foreign students and scholars.* Washington, DC: NAFSA: Association of International Educators.

Young, R. (Ed.). (1989). [Special issue] *English for Specific Purposes, 8*(2).

Young, R. (1992). A systems approach to curriculum innovation in intensive English programs. *Southern Illinois Working Papers in Linguistics and Language Teaching, 1,* 75–94.

Young, R., & Lee, S. (1985). EFL curriculum innovation and teachers' attitudes. In P. Larson, E. Judd, & D. S. Messerschmitt (Eds.), *On TESOL '84: A brave new world for TESOL* (pp. 183–194). Washington, DC: TESOL.

CONTRIBUTORS

Marian E. Blaber has been both an administrator and a classroom teacher in ESL education since 1977, working in the United States, Latin America, and Eastern Europe. Her graduate studies include work in TESL and administration in higher education. Her research interests are professionalization in ESL and computer-assisted language learning.

Susan Carkin has been teaching ESL at Utah State University (USU) for more than 20 years. Her teaching and research interests center around the development of academic expertise among ESL students; her administrative interests, based on 9 years of directing the USU intensive English program, focus on the role and status of intensive English professionals and programs in American and foreign universities.

Mary Ann Christison, co-editor of this volume, is a professor and the director of the International Center at Snow College. She has been a language program administrator for 17 years. She is the author of numerous teacher resource books and articles on administration, methodology, and second language acquisition. Mary Ann has served on the TESOL board of directors and will serve as president of TESOL, 1997–1998.

Janet C. Constantinides is a professor of English and chair of the Department of English at the University of Wyoming. Her teaching and research interests center on composition—including scientific and technical writing for both native and non-native speakers—and training international teaching assistants. She is past-president of NAFSA and is currently a member of the TESOL Accreditation Advisory Committee.

Joseph O. Davidson is the director of the Language and Culture Center at the University of Houston. He was a field linguist with the Peace Corps in Bolivia. Active in both TESOL and NAFSA, he has chaired the TESOL Program Administration Interest Section and has been a member-at-large on NAFSA's ATESL team.

David E. Eskey is an associate professor of Education and the director of the American Language Institute at the University of Southern California. He is both a co-editor and co-author of *Teaching Second Language Reading for Academic Purposes* (1986), *Research in Reading in English as a Second Language* (1987), and *Interactive Approaches to Second Language Reading* (1988).

Joann M. Geddes is the director of the Lewis and Clark College intensive English program and has also served as the institution's director of summer sessions. Other experience in program development and administration includes the coordination of the Beaverton Public School District ESL program. She has taught ESL to students from elementary grades through university levels, and TESL/TEFL at Lewis and Clark College and overseas.

Deborah Healey is currently the technology coordinator of Oregon State University's English Language Institute. She is the editor of *CÆLL (Computer-Assisted English Language Learning) Journal* and the author of *Something to Do on Tuesday* (1995). She is a former chair of TESOL's CALL Interest Section.

Frederick L. Jenks is a professor and the coordinator of multilingual multicultural education at Florida State University, where he is also the director of the Center for Intensive English Studies. He has been an active member in ACTFL, NAFSA, and TESOL. He has published recently in areas related to the efficacy of ESL promotional materials and the maintenance of foreign language skills.

Robert B. Kaplan is a professor emeritus of Applied Linguistics and a past director of the American Language Institute at the University of Southern California. He has served as president of NAFSA, TESOL, and AAAL. During his distinguished career, he has taught courses and published papers on language program administration and has evaluated language programs in the United States and abroad. He is now retired and currently resides in Port Angeles, Washington.

Sarah J. Klinghammer is the director of the American English Institute at the University of Oregon, where she has held various administrative positions for more than 15 years. She has taught ESL methodology for both the Linguistics Department and the School of Education, has been a Fulbright scholar and Peace Corps TESL consultant, and has conducted teacher training in Mexico, the Czech Republic, and Slovakia.

Peter S. Levitov is the associate dean of International Affairs at the University of Nebraska Lincoln and Special Assistant General Counsel (Immigration) for the University of Nebraska System. He has worked with foreign students and scholars since 1972 and written and spoken extensively on immigration law and regulations related to the academic community. Levitov has served in numerous leadership positions for NAFSA: Association of International Educators.

Doris R. Marks is the principal of Beaver Acres Elementary School in Beaverton, Oregon. Previous work experience includes coordinating the ESL program and administrating various special education programs in the Beaverton school district. She has taught ESL to students at the elementary through university levels, and has taught English and French to high school students.

Charles Mickelson has been the director of the Ohio Program of Intensive English

(OPIE) at Ohio University since 1984. During that time, the OPIE has designed, bid, and implemented projects funded by private student tuition, internal Ohio University units, U.S. government and nonprofit agencies, U.S. businesses, and international public and private institutions.

Bradley D. Miller is currently the associate director at the Center for Quality Assurance in International Education/Global Alliance for Transnational Education. He was the coordinator for international program development at the University of Arizona's Center for English as a Second Language for 5 years; he was responsible for international student recruitment, special program development, and outreach.

Lee Ann Rawley is the assistant director of the Intensive English Language Institute at Utah State University. Her administrative interests include curriculum development, language program fit within institutions of higher education, and student orientation to American colleges and universities. She has served as chair of the TESOL Awards Committee and as president of Intermountain TESOL.

Alexandra Rowe Henry directs the English Programs for Internationals and serves on the Linguistics faculty at the University of South Carolina. She is author of *Second Language Rhetorics in Process: A Comparison of Arabic, Chinese, and Spanish* (1993).

Rebecca Smith Murdock is the director of the Intensive English Language Institute at the University of North Texas. Before that, she was director of a language program at the University of Arkansas in Little Rock. She is an active member of NAFSA, TESOL, AAIEP, and UCIEP. She was chair of NAFSA's ATESL from 1995 to 1996.

Elizabeth (Betty) F. Soppelsa has been the director of the Applied English Center, University of Kansas, since 1980. She has been active in TESOL and NAFSA and has held a number of local and national offices. Her research interests include faculty and program evaluation. Betty has lectured in Japan, Poland, the Czech Republic, and Slovakia. She got her start in TESL in the Peace Corps in the Ivory Coast.

John J. Staczek is a professor and the chair of the Department of Modern Languages at Thunderbird, The American Graduate School of International Management. He has held Senior Fulbrights to Nicaragua, Colombia, and Poland. His research interests include English, Polish, and Spanish language variation and change; textual analysis; language awareness; and program administration.

Fredricka L. Stoller, co-editor of this volume, is an associate professor at Northern Arizona University where she teaches in the TESL and Applied Linguistics programs. As director of the Program in Intensive English at the same institution, she is responsible for all administrative matters including faculty development, curriculum design, budgeting, student advising, and liaison with on-campus and off-campus entities.

Joy S. Tesh is the associate director of the Language and Culture Center at the University of Houston. She began her work in ESL as a Peace Corps volunteer in Liberia, West Africa. A frequent presenter at TESOL conventions, she is a former chair of the Intensive English Programs Interest Section of TESOL.

Michael Witbeck is at Oregon State University where he serves as finance coordinator of the English Language Institute (ELI) and works for the Office of Continuing Higher Education. His duties include network management and other computer support services. A former acting director of the ELI, Michael has also worked as an ESL instructor and program administrator in Europe, Asia, and the Middle East.

AUTHOR INDEX

SUBJECT INDEX